SCHOLASTIC Pocket
Thesaurus

SCHOLASTIC Pocket
Thesaurus

John K. Bollard

SCHOLASTIC REFERENCE

An imprint of

Editorial Assistant: Catrin Lloyd-Bollard
Curriculum Consultant: Bob Stremme
Book design: Nancy Sabato
Composition: Brad Walrod/High Text Graphics, Inc.

Previously published as the *Scholastic Student Thesaurus*

ISBN 978-0-439-62037-6

10 9   11 12 13 14

Printed in the U.S.A.   08
First printing, July 2005

Cover photo credit: Spike Mafford/Photodisc/PictureQuest

Contents

Introduction

The Web of Words

I magine a large, beautiful spiderweb. Its strands run from point to point creating intricate and fascinating patterns wherever you look. The English language is just such a web, but it is a web of words. Many words are connected by strands of meaning to other similar words, called *synonyms*. Those words, in turn, are connected to still other synonyms, moving you gradually from one idea to another. How can you find your way around this web of words? How can you find just the right word when you need it? A thesaurus helps you to do just that. The *Scholastic Pocket Thesaurus* is designed to move you around in the web of words. If you start with a word you know, your thesaurus will help you find synonyms to choose from.

Why Use a Thesaurus?

You already know thousands of words. These words are usually all you need. But sometimes, even though you know you have a good idea, you just can't think of quite the right word to express it the way you want. Here are some of the ways in which the *Scholastic Pocket Thesaurus* can be helpful:

To avoid repetition. Suppose you have used the same word three or four times in one paragraph or page. Rather than use that word again, you would like to find a different way to express the same idea. Your thesaurus provides you with a variety of synonyms.

To make your meaning clear and precise. When you speak or write, you usually think about what you *mean*, not about the words you are using. But sometimes the meaning doesn't come out as easily or as clearly as you had hoped. Your thesaurus can help you find words that express your idea more effectively than the words you began with. You may find that looking through the synonyms of a word brings to mind different ways to express your idea. It may even help you understand the idea better yourself. Sometimes a word you have used may be too vague. Sometimes its meaning or its tone is not exactly what you want. You want your readers to understand exactly how you felt, what you saw, or what you thought. Your thesaurus can give you synonyms that are more precise and effective.

To avoid overused terms. There are a few words that get used so often in so many different ways that they have run out of energy. They no longer have a sharply defined meaning, even though they give a general impression of what we want to say. It may be easier just to use these words, but they don't say anything specific. Often they lead us into clichés or vague thinking. If you find yourself using such general words as **nice** or **pretty** or **good**, try to pin down your thoughts with synonyms that more specifically describe what you are talking about. Your thesaurus can help you replace those words with synonyms like "delightful," "striking," or "favorable." This will make your writing more energetic and original.

To achieve the proper tone. Sometimes the word you thought of is too informal to be used in a school assignment or for a letter you want to write. You want a more serious word, but can't think of one. Or the opposite may be true. You may be writing a story or poem in a conversational or informal style. The synonyms in your thesaurus cover a broad range of vocabulary from informal to colloquial to formal. Some words are labeled as *informal* in your thesaurus. You should avoid using these in your serious writing. For example, "chicken" and "yellow" are informal synonyms of **cowardly**. You may not want to use them in an essay or assignment, but they might be just right for a character's speech in a story. When selecting any synonym, you should always take a moment to consider whether it is suitable for the style in which you are writing or speaking.

You already know many of the words in the *Scholastic Pocket Thesaurus*, but you will also find many new words here. Your thesaurus will guide you through this web of words in order to make your writing more clear, more mature, and even more elegant. Most importantly, the *Scholastic Pocket Thesaurus* will help you to write accurately and precisely. In this way, you can communicate your thoughts more easily to others. And that is what you are always trying to do when you speak or write.

At-a-Glance

A thesaurus is a reference book that lists words that mean the same thing or almost the same thing. Such words are called *synonyms*. In some cases, your thesaurus also helps you find words that mean the opposite or almost the opposite. These words are called *antonyms*. The different parts of your *Scholastic Pocket Thesaurus* are identified in the sample page below.

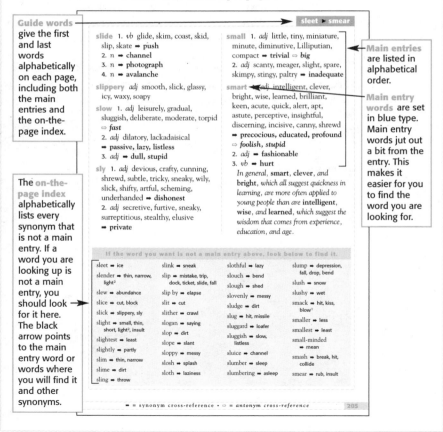

Guide words give the first and last words alphabetically on each page, including both the main entries and the on-the-page index.

The **on-the-page index** alphabetically lists every synonym that is not a main entry. If a word you are looking up is not a main entry, you should look for it here. The black arrow points to the main entry word or words where you will find it and other synonyms.

Main entries are listed in alphabetical order.

Main entry words are set in blue type. Main entry words jut out a bit from the entry. This makes it easier for you to find the word you are looking for.

sleet ► smear

slide 1. *vb* glide, skim, coast, skid, slip, skate ► push
2. *n* ► channel
3. *n* ► photograph
4. *n* ► avalanche

slippery *adj* smooth, slick, glassy, icy, waxy, soapy

slow 1. *adj* leisurely, gradual, sluggish, deliberate, moderate, torpid ⇨ fast
2. *adj* dilatory, lackadaisical ► passive, lazy, listless
3. *adj* ► dull, stupid

sly 1. *adj* devious, crafty, cunning, shrewd, subtle, tricky, sneaky, wily, slick, shifty, artful, scheming, underhanded ► dishonest
2. *adj* secretive, furtive, sneaky, surreptitious, stealthy, elusive ► private

small 1. *adj* little, tiny, miniature, minute, diminutive, Lilliputian, compact ► trivial ⇨ big
2. *adj* scanty, meager, slight, spare, skimpy, stingy, paltry ► inadequate

smart *adj* intelligent, clever, bright, wise, learned, brilliant, keen, acute, quick, alert, apt, astute, perceptive, insightful, discerning, incisive, canny, shrewd ► precocious, educated, profound ⇨ foolish, stupid
2. *adj* ► fashionable
3. *vb* ► hurt
In general, **smart**, **clever**, *and* **bright**, *which all suggest quickness in learning, are more often applied to young people than are* **intelligent**, **wise**, *and* **learned**, *which suggest the wisdom that comes from experience, education, and age.*

If the word you want is not a main entry above, look below to find it.

sleet ► ice	slink ► sneak	slothful ► lazy	slump ► depression, fall, drop, bend
slender ► thin, narrow, light²	slip ► mistake, trip, dock, ticket, slide, fall	slouch ► bend	slush ► snow
slew ► abundance	slip by ► elapse	slough ► shed	slushy ► wet
slice ► cut, block	slit ► cut	slovenly ► messy	smack ► hit, kiss, blow¹
slick ► slippery, sly	slither ► crawl	sludge ► dirt	smaller ► less
slight ► small, thin, short, light², insult	slogan ► saying	slug ► hit, missile	smallest ► least
slightest ► least	slop ► dirt	sluggard ► loafer	small-minded ► mean
slightly ► partly	slope ► slant	sluggish ► slow, listless	smash ► break, hit, collide
slim ► thin, narrow	sloppy ► messy	sluice ► channel	
slime ► dirt	slosh ► splash	slumber ► sleep	smear ► rub, insult
sling ► throw	sloth ► laziness	slumbering ► asleep	

► = synonym cross-reference • ⇨ = antonym cross-reference   205

Thesaurus Entries Close-up

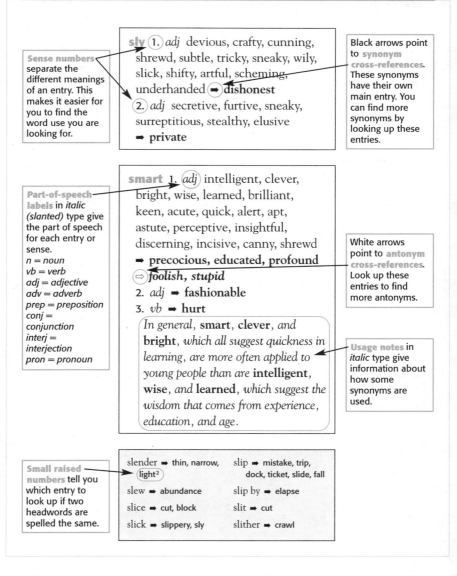

Sense numbers separate the different meanings of an entry. This makes it easier for you to find the word use you are looking for.

sly (1.) *adj* devious, crafty, cunning, shrewd, subtle, tricky, sneaky, wily, slick, shifty, artful, scheming, underhanded ➡ **dishonest**
(2.) *adj* secretive, furtive, sneaky, surreptitious, stealthy, elusive
➡ **private**

Black arrows point to **synonym cross-references**. These synonyms have their own main entry. You can find more synonyms by looking up these entries.

Part-of-speech labels in *italic (slanted)* type give the part of speech for each entry or sense.
n = noun
vb = verb
adj = adjective
adv = adverb
prep = preposition
conj = conjunction
interj = interjection
pron = pronoun

smart 1. *adj* intelligent, clever, bright, wise, learned, brilliant, keen, acute, quick, alert, apt, astute, perceptive, insightful, discerning, incisive, canny, shrewd
➡ **precocious, educated, profound**
⇨ *foolish, stupid*
2. *adj* ➡ **fashionable**
3. *vb* ➡ **hurt**

In general, **smart**, **clever**, *and* **bright**, *which all suggest quickness in learning, are more often applied to young people than are* **intelligent**, **wise**, *and* **learned**, *which suggest the wisdom that comes from experience, education, and age.*

White arrows point to **antonym cross-references**. Look up these entries to find more antonyms.

Usage notes in *italic* type give information about how some synonyms are used.

Small raised numbers tell you which entry to look up if two headwords are spelled the same.

slender ➡ thin, narrow, (light²)

slew ➡ abundance

slice ➡ cut, block

slick ➡ slippery, sly

slip ➡ mistake, trip, dock, ticket, slide, fall

slip by ➡ elapse

slit ➡ cut

slither ➡ crawl

How to Use This Book

The *Scholastic Pocket Thesaurus* will help you find synonyms for a word that you have in mind. The three main features of the thesaurus are explained below: **main entries**, **cross-references**, and the **on-the-page index**.

Main Entry Words

Synonyms are grouped together after **main entry words**. These **main entries** are listed alphabetically and printed in blue boldface type. Suppose you need a synonym for **exaggerate**. Your thesaurus has a main entry for **exaggerate** with nine synonyms:

exaggerate *vb* overstate, overdo, inflate, embellish, embroider, elaborate, gild, magnify, dramatize

If a main entry word has more than one sense or use, the synonyms are grouped in numbered senses, as in the entry for **boast**, which can be either a verb or a noun:

boast 1. *vb* brag, gloat, crow, show off, vaunt, swagger, exult
2. *n* brag, bragging, vaunt, claim, assertion, bluster, swagger, bravado

If two main entries have the same spelling, a small raised number is used to tell them apart, as at live[1] and live[2]. The same raised numbers are used in the index.

live[1] 1. *vb* exist, be, thrive, subsist, breathe → **experience**
2. *vb* survive, outlive, outlast, persevere, persist → **continue**
⇨ *die*
3. *vb* reside, dwell, stay, abide, inhabit, lodge, room, sojourn
→ **occupy**
live[2] *adj* → **lively, alive, active**

Part-of-speech labels

Each entry or numbered sense has a **part-of-speech label** that
identifies the part of speech of the main entry and the synonyms of
each sense. The part-of-speech labels are:

n	noun	*prep*	preposition
vb	verb	*conj*	conjunction
adj	adjective	*interj*	interjection
adv	adverb	*pron*	pronoun

Usage labels and usage notes

Some synonyms are followed by a **usage label** printed in *italics*
inside parentheses. A usage label helps you recognize how that
synonym is used. For example, there are two usage labels at the
entry for **wig**:

wig *n* hairpiece, fall, toupee, periwig *(historical)*, rug *(informal)*
→ **hair**

The *(historical)* label indicates that "periwig" is used in historical
contexts. You can learn from a dictionary that it is a term for a type
of wig popular in the 17th and 18th centuries. The *(informal)* label

is the most common usage label in this thesaurus. It warns you that a synonym should not be used in serious or formal writing or speech. Other usage labels may indicate the language of origin of a term, such as *"adios (Spanish), au revoir (French)"* at the entry **good-bye**, or a field of reference to which it is restricted, such as "petrol *(British)"* at **gasoline**.

Some entries are followed by a usage note, which gives information about how the synonyms are used or how they are different from each other. For an example, see the usage note at **maybe**:

> *All of these words express uncertainty about something.* **Maybe** *and* **perhaps** *are very close synonyms and it usually makes no difference which one you use.* **Possibly** *stresses the uncertainty more than* **maybe**. **Conceivably** *and* **feasibly** *suggest even greater uncertainty.* **Perchance** *is a more formal and less common synonym.*

Cross-references

Many entries include a boldface cross-reference, indicated by an arrow, that directs you to a related main entry. If you don't find a synonym that you want at one main entry, the cross-references direct you to other entries where you will find more choices. There are two types of cross-references: ➡ **synonym cross-references** and ⇨ *antonym cross-references.*

➡ Synonym cross-references
Synonym cross-references direct you to other main entries that are related to the main entry you looked up. Synonym cross-references

are printed in **boldface** type following a black arrow ➡, as at the entry for **patriotic**:

patriotic *adj* loyal, zealous, nationalistic, chauvinistic ➡ **faithful**

If the main entry you looked up does not have a synonym you want, the synonym cross-reference points you to another main entry that might be helpful.

Sometimes more than one synonym cross-reference is given, as at **tolerant**:

tolerant *adj* permissive, lenient, indulgent, easygoing ➡ **liberal, kind, patient**

In these cases, look first at the entry that seems closest to the idea you have in mind. And remember that the cross-reference itself may be a synonym for you to use.

In some main entries, you will find a sense number with only a cross-reference and no other synonyms. This cross-reference indicates that the synonyms for that sense are given at the cross-reference entry, as at the entry for **house**:

house 1. *n* ➡ **home**
2. *vb* accommodate, board, lodge, put up, shelter, quarter, billet

At the entry for **home**, you will find the noun "house" with 17 other synonyms and two more cross-references.

⇨ Antonym cross-references
Sometimes you can find a clearer way to express your idea by putting it in opposite terms. **Antonym cross-references** direct you to main entries that are approximate opposites, or *antonyms*, of the

entry where they are found. If you are not quite satisfied with any of the synonyms you have found, it may be helpful to check the antonym cross-references. Antonym cross-references are printed in **_boldface italic_** type following a white arrow ⇨, as at **punctual**:

punctual *adj* timely, prompt, precise, expeditious, punctilious
⇨ **_late_**

On-the-page Index

All of the synonyms in the *Scholastic Pocket Thesaurus* are listed alphabetically in the **on-the-page index** in the bottom portion of the page. Each word in the index is followed by a black arrow ➡ with one or more **main entries** where the index word is listed as a synonym:

clash ➡ bang, fight
classic ➡ masterpiece, model
classified ➡ secret
classify ➡ arrange

If a word you are looking for is not a main entry, you should look in the **on-the-page index** on the same page where you looked for it as a main entry. Having the **on-the-page index** on the same pages as the main entries means that you will not have to look in two parts of the book just to get started in your search for the right word. For example, if you look up the word **silly**, you will find that it is not a main entry on page 203. The main entries go from **sideways** to **singer**. On the bottom of that same page, however, you will find "silly" in the **on-the-page index**:

silly ➡ foolish

All you need to do now is turn to the main entry for **foolish**, where there are 10 synonyms, including "silly," and three more cross-references.

Guide Words

The **guide words** at the top left and right corners of the pages give the first and last words alphabetically on each page, including both the **main entries** and the **on-the-page index**.

An Important Reminder

Teachers have one common complaint about the way thesauruses are used. They complain that often students will pick an unfamiliar synonym without realizing that it does not fit properly into the sentence where they put it. Remember that **no two synonyms mean *exactly* the same thing**. Sometimes synonyms are used in different grammatical constructions. If you have a feeling that a synonym is not quite right, trust your instincts. You can either look in a dictionary to find out more about it or pick another synonym that you are more sure of. Anytime you are not certain whether a synonym is just the one you want, or if you are not sure what it means, look it up in a dictionary. Or ask someone whose judgment and knowledge of the language you can trust.

A

abandon 1. *vb* quit, cease, discontinue, concede, abdicate, renounce, resign, forfeit, scuttle ➡ **surrender, discard**
2. *vb* ➡ **leave, betray**

abandoned *adj* deserted, desolate, forsaken, uninhabited, neglected, rejected, derelict ➡ **empty**

abbreviation *n* acronym, initialism, contraction, abridgment, shortening

ability *n* capability, capacity, competence, aptitude, proficiency, ingenuity, faculty, power, efficacy ➡ **strength, talent**

able 1. *adj* capable, competent, qualified, eligible, authorized, suitable, fit
2. *adj* accomplished, proficient, skillful, adept, clever, handy, dexterous, deft ➡ **smart, expert, practical**

abolish *vb* end, eradicate, exterminate, eliminate, revoke, cancel, obliterate, repeal, rescind, annul, nullify, countermand, disallow, veto, overrule ➡ **finish, destroy, erase** ⇨ *save*

about 1. *adv* approximately, around, roughly, nearly, almost ➡ **practically**
2. *adv* around, round, all around, everywhere, nearby
3. *prep* concerning, regarding, touching, relating to
4. *prep* around, near, at

above 1. *prep* over, on, higher than, upon ⇨ *under*
2. *prep* over, more than, beyond, exceeding
3. *adv* over, overhead, up, upward, upwards, aloft ⇨ *under*

If the word you want is not a main entry above, look below to find it.

abase ➡ shame

abash ➡ embarrass, confuse

abashed ➡ ashamed

abate ➡ decrease

abbess ➡ religious

abbey ➡ monastery

abbot ➡ religious

abbreviate ➡ condense

abbreviated ➡ short

abdicate ➡ abandon

abdication ➡ surrender

abdomen ➡ stomach

abduct ➡ seize

aberration ➡ oddity, departure

abhor ➡ hate

abhorrence ➡ hatred

abide ➡ bear, live[1], wait

abiding ➡ permanent

abject ➡ poor, servile

ablaze ➡ burning

abnormal ➡ strange

abnormality ➡ oddity

abode ➡ home

abominable ➡ bad

abominate ➡ hate

aboriginal ➡ primitive, native

abortive ➡ useless

abounding ➡ abundant

above all ➡ best

---

abroad *adj* overseas, away, traveling, touring

abrupt 1. *adj* blunt, hurried, impetuous, brusque, curt, short, gruff ➡ **rude, thoughtless**
2. *adj* ➡ **steep**
3. *adj* ➡ **sudden, sharp**

absence 1. *n* nonattendance, truancy, absenteeism ⇨ *presence*
2. *n* deficiency, dearth, lack ➡ **want**

absent *adj* away, missing, elsewhere, astray, AWOL ➡ **lost** ⇨ *present*

absentminded *adj* forgetful, preoccupied, distracted, inattentive, oblivious, scatterbrained, spacey (*informal*) ➡ **absorbed**

absorb 1. *vb* soak (up), digest, suck up, sop up
2. *vb* ➡ **learn, interest**

absorbed *adj* engrossed, engaged, intent, involved, preoccupied, immersed ➡ **thoughtful, absent-minded**

abstain *vb* refrain, forbear, forgo, renounce, shun, eschew ➡ **avoid**

abstinence *n* temperance, forbearance, denial, self-denial, self-restraint, austerity, moderation, celibacy

abundance *n* profusion, wealth, surplus, plethora, excess, plenty, lot, peck, slew, load, ton, glut

abundant *adj* plentiful, copious, ample, profuse, plenteous, generous, voluminous, abounding, bountiful, bounteous, prodigal, much ➡ **big, enough**

abuse 1. *vb* misuse, mistreat, torment, oppress, suppress, repress, ill-treat, maltreat, torture, persecute, victimize, molest, harass ➡ **hurt, insult, punish**
2. *n* misuse, mistreatment, ill-treatment, injury, harm, punishment, torture

---

If the word you want is not a main entry above, look below to find it.

abrade ➡ rub

abrasion ➡ friction

abreast ➡ parallel

abridge ➡ condense

abridged ➡ short

abridgment ➡ abbreviation, summary

abscess ➡ sore

absentee ➡ runaway

absenteeism ➡ absence

absolute ➡ complete, certain, unconditional, dictatorial

absolutely ➡ very, certainly

absolution ➡ forgiveness

absolutism ➡ tyranny

absolve ➡ forgive

absorbing ➡ interesting

abstinent ➡ celibate

abstract ➡ theoretical, summary

abstruse ➡ obscure

absurd ➡ foolish, illogical

absurdity ➡ nonsense

abut ➡ border

abutting ➡ adjacent

abyss ➡ hole

accent 1. *n* stress, emphasis, prominence, beat, cadence, diacritic 2. *n* pronunciation, inflection, drawl, twang, burr ➡ **dialect** 3. *n* ➡ **decoration** 4. *vb* ➡ **emphasize**

accident 1. *n* mishap, setback ➡ **collision, disaster, emergency** 2. *n* ➡ **chance**

accidental *adj* incidental, coincidental, unintentional, fortuitous, inadvertent, unplanned, chance ➡ **lucky**

accidentally *adv* unintentionally, inadvertently, unwittingly, unconsciously, fortuitously, incidentally ⇨ *purposely*

accompany *vb* escort, attend, chaperon, chaperone, convoy ➡ **lead**

accuracy *n* exactness, precision, correctness, exactitude ➡ **truth**

acquisition 1. *n* attainment, procurement, takeover, appropriation 2. *n* purchase, inheritance, possession, accession ➡ **property**

If the word you want is not a main entry above, look below to find it.

academic
➡ theoretical, intellectual, teacher

academy ➡ school

accede ➡ agree, surrender

accelerate ➡ hurry

acceleration ➡ speed

accentuate
➡ emphasize

accept ➡ agree, approve, believe, receive, bear

acceptable ➡ fair

acceptance
➡ approval

access ➡ door

accessible ➡ available, open

accession
➡ acquisition

accessory ➡ partner

acclaim ➡ approve, praise

acclamation ➡ praise

acclimatize ➡ adjust

accommodate
➡ adjust, house, contain, condescend

accommodation
➡ loan

accomplice ➡ partner

accomplish ➡ do

accomplished ➡ able, successful

accomplishment
➡ act, work, success

accord ➡ agree, agreement

accordingly
➡ therefore

accost ➡ approach, call

account ➡ story, description, supply

accoutrement
➡ equipment

accumulate ➡ gather

accurate ➡ correct, careful

accurately ➡ correctly

accusation
➡ complaint

accuse ➡ blame

accused ➡ defendant

accustomed ➡ usual

ace ➡ expert

ache ➡ pain, hurt

achieve ➡ do, win

achievement ➡ act, event, success

acid ➡ sour

acidic ➡ sour

acknowledge ➡ admit, answer, believe

acknowledgment
➡ gratitude, apology

acme ➡ top

acquaint ➡ introduce

acquaintance
➡ friend, introduction

acquiesce ➡ surrender

acquiescence
➡ surrender

acquire ➡ get

acquisitive ➡ greedy

acquit ➡ forgive

acrid ➡ smelly

➡ = synonym cross-reference • ⇨ = antonym cross-reference   3

acrobat n gymnast, tumbler, aerialist, trapeze artist ➡ **athlete**

act 1. vb perform, work, function, operate, execute, stage, carry out, ply, serve, go ➡ **do**
2. vb behave, seem, appear
3. vb perform, play, enact, stage, portray, dramatize, impersonate, pose, render ➡ **pretend**
4. n deed, action, feat, accomplishment, achievement, exploit, undertaking, step ➡ **work**
5. n bill, law, decree, statute, ordinance, legislation ➡ **rule**
6. n performance, routine, number, sketch, bit, skit ➡ **pretense**

active adj animated, spirited, dynamic, busy, vibrant, bustling, frenetic, hyperactive, strenuous, athletic ➡ **lively, alive** ⇨ *passive*

activity 1. n action, motion, liveliness, commotion, bustle ➡ **movement** ⇨ *calm*
2. n ➡ **pastime, exercise**

actor n actress, performer, player, entertainer, star, thespian, ham ➡ **celebrity, comic, artist**

add 1. vb sum, total, calculate, compute, tally, count, score ⇨ *subtract*
2. vb combine, include, append, annex, supplement, incorporate, integrate ➡ **join**

addition 1. n reckoning, computing, summation, tabulating, counting ⇨ *subtraction*
2. n extension, expansion, annex, enlargement, appendix, complement, supplement, amendment, rider, codicil

adhesive 1. n glue, paste, mucilage, cement, epoxy, tape, Scotch tape (*trademark*), adhesive tape, masking tape, duct tape
2. adj ➡ **sticky**

If the word you want is not a main entry above, look below to find it.

acrobatics ➡ **gymnastics**

acronym ➡ **abbreviation**

across from ➡ **opposite**

acting ➡ **temporary**

action ➡ **act, activity, fight, suit**

action figure ➡ **doll**

activate ➡ **start**

actress ➡ **actor**

actual ➡ **real**

actuality ➡ **certainty, event**

actually ➡ **really**

acute ➡ **sharp, smart, urgent**

ad ➡ **advertisement**

adage ➡ **saying**

adamant ➡ **resolute, hard**

adapt ➡ **adjust, prepare**

adaptation ➡ **translation**

added ➡ **more**

addict ➡ **fan**

addiction ➡ **habit**

additional ➡ **more**

additionally ➡ **more, besides**

address ➡ **approach, welcome, speech, destination**

adept ➡ **able**

adequate ➡ **enough, fair**

adequately ➡ **well**

adhere ➡ **stick, obey**

adhesive tape ➡ **adhesive**

adjacent 1. *adj* adjoining, neighboring, bordering, abutting, tangent, next, next door ➡ **near**
2. *prep* ➡ **beside**

adjust *vb* alter, modify, regulate, adapt, tailor, accommodate, conform, acclimatize, orient ➡ **change, fix, arrange**

admit 1. *vb* acknowledge, confess, own, concede, confirm, allow ➡ **reveal**
2. *vb* ➡ **receive**

adopt 1. *vb* embrace, appropriate, assume, espouse ➡ **approve, choose, use**
2. *vb* foster, take in, raise, rear

adult 1. *adj* grown-up, mature, full-grown, ripe

2. *n* grown-up, man, woman ⇨ **child, baby**

advantage *n* benefit, profit, superiority, convenience, vantage, upper hand, asset, virtue, plus, avail

adventure *n* exploit, escapade, venture, enterprise, spree, lark, fling ➡ **event**

advertise *vb* publicize, announce, promote, proclaim, declare, broadcast, pitch, parade, flaunt, plug ➡ **tell, show**

advertisement *n* commercial, ad, notice, circular, flier, billboard, poster, promotion, pitch, plug ➡ **announcement**

advertising *n* promotion, publicity, hype, propaganda ➡ **advertisement**

if the word you want is not a main entry above, look below to find it.

adieu ➡ good-bye
adios ➡ good-bye
adjoin ➡ border
adjoining ➡ adjacent, beside
adjudge ➡ decide
adjudicate ➡ try
adjustment ➡ repair, correction
ad-lib ➡ invent
administer ➡ lead, govern
administration ➡ government, leadership

administrator ➡ official, principal
admirable ➡ good
admiration ➡ respect
admire ➡ love, respect
admission ➡ ticket
admonish ➡ scold, warn
admonition ➡ warning, advice
adolescence ➡ childhood
adolescent ➡ teenager, young
adorable ➡ cute
adoration ➡ love

adore ➡ love, worship
adoring ➡ loving
adorn ➡ decorate
adornment ➡ decoration
adroit ➡ expert
adroitness ➡ talent, agility
adulate ➡ flatter
adulation ➡ praise, worship
adulterate ➡ weaken
adulthood ➡ maturity
advance ➡ approach, go, promote, lend,

progress, loan, forward
advanced ➡ gifted
advancement ➡ progress, promotion
advantageous ➡ useful
advent ➡ approach
adventuresome ➡ brave
adventurous ➡ brave
adversary ➡ enemy, opponent
adverse ➡ unfortunate, destructive
adversity ➡ hardship

advice *n* guidance, counsel, recommendation, suggestion, caution, admonition ➡ **tip, warning**

adviser *n* advisor, counselor, counsel, consultant, attorney, lawyer, advocate ➡ **teacher**

affect 1. *vb* influence, impress, move, sway
2. *vb* ➡ **act, pretend**
3. *n* ➡ **emotion**
In the most common or frequent uses of **affect** *and* **effect**, **affect** *is a verb and* **effect** *is a noun. There is also a verb* **effect**, *which you should be careful not to confuse with the verb* **affect**. *See* **effect**.

afford *vb* pay for, support, bear, manage

afraid *adj* scared, frightened, alarmed, terrified, petrified, aghast, scared, timorous ➡ **anxious, nervous, cowardly** ⇨ *brave*

afternoon *n* p.m., midday, lunchtime, teatime ➡ **day, evening**

again *adv* once more, anew, afresh, over ➡ **encore**

agent 1. *n* representative, intermediary, middleman, broker, executor, liaison, delegate, spokesperson, go-between, handler ➡ **seller**
2. *n* ➡ **spy**

agile *adj* nimble, spry, quick, sprightly, dexterous, supple, limber ➡ **active**

agility *n* dexterity, nimbleness, adroitness, spryness ➡ **talent**

If the word you want is not a main entry above, look below to find it.

advise ➡ **suggest, warn**

advisor ➡ **adviser**

advocate ➡ **prefer, adviser**

aerate ➡ **fan**

aerialist ➡ **acrobat**

aerobatics ➡ **gymnastics**

aerobics ➡ **gymnastics**

aeronaut ➡ **pilot**

aeronautics ➡ **flight**

affable ➡ **nice**

affair ➡ **business**

affectation ➡ **pretense, habit**

affection ➡ **love**

affectionate ➡ **loving**

affidavit ➡ **document**

affiliate ➡ **member, department**

affiliation ➡ **link**

affinity ➡ **link, similarity, relationship**

affirm ➡ **believe, testify, approve**

affirmative ➡ **yes**

afflict ➡ **hurt, trouble**

affliction ➡ **hardship, illness, disability**

affluence ➡ **wealth**

affluent ➡ **rich**

affordable ➡ **cheap**

affront ➡ **insult**

aficionado ➡ **fan**

afire ➡ **burning**

afresh ➡ **again**

aft ➡ **back**

after ➡ **past**

aftermath ➡ **effect**

aftershock ➡ **earthquake**

afterword ➡ **conclusion**

against ➡ **beside, opposite**

age ➡ **period, weather**

aged ➡ **old**

agency ➡ **department**

agenda ➡ **list**

aggravate ➡ **bother**

aggravated ➡ **angry**

aggregate ➡ **total**

aggression ➡ **violence, anger**

aggressive ➡ **belligerent, ambitious**

aghast ➡ **afraid**

---

agree 1. *vb* consent, assent, concur, accept, accede ⇨ *argue, object*
2. *vb* match, correspond, coincide, harmonize, accord, jibe ➡ **suit**

agreement 1. *n* bargain, deal, contract, lease, treaty, pact, accord, covenant, compact, arrangement, compromise, understanding
2. *n* consent, assent, consensus, concurrence, compliance, conformity, sympathy, harmony ➡ **unity**

air 1. *n* sky, heaven, atmosphere, stratosphere, troposphere ➡ **space**
2. *n* breath, ventilation, oxygen ➡ **wind**
3. *n* ➡ **quality, appearance**
4. *vb* ➡ **broadcast, play, say**

airplane *n* aircraft, plane, flying machine ➡ **vehicle**

alert 1. *adj* attentive, wide-awake, watchful, vigilant, aware, conscious ➡ **awake**
2. *adj* ➡ **smart**
3. *vb* ➡ **warn**

alibi *n* defense, excuse, cover story

alike 1. *adj* similar, like, analogous, comparable, equivalent, parallel, close, akin ➡ **same** ⇨ *different*
2. *adv* similarly, likewise, comparably, analogously

alive *adj* living, live, animate, animated, vital, viable, quick, organic ➡ **lively, active** ⇨ *dead*

all 1. *n, pron* everything, everyone, everybody, sum, whole, totality ➡ **total**
2. *adj* every, entire, each, complete, whole, total
3. *adv* ➡ **completely**

If the word you want is not a main entry above, look below to find it.

agitate ➡ disturb, fan, excite

agitated ➡ tense

agitation ➡ excitement

agnostic ➡ atheist

agonizing ➡ uncomfortable

agony ➡ misery

agrarian ➡ farming

agreeable ➡ nice, pleasant, compatible

agricultural ➡ farming

agriculture ➡ farming

ahead ➡ forward

ahead of ➡ before

aid ➡ help, back

aide ➡ helper

ail ➡ trouble

ailing ➡ sick

ailment ➡ illness

aim ➡ object, plan, intend

aimless ➡ indiscriminate

aircraft ➡ airplane

airfield ➡ field

airless ➡ stuffy

airman ➡ pilot

airport ➡ field

airtight ➡ tight

airy ➡ windy

ajar ➡ open

akin ➡ alike

alarm ➡ fear, scare, warning

alarmed ➡ afraid

alcohol ➡ drink

alcoholic ➡ drunkard

alcove ➡ bay

alertness ➡ attention

alfalfa ➡ hay

alfresco ➡ outside

alias ➡ pseudonym

alien ➡ foreign, foreigner

alight ➡ descend

align ➡ straighten

aligned ➡ parallel

alignment ➡ order

all around ➡ about

allay ➡ relieve

---

alone *adj* lone, solitary, isolated, unaccompanied, unattended, solo, single-handed ➡ **lonely, single**

alternate 1. *vb* reciprocate, oscillate, fluctuate, switch
2. *adj* alternating, every other ➡ **periodic**
3. *n* substitute, replacement, backup, surrogate, double

amateur 1. *n* nonprofessional, novice, beginner, dilettante, apprentice, neophyte
2. *adj* amateurish, unskilled, inexperienced, untrained, inexpert,

unpaid, green ➡ **clumsy, incompetent, naive**

ambition 1. *n* aspiration, drive, enterprise, eagerness, desire, will, get-up-and-go, initiative ➡ **hope, enthusiasm, energy**
2. *n* ➡ **object**

ambitious 1. *adj* eager, zealous, enterprising, determined, aggressive, industrious, resourceful ➡ **competitive** ⇨ *lazy*
2. *adj* ➡ **hard**

If the word you want is not a main entry above, look below to find it.

allegation ➡ complaint

allege ➡ argue

allegiance ➡ loyalty

alleviate ➡ relieve

alley ➡ road

alliance ➡ union

allocate ➡ budget

allot ➡ budget

allotment ➡ share, budget

allow ➡ let, admit

allowable ➡ legal

allowance ➡ share, wage, budget, loan

all right ➡ cool

allude ➡ mention

allure ➡ attraction, enchantment, personality

alluring ➡ attractive

ally ➡ friend

almighty ➡ strong

almost ➡ about

alms ➡ gift

aloft ➡ above

alongside ➡ beside, parallel

aloof ➡ cool

alphabetical ➡ consecutive

already ➡ before

also ➡ besides

alter ➡ change, adjust

alteration ➡ change

altercation ➡ fight

alternately ➡ instead

alternating ➡ alternate

alternative ➡ choice

alternatively ➡ instead

although ➡ but

altitude ➡ height

altogether ➡ completely

altruistic ➡ generous

always ➡ forever, regularly

a.m. ➡ morning

amalgam ➡ mixture

amalgamation ➡ union, mixture

amass ➡ gather

amateurish ➡ amateur

amaze ➡ surprise

amazed ➡ dumbfounded

amazement ➡ surprise

amazing ➡ awesome

ambassador ➡ diplomat, messenger

ambiance ➡ setting

ambiguity ➡ problem

ambiguous ➡ obscure

ambivalent ➡ doubtful

amble ➡ walk

ambush ➡ attack

amen ➡ yes

amend ➡ perfect, correct

amendment ➡ addition

amiability ➡ hospitality

amiable ➡ friendly

amicable ➡ peaceful

---

n = noun • *vb* = verb • *adj* = adjective • *adv* = adverb • *prep* = preposition • *conj* = conjunction

ammunition *n* munitions, matériel, ammo (*informal*), bullets, shells

ancestor *n* forebear, forefather, progenitor, forerunner, predecessor, antecedent, patriarch, matriarch, elder ➡ **parent**

ancestry *n* lineage, birth, descent, extraction, blood ➡ **family**

anchor 1. *n* mooring, grapnel, stay, mainstay ➡ **support, protection**
2. *n* ➡ **reporter**
3. *vb* ➡ **dock, join**

angel *n* spirit, sprite, archangel, seraph, cherub

anger 1. *n* rage, fury, wrath, temper, indignation, hostility, animosity, annoyance, ire, aggression, belligerence
2. *vb* infuriate, enrage, madden, incense, exasperate, outrage, upset, provoke, rile, antagonize, embitter ➡ **bother**

angry *adj* mad, furious, upset, annoyed, irritated, aggravated, exasperated, indignant, irate, infuriated, livid, bitter, sore ➡ **cross, belligerent, violent**

animal 1. *n* creature, beast, brute, being, organism ➡ **monster**
2. *adj* bestial, beastly, brutish

announcement *n* declaration, notice, notification, proclamation, report, statement, pronouncement, news, revelation, bulletin, message, tidings ➡ **advertisement**

If the word you want is not a main entry above, look below to find it.

amid ➡ between

amidst ➡ between

amigo ➡ friend

amiss ➡ wrong

amity ➡ friendship, peace

ammo ➡ ammunition

amnesty ➡ forgiveness

among ➡ between, through

amongst ➡ between

amorous ➡ loving

amount ➡ number, total, price, measure

amphibian ➡ reptile

amphitheater ➡ hall

ample ➡ enough, abundant

amplify ➡ strengthen, lengthen, grow

amputate ➡ cut

amuse ➡ entertain

amusement ➡ entertainment, pleasure, humor, toy

amusement park ➡ carnival

amusing ➡ funny

analogous ➡ alike

analogously ➡ alike

analogue ➡ duplicate

analogy ➡ similarity

analysis ➡ study, reason

analyze ➡ study

anarchy ➡ confusion

anatomy ➡ body

anchorage ➡ harbor

ancient ➡ old

anecdote ➡ story

anesthetic ➡ drug

anew ➡ again

angelic ➡ innocent

angle ➡ corner, perspective

angleworm ➡ worm

anguish ➡ misery, sorrow

animal farm ➡ zoo

animals ➡ livestock

animate ➡ alive

animated ➡ alive, active

animation ➡ life

animosity ➡ anger, hatred

annex ➡ add, addition

annihilate ➡ destroy, kill

annihilation ➡ murder

announce ➡ tell, advertise

➡ = synonym cross-reference • ⇨ = antonym cross-reference   9

anonymous *adj* unsigned, unnamed, unknown, pseudonymous, nameless, secret

answer 1. *n* reply, response, retort, rejoinder, riposte, reaction, reciprocation ⇨ **question**
2. *n* solution, key, result, explanation, resolution, product ⇨ **problem, question**
3. *vb* reply, respond, retort, acknowledge, echo, counter, react, reciprocate ⇨ **question**
4. *vb* ➡ **solve**
5. *vb* ➡ **satisfy**

anticipate 1. *vb* foresee, expect, look forward to ➡ **predict**
2. *vb* ➡ **hope**

antique 1. *n* heirloom, relic, curio, artifact, antiquity
2. *adj* ➡ **old**

anxious 1. *adj* worried, apprehensive, uneasy, disturbed, insecure ➡ **afraid, nervous, tense**
2. *adj* ➡ **eager**

any *pron* each, some, every, either ➡ **few**

anyway *adv* anyhow, nevertheless, nonetheless, however, regardless, notwithstanding, still

apart *adv* asunder, separately, independently ⇨ **together**

apathetic *adj* indifferent, unconcerned, unresponsive, uncaring, disinterested, nonchalant ➡ **listless, lazy, cool** ⇨ **eager**

apathy *n* indifference, unconcern, nonchalance, disinterest ➡ **boredom** ⇨ **enthusiasm**

If the word you want is not a main entry above, look below to find it.

annoy ➡ bother

annoyance ➡ anger, nuisance

annoyed ➡ angry

annoying ➡ inconvenient

annual ➡ flower

annuity ➡ pension

annul ➡ abolish

anoint ➡ rub, bless

anomaly ➡ oddity

anon ➡ soon

another ➡ more, different

antagonism ➡ opposition, competition

antagonist ➡ enemy, opponent

antagonistic ➡ unfriendly, competitive

antagonize ➡ anger

antarctic ➡ cold

ante ➡ bet

antecedent ➡ ancestor, past

antedate ➡ precede

anteroom ➡ hall

anthem ➡ hymn

antibiotic ➡ drug

antic ➡ joke, funny

anticipated ➡ due

anticipation ➡ foresight, suspense

antidepressant ➡ drug

antidote ➡ cure

antipathy ➡ opposition, hatred

antiquated ➡ old

antiquity ➡ antique, past

antiseptic ➡ sterile

antisocial ➡ unfriendly

antithesis ➡ opposite

antithetical ➡ opposite

anxiety ➡ worry, fear

anyhow ➡ anyway

apartment ➡ home, room

ape ➡ boor, imitate

---

apology *n* excuse, acknowledgment, regrets, explanation

apparently 1. *adv* evidently, seemingly, presumably, supposedly, reputedly ➡ **probably**
2. *adv* clearly, obviously, plainly, patently

appeal 1. *vb* petition, pray, supplicate, sue, invoke ➡ **beg, ask**
2. *vb* ➡ **fascinate**
3. *n* request, plea, claim, petition, application ➡ **invitation**
4. *n* ➡ **attraction**

appear 1. *vb* emerge, arise, rise, surface, materialize, come into view, show up, turn up, form ➡ **come**
2. *vb* ➡ **act**
3. *vb* ➡ **look**

appearance 1. *n* look, looks, aspect, features, countenance, demeanor, air, atmosphere, bearing, mien, visage
2. *n* ➡ **approach**

appetite *n* hunger, thirst, craving ➡ **desire**

appointment 1. *n* selection, nomination, election, designation, assignment, delegation, installation, investiture, ordination ➡ **choice**
2. *n* ➡ **meeting, visit**
3. *n* ➡ **profession**

appreciate 1. *vb* value, prize, cherish, treasure, relish, savor ➡ **respect**
2. *vb* thank, enjoy ➡ **welcome**
3. *vb* ➡ **understand**

If the word you want is not a main entry above, look below to find it.

aperture ➡ hole

apex ➡ top

aphorism ➡ saying

apocryphal ➡ legendary

apogee ➡ top

apologetic ➡ sorry

apologize ➡ regret

appall ➡ shock, disgust

appalling ➡ awful, scary

apparatus ➡ equipment, tool

apparel ➡ clothes

apparent ➡ obvious, likely

apparition ➡ ghost, illusion

appealing ➡ pleasant, attractive

appease ➡ pacify, soften, satisfy

appellation ➡ name

append ➡ add

appendage ➡ limb

appendix ➡ addition, table

appertain ➡ concern

appetizing ➡ delicious

applaud ➡ approve, clap

applause ➡ praise

appliance ➡ tool

applicable ➡ fit[1], relevant

applicant ➡ candidate

application ➡ use, diligence, appeal

apply ➡ belong, use, ask

appoint ➡ name, hire

apportion ➡ share, divide

apposite ➡ relevant, fit[1]

appraisal ➡ estimate

appreciation ➡ gratitude, wisdom

appreciative ➡ grateful

apprehend ➡ arrest, know

apprehension ➡ worry, fear, suspense, arrest

apprehensive ➡ anxious, suspicious

apprentice ➡ amateur

apprise ➡ introduce

---

approach 1. *vb* come near, draw near, near, advance, loom, gravitate toward ➡ **come**
2. *vb* address, accost, speak to ➡ **talk** ⇨ *avoid*
3. *n* coming, arrival, appearance, advent, entry
4. *n* ➡ **method, treatment**

approval 1. *n* acceptance, passage, ratification, enactment ➡ **support, praise**
2. *n* ➡ **permission**

approve 1. *vb* endorse, support, authorize, sanction, certify, ratify, validate, legalize, affirm ➡ **agree, back**
2. *vb* accept, favor, applaud, recommend, acclaim, commend ➡ **appreciate**

approximate 1. *adj* rough, inexact, estimated, close, near, ballpark, general
2. *vb* ➡ **estimate**
3. *vb* ➡ **resemble**

arbitrary 1. *adj* chance, random, subjective, unpredictable, unscientific, haphazard, unplanned, careless, stray ➡ **indiscriminate**
2. *adj* capricious, frivolous, impulsive, whimsical ➡ **illogical**
3. *adj* willful, unreasonable ➡ **dictatorial**

argue 1. *vb* quarrel, debate, dispute, disagree, bicker, squabble, quibble, wrangle ➡ **fight** ⇨ *agree*
2. *vb* claim, maintain, plead, assert, contend, allege, charge, protest

argument *n* quarrel, dispute, debate, controversy, discussion, squabble, row, fuss, falling-out, disagreement, misunderstanding, spat, tiff ➡ **fight, disagreement**

If the word you want is not a main entry above, look below to find it.

approaching ➡ future

appropriate ➡ fit¹, correct, take, adopt

appropriately ➡ correctly

appropriation ➡ acquisition

approved ➡ official

approvingly ➡ well

approximately ➡ about

approximation ➡ estimate

apricot ➡ orange

apropos ➡ relevant

apt ➡ likely, fit¹, smart

aptitude ➡ talent, ability

aquarium ➡ zoo

aqueduct ➡ channel

aqueous ➡ liquid

arbiter ➡ judge

arbitrate ➡ negotiate, decide

arboretum ➡ greenhouse

arc ➡ curve

arcane ➡ secret

arch ➡ bend, curve

archaic ➡ old, early

archangel ➡ angel

archetypal ➡ model

archetype ➡ model

archfiend ➡ devil

archipelago ➡ island

architect ➡ creator

arctic ➡ cold

ardent ➡ eager, loving

ardor ➡ enthusiasm

arduous ➡ hard

area ➡ space, zone, field

arena ➡ field, hall

argot ➡ dialect

arid ➡ dry, sterile

arise ➡ ascend, descend, appear, happen

aristocracy *n* nobility, gentry, elite, upper class, society, high society, haut monde (*French*), jet set, rich

arm 1. *n* forelimb, forearm ➡ **limb**
2. *n* ➡ **branch**
3. *n* ➡ **bay**

arms *n* weapons, weaponry, armament, ordnance, artillery, matériel, armor ➡ **gun**

army 1. *n* force, armed force, troops, military, service, militia, legion ➡ **troop, soldier**
2. *n* ➡ **crowd**

arrange 1. *vb* organize, sort, classify, order, file, systematize, categorize, determine, array, structure, place, rank, orient, orientate ➡ **adjust, straighten**
2. *vb* plan, devise, set up, schedule

arrest 1. *vb* apprehend, detain, take prisoner, bust (*informal*), collar (*informal*), nab (*informal*) ➡ **catch, seize**
2. *vb* ➡ **stop**
3. *n* capture, seizure, detention, apprehension

art *n* skill, craft, technique, artistry, craftsmanship, creativity, artifice ➡ **talent**

articulate 1. *adj* intelligible, understandable, eloquent, lucid, fluent, clear, coherent
2. *vb* ➡ **pronounce**

artist *n* painter, sculptor, artisan, craftsman ➡ **musician, actor, photographer, writer, creator**

ascend *vb* climb, rise, mount, arise ⇨ *descend*

If the word you want is not a main entry above, look below to find it.

aristocrat ➡ noble
aristocratic ➡ noble
armada ➡ navy
armament ➡ arms
armed ➡ military
armed force ➡ army
armistice ➡ truce
armoire ➡ closet
armor ➡ arms
armory ➡ warehouse
aroma ➡ smell
aromatic ➡ fragrant
around ➡ about, through

arouse ➡ wake, excite, fan
arraign ➡ try
arrangement ➡ order, structure, display, bouquet, agreement, score
array ➡ assortment, display, arrange, deploy, dress
arrears ➡ debt
arrival ➡ approach, return
arrive ➡ come
arrivederci ➡ good-bye

arrogance ➡ pride
arrogant ➡ proud, dogmatic
arrow ➡ missile
arroyo ➡ canyon
arsenal ➡ warehouse
artery ➡ blood vessel, channel, road
artful ➡ sly
art gallery ➡ gallery
article ➡ object, report
articulation ➡ speech, word
artifact ➡ antique

artifice ➡ art, trick
artificial ➡ fake, manufactured
artillery ➡ arms
artisan ➡ artist
artistic ➡ talented
artistry ➡ art
artless ➡ naive
as ➡ because
ascendancy ➡ victory
ascension ➡ climb
ascent ➡ slant, climb
ascertain ➡ learn, verify, infer

---

ashamed *adj* humiliated, mortified, chagrined, embarrassed, shamed, abashed ➡ **sorry**

ask *vb* inquire, request, question, interrogate, query, quiz, examine, interview, grill, petition, apply ➡ **beg**

asleep *adj* sleeping, dozing, napping, resting, dreaming, somnolent, slumbering, dormant, hibernating ➡ **unconscious** ⇨ *awake*

assembly 1. *n* ➡ meeting, committee, government

2. *n* construction, building, creation, erection, fabrication, production, manufacture, formation

assortment *n* variety, mix, selection, collection, compilation, array, miscellany, range, series, gamut, medley, potpourri, hash ➡ **pile, mess**

assume 1. *vb* presume, postulate, presuppose, surmise, gather ➡ **guess, believe, pretend**
2. *vb* ➡ **adopt, bear**

If the word you want is not a main entry above, look below to find it.

ascetic ➡ hermit

ascot ➡ tie, scarf

ascribe ➡ attribute

ashen ➡ pale

ashram ➡ monastery

asinine ➡ foolish

askance ➡ sideways

askew ➡ zigzag

aspect ➡ appearance, part

asphyxiate ➡ choke

aspirant ➡ candidate

aspiration ➡ ambition, hope

aspire ➡ hope

assail ➡ attack

assailant ➡ enemy

assassin ➡ killer

assassinate ➡ kill

assassination ➡ murder

assault ➡ attack

assemble ➡ build, gather

assembly plant ➡ factory

assent ➡ agree, agreement

assert ➡ insist, argue

assertion ➡ boast

assertive ➡ certain

assess ➡ estimate, charge

assessment ➡ estimate, tax

asset ➡ advantage

assets ➡ property, wealth

assiduous ➡ patient, diligent

assign ➡ name, attribute, place

assignment ➡ appointment, job, lesson

assimilate ➡ learn

assist ➡ help

assistance ➡ support, help

assistant ➡ helper

associate ➡ friend, partner, join, mix

association ➡ organization, union, link

assonant ➡ musical

assorted ➡ different

assuage ➡ soften

assumption ➡ theory, conclusion

assurance ➡ promise, certainty

assure ➡ guarantee, promise, verify

assured ➡ certain, resolute

asteroid ➡ meteor

astonish ➡ surprise

astonished ➡ dumbfounded

astonishing ➡ awesome

astonishment ➡ surprise

astound ➡ shock

astounding ➡ great

astray ➡ absent

astrologer ➡ prophet

astute ➡ smart

asunder ➡ apart

---

n = noun • *vb* = verb • *adj* = adjective • *adv* = adverb • *prep* = preposition • *conj* = conjunction

atheist *n* agnostic, deist, freethinker, unbeliever, nonbeliever, infidel, heathen ➡ **skeptic**

athlete *n* player, competitor, contender, sportsman, sportswoman, jock *(informal)* ➡ **contestant**

atom *n* molecule

attack 1. *vb* invade, assault, charge, ambush, waylay, mug, storm, raid, beseige, harry, assail, ravage, bombard, strike ➡ **fight, argue, pillage** ⇨ *protect*
2. *n* assault, raid, invasion, charge, offensive, offense, incursion, strike, sally, sortie, foray, onset, onslaught, counterattack, operation, sack
3. *n* ➡ **fit²**

attention 1. *n* concentration, awareness, alertness, thought, consideration ➡ **diligence**
2. *n* ➡ **notice**

attic *n* loft, garret, dormer ➡ **room**

attraction *n* allure, appeal, charm, draw, fascination, enticement, temptation, lure, seduction ➡ **pull, personality**

attractive *adj* appealing, fascinating, captivating, magnetic, alluring, inviting, desirable, intriguing, charming, charismatic, winning ➡ **pretty, pleasant**

attribute 1. *n* ➡ **quality**
2. *vb* ascribe, assign, attach, credit ➡ **join**

audacity 1. *n* ➡ **courage**
2. *n* nerve, cheek, impertinence, insolence, temerity, gall

audible *adj* perceptible, discernible, distinct, clear ➡ **loud** ⇨ *quiet*

If the word you want is not a main entry above, look below to find it.

asylum ➡ **protection**

at ➡ **about**

athletic ➡ **strong, active**

athletic field ➡ **field**

atmosphere ➡ **air, appearance, quality**

atoll ➡ **island**

atone ➡ **pay**

atrium ➡ **court**

atrocious ➡ **awful**

attach ➡ **join, attribute**

attaché ➡ **diplomat**

attached ➡ **married**

attachment ➡ **link, love**

attacker ➡ **enemy**

attain ➡ **finish, come**

attainment ➡ **acquisition, success**

attempt ➡ **try**

attend ➡ **accompany, frequent, concentrate, listen**

attendance ➡ **presence**

attendant ➡ **servant, doorman**

attendants ➡ **court**

attentive ➡ **alert, loving**

attentiveness ➡ **diligence**

attenuate ➡ **weaken**

attest ➡ **testify**

attire ➡ **clothes, dress**

attitude ➡ **belief, perspective, posture**

attorney ➡ **adviser**

attract ➡ **pull, fascinate**

attractiveness ➡ **beauty**

auction ➡ **sale**

audacious ➡ **brave, rude**

---

audience n spectators, viewers, onlookers, readers, listeners, patrons, congregation, gallery ➡ **meeting, patron**

automatic 1. *adj* automated, mechanical, mechanized, motorized, self-starting, self-acting, computerized
2. *adj* habitual, involuntary, instinctive, mechanical, spontaneous, reflex, unintentional

available *adj* accessible, usable, convenient, handy ➡ **ready**

avalanche n slide, landslide, mudslide, rockslide

average 1. *adj* unexceptional, mediocre, unremarkable, standard, routine, medium, modest ➡ **common, normal**
2. n mean, median, midpoint, standard, medium, par, norm

avoid *vb* shun, dodge, evade, shirk, duck, sidestep, elude, avert, bypass, circumvent ➡ **escape**

awake 1. *adj* conscious, up, sleepless, wakeful ➡ **alert** ⇨ *asleep*
2. *vb* ➡ **wake**

If the word you want is not a main entry above, look below to find it.

audiobook ➡ book

audition ➡ tryout

auditorium ➡ hall

auf Wiedersehen ➡ good-bye

augment ➡ strengthen, grow

augur ➡ predict

augury ➡ prediction

august ➡ grand, dignified

au revoir ➡ good-bye

aurora ➡ halo

auspicious ➡ lucky, successful

austere ➡ empty, hard, plain, strict

austerity ➡ abstinence, economy

authentic ➡ real, correct, official

authenticate ➡ verify

authentication ➡ proof

authenticity ➡ truth

author ➡ writer, creator, write

authoritarian ➡ dictator, dictatorial

authoritative ➡ infallible, model

authorities ➡ police

authority ➡ basis, right, expert, permission, rule

authorization ➡ permission

authorize ➡ approve, let

authorized ➡ official, able

autocrat ➡ dictator

autocratic ➡ dictatorial

autograph ➡ signature, sign

automated ➡ automatic

automobile ➡ vehicle

autonomous ➡ free

autonomy ➡ freedom

auxiliary ➡ subordinate

avail ➡ help, advantage

avarice ➡ greed

avaricious ➡ greedy

avenge ➡ revenge

avenging ➡ revengeful

avenue ➡ road

averse ➡ reluctant

aversion ➡ opposition, hatred

avert ➡ prevent, avoid

aviary ➡ zoo

aviation ➡ flight

aviator ➡ pilot

avid ➡ eager

avocation ➡ pastime, profession

await ➡ wait

awaken ➡ wake

award 1. *n* honor, decoration, medal, ribbon, citation ➡ **prize**
2. *n* grant, scholarship, fellowship ➡ **prize**
3. *vb* ➡ **give**

awesome 1. *adj* amazing, impressive, astonishing, miraculous, terrific, sensational ➡ **grand, great**
2. *adj* ➡ **scary**

awful *adj* terrible, horrible, dreadful, dire, ghastly, appalling, wretched, grievous, disagreeable, atrocious, outrageous, disgraceful, hateful, odious ➡ **bad, gruesome**

ax, axe *n* hatchet, tomahawk, broadax, pickax, poleax

axis *n* pivot, fulcrum, swivel, hinge ➡ **middle**

If the word you want is not a main entry above, look below to find it.

aware ➡ alert

awareness ➡ attention, knowledge

away ➡ absent, abroad

awe ➡ respect, shock

awe-inspiring ➡ grand

awfully ➡ very

awkward ➡ clumsy, inconvenient

AWOL ➡ absent

awry ➡ wrong

axiom ➡ saying, rule

aye ➡ yes

azure ➡ blue

baby 1. *n* infant, newborn, toddler, babe, tot ➡ **child** ⇨ *adult*
2. *vb* ➡ **pamper**

back 1. *n* rear, posterior, end, rear end, backside, stern (*of a boat or ship*), aft (*of a boat or ship*), tail (*of an animal or plane*), hindquarters (*of an animal*), rump (*of an animal*), haunch (*of an animal*), reverse (*of a coin or page*) ⇨ **front**
2. *vb* aid, finance, sponsor, fund, promote ➡ **approve, support, help**
3. *vb* back up, reverse ➡ **retreat**
4. *adj, adv* ➡ **backward**

background 1. *n* backdrop, distance, landscape ➡ **setting**
2. *n* ➡ **experience**

backward 1. *adj* backwards, rearward, reversed, behind, retrograde, regressive
➡ **underdeveloped** ⇨ *forward*
2. *adv* backwards, back, rearward, behind, regressively, reversed

bad 1. *adj* evil, sinful, naughty, infamous, villainous, nefarious, incorrigible, disreputable ➡ **wicked, improper, mischievous, dishonest, immoral** ⇨ *good*
2. *adj* unpleasant, disagreeable, undesirable, objectionable, miserable, lousy, nasty, offensive, abominable, repulsive, detestable, despicable, vile, nauseating, sickening, unsavory, disgusting, obnoxious, distasteful ➡ **awful**
3. *adj* rotten, spoiled, rancid, decayed, putrid, moldy ➡ **stale**
4. *adj* ➡ **sad**
5. *adj* ➡ **unhealthy**
6. *adj* ➡ **wrong**

badge *n* insignia, emblem, shield, medallion, escutcheon

---

babble ➡ chatter

babe ➡ baby

baby blue ➡ blue

baby doll ➡ doll

babyhood
➡ childhood

back down ➡ retreat

backdrop
➡ background, setting

backer ➡ support

backing ➡ support

back out ➡ retreat

backpack ➡ bag

backside ➡ back

backslide ➡ relapse

backup ➡ alternate

backwards
➡ backward

backwoods ➡ country, rural

backwoodsman
➡ pioneer

badger ➡ bother

badlands ➡ desert

bad-tempered ➡ cross

baffle ➡ confuse

bafflement
➡ confusion

baffling ➡ mysterious

---

bag 1. *n* sack, pouch, purse, handbag, pocketbook, satchel, tote bag, tote, backpack, pack, knapsack, fanny pack ➡ **container, luggage, wallet**
2. *n* ➡ **base**
3. *vb* ➡ **catch**

balance 1. *n* stability, equilibrium, footing, poise
2. *n* symmetry, harmony, counterbalance, proportion, equilibrium
3. *n* ➡ **remainder**
4. *vb* stabilize, counterbalance, steady, poise, counterpoise, neutralize, equalize, redeem, compensate, coordinate, offset

bald 1. *adj* hairless, bald-headed, bare ➡ **naked**
2. *adj* flagrant, outright, unadorned, blunt, forthright ➡ **obvious**

ball 1. *n* globe, sphere, orb, globule, drop, pellet, bead, pearl
2. *n* ➡ **dance**
3. *n* ➡ **foot**

ballot *n* slate, ticket, lineup ➡ **vote, choice**

ban 1. *vb* ➡ **forbid**
2. *n* prohibition, embargo, proscription, restriction, injunction, boycott, sanction

band 1. *n* ➡ **group**
2. *n* group, orchestra, ensemble, combo
3. *n* stripe, ribbon, belt, girdle, sash, tape, border, strip, streak, seam, vein ➡ **row, zone, ring**

bandage 1. *n* dressing, compress, Band-Aid (*trademark*), gauze
2. *vb* dress, bind, wrap, swathe

bang 1. *n* crash, crack, pop, boom, blast, explosion, report, thud, detonation, clang, rumble, clap, thunder ➡ **noise, knock**
2. *vb* rattle, clatter, clash, clank, bump ➡ **knock, hit, collide**

banish *vb* deport, exile, expel, expatriate, drive out, drive away, dispel, evict, ostracize ➡ **exclude, oust**

If the word you want is not a main entry above, look below to find it.

baggage ➡ luggage

baggage carrier ➡ porter

baguette ➡ bread

bailiwick ➡ field

bait ➡ tempt

bake ➡ cook

baked goods ➡ pastry

baker ➡ cook

balanced ➡ sane

balderdash ➡ nonsense

bald-headed ➡ bald

baleful ➡ ominous

balk ➡ hesitate

ballad ➡ song

balloon ➡ swell

ballpark ➡ approximate

ball-peen hammer ➡ hammer

ballpoint ➡ pen

baloney ➡ nonsense

banal ➡ trite, common

banality ➡ cliché

Band-Aid® ➡ bandage

bandanna ➡ scarf

bandit ➡ criminal

bane ➡ poison

banishment ➡ exile, suspension

---

bank 1. *n* ➡ **hill, shore, cliff**
2. *n* savings bank, credit union, trust company, savings and loan, treasury, exchequer, repository, depository
3. *vb* save, deposit, invest
4. *vb* ➡ **slant**

bar 1. *n* rod, shaft, pole, crossbar, boom, rib, rail, stake, stripe, strip ➡ **stick**
2. *n* tavern, saloon, barroom, pub, cocktail lounge, lounge, nightclub, cabaret, brewery
3. *n* ➡ **block**
4. *n* ➡ **table**
5. *n* ➡ **court**
6. *vb* ➡ **lock**
7. *vb* block, obstruct, impede, thwart, hinder, restrict, handicap ➡ **prevent, exclude, forbid, delay**

bargain 1. *n* ➡ **agreement**
2. *n* discount, deal, good deal, buy, reduction, steal (*informal*) ➡ **sale**
3. *vb* ➡ **negotiate**

bark 1. *vb*, *n* yelp, yap, yip, howl, snarl, growl, woof ➡ **cry**

2. *n* ➡ **boat**
3. *n* ➡ **peel**

barn *n* stable, stall, cow barn, cowshed, byre ➡ **shed, pen, building**

barrel *n* keg, vat, drum, cask, tub, hogshead, tun ➡ **container**

barrier *n* obstacle, obstruction, hindrance, hurdle, difficulty, impediment, barricade, roadblock, blockade, palisade, clog ➡ **divider**

base 1. *n* foundation, bottom, support, footing, foot, root ➡ **floor** ⇨ *top*
2. *n* ➡ **basis**
3. *n* headquarters, home, home base, base camp, camp, station, terminal
4. *n* plate, goal, bag, sack
5. *vb* found, ground, predicate, establish
6. *vb* locate, station, post, situate

basement *n* cellar, crypt, bunker, storm cellar, crawl space ➡ **room**

If the word you want is not a main entry above, look below to find it.

bankrupt ➡ ruin	barbecue ➡ cook, fireplace	baritone ➡ low	barring ➡ but
banner ➡ flag	bard ➡ musician	barkeep ➡ host	barroom ➡ bar
banquet ➡ feast, meal	bare ➡ empty, naked, bald, reveal	barrage ➡ flood	barrow ➡ grave
banter ➡ joke		barren ➡ sterile	bartender ➡ host
baptize ➡ bless	barely ➡ only, seldom	barrens ➡ desert	barter ➡ trade, buy, sell
barb ➡ thorn	barf ➡ vomit	barricade ➡ barrier, wall	base camp ➡ base
barbarian ➡ vandal			

basic *adj* elemental, elementary, fundamental, staple, rudimentary, primitive, introductory, primary ➡ **necessary**

basis *n* foundation, support, justification, grounds, authority, underpinning, raison d'être, cornerstone, rudiment ➡ **base, cause**

bat 1. *n* club, stick, pole, mallet
2. *vb* ➡ **hit**

bathrobe *n* robe, dressing gown, negligee, peignoir

bathroom *n* washroom, rest room, lavatory, toilet, bath, women's room, men's room, latrine, head, facilities ➡ **room**

bay 1. *n* inlet, cove, bayou, lagoon, estuary, gulf, arm ➡ **harbor**
2. *n* alcove, niche, nook, recess
3. *vb* ➡ **cry**
4. *adj* ➡ **brown**

beam 1. *n* timber, rafter, stud, joist ➡ **bar, board**
2. *n* ➡ **light**[1]
3. *vb* ➡ **shine**
4. *vb* ➡ **smile**
5. *vb* ➡ **broadcast**

bear 1. *vb* endure, stand, tolerate, abide, stomach, suffer, accept, brook, take, shoulder, assume, undertake ➡ **experience**
2. *vb* ➡ **carry**
3. *vb* ➡ **support, afford**
4. *vb* ➡ **give**

beard *n* whiskers, goatee, Vandyke, stubble, five o'clock shadow, sideburns ➡ **hair**

bearing 1. *n* carriage, demeanor, manner, deportment, presence, mien ➡ **behavior, personality**
2. *n* ➡ **relevance**
3. *n* ➡ **course**
4. *n* ➡ **appearance, posture**

If the word you want is not a main entry above, look below to find it.

bash ➡ hit
bashful ➡ shy
basically ➡ chiefly, practically
basin ➡ bowl, sink, valley
bass ➡ low
bassinet ➡ bed
baste ➡ sew

batch ➡ number
bath ➡ bathroom, cleaning
bathe ➡ clean, swim
bathing ➡ swim
baton ➡ stick
batter ➡ hit
battle ➡ fight
battlefield ➡ field

battleground ➡ field
bauble ➡ trinket
bawdy ➡ dirty
bawl ➡ cry
bayou ➡ bay, swamp
bazaar ➡ market
be ➡ live[1]
beach ➡ shore

beacon ➡ light[1]
bead ➡ trinket, drop, ball
beak ➡ nose
beaker ➡ glass
bear on ➡ concern
beast ➡ animal, monster
beastly ➡ animal

---

beautiful *adj* gorgeous, glamorous, exquisite, beauteous, elegant, stunning, ravishing, dazzling, magnificent ➡ **pretty** ⇨ *ugly*

beauty *n* attractiveness, loveliness, prettiness, elegance, winsomeness, pulchritude, grace, charm, good looks

because *conj* since, due to, for, as, on account of

bed 1. *n* couch, cot, futon, mattress, bedstead, bunk, berth, crib, cradle, bassinet, gurney, stretcher, litter
2. *n* ➡ **floor**

bedroom *n* bedchamber, boudoir, dormitory, guest room, nursery ➡ **room**

before 1. *adv* previously, formerly, earlier, already, beforehand, yet

2. *prep* prior to, ahead of, preceding ➡ **until**

beg *vb* implore, entreat, beseech, plead, urge, solicit, importune ➡ **ask**

beggar 1. *n* panhandler, tramp, bum, hobo, pauper, wretch, derelict, vagrant
2. *vb* ➡ **ruin**

beginning *n* origin, source, outset, onset, commencement, initiation, inauguration, start, birth, conception, genesis, infancy, threshold ➡ **front** ⇨ *finish, conclusion*

behavior 1. *n* conduct, manners, etiquette, decorum ➡ **bearing**
2. *n* performance, function, operation, execution

If the word you want is not a main entry above, look below to find it.

beat ➡ hit, defeat, mix, tick, accent, rhythm, round

beatify ➡ bless

beating ➡ defeat

beauteous ➡ beautiful

beautification ➡ decoration

beautify ➡ decorate

beckon ➡ call, wave

become ➡ suit

becoming ➡ pretty, correct

bed-and-breakfast ➡ hotel

bedazzle ➡ surprise

bedchamber ➡ bedroom

bedeck ➡ decorate

bedraggled ➡ messy

bedspread ➡ blanket

bedstead ➡ bed

bedtime ➡ night

befall ➡ happen

befit ➡ suit

be fond of ➡ like

beforehand ➡ before

befoul ➡ dirty

befuddle ➡ confuse

beget ➡ reproduce

begin ➡ start

beginner ➡ amateur

begrudge ➡ envy

begrudging ➡ jealous

beguile ➡ cheat, entertain, enchant

behave ➡ obey, act

behemoth ➡ giant

behest ➡ order

behind ➡ backward, late, past

behindhand ➡ late

behold ➡ see

beholden ➡ grateful

beige ➡ brown

being ➡ life, existence, animal, human being

belated ➡ late

belatedly ➡ late

belfry ➡ tower

---

belief 1. *n* conviction, opinion, view, notion, mind, instinct, hunch, suspicion, attitude, sentiment
➡ **theory, idea, feeling, perspective**
2. *n* faith, trust, confidence, credit, credence, understanding
➡ **certainty**
3. *n* creed, doctrine, dogma, credo, principle ➡ **religion, philosophy, superstition**

believe 1. *vb* accept, think, hold, deem, trust, acknowledge, affirm, view ⇨ *deny*
2. *vb* ➡ **guess**

bell *n* chime, gong, carillon, buzzer, signal

belligerent *adj* hostile, aggressive, combative, contentious, bellicose, pugnacious, militant ➡ **angry, violent, unfriendly**

belong *vb* fit, go, fit in, pertain, apply, relate, concern

bend 1. *vb* twist, curve, wind, arch, warp, flex, buckle, bow, droop, veer, meander, thread, contort, distort
➡ **turn, slant** ⇨ *straighten*
2. *vb* bow, curtsy, genuflect, stoop, kneel, crouch, squat, duck, hunch, slouch, slump
3. *n* twist, kink, crimp, curl, tangle
➡ **curve, corner**

bent *adj* curved, twisted, warped, bowed, crooked, contorted, misshapen, gnarled ⇨ *straight*

beside *prep* next to, alongside, adjoining, adjacent to, against, near, with

besides 1. *adv* moreover, furthermore, plus, also, too, additionally
2. *prep* ➡ **but**

If the word you want is not a main entry above, look below to find it.

believable ➡ **possible**

belittle ➡ **ridicule, underestimate**

bellboy ➡ **porter**

belles lettres ➡ **literature**

bellhop ➡ **porter**

bellicose ➡ **belligerent, military**

belligerence ➡ **anger**

bellow ➡ **yell, cry**

belly ➡ **stomach**

belongings ➡ **property**

beloved ➡ **love, valuable**

below ➡ **under**

belowground ➡ **underground**

belt ➡ **band, zone, punch**

bemoan ➡ **regret**

bench ➡ **seat, court**

benchmark ➡ **measure**

bendable ➡ **flexible**

beneath ➡ **under**

benefactor ➡ **patron**

beneficial ➡ **useful**

benefit ➡ **worth, advantage, pension, help, prosper**

benevolence ➡ **generosity**

benevolent ➡ **kind**

benign ➡ **kind**

bequeath ➡ **leave, give**

bequest ➡ **inheritance, will**

berate ➡ **scold**

berry ➡ **fruit**

berserk ➡ **violent, insane**

berth ➡ **dock, bed**

beseech ➡ **beg**

beseige ➡ **attack**

beset ➡ **infest**

besotted ➡ **drunk**

---

best 1. *adj* finest, choicest, first, prime, premium, optimum, preeminent, leading, unparalleled, unsurpassed, superlative, foremost, ultimate, supreme, prime, top, upper ➡ **good** ⇨ *worst*
2. *adv* most, above all ⇨ *least*
3. *vb* ➡ **defeat, exceed**

bet *n, vb* wager, venture, gamble, risk, stake, ante

betray 1. *vb* deceive, trick, tell on, inform on, double-cross, abandon ➡ **cheat**
2. *vb* ➡ **reveal**

better 1. *adj* finer, greater, preferable, improved, superior ➡ **good, best**
2. *adj* improved, improving, convalescent, convalescing ➡ **healthy**
3. *adv* ➡ **more**

4. *vb* ➡ **exceed**
5. *vb* ➡ **defeat**

between *prep* among, amid, amongst, amidst, betwixt ➡ **through**
Note that **among** *refers to more than two people or things, and* **between** *most often refers to two, but sometimes more than two.*

big *adj* large, generous, substantial, considerable, giant, stout, stocky, great ➡ **huge, heavy, fat, infinite, abundant, high** ⇨ *small*

bill 1. *n* check, tab, invoice, charge, tally, statement ➡ **price, debt**
2. *n* ➡ **act**
3. *n* ➡ **nose**
4. *n* visor, peak, brim
5. *vb* ➡ **charge**

binge *n* spree, bout, fling

bird *n* fowl, songbird, seagull, waterfowl, wader, chick, fledgling ➡ **animal**

If the word you want is not a main entry above, look below to find it.

bestial ➡ animal
best-liked ➡ favorite
bestow ➡ give, leave
betrayal ➡ treason
betrothed ➡ married
betting ➡ gambling
betwixt ➡ between
beverage ➡ drink
bevy ➡ herd
bewail ➡ grieve, regret

bewilder ➡ confuse
bewildered ➡ dumbfounded
bewilderment ➡ confusion
bewitch ➡ enchant
bewitching ➡ magic
beyond ➡ above, past
bias ➡ prejudice, tendency

biased ➡ prejudiced
bicker ➡ argue
bicyclist ➡ rider
bid ➡ order, offer, try, estimate
bidding ➡ invitation
bifocals ➡ glasses
big house ➡ jail
bigoted ➡ prejudiced
bigotry ➡ prejudice

billboard ➡ advertisement
billet ➡ house
billfold ➡ wallet
billow ➡ wave, cloud
bind ➡ tie, wrap, bandage
binocular ➡ glass
biographer ➡ writer

birth 1. *n* childbirth, delivery, nativity ⇨ *death*
2. *n* ➡ **beginning**
3. *n* ➡ **ancestry**

bit 1. *n* piece, fragment, particle, scrap, shred, chip, flake, fleck, trifle, snippet, snatch ➡ **bite, block, part**
2. *n* trace, hint, suggestion, shade, touch, lick, glimmer, dash, pinch, tang, modicum, jot, iota, shred
3. *n* ➡ **role, act**

bite 1. *vb* chew, gnaw, nibble, munch, taste, chomp, nip, snap
2. *n* morsel, taste, mouthful, nibble, scrap ➡ **bit, meal**

black *adj, n* ebony, jet, sable, raven, inky, pitch-black, coal-black ➡ **dark** ⇨ *white*

blame 1. *vb* censure, criticize, condemn, denounce, accuse, implicate, charge ➡ **try, scold** ⇨ *forgive*
2. *n* ➡ **guilt**

blank 1. *adj* ➡ **empty, clean**
2. *adj* expressionless, vacuous, impassive, vacant, deadpan, poker-faced

blanket 1. *n* cover, quilt, comforter, duvet, featherbed, bedspread, sheet, shroud
2. *n* ➡ **coat**
3. *adj* ➡ **comprehensive**
4. *vb* ➡ **cover**

bleach *vb* fade, whiten, blanch, lighten, pale

bleak *adj* dreary, desolate, somber, grim, depressing, drear, hopeless, cheerless, gloomy, oppressive, dismal, dour ➡ **sad, sterile, pessimistic**

bless *vb* consecrate, sanctify, dedicate, exalt, hallow, beatify, glorify, anoint, baptize, ordain

blind 1. *adj* sightless, visually impaired, visionless, eyeless, unseeing
2. *adj* ➡ **unaware**

If the word you want is not a main entry above, look below to find it.

birthplace ➡ source
biscuit ➡ bread
bishop ➡ priest
bistro ➡ restaurant
biting ➡ sharp
bitter ➡ sour, sharp, hard, angry
bizarre ➡ strange
blackfly ➡ fly

blackness ➡ dark
blade ➡ knife
blameless ➡ innocent
blameworthy ➡ guilty
blanch ➡ bleach
bland ➡ insipid
blasé ➡ bored
blaspheme ➡ curse

blasphemy ➡ curse
blast ➡ bang, blow[1], wind, shoot
blatant ➡ obvious
blather ➡ chatter
blaze ➡ burn, fire
blazer ➡ coat
blazing ➡ bright, burning

bleached ➡ fair
bleachers ➡ seat
bleeding ➡ bloody
blemish ➡ spot, defect, scar
blend ➡ mix, mixture
blessed ➡ holy
blight ➡ disease, fungus, destroy

---

blink *vb* wink, flicker, flash, twinkle ➡ **shine**

block 1. *n* piece, chunk, cube, cake, slice, slab, bar, hunk, wedge ➡ **bit, part**
2. *n* ➡ **neighborhood, building**
3. *vb* ➡ **hide**
4. *vb* ➡ **bar**

blood vessel *n* artery, vein, capillary, duct

bloody *adj* bleeding, gory, bloodstained

blossom 1. *n* ➡ **flower**
2. *vb* bloom, flower, bud ➡ **grow, prosper**

blow[1] 1. *n* hit, stroke, strike, punch, slap, jab, lick, swat, kick, stab, poke, whack, thwack, smack ➡ **push**
2. *n* blast, impact, concussion, shock, wallop, jolt
3. *n* ➡ **shock**

blow[2] 1. *vb* waft, float, sail, drift ➡ **wave**
2. *vb* honk, toot, sound ➡ **play**
3. *vb* ➡ **breathe**
4. *n* ➡ **wind**

blue 1. *adj, n* navy, azure, turquoise, royal blue, powder blue, baby blue, sky blue
2. *adj* ➡ **sad**

blush *vb* flush, redden, color, glow

board 1. *n* plank, beam, slat, timber, lumber, rafter, joist, two-by-four
2. *n* meals, fare, keep ➡ **food**
3. *n* ➡ **committee**
4. *vb* ➡ **enter**
5. *vb* ➡ **house**

boast 1. *vb* brag, gloat, crow, show off, vaunt, swagger, exult
2. *n* brag, bragging, vaunt, claim, assertion, bluster, swagger, bravado

boat *n* ship, vessel, craft, bark

If the word you want is not a main entry above, look below to find it.

bliss ➡ heaven, pleasure
blissful ➡ ecstatic
blizzard ➡ storm, snow
blob ➡ lump
bloc ➡ group, party
blockade ➡ barrier
blockhead ➡ fool
blond, blonde ➡ fair, yellow

blood ➡ ancestry
bloodshed ➡ murder
bloodstained ➡ bloody
bloodthirsty ➡ predatory
bloom ➡ flower, blossom
blooper ➡ mistake
blot ➡ spot
blotch ➡ spot

blow up ➡ explode
blue-blooded ➡ noble
bluebottle ➡ fly
blueprint ➡ pattern
bluff ➡ cheat, cliff
blunder ➡ mistake
blunderbuss ➡ gun
blunt ➡ dull, bald, abrupt, straightforward

blurry ➡ dim
blushing ➡ red
bluster ➡ boast
blustery ➡ stormy, windy
B.O. ➡ sweat
boards ➡ stage
boating ➡ nautical
boatman ➡ sailor
bobby pin ➡ pin

body 1. *n* build, physique, frame, anatomy, figure, form, torso, trunk
2. *n* corpse, carcass, cadaver, remains, skeleton, bones
3. *n* ➡ **human being**
4. *n* ➡ **group**
5. *n* ➡ **matter**
6. *n* ➡ **density**

bogeyman *n* bogey, bugaboo, goblin, hobgoblin, bugbear

boil 1. *vb* simmer, stew, seethe, parboil, bubble, poach ➡ **cook**
2. *n* ➡ **sore**

bond 1. *n* shackle, chain, fetter, manacle, handcuff, restraint
2. *n* ➡ **link**

book *n* volume, publication, text, paperback, hardcover, work, tome, manual, handbook, audiobook, manuscript, script, libretto ➡ **pamphlet**

boor *n* lout, oaf, churl, bumpkin, yahoo, Philistine, ape, lummox, dullard

booth *n* stall, counter, kiosk, stand, cubicle, compartment, enclosure

booty *n* loot, plunder, spoils, winnings, contraband, pillage ➡ **prize**

border 1. *n* frontier, boundary, march, borderland ➡ **edge, circumference, band**
2. *vb* abut, adjoin, neighbor, bound, skirt, flank ➡ **join**

bored *adj* uninterested, jaded, blasé ➡ **tired**

boredom *n* ennui, apathy, tedium, monotony

borrow *vb* rent, hire, bum (*informal*), scrounge (*informal*), mooch (*informal*) ➡ **adopt, get, use**

If the word you want is not a main entry above, look below to find it.

bodily ➡ physical
body odor ➡ sweat
bog ➡ swamp
bogey ➡ bogeyman
bogus ➡ fake
boiler ➡ furnace
boiling ➡ hot
boisterous ➡ loud
bold ➡ brave, rude
boldness ➡ courage

bolster ➡ cushion, support
bolt ➡ lock, nail, missile, run, escape, eat
bombard ➡ attack
bombardment ➡ fire
bombastic ➡ pompous
bona fide ➡ real
bondage ➡ slavery
bones ➡ body
bonfire ➡ fire

bong ➡ ring
bonjour ➡ hello
bon mot ➡ joke
bonnet ➡ hat
bonus ➡ prize, tip
boo ➡ yell
boo-boo ➡ mistake
bookish ➡ educated
booklet ➡ pamphlet
boom ➡ bang, bar
boon ➡ gift

boondocks ➡ country
boorishness ➡ rudeness
boost ➡ lift, strengthen
boot ➡ shoe, kick
bordering ➡ adjacent
borderland ➡ border
bore ➡ dig, well, tire
boring ➡ dull
borough ➡ town, neighborhood

➡ = synonym cross-reference • ⇨ = antonym cross-reference   27

boss 1. *n* chief, leader, head, director, employer, foreman, manager, supervisor, superior, captain, commander, skipper ➡ **principal, chairperson**
2. *vb* ➡ **lead, control**

bother 1. *vb* annoy, vex, tease, plague, pester, needle, aggravate, irk, nag, hound, badger, harass, bug, irritate, chafe, rankle ➡ **disturb, worry**
2. *n* ➡ **nuisance**

bottle *n* jug, pitcher, flask, canteen, carafe, ewer, crock, cruet ➡ **container**

bouquet 1. *n* bunch, posy, nosegay, arrangement, spray, garland
2. *n* ➡ **smell**

bowl *n* dish, vessel, basin, tureen, crock ➡ **container, kettle, plate**

braid 1. *n* plait, pigtail, queue, twist
2. *vb* ➡ **weave**

branch 1. *n* limb, arm, wing, offshoot, fork, projection, tributary ➡ **stick, department**
2. *vb* ➡ **divide**

brave 1. *adj* courageous, heroic, fearless, valiant, valorous, gallant, bold, stalwart, daring, audacious, intrepid, dauntless, undaunted, adventurous, adventuresome, plucky, dashing ⇨ *afraid*
2. *vb* ➡ **face**

If the word you want is not a main entry above, look below to find it.

bosom ➡ chest

botch ➡ fumble

bothersome ➡ inconvenient

bottom ➡ base, floor, essence

bottomland ➡ swamp

boudoir ➡ bedroom

bough ➡ limb

boulder ➡ rock

boulevard ➡ road

bounce ➡ jump, reflect

bound ➡ jump, border

boundary ➡ edge, border, hedge

boundless ➡ infinite

bounteous ➡ abundant

bountiful ➡ abundant

bounty ➡ generosity

bourgeoisie ➡ people

bout ➡ game, period, binge

bow ➡ bend, curve, play, surrender, front

bowed ➡ bent

bow tie ➡ tie

box ➡ container, square, punch

boy ➡ child, man

boycott ➡ ban, forbid

boyfriend ➡ friend, love

boyhood ➡ childhood

boyish ➡ young

brace ➡ support, strengthen, pair

bracing ➡ brisk, cool

brackish ➡ salty

brad ➡ nail

brag ➡ boast

bragging ➡ boast

brain ➡ mind, genius

brake ➡ stop

bramble ➡ thorn

brand ➡ make, label

brandish ➡ swing

brand name ➡ make

brand-new ➡ new

brash ➡ rude

brat ➡ urchin

brava ➡ encore

bravado ➡ boast

bravery ➡ courage

bravissimo ➡ encore

bravo ➡ encore

brawl ➡ fight

brawny ➡ fat

breach ➡ break

bread n loaf, biscuit, roll, baguette, tortilla ➡ **cake, pastry**

break 1. vb crack, shatter, smash, fracture, split, snap, crash, splinter, burst, rupture, crush, squash, chip ➡ **destroy, explode, separate**
2. n fracture, split, crack, rift, breach, gap, opening, chip, schism
3. n pause, recess, intermission, breather, respite, delay, interlude, interruption, lull, hiatus, suspension, disruption ➡ **vacation, rest, truce**
4. vb ➡ **disobey**
5. vb ➡ **defeat**
6. n ➡ **luck**

breakable adj fragile, delicate, dainty, brittle, flimsy, friable, crumbly ➡ **weak** ⇨ *unbreakable*

breath 1. n respiration, inhalation, exhalation, breathing
2. n ➡ **life**
3. n ➡ **air, wind**

breathe 1. vb inhale, exhale, respire, expire, pant, gasp, wheeze, puff, huff, gulp ➡ **mumble**
2. vb ➡ **live**[1]

brevity n conciseness, concision, succinctness, economy, terseness

bridge 1. n span, overpass, catwalk, gangway, gangplank, viaduct
2. n ➡ **link**
3. vb cross, connect, span ➡ **join**

bright 1. adj brilliant, glowing, radiant, sunny, dazzling, glaring, blazing, intense, luminous, colorful, gay, vivid, flashy ➡ **fair, shiny** ⇨ *dim, dull*
2. adj ➡ **happy**
3. adj ➡ **smart**

bring vb fetch, deliver, lead, conduct, escort ➡ **take, lead, carry, pull**

If the word you want is not a main entry above, look below to find it.

breadth ➡ width	breast ➡ chest	breeze ➡ wind	brighten ➡ light[1]
breadwinner ➡ worker	breather ➡ break	breezeway ➡ porch	brightness ➡ light[1]
breaker ➡ wave	breathing ➡ breath	breezy ➡ windy	brilliance ➡ light[1]
breakfast nook ➡ dining room	breathtaking ➡ exciting	brew ➡ cook	brilliant ➡ bright, smart, jewel
break out ➡ escape	breed ➡ reproduce, grow, type	brewery ➡ bar	brim ➡ bill, edge
breakthrough ➡ event, invention	breeder ➡ farmer	briar ➡ thorn	brimful ➡ full
break up ➡ separate	breeding ➡ class, civilization	bride ➡ spouse	bring up ➡ broach
breakwater ➡ jetty		brief ➡ short	brink ➡ edge
		brier ➡ thorn	briny ➡ salty
		brig ➡ jail	

➡ = synonym cross-reference • ⇨ = antonym cross-reference

brisk 1. *adj* crisp, bracing, invigorating ➡ **cold, cool**
2. *adj* ➡ **lively**

broach *vb* mention, bring up, introduce, raise ➡ **say**

broad *adj* wide, thick, deep, expansive, extensive, capacious ➡ **big** ⇨ *narrow*
Note that **broad** and **wide** are close synonyms in that both refer to the distance across something, as in "a **broad** street" or "a **wide** street." However, **broad** suggests the whole area or expanse of the surface itself and **wide** stresses more the distance from one side to the other. If you want to give the actual distance, use **wide**: three feet **wide**, a yard **wide**.

broadcast 1. *vb* transmit, beam, air, televise, telecast, relay ➡ **send, play**
2. *vb* ➡ **advertise**
3. *vb* ➡ **plant**
4. *n* ➡ **program**

broken 1. *adj* cracked, shattered, fractured, damaged, defective, faulty, malfunctioning, disabled, broken-down, down, unusable, out of order ➡ **useless**
2. *adj* ➡ **tame**

brown *adj, n* tan, chestnut, beige, fawn, tawny, khaki, bay, bronze, chocolate, taupe, umber ➡ **dark**

brush 1. *n* underbrush, undergrowth, shrubbery, scrub, thicket, bushes ➡ **hedge**
2. *n* ➡ **meeting**
3. *vb* ➡ **clean, sweep, rub**
4. *vb* ➡ **comb**

If the word you want is not a main entry above, look below to find it.

brittle ➡ breakable
broadax ➡ ax, axe
broad-minded ➡ liberal
broadside ➡ sideways
broadsword ➡ sword
brochure ➡ pamphlet
broil ➡ cook
broiling ➡ hot
broke ➡ poor

broken-down ➡ broken, shabby
broker ➡ agent
bromide ➡ cliché
bronze ➡ brown, statue
brooch ➡ pin
brood ➡ worry, mope, herd
brook ➡ river, bear
brother ➡ religious

brotherhood ➡ friendship
brownie ➡ fairy
browse ➡ read, eat
bruise ➡ hurt
bruised ➡ sore
brunette ➡ dark
brusque ➡ abrupt
brutal ➡ sharp, mean
brutality ➡ violence
brute ➡ animal, monster

brutish ➡ animal
bubble ➡ boil
bubbles ➡ foam
buccaneer ➡ pirate
bucket ➡ container
buckle ➡ clasp, join, bend
bud ➡ flower, blossom, shoot
buddy ➡ friend

---

budget 1. *n* finances, expenses, allotment, allowance, resources
2. *vb* allot, allocate, ration, estimate ➡ **share**
3. *adj* ➡ **cheap**

bug 1. *n* insect, beetle, spider, vermin, pest
2. *n* ➡ **disease, germ**
3. *vb* ➡ **bother**

build 1. *vb* construct, erect, assemble, raise, fabricate, fashion ➡ **form, invent, make** ⇨ *destroy*
2. *vb* ➡ **strengthen**
3. *n* ➡ **body**

building 1. *n* structure, edifice, block, shelter ➡ **house, hall**
2. *n* ➡ **assembly**

bulge 1. *n* bump, lump, hump, knob, swelling, protrusion, protuberance
2. *vb* ➡ **swell**

bully 1. *n* ruffian, troublemaker, tyrant, tormentor, tough, rowdy, hooligan ➡ **rascal, criminal**
2. *vb* ➡ **threaten**

If the word you want is not a main entry above, look below to find it.

budge ➡ move

budgetary ➡ financial

buff ➡ shine

buffer ➡ cushion, protection

buffet ➡ hit, cupboard

buffoon ➡ fool

bugaboo ➡ bogeyman

bugbear ➡ bogeyman

buggy ➡ wagon

bulb ➡ seed, flower, light[1]

bulk ➡ size, density, most

bulky ➡ clumsy, heavy

bulldoze ➡ dig

bullet ➡ missile

bulletin ➡ announcement

bullets ➡ ammunition

bullfrog ➡ frog

bullish ➡ optimistic

bullwhip ➡ whip

bulwark ➡ jetty

bum ➡ beggar, borrow

bumbling ➡ clumsy

bump ➡ hit, bang, bulge

bumpkin ➡ boor

bumpy ➡ rough

bunch ➡ group, number, bouquet

buncombe ➡ nonsense

bundle ➡ package, number

bung ➡ top

bungalow ➡ home

bungle ➡ fumble

bunk ➡ bed, nonsense

bunker ➡ basement

buoyant ➡ light[2]

burden ➡ load, worry

bureau ➡ chest, department

bureaucrat ➡ official

burglar ➡ criminal

burglarize ➡ steal

burglary ➡ theft

burial ground ➡ cemetery

buried ➡ underground

burlesque ➡ parody

burly ➡ strong

➡ = synonym cross-reference • ⇨ = antonym cross-reference

burn 1. *vb* blaze, flare, incinerate, scorch, singe, sear, char, glow ➡ **smoke, cook**
2. *vb* ➡ **hurt**

burning *adj* flaming, fiery, blazing, ablaze, afire, inflamed, smoldering ➡ **hot**

bury *vb* inter, entomb, lay to rest, enshrine, mummify, cremate ➡ **hide**

business 1. *n* industry, commerce, trade, traffic, manufacturing, finance, economics
2. *n* affair, matter, concern, transaction ➡ **job**

3. *n* company, firm, establishment, corporation, enterprise, outfit, partnership, concern ➡ **factory**

but 1. *conj* however, although, though, yet, except, nevertheless
2. *prep* except, besides, save, excluding, barring

buy 1. *vb* purchase, pay for, barter, shop ➡ **get, hire**
2. *n* ➡ **bargain**

If the word you want is not a main entry above, look below to find it.

burnable ➡ inflammable

burner ➡ furnace

burnish ➡ shine

burr ➡ accent

burro ➡ donkey

burrow ➡ dig, den

burst ➡ break, explode

bush ➡ country, plant

bushes ➡ brush, hedge

businessman, businessperson, businesswoman ➡ tycoon

buss ➡ kiss

bust ➡ chest, statue, arrest

bustle ➡ activity

bustling ➡ active

busy ➡ active, employed

C

cake 1. *n* layer cake, coffee cake, fruitcake, cupcake, torte ➡ **pastry, bread**
2. *n* ➡ **block**
3. *vb* ➡ **harden**

call 1. *vb* summon, beckon, invite, page, accost ➡ **welcome, visit**
2. *vb, n* ➡ **yell**
3. *vb* phone, telephone, ring, dial, buzz
4. *vb* ➡ **name**
5. *n* ➡ **attraction**
6. *n* ➡ **reason**

calm 1. *adj* peaceful, serene, tranquil, placid, undisturbed, untroubled, composed, self-possessed, relaxed, poised ➡ **quiet, gentle**
2. *n* quiet, tranquility, peacefulness, serenity, stillness, composure, silence, hush ➡ **peace** ⇨ *activity*
3. *vb* quiet, relax, soothe, ease, comfort, compose, lull ➡ **pacify** ⇨ *excite*

candidate *n* nominee, aspirant, applicant, office-seeker, front-runner, dark horse, favorite son ➡ **contestant**

If the word you want is not a main entry above, look below to find it.

cab ➡ taxi

cabal ➡ party

cabaret ➡ bar

cabin ➡ shack, home

cabinet ➡ cupboard, committee

cable ➡ rope

cache ➡ supply

cackle ➡ laugh

cacophonous ➡ loud

cadaver ➡ body

cadence ➡ rhythm, accent

cadet ➡ soldier

café ➡ restaurant

cafeteria ➡ restaurant

cage ➡ pen

cajole ➡ persuade

calamitous ➡ destructive

calamity ➡ disaster

calcify ➡ harden

calculate ➡ add, estimate

calculation ➡ mathematics

calendar ➡ diary

caliber ➡ class

caliph ➡ emperor

caller ➡ visitor

calligraphy ➡ handwriting

calling ➡ profession

callous ➡ insensitive

camaraderie ➡ friendship

Camelot ➡ utopia

cameraman ➡ photographer

camouflage ➡ hide, disguise

camp ➡ base

campaign ➡ movement

campanile ➡ tower

campfire ➡ fire

can ➡ container, fire

canal ➡ channel

canard ➡ lie

cancel ➡ abolish

cancer ➡ growth

candid ➡ straightforward

candor ➡ truth, honesty

cane ➡ stick, whip

canine ➡ dog

cannon ➡ gun

canny ➡ smart

canon ➡ rule

canopy ➡ tent

canyon *n* ravine, gorge, gully, arroyo, crevasse, crevice, chasm, gulch ➡ **valley**

cape 1. *n* peninsula, promontory, point, headland, neck, spit
2. *n* ➡ **wrap**

carefree *adj* lighthearted, easygoing, nonchalant, casual, informal, untroubled, devil-may-care, laid-back, mellow ➡ **happy, calm**

careful 1. *adj* painstaking, thorough, exact, accurate, particular, precise, meticulous, conscientious, studious, scrupulous, nice

2. *adj* cautious, wary, prudent, concerned, circumspect, politic, discreet, judicious, guarded ➡ **alert, suspicious** ⇨ **thoughtless**

carefully 1. *adv* precisely, meticulously, deliberately, faithfully, thoroughly
2. *adv* cautiously, warily, prudently, discreetly, mindfully, gingerly, delicately

carnival *n* fair, circus, festival, amusement park, theme park

If the word you want is not a main entry above, look below to find it.

cant ➡ slant, dialect

cantankerous ➡ cross

cantata ➡ hymn

canteen ➡ restaurant, bottle

canter ➡ run

canto ➡ stanza

cantor ➡ singer

canvass ➡ study

cap ➡ top, hat, climax

capability ➡ ability, sense

capable ➡ able

capacious ➡ broad

capacity ➡ function, ability, size, measure

caper ➡ joke, dance

capillary ➡ blood vessel

capital ➡ property, money, good

capitalist ➡ tycoon

capitulate ➡ surrender

capitulation ➡ surrender

caprice ➡ fancy, impulse

capricious ➡ arbitrary

capsize ➡ upset

capsule ➡ medicine

captain ➡ boss, control

caption ➡ headline

captivate ➡ fascinate

captivating ➡ attractive

captive ➡ prisoner

capture ➡ catch, arrest

car ➡ vehicle

carafe ➡ bottle

carapace ➡ shell

carbine ➡ gun

carcass ➡ body

card ➡ letter

cardinal ➡ important, priest

care ➡ worry, diligence, protection, treatment

career ➡ profession, life

care for ➡ like

carefulness ➡ diligence

careless ➡ thoughtless, arbitrary

caress ➡ pet, embrace, touch

caretaker ➡ guardian, doorman

cargo ➡ load

caricature ➡ parody, imitate

carillon ➡ bell

caring ➡ loving

carjack ➡ seize

carmine ➡ red

carnage ➡ murder

carnivorous ➡ predatory

carol ➡ hymn

carouse ➡ celebrate

carpet ➡ rug, cover

carpeting ➡ rug

carport ➡ garage

carry 1. *vb* move, transport, convey, bear, cart, pack, haul, transfer, tote, lug *(informal)* ➡ **take**
2. *vb* ➡ **sell**
3. *vb* ➡ **support**

carve *vb* sculpt, sculpture, whittle, etch, inscribe, engrave, incise, hew, chisel ➡ **cut**

cash register *n* register, till, cash box ➡ **safe**

castle *n* fortress, fort, garrison, fortification, stronghold, citadel, keep, donjon, palace

casualty 1. *n* victim, death, injury, fatality, dead
2. *n* ➡ **disaster**

catch 1. *vb* capture, trap, grasp, take, bag, snag, clasp, snare, ensnare, entangle, mire, enslave ➡ **seize, arrest** ⇨ *free*
2. *vb* pass, overtake, outrun, outstrip
3. *vb* contract, develop, come down with, incur ➡ **get**
4. *n* grab, snag, scoop
5. *n* ➡ **clasp, lock**
6. *n* ➡ **trap**

cause 1. *vb* produce, create, effect, generate, prompt, inspire, motivate, engender ➡ **start, make, do**
2. *n* origin, source, stimulus, basis ➡ **reason**
3. *n* principle, conviction ➡ **movement**

cave *n* cavern, tunnel, grotto, chamber ➡ **hole, den**

If the word you want is not a main entry above, look below to find it.

carriage ➡ wagon, posture, bearing, gait

carrier ➡ messenger

carry on ➡ continue

carry out ➡ do, act, commit

cart ➡ carry, wagon

cartel ➡ monopoly

carton ➡ container

cartoon ➡ picture

cascade ➡ flood, flow

case ➡ container, example, suit

cash ➡ money

cash box ➡ cash register

casing ➡ shell

cask ➡ barrel

cast ➡ throw, form

castigate ➡ scold

cast off ➡ shed

castrate ➡ sterilize

casual ➡ carefree, spontaneous

cataclysm ➡ disaster

catacomb ➡ grave, cemetery

catalog ➡ list, table

catalogue ➡ list

catapult ➡ throw

catastrophe ➡ disaster

catastrophic ➡ destructive, unfortunate

catching ➡ contagious

categorization ➡ stereotype

categorize ➡ arrange, stereotype

category ➡ type

caterpillar ➡ larva

cathedral ➡ church

catholic ➡ universal

catnap ➡ sleep

cat-o'-nine-tails ➡ whip

cattle ➡ livestock

catwalk ➡ bridge

cauldron ➡ pot

caustic ➡ sharp, sarcastic

caution ➡ warn, warning, advice, protection

cautious ➡ careful

cautiously ➡ carefully

cavalcade ➡ parade

caveat ➡ warning

cavern ➡ cave

cavity ➡ hole

cavort ➡ dance

cay ➡ island

celebrate 1. *vb* observe, commemorate, keep, solemnize, honor ➡ **praise**
2. *vb* rejoice, carouse, revel, party

celebrity 1. *n* ➡ **fame**
2. *n* notable, luminary, personage, personality, name, star, superstar, dignitary, VIP ➡ **actor**

celibate *adj* abstinent, chaste, virginal, unmarried

cemetery *n* graveyard, burial ground, memorial park, churchyard, crypt, sepulcher, catacomb ➡ **grave, monument**

ceremony 1. *n* service, ritual, rite, celebration, tradition, commemoration, festival
2. *n* formality, pomp, solemnity, protocol

certain 1. *adj* sure, positive, confident, definite, assertive, forceful, vehement, self-confident, assured, convinced
2. *adj* undeniable, unquestionable, definite, absolute, inevitable, inescapable, unavoidable ➡ **reliable, conclusive, infallible**
3. *adj* ➡ **special**
4. *adj* ➡ **reliable**

certainly *adv, interj* absolutely, positively, definitely, perfectly, completely, surely, truly, undoubtedly, unquestionably, indeed, really ➡ **finally**

certainty 1. *n* certitude, assurance, conviction, confidence, self-confidence ➡ **belief**
2. *n* fact, reality, truth, actuality, truth, foregone conclusion, sure thing

chairperson *n* chair, chairman, chairwoman, head ➡ **boss, host**

If the word you want is not a main entry above, look below to find it.

cease ➡ stop, abandon

cease-fire ➡ truce

celebrated ➡ famous

celebration ➡ party, ceremony

celerity ➡ speed

celestial ➡ heavenly

celestial body ➡ planet

celibacy ➡ abstinence

cell ➡ jail

cellar ➡ basement

cement ➡ adhesive, join

censor ➡ forbid

censure ➡ blame

census ➡ study

center ➡ middle

central ➡ middle

ceramics ➡ pottery

cerebral ➡ intellectual, profound

ceremonious ➡ dignified

certificate ➡ document

certification ➡ proof

certify ➡ guarantee, approve, testify

certitude ➡ certainty

chafe ➡ rub, bother

chagrin ➡ embarrass, shame

chagrined ➡ ashamed

chain ➡ bond, row

chair ➡ seat, chairperson, lead

chairman ➡ chairperson

chairwoman ➡ chairperson

chalet ➡ home

chalky ➡ pale

challenge ➡ contradict, face, dare

challenger ➡ opponent

chance 1. *n* fate, fortune, luck, destiny, lot, accident, coincidence, happenstance, serendipity
2. *n* ➡ **possibility**
3. *n* ➡ **opportunity**
4. *adj* ➡ **arbitrary, accidental**
5. *vb* ➡ **happen**

change 1. *vb* alter, vary, modify, transform, convert, mutate, shift, innovate ➡ **correct, adjust, distort, tinker**
2. *vb* switch, exchange, replace, interchange, substitute, swap, reverse, invert, transpose ➡ **trade**
3. *n* alteration, variation, shift, deviation, evolution, mutation, transformation, revolution, modification, metamorphosis, transition, vicissitude

channel *n* trough, chute, gutter, sluice, shaft, ramp, slide, groove, furrow, trench, rut, ditch, moat, aqueduct, canal, waterway, artery ➡ **pipe, course**

charge 1. *vb* bill, assess, invoice
2. *vb* ➡ **attack**
3. *vb* ➡ **argue, blame, try**
4. *n* ➡ **bill, price**
5. *n* ➡ **duty**
6. *n* ➡ **rule, order**
7. *n* ➡ **complaint**

If the word you want is not a main entry above, look below to find it.

chamber ➡ **room, cave**

chamois ➡ **hide, cloth**

champ ➡ **winner**

champion ➡ **winner, savior, support**

chandelier ➡ **light**[1]

changeable ➡ **variable, fickle**

change purse ➡ **wallet**

chant ➡ **sing, hymn**

chaos ➡ **confusion**

chaotic ➡ **frantic**

chap ➡ **man**

chapeau ➡ **hat**

chapel ➡ **church**

chaperon, chaperone ➡ **accompany, host**

chaplain ➡ **minister**

chaplet ➡ **crown**

chapter ➡ **division, department**

char ➡ **burn**

character ➡ **personality, reputation, quality, role**

characteristic ➡ **quality**

characterization ➡ **description, stereotype**

characterize ➡ **describe, stereotype**

chargé d'affaires ➡ **diplomat**

charisma ➡ **personality**

charismatic ➡ **attractive**

charitable ➡ **generous, kind**

charitableness ➡ **generosity**

charity ➡ **kindness, generosity**

charlatan ➡ **cheat, rascal**

charm ➡ **beauty, attraction,** personality, curse, enchantment, enchant, fascinate

charmed ➡ **magic**

charming ➡ **nice, attractive, cute, suave**

chart ➡ **table, plan**

charter ➡ **hire, license**

chartreuse ➡ **green**

chase ➡ **follow, hunt**

chasm ➡ **canyon, hole**

chassis ➡ **framework**

chaste ➡ **innocent, celibate**

chastise ➡ **scold**

chastity ➡ **virtue**

chatter *vb* prattle, babble, gibber, jabber, gossip, tattle, ramble, prate, blather ➡ **talk**

cheap 1. *adj* inexpensive, reasonable, affordable, economical, low-priced, cut-rate, budget ⇨ *expensive*
2. *adj* inferior, shoddy, mediocre, second-rate, chintzy
3. *adj* thrifty, frugal, prudent, stingy, miserly, niggardly, tight-fisted, penny-pinching, cheeseparing, penurious, tight

cheat 1. *vb* trick, deceive, swindle, chisel, hoodwink, beguile, bluff, defraud, dupe, con, gyp, prey on ➡ **fool**
2. *n* cheater, swindler, quack, charlatan, fraud, shyster, imposter, fake, humbug ➡ **criminal, hypocrite**

chest 1. *n* trunk, footlocker, locker, bureau, dresser, chiffonier
➡ **container, safe**
2. *n* breast, bosom, bust, ribcage, ribs, trunk, thorax

chiefly *adv* mainly, primarily, essentially, principally, particularly, substantially, especially, notably, importantly, fundamentally, predominantly, basically, generally, mostly

child 1. *n* juvenile, youngster, minor, kid (*informal*), youth, boy, girl ➡ **baby, teenager, urchin** ⇨ *adult*
2. *n* daughter, son, offspring, progeny, descendant

childhood *n* infancy, babyhood, youth, minority, boyhood, girlhood, adolescence, puberty, immaturity

childish *adj* childlike, infantile, immature, juvenile, puerile, sophomoric ➡ **young**

If the word you want is not a main entry above, look below to find it.

chat ➡ talk

chateau ➡ home

chatty ➡ talkative

chauvinistic ➡ patriotic

cheapskate ➡ miser

cheater ➡ cheat

check ➡ prevent, stop, try, bill, tick

check mark ➡ tick

cheek ➡ audacity

cheeky ➡ rude

cheep ➡ peep

cheer ➡ clap, entertain

cheerful ➡ happy, optimistic

cheerio ➡ good-bye

cheerless ➡ bleak

cheeseparing ➡ cheap

chef ➡ cook

cherish ➡ love, appreciate, respect

cherished ➡ valuable

cherub ➡ angel

chestnut ➡ brown

chew ➡ bite

chic ➡ fashionable

chick ➡ bird

chicken ➡ cowardly

chide ➡ scold

chief ➡ boss, important

chiffonier ➡ chest

childbirth ➡ birth

childless ➡ sterile

childlike ➡ childish

chill ➡ cool

chilly ➡ cool

chime ➡ bell, ring

chimney ➡ fireplace

china ➡ plate, pottery

chintzy ➡ cheap

chip ➡ bit, break

chirp ➡ peep, sing

choice 1. *n* alternative, option, selection, pick, preference, way, recourse, vote, voice ➡ **preference**
2. *adj* ➡ **good, favorite, special**

choir *n* chorus, chorale, glee club, ensemble ➡ **singer**

choke *vb* strangle, suffocate, asphyxiate, stifle, smother, drown ➡ **die, kill**

choose *vb* select, pick, elect, opt, name, take, designate, vote ➡ **decide, prefer** ⇨ *exclude*

choosy *adj* finicky, fussy, particular, picky, dainty, fastidious

chorus 1. *n* ➡ **choir**
2. *n* refrain, theme, strain, motif, leitmotif

church 1. *n* cathedral, temple, synagogue, mosque, chapel, mission ➡ **building**
2. *n* congregation, parish, parishioners, flock

circle 1. *n* ring, loop, hoop, disk, coil, circuit, circumference, perimeter, periphery, revolution, orbit ➡ **round**
2. *vb* ➡ **ring**

circumference *n* perimeter, periphery, circuit, outline, contour, silhouette ➡ **edge, border, circle**

circumstantial *adj* indirect, inferential, inconclusive, incidental

citizen *n* inhabitant, subject, native, resident, national, denizen ➡ **occupant**

If the word you want is not a main entry above, look below to find it.

chisel ➡ carve, cheat

chitchat ➡ talk

chivalric ➡ noble

chivalrous ➡ polite, noble

chocolate ➡ brown

choicest ➡ best

chomp ➡ bite

chop ➡ cut

choppy ➡ rough

chorale ➡ choir

chore ➡ job

chorister ➡ singer

christen ➡ name

chronic ➡ continual, frequent

chronicle ➡ diary, story

chronograph ➡ clock

chronometer ➡ clock

chubby ➡ fat

chuck ➡ throw

chuckle ➡ laugh

chum ➡ friend

chunk ➡ block, lump

churchgoing ➡ religious

churchyard ➡ cemetery

churl ➡ boor

churn ➡ mix

chute ➡ channel

ciao ➡ good-bye, hello

cicatrix ➡ scar

cinema ➡ movies

cinematographer ➡ photographer

cipher ➡ zero, number

circlet ➡ crown, ring

circuit ➡ circle, circumference, round

circuitous ➡ indirect

circular ➡ round, advertisement

circulate ➡ spread

circulation ➡ flow

circumspect ➡ careful

circumspection ➡ tact

circumstance ➡ event, state

circumvent ➡ avoid

circus ➡ carnival

cistern ➡ well

citadel ➡ castle

citation ➡ award, document

cite ➡ quote

citizenry ➡ people

city ➡ town, urban

➡ = synonym cross-reference • ⇨ = antonym cross-reference · **39**

civilization 1. *n* cultivation, culture, enlightenment, refinement, breeding, polish ➡ **progress**
2. *n* ➡ **people**

clap 1. *vb* applaud, cheer, root ➡ **praise**
2. *n* ➡ **bang**

clarity *n* clearness, lucidity, simplicity, transparency, definition, focus, sharpness, resolution

clasp 1. *n* fastener, clamp, buckle, zipper, button, catch, snap, clip ➡ **lock**
2. *vb* ➡ **join, squeeze, embrace, catch**

class 1. *n* ➡ **type, group, grade**
2. *n* refinement, polish, quality, panache, grace, style, breeding,

cultivation, caliber ➡ **elegance**
3. *n* ➡ **lesson, course**

clean 1. *vb* wash, cleanse, rinse, scrub, scrape, scour, launder, bathe, brush, tidy, purify, sterilize, filter ➡ **shine, sweep**
2. *adj* spotless, washed, unblemished, unused, unsoiled, fresh, blank, pristine, immaculate ➡ **neat, sterile** ⇨ *dirty*

cleaning *n* washing, wash, bath, shower, rinse, soak, scrub ➡ **laundry**

cliché *n* platitude, truism, commonplace, bromide, banality ➡ **saying, stereotype**

cliff *n* bluff, crag, precipice, escarpment, bank, promontory, palisade ➡ **hill, mountain**

If the word you want is not a main entry above, look below to find it.

civic ➡ **public, urban**

civil ➡ **polite, public**

civil servant ➡ **official**

clack ➡ **tick**

claim ➡ **boast, argue, appeal, interest**

clairvoyant ➡ **prophet**

clamber ➡ **climb**

clammy ➡ **damp**

clamor ➡ **noise**

clamorous ➡ **loud**

clamp ➡ **clasp**

clan ➡ **family**

clandestine ➡ **secret**

clang ➡ **bang, ring**

clank ➡ **bang**

claptrap ➡ **nonsense**

clarify ➡ **explain**

clash ➡ **bang, fight**

classic ➡ **masterpiece, model**

classified ➡ **secret**

classify ➡ **arrange**

clatter ➡ **bang**

clause ➡ **term, excerpt**

claustrophic ➡ **stuffy**

claw ➡ **foot**

clawhammer ➡ **hammer**

clean out ➡ **empty**

cleanse ➡ **clean**

clear ➡ **transparent, fair, legible, obvious, articulate, audible, open, forgive**

clearance ➡ **sale**

clearing ➡ **field**

clearly ➡ **apparently**

clearness ➡ **clarity**

cleave ➡ **cut, separate, stick**

cleaver ➡ **knife**

cleft ➡ **cut, hole**

clemency ➡ **pity, forgiveness**

clementine ➡ **orange**

clench ➡ **tighten, embrace**

clergy ➡ **minister**

clergyman ➡ **minister**

clergywoman ➡ **minister**

cleric ➡ **minister**

clerical ➡ **religious**

clever ➡ **able, smart**

clichéd ➡ **trite**

click ➡ **peep, tick**

client ➡ **patron**

climax 1. *n* ➡ **top**
2. *vb* crest, peak, culminate, cap, consummate, crown ➡ **finish**

climb 1. *vb* scale, clamber, scramble, crawl ➡ **ascend**
2. *n* ascent, ascension, rise ➡ **growth, slant**

clock *n* timepiece, watch, wristwatch, stopwatch, chronometer, chronograph, timer, hourglass, egg timer, sundial

close 1. *vb* shut, fasten, slam ➡ **lock**
2. *vb* plug, seal, stop, clog, obstruct, fill
3. *adj* ➡ **near**
4. *adj* ➡ **alike, approximate**
5. *adj* ➡ **narrow**
6. *adj* ➡ **friendly**
7. *adj* ➡ **thick**
8. *adj* ➡ **stuffy**
   In general, **shut** *is a stronger or more forceful word than* **close,** *and it suggests the action of moving the door, lid, cover, etc., to a closed and fastened position.*

closet *n* armoire, wardrobe, cloakroom, locker, storeroom, pantry, larder ➡ **cupboard**

cloth 1. *n* fabric, material, textile, weave
2. *n* dustcloth, dishrag, dishcloth, washcloth, chamois, rag, remnant

clothes *n* clothing, dress, apparel, wardrobe, garments, attire, garb, vestments, finery, habit
   Note that **clothes** *is a plural noun and always takes a plural verb: "My* **clothes** *are on fire!"* **Clothing** *is a collective noun; it may refer to clothes in general or to all of the clothes you are wearing, but it always takes a singular verb: "Warm* **clothing** *is necessary in the winter."*

cloud 1. *n* haze, mist, billow, vapor ➡ **fog, smoke**
2. *n* shadow, pall, gloom

cloudy 1. *adj* overcast, hazy, lowering ➡ **dim** ⇨ *fair*
2. *adj* ➡ **obscure**

If the word you want is not a main entry above, look below to find it.

climate ➡ weather, setting

clime ➡ weather

clinch ➡ finish, join

cling ➡ stick

clinic ➡ hospital

clink ➡ peep, jail

clip ➡ cut, pin, clasp

clique ➡ group

cloak ➡ wrap, hide

cloakroom ➡ closet

clobber ➡ hit

clog ➡ close, barrier

clogged ➡ stuffy

cloister ➡ court, monastery

clone ➡ reproduce

closed ➡ impassable

close-fitting ➡ tight

closeness ➡ presence

closeout ➡ sale

closing ➡ last

clot ➡ lump, harden

clothe ➡ dress, wrap

clothing ➡ clothes

cloudburst ➡ rain

clown ➡ comic, fool

clowning ➡ play

cloying ➡ rich

clumsy 1. *adj* (*in reference to people*) awkward, ungraceful, ungainly, inept, fumbling, bumbling, uncoordinated, gauche ➡ **amateur** 2. *adj* (*in reference to objects*) awkward, bulky, cumbersome, unwieldy, unmanageable

coat 1. *n* overcoat, jacket, blazer, sport coat, sport jacket, raincoat, windbreaker, parka, trench coat 2. *n* fur, wool, fleece ➡ **hair, hide** 3. *n* coating, film, covering, blanket, mantle, veneer, crust, scale ➡ **layer** 4. *vb* ➡ **cover**

cold *adj* frosty, icy, freezing, frigid, arctic, polar, antarctic, raw ➡ **cool** ⇨ **hot**

college *n* university, institute, institution, community college, junior college ➡ **school**

collide *vb* crash, smash, impact, sideswipe, rear-end ➡ **hit, knock**

collision *n* crash, impact, wreck, fender-bender (*informal*) ➡ **accident**

colony 1. *n* possession, dependency, settlement, satellite ➡ **state, country** 2. *n* ➡ **herd**

color 1. *n* shade, hue, tinge, tone, tint 2. *vb* ➡ **draw** 3. *vb* ➡ **blush**

If the word you want is not a main entry above, look below to find it.

club ➡ bat, stick, organization

clue ➡ sign

clump ➡ lump, pile

cluster ➡ group, flower

clutch ➡ seize, touch

clutter ➡ mess

coach ➡ teach, teacher, wagon

coagulate ➡ harden

coal-black ➡ black

coarse ➡ rough, common, rude, dirty

coarseness ➡ rudeness

coast ➡ shore, slide

coating ➡ coat

coax ➡ persuade, urge

cobblestone ➡ rock

cocktail lounge ➡ bar

coda ➡ conclusion

coddle ➡ pamper

code ➡ rule

codicil ➡ addition

coerce ➡ force

coffee cake ➡ cake

coffeehouse ➡ restaurant

coffeepot ➡ pot

coffer ➡ safe

cogent ➡ valid

cogitate ➡ think

cohere ➡ stick

coherent ➡ articulate

coil ➡ turn, circle

coin ➡ money

coincide ➡ agree

coincidence ➡ chance

coincident ➡ simultaneous

coincidental ➡ accidental

coinciding ➡ simultaneous

Coke® ➡ soda

cola ➡ soda

cold-blooded ➡ mean, insensitive

coldhearted ➡ insensitive

coliseum ➡ field

collaborate ➡ help

collaborative ➡ common

collapse ➡ fall

collar ➡ arrest

collateral ➡ parallel

colleague ➡ member, worker

collect ➡ gather, earn

collection ➡ assortment

collective ➡ common

collectively ➡ together

colloquium ➡ course

colonist ➡ pioneer

colonizer ➡ pioneer

colorful ➡ bright

colors ➡ flag

---

comb 1. *vb* brush, untangle, disentangle, straighten, groom, tease, curry
2. *vb* ➡ **hunt**

come *vb* arrive, reach, appear, attain ➡ **approach, descend** ⇨ **go**

comfort 1. *n* contentment, ease, relaxation, repose ➡ **pleasure**
2. *n* succor, consolation, solace ➡ **pity, help, support, kindness**
3. *vb* console, solace, condole, reassure ➡ **calm, support**
4. *vb* ➡ **pity**

comfortable 1. *adj* cozy, snug, comfy, restful, homey, roomy,

spacious ⇨ *uncomfortable*
2. *adj* ➡ **rich**

comic 1. *n* comedian, comedienne, joker, humorist, clown ➡ **actor**
2. *adj* ➡ **funny**

commit 1. *vb* perpetrate, enact, carry out ➡ **act, do**
2. *vb* ➡ **entrust**
3. *vb* ➡ **dedicate**
4. *vb* ➡ **jail**

committee *n* board, council, panel, commission, subcommittee, delegation, mission, cabinet, assembly

---

If the word you want is not a main entry above, look below to find it.

colossal ➡ huge

colossus ➡ giant

colt ➡ horse

column ➡ post, row

comatose ➡ unconscious

combat ➡ fight

combatant ➡ soldier

combative ➡ belligerent, unfriendly, military

comber ➡ wave

combination ➡ mixture, union

combine ➡ mix, add

combo ➡ band

combustible ➡ inflammable

combustion ➡ fire

come across ➡ find

come back ➡ return

comedian ➡ comic

comedienne ➡ comic

come down with ➡ catch

comedy ➡ humor, play

come into view ➡ appear

comely ➡ pretty

come near ➡ approach

comet ➡ meteor

comforter ➡ blanket

comfy ➡ comfortable

comical ➡ funny

coming ➡ approach

command ➡ control, order, rule

commandeer ➡ take

commander ➡ boss

commanding ➡ grand

commandment ➡ order

commemorate ➡ celebrate, remember

commemoration ➡ ceremony

commence ➡ start

commencement ➡ beginning

commend ➡ praise, approve

commendable ➡ praiseworthy

comment ➡ remark

commentary ➡ remark

commerce ➡ business

commercial ➡ advertisement, financial

commiserate ➡ pity

commiseration ➡ pity

commission ➡ committee

commitment ➡ promise

committed ➡ faithful

commodity ➡ product

---

common 1. *adj* ordinary, typical, familiar, everyday, widespread, average, unpretentious, humble, commonplace, pedestrian, popular, prevalent ➡ **general, normal, usual, plain** ⇨ *strange*
2. *adj* vulgar, coarse, commonplace, crass, crude, banal, plebeian ➡ **cheap, dirty**
3. *adj* communal, mutual, joint, collective, collaborative, shared ➡ **unanimous, public**
4. *n* ➡ **park**

compare *vb* contrast, juxtapose, parallel, liken, match, correlate ➡ **study, distinguish**

compatible *adj* similar, harmonious, agreeable, congruous ➡ **friendly**

compete *vb* contend, rival, play, contest, vie ➡ **fight, face**

competition 1. *n* rivalry, contention, antagonism ➡ **fight, game**
2. *n* ➡ **opponent**

competitive *adj* rival, contentious, antagonistic, vying ➡ **ambitious**

complain *vb* protest, gripe, grouch, grumble, whine, nag, fuss, moan, groan, squawk *(informal)* ➡ **mumble, object**

complaint 1. *n* objection, grievance, criticism, lament, charge, accusation, allegation, indictment, denunciation, reproach, outcry, grudge ➡ **protest**
2. *n* ➡ **illness, hardship**

If the word you want is not a main entry above, look below to find it.

commonplace
➡ **common, cliché**

common sense
➡ **wisdom**

commonwealth
➡ **country, state**

commotion
➡ **disturbance, noise, activity**

communal
➡ **common, public**

communicable
➡ **contagious**

communicate ➡ **talk, tell**

communication
➡ **speech, mail**

communications
➡ **media**

community ➡ **town, neighborhood, people**

community college
➡ **college**

commute ➡ **travel**

commuter ➡ **traveler**

compact ➡ **firm, small, short, thick, agreement**

companion ➡ **friend**

companionship
➡ **friendship**

company ➡ **business, friendship, visitor, team, troop**

comparable ➡ **alike**

comparably ➡ **alike**

comparison
➡ **similarity, estimate**

compartment
➡ **booth**

compass ➡ **range**

compassion ➡ **pity, kindness**

compassionate ➡ **kind**

compatibility
➡ **relationship**

compeer ➡ **equal**

compel ➡ **force**

compelling
➡ **interesting, urgent**

compensate ➡ **pay, balance, refund**

compensation
➡ **wage, refund, revenge**

competence ➡ **ability**

competent ➡ **able, efficient**

competently ➡ **well**

competitor ➡ **athlete, contestant, opponent**

compilation
➡ **assortment**

compile ➡ **gather, write**

complacent
➡ **satisfied**

complete 1. *adj* entire, full, total, whole, absolute, utter, uncut, intact, unbroken, exhaustive, thorough, unabridged, uncensored ➡ **all, comprehensive, perfect**
2. *vb* ➡ **finish**

completely 1. *adv* fully, totally, entirely, utterly, wholly, altogether, quite, thoroughly, stark
2. *adv* ➡ **certainly**

complicated *adj* complex, intricate, elaborate, sophisticated, involved, subtle ➡ **hard**

comprehensive *adj* thorough, inclusive, exhaustive, blanket
➡ **complete, general**

concentrate 1. *vb* focus, devote, attend ➡ **meditate, think, study**
2. *vb* focus, converge, consolidate, condense, compress, intensify, thicken, distill ➡ **gather**

concern 1. *vb* involve, touch, pertain, appertain, regard, bear on, refer to, encompass ➡ **affect, belong**
2. *vb* ➡ **worry**
3. *n* ➡ **worry, interest**
4. *n* ➡ **business**

If the word you want is not a main entry above, look below to find it.

complement ➡ suit, addition

completion ➡ finish

complex
➡ complicated

compliance
➡ agreement

compliant ➡ passive

complicate ➡ confuse

compliment ➡ praise

complimentary ➡ free

comply ➡ obey

component ➡ part, division

compose ➡ calm, make, write

composed ➡ calm

composer ➡ musician

composite ➡ mixture

composition
➡ structure, work, report, score

composure ➡ calm

compound ➡ mix, mixture

comprehend ➡ know, read

comprehension
➡ wisdom

compress
➡ concentrate, condense, squeeze, bandage

comprise ➡ contain

compromise
➡ agreement

compulsion
➡ obsession

compulsory
➡ necessary

compunction ➡ regret

computation
➡ mathematics

compute ➡ add

computerized
➡ automatic

computing ➡ addition

comrade ➡ friend

comradeship
➡ friendship

con ➡ cheat

con artist ➡ hypocrite

conceal ➡ hide

concealed ➡ invisible

concede ➡ admit, surrender, abandon

conceit ➡ pride

conceited ➡ proud

conceivable
➡ possible

conceivably ➡ maybe

conceive ➡ imagine, invent

concentration
➡ attention

concept ➡ idea

conception
➡ beginning

concerned ➡ careful

concerning ➡ about

concert ➡ program

concerted
➡ unanimous

concession
➡ surrender

conciliatory
➡ peaceful

concise ➡ short

conciseness ➡ brevity

concision ➡ brevity

---

conclusion 1. *n* inference, assumption, deduction ➡ **decision** ⇨ *beginning*
2. *n* afterword, epilogue, postscript, postlude, coda ⇨ *introduction*
3. *n* ➡ **finish**

conclusive *adj* decisive, definitive, undeniable ➡ **certain**

condense *vb* shorten, contract, abbreviate, abridge, compress, telescope, cut, prune ➡ **decrease, shrink, concentrate** ⇨ *lengthen*

condescend *vb* stoop, deign, vouchsafe, demean, degrade, humble, accommodate, patronize

confuse *vb* perplex, puzzle, bewilder, confound, complicate, baffle, disconcert, disorient, befuddle, abash, stymie, mystify, throw, stump

confusion 1. *n* disorder, chaos, anarchy, turmoil, discord, mayhem, lawlessness ➡ **excitement, hysteria, violence**
2. *n* perplexity, bewilderment, bafflement, puzzlement, consternation, nervousness ➡ **misunderstanding**

If the word you want is not a main entry above, look below to find it.

conclude ➡ finish, decide, infer

concluding ➡ last

conclusively ➡ finally

concoct ➡ invent

concoction ➡ mixture, lie

concord ➡ peace, unity

concordance ➡ dictionary

concrete ➡ real

concur ➡ agree

concurrence ➡ agreement

concurrent ➡ simultaneous

concurrently ➡ together

concussion ➡ blow[1]

condemn ➡ blame

condensation ➡ summary

condensed ➡ thick

condescending ➡ pompous

condition ➡ state, health, exercise, term

conditioning ➡ exercise

conditions ➡ weather

condo ➡ home

condole ➡ comfort

condolence ➡ pity

condominium ➡ home

condone ➡ forgive

conduct ➡ behavior, lead, bring

conductor ➡ guide

conduit ➡ pipe

confederate ➡ partner

confer ➡ talk, negotiate, give

conference ➡ meeting

confess ➡ admit, reveal

confide ➡ entrust

confidence ➡ certainty, secrecy, secret, belief

confident ➡ certain, optimistic

confidential ➡ secret

configuration ➡ pattern

confine ➡ jail

confinement ➡ privacy

confirm ➡ verify, admit

confirmation ➡ proof

confiscate ➡ take

conflagration ➡ fire

conflict ➡ fight

conflicting ➡ opposite

confluence ➡ union

conform ➡ adjust

conformity ➡ agreement

confound ➡ confuse

confront ➡ face

confrontation ➡ fight, meeting

confronting ➡ opposite

confused ➡ delirious

congeal ➡ harden, cool

---

consecutive *adj* successive, continuous, progressive, ensuing, numerical, alphabetical, sequential, serial

conservative *adj* conventional, traditional, orthodox, moderate, reactionary, right-wing, illiberal
➡ **stuffy** ⇨ *liberal*

consider *vb* reflect, weigh, entertain, contemplate ➡ **study, think**

contagious *adj* infectious, catching, communicable, transmissible, transmittable, spreadable, epidemic

If the word you want is not a main entry above, look below to find it.

congenial ➡ pleasant
congenital ➡ natural
congested ➡ stuffy
congratulate ➡ praise
congratulations ➡ praise
congregate ➡ gather
congregation ➡ audience, church
congress ➡ government
congruity ➡ similarity
congruous ➡ compatible
conifer ➡ tree
conjectural ➡ theoretical
conjecture ➡ theory
conjurer ➡ magician
connect ➡ join, bridge
connection ➡ link, junction, relevance
conniption ➡ fit²
connive ➡ plan
connoisseur ➡ expert
connotation ➡ meaning
connote ➡ mean

conquer ➡ defeat
conqueror ➡ winner
conquest ➡ defeat, victory
conscientious ➡ reliable, careful
conscious ➡ alert, awake
consciously ➡ purposely
consciousness ➡ life, mind
conscript ➡ soldier
consecrate ➡ bless
consecrated ➡ holy
consensus ➡ agreement
consent ➡ agree, agreement, permission
consequence ➡ effect, importance, punishment
consequently ➡ therefore
conservation ➡ economy
conservatory ➡ greenhouse
conserve ➡ save

considerable ➡ big
considerably ➡ far
considerate ➡ kind, thoughtful
consideration ➡ kindness, attention, price
consign ➡ entrust
consistency ➡ density
consistent ➡ same, continual
consist of ➡ contain
consolation ➡ comfort
console ➡ comfort
consolidate ➡ concentrate, mix, unify
consolidation ➡ union
consort ➡ mix, spouse
consortium ➡ monopoly
conspicuous ➡ obvious, striking
conspiracy ➡ plan
conspire ➡ plan
constable ➡ police officer

constant ➡ continual, faithful
constantly ➡ regularly
consternation ➡ confusion, fear
constituent ➡ matter, member
constitute ➡ make
constitutional ➡ legal
constrain ➡ force
constrict ➡ shrink
constricted ➡ narrow
constricting ➡ tight
construct ➡ build
construction ➡ assembly
consul ➡ diplomat
consult ➡ talk
consultant ➡ adviser
consultation ➡ talk
consume ➡ eat, use
consummate ➡ climax
consumption ➡ use
contact ➡ touch, link
contact lenses ➡ glasses
contacts ➡ glasses
contagion ➡ disease

contain 1. *vb* hold, include, consist of, comprise, accommodate ➠ **carry, embody**
2. *vb* restrain, limit, suppress, curb, quell, quash, quench, control, repress, swallow ➠ **stop, extinguish, prevent**

container *n* receptacle, box, carton, case, crate, can, jar, cup, glass, bucket, pail, tank, tub, tube ➠ **bag, bowl, barrel, chest, package, bottle, wrapper**

contestant *n* competitor, participant, contender, player, entry ➠ **athlete, opponent, candidate**

continual *adj* continuous, incessant, unceasing, constant, persistent, relentless, steady, chronic, unvarying, invariable, unchanging, ongoing, consistent, nonstop, unbroken ➠ **frequent, permanent**

continue 1. *vb* last, endure, remain, persist, persevere, carry on, proceed
2. *vb* resume, recommence, renew, pick up ➠ **start**

contradict *vb* deny, refute, challenge, dispute ➠ **object, discredit**

contradiction *n* disagreement, discrepancy, inconsistency, incongruity, paradox, oxymoron ➠ **problem, disagreement**

If the word you want is not a main entry above, look below to find it.

contaminate ➠ dirty

contaminated ➠ dirty

contemplate ➠ consider, meditate

contemplative ➠ thoughtful

contemporaneous ➠ simultaneous

contemporaneously ➠ together

contemporary ➠ modern, fashionable, simultaneous

contempt ➠ hatred

contemptible ➠ shameful

contend ➠ argue, compete

contender ➠ athlete, contestant

content ➠ part, pleasure, please, satisfied

contented ➠ satisfied

contention ➠ competition, disagreement

contentious ➠ belligerent, competitive

contentment ➠ satisfaction, comfort

contest ➠ game, compete

context ➠ setting

continually ➠ regularly

continuous ➠ continual, consecutive

contort ➠ bend

contorted ➠ bent

contour ➠ circumference

contraband ➠ booty

contract ➠ agreement, catch, condense, shrink, tighten

contraction ➠ abbreviation

contradictory ➠ opposite

contrary ➠ opposite

contrast ➠ compare, differ, difference

contrasting ➠ opposite

contribute ➠ give

contribution ➠ gift

contributor ➠ patron

contrite ➠ sorry

contrition ➠ shame

contrivance ➠ invention

contrive ➠ invent, plan

---

control 1. *vb* command, direct, manage, dominate, subject, regulate, engineer, tame, captain, cope, handle, harness ➡ **govern, lead, contain**
2. *vb* ➡ **contain**
3. *n* ➡ **rule, discipline**

cook 1. *vb* fry, bake, broil, roast, grill, stew, sauté, steam, barbecue, microwave, brew ➡ **boil, prepare**
2. *n* chef, sous-chef, pastry chef, baker ➡ **servant**

cool 1. *adj* chilly, chill, brisk, fresh, bracing, nippy ➡ **cold**
2. *adj* remote, aloof, distant, reserved, chilly, impersonal ➡ **calm,**

apathetic, unfriendly
3. *adj* excellent, all right, fashionable ➡ **good**
4. *vb* chill, refrigerate, freeze, congeal ➡ **fan**

copy 1. *n* reproduction, facsimile, photocopy, likeness ➡ **duplicate**
2. *vb* ➡ **reproduce, imitate**

corner 1. *n* angle, turn ➡ **bend, curve**
2. *n* intersection, turn, junction, juncture, crossroad
3. *n* ➡ **monopoly**
4. *vb* ➡ **catch**

If the word you want is not a main entry above, look below to find it.

controls ➡ wheel

controversy ➡ argument

controvert ➡ disprove

conundrum ➡ problem

convalescence ➡ cure

convalescent ➡ better, patient

convalescing ➡ better

convene ➡ gather

convenience ➡ advantage

convenient ➡ available

convent ➡ monastery

convention ➡ meeting

conventional ➡ normal, conservative, stuffy

converge ➡ concentrate

convergence ➡ junction

conversation ➡ talk

converse ➡ talk, opposite

convert ➡ change, translate

convey ➡ carry, give, send, take, tell

conveyance ➡ movement

convict ➡ criminal, decide

conviction ➡ belief, cause, certainty, will

convince ➡ persuade

convinced ➡ certain

convincing ➡ valid

convivial ➡ friendly

convoy ➡ accompany

convulsion ➡ fit²

cookhouse ➡ kitchen

cookie ➡ pastry

cooler ➡ refrigerator

coop ➡ pen

cooperate ➡ help

cooperation ➡ help

cooperatively ➡ together

coordinate ➡ balance

cop ➡ police officer

cope ➡ control

copious ➡ abundant

copse ➡ forest

copyright ➡ license

coral ➡ orange

cord ➡ string

cordial ➡ friendly

cordiality ➡ hospitality

core ➡ middle, essence

cork ➡ top

cornerstone ➡ basis

cornfield ➡ field

corona ➡ halo

coronet ➡ crown

---

correct 1. *adj* accurate, right, exact, precise, true, faultless, flawless, authentic, faithful, factual ➡ **perfect** ⇨ *wrong*
2. *adj* respectable, decent, proper, fitting, appropriate, seemly, decorous, becoming ➡ **fit, prim**
3. *vb* remedy, rectify, revise, edit, amend, emend, reconcile, improve, reform, redress ➡ **fix, adjust, perfect, change**
4. *vb* ➡ **punish**

correction *n* revision, remedy, adjustment, emendation, reparation, rectification ➡ **repair**

correctly *adv* properly, accurately, appropriately, right, satisfactorily ➡ **precisely**

corrode *vb* erode, rust, rot, oxidize, tarnish ➡ **decay, melt**

cosmopolitan 1. *adj* ➡ **urban**
2. *adj* sophisticated, worldly, experienced ➡ **suave**

If the word you want is not a main entry above, look below to find it.

corporal ➡ physical

corporation ➡ business, organization

corporeal ➡ physical

corps ➡ troop

corpse ➡ body

corpulent ➡ fat

corral ➡ pen

correctional facility ➡ jail

correctness ➡ accuracy

correlate ➡ compare

correlation ➡ link

correspond ➡ agree, resemble

correspondence ➡ mail, similarity

correspondent ➡ reporter

corresponding ➡ same

corridor ➡ hall

corroborate ➡ verify

corroboration ➡ proof

corroded ➡ rusty

corrosion ➡ decay

corrupt ➡ dishonest, wrong

corruption ➡ dishonesty

corsair ➡ pirate

cortege ➡ court

cosmetic ➡ superficial

cosmic ➡ universal

cosmos ➡ space

cost ➡ price

cost-effective ➡ efficient

costly ➡ expensive

costume ➡ disguise, dress, suit

cot ➡ bed

coterie ➡ following

cottage ➡ home

cotter pin ➡ pin

couch ➡ seat, bed

council ➡ committee, meeting

counsel ➡ advice, adviser, suggest, warn

counselor ➡ adviser

count ➡ add, matter, score

countenance ➡ appearance, face

counter ➡ answer, booth, shelf, table, opposite

counterattack ➡ attack

counterbalance ➡ balance

counterespionage ➡ spying

counterfeit ➡ fake, invent

counterintelligence ➡ spying

countermand ➡ abolish

counterpart ➡ duplicate

counterpoise ➡ balance

counterproductive ➡ useless

countersign ➡ sign

counterspy ➡ spy

counting ➡ addition

countless ➡ infinite, many

count on ➡ depend

---

country 1. *n* nation, republic, kingdom, dominion, realm, commonwealth, land, domain, homeland, fatherland, motherland ➡ **state, colony**
2. *n* countryside, landscape, hinterland, wilderness, wild, backwoods, frontier, bush, boondocks (*informal*), sticks (*informal*)
3. *n* ➡ **music**

courage *n* bravery, valor, fortitude, boldness, spirit, gallantry, heroism, daring, audacity, nerve, mettle, grit, stomach, guts (*informal*)

course 1. *n* path, route, direction, heading, bearing, way, itinerary
2. *n* track, racetrack, trail ➡ **road**
3. *n* class, subject, seminar, program, major, minor, colloquium, elective

court 1. *n* courtyard, square, quadrangle, quad, atrium, patio, plaza, piazza, cloister
2. *n* ➡ **field**
3. *n* tribunal, law court, bench, bar, judiciary, forum
4. *n* courthouse, courtroom
5. *n* retinue, entourage, cortege, royal household, attendants
6. *vb* woo, date, romance, flirt ➡ **love**

cover 1. *vb* cover up, blanket, carpet, spread, coat, overspread, surface, pave, flag ➡ **wrap, protect, plate**
2. *vb* ➡ **hide**
3. *n* ➡ **top**
4. *n* ➡ **blanket, wrapper**
5. *n* ➡ **protection**

cowardly *adj* timid, timorous, fearful, cowering, fainthearted, yellow (*informal*), chicken (*informal*) ➡ **afraid** ⇨ **brave**

if the word you want is not a main entry above, look below to find it.

countryside ➡ country
coup ➡ revolution
coup d'état ➡ revolution
couple ➡ pair, few, join
coupling ➡ union
courageous ➡ brave
courier ➡ messenger
courteous ➡ polite
courtesy ➡ kindness, respect, hospitality

courthouse ➡ court
courtly ➡ noble
courtroom ➡ court
courtyard ➡ court
cove ➡ bay
covenant ➡ agreement, promise
covered ➡ underground

covering ➡ coat, wrapper
cover story ➡ alibi
covert ➡ secret, den
covet ➡ envy
covetous ➡ greedy
covetousness ➡ envy
cow ➡ scare
cow barn ➡ barn
cower ➡ fear, jump

cowering ➡ cowardly
co-worker ➡ partner
cowshed ➡ barn
coxswain ➡ pilot
cozy ➡ comfortable
crack ➡ hole, bang, break
cracked ➡ broken
crackle ➡ rustle
cradle ➡ bed, source

➡ = synonym cross-reference • ⇨ = antonym cross-reference

crawl 1. *vb* creep, squirm, wiggle, wriggle, slither, grovel, drag, inch ➡ **walk, climb** 2. *n* ➡ **swim**

creator *n* author, originator, architect, framer, designer, engineer, inventor, pioneer, innovator, founder ➡ **artist**

crime *n* offense, violation, sin, evil, wrong, wrongdoing, misdeed, trespass, transgression, infraction, felony, misdemeanor ➡ **theft, treason, murder**

criminal 1. *n* crook, thief, bandit, outlaw, desperado, convict, felon, offender, robber, burglar, perpetrator, wrongdoer, malefactor, lawbreaker, culprit ➡ **cheat, vandal, pirate** 2. *adj* ➡ **illegal**

If the word you want is not a main entry above, look below to find it.

craft ➡ art, profession, boat

craftsman ➡ artist

craftsmanship ➡ art

crafty ➡ sly

crag ➡ cliff

cram ➡ load

crammed ➡ full

cramp ➡ pain

cramped ➡ uncomfortable

cranky ➡ cross

crash ➡ bang, break, collide, collision, depression

crass ➡ rude, common

crate ➡ container

crater ➡ hole

cravat ➡ tie

crave ➡ want

craving ➡ appetite

crawl space ➡ basement

craze ➡ fashion

crazed ➡ insane

crazy ➡ insane, foolish

creak ➡ squeak

creamy ➡ rich, fair, white

crease ➡ fold, wrinkle

create ➡ cause, make

creation ➡ invention, work, assembly, earth

creative ➡ talented

creativity ➡ art, imagination

creature ➡ animal

credence ➡ belief

credentials ➡ document

credible ➡ possible

credit ➡ loan, belief, attribute

credit union ➡ bank

creditable ➡ praiseworthy

credo ➡ belief

credulous ➡ naive, superstitious

creed ➡ belief

creek ➡ river

creep ➡ crawl, sneak, tingle

cremate ➡ bury

creole ➡ dialect

crepe paper ➡ paper

crescent ➡ curve

crest ➡ climax, top

crevasse ➡ canyon, hole

crevice ➡ hole, canyon

crew ➡ group, team

crib ➡ bed

crimp ➡ bend, wrinkle

crimson ➡ red

cringe ➡ jump

crinkle ➡ wrinkle

cripple ➡ paralyze, weaken

crippled ➡ lame

crisis ➡ emergency

crisp ➡ brisk

criterion ➡ measure

critic ➡ judge

critical ➡ important

criticism ➡ complaint

criticize ➡ blame, study

croak ➡ grunt

crock ➡ bottle, bowl

crook ➡ criminal, curve

crooked ➡ bent, zigzag, dishonest

crookedness ➡ dishonesty

croon ➡ sing

crop ➡ growth, whip

cross 1. *adj* grouchy, irritable, disagreeable, cranky, fussy, peevish, cantankerous, ill-tempered, bad-tempered, ill-natured, petulant, grumpy, testy, sullen, surly ➡ **angry, rude, abrupt** ⇨ *happy*
2. *n* ➡ **tick**
3. *n* ➡ **hybrid**
4. *vb* ➡ **bridge**

crowd *n* mob, multitude, host, throng, army, legion, horde, swarm, flock ➡ **band, group, troop**

crown 1. *n* diadem, coronet, tiara, circlet, garland, chaplet, wreath
2. *vb* enthrone, invest, install, induct, inaugurate ➡ **bless**
3. *vb* ➡ **climax**

cry 1. *vb* weep, sob, wail, bawl, whimper, whine, moan, groan
2. *n, vb* shout, scream, howl, screech, bellow, shriek, roar, whoop, squeal, bay, yowl, wail, squawk ➡ **noise, yell, bark**

cupboard *n* cabinet, sideboard, buffet, locker ➡ **closet**

cure 1. *n* remedy, treatment, antidote, curative, therapy ➡ **medicine**
2. *n* recovery, recuperation, healing, rehabilitation, convalescence
3. *vb* ➡ **heal**

If the word you want is not a main entry above, look below to find it.

crossbar ➡ bar

crossbreed ➡ hybrid

crossroad ➡ corner

crouch ➡ bend

crow ➡ boast

crowded ➡ full

crucial ➡ urgent

crude ➡ primitive, common, rude

crudeness ➡ rudeness

crude oil ➡ oil

crudity ➡ rudeness

cruel ➡ mean

cruet ➡ bottle

cruise ➡ patrol, travel, trip

crumble ➡ decay, grind

crumbly ➡ breakable

crumple ➡ fall, wrinkle

crumpled ➡ rough

crusade ➡ movement

crush ➡ break, grind, trample, defeat

crust ➡ coat

crypt ➡ cemetery, grave, basement

cryptic ➡ obscure, secret

crystalline ➡ transparent

cube ➡ block

cubicle ➡ booth

cuddle ➡ embrace, snuggle

cue ➡ reminder

cuisine ➡ food

culminate ➡ climax

culmination ➡ finish

culpability ➡ guilt

culpable ➡ guilty

culprit ➡ criminal, defendant

cult ➡ religion

cultivate ➡ dig, grow

cultivation ➡ farming, civilization, class

culture ➡ civilization

cultured ➡ suave

cumbersome ➡ clumsy, heavy

cunning ➡ sly, dishonesty

cup ➡ container, glass

cupcake ➡ cake

cur ➡ dog

curative ➡ medicinal, cure

curator ➡ guardian

curb ➡ contain

---

curious 1. *adj* inquisitive, prying, nosy, inquiring ➡ **meddlesome**
2. *adj* ➡ **strange**

curse 1. *n* oath, profanity, blasphemy, expletive
2. *n* hex, charm, spell, jinx
3. *vb* swear, blaspheme, damn, revile, vilify, cuss (*informal*)

curve 1. *n* bow, bend, turn, arch, arc, crook, trajectory, curvature, crescent, horseshoe, oxbow
2. *vb* ➡ **bend**

cushion 1. *n* pad, mat, pillow, bolster, pallet
2. *n* padding, buffer, shock absorber ➡ **protection**
3. *vb* ➡ **protect**

cut 1. *vb* chop, slice, dice, mince, shred, grate, carve, cleave, gouge, hew, hack, lacerate, amputate ➡ **rip, peel, carve**
2. *vb* trim, shave, clip, snip, shear, prune, mow, reap
3. *vb* ➡ **condense, decrease**
4. *n* gash, slash, wound, injury, incision, laceration, scrape, scratch, nick, gouge, cleft, notch, slit ➡ **rip, hole, sore**

cute *adj* adorable, charming, quaint, cutesy ➡ **pretty**

If the word you want is not a main entry above, look below to find it.

curio ➡ novelty, antique

curiosity ➡ interest, novelty

curious ➡ strange

curl ➡ bend, lock

currency ➡ money

current ➡ energy, flood, modern

curry ➡ comb

cursive ➡ handwriting

cursory ➡ superficial, fast

curt ➡ abrupt

curtail ➡ decrease

curtain ➡ divider

curtsy ➡ bend

curvature ➡ curve

curved ➡ bent

cuss ➡ curse

custodian ➡ guardian

custody ➡ possession

custom ➡ habit, rule

customarily ➡ usually

customary ➡ usual

customer ➡ patron

cutesy ➡ cute

cutlass ➡ sword

cut-rate ➡ cheap

cutting ➡ sharp

cycle ➡ period, round, periodic

cyclical ➡ periodic

cyclist ➡ rider

cyclone ➡ storm

cylindrical ➡ round

cynic ➡ skeptic

cynical ➡ pessimistic

cyst ➡ growth

czar ➡ emperor

czarina ➡ empress

D

dam *n* embankment, dike, levee, weir ➥ **wall**

damage 1. *n* destruction, wreckage, wear, devastation, desolation, ruin, havoc, mayhem, injury, sabotage ➥ **decay, harm**
2. *vb* impair, mar, deface, scratch, scrape, scar, disfigure, deform, distort ➥ **hurt, break, destroy**

damp *adj* moist, humid, clammy, dank, muggy, sultry, sticky ➥ **wet, liquid**

dance 1. *n* ball, prom, social, mixer, gala ➥ **party**
2. *vb* step, trip, glide, pirouette, whirl
3. *vb* gambol, frolic, scamper, caper, cavort, romp ➥ **jump**

danger *n* risk, threat, peril, hazard, menace, jeopardy

dangerous *adj* harmful, perilous, hazardous, unsafe, risky, treacherous, precarious, explosive ➥ **deadly, destructive** ⇨ *safe*

dare 1. *vb* hazard, presume, risk ➥ **try**
2. *vb* defy, challenge, provoke ➥ **face**

dark 1. *adj* gloomy, murky, dusky, shady, unlit, somber, overcast, pitch-black, black, opaque ➥ **dim**
2. *adj* brunette, brown, tan, black, swarthy, sable, ebony
3. *n* darkness, dusk, gloom, blackness, shade, shadow ➥ **night**

If the word you want is not a main entry above, look below to find it.

dab ➥ rub

dabble ➥ tinker

dagger ➥ knife

daily ➥ paper

dainty ➥ breakable, choosy

dais ➥ platform

dale ➥ valley

dally ➥ wait

damaged ➥ broken

damaging ➥ destructive

damn ➥ curse

dampen ➥ wet

dampness ➥ humidity

dangle ➥ hang

Danish ➥ pastry

dank ➥ damp

dapper ➥ fashionable

dappled ➥ speckled

daring ➥ brave, courage

dark horse ➥ candidate

darkness ➥ dark

darling ➥ favorite, love

dart ➥ run, missile

dash ➥ bit, race, hurry, run

dashing ➥ fashionable, brave

data ➥ knowledge, proof

date ➥ day, period, meeting, court

datebook ➥ diary

daub ➥ rub

daughter ➥ child

daunt ➥ discourage

dauntless ➥ brave

dawdle ➥ lag

dawn ➥ morning

➥ = synonym cross-reference • ⇨ = antonym cross-reference

day n daylight, daytime, light, midday, date ➡ **morning, afternoon** ⇨ **night**

dead 1. adj deceased, departed, late, lifeless, extinct, defunct, inanimate ⇨ **alive**
2. adj inert, still, stagnant, motionless ➡ **calm**
3. adj ➡ **tired**
4. adv ➡ **completely**
5. n ➡ **casualty**

deadly 1. adj fatal, mortal, lethal, deathly, murderous, homicidal, terminal, incurable
2. adj poisonous, venomous, virulent, malignant, toxic, noxious ➡ **dangerous**

3. adj ➡ **dull**
4. adv terminally ➡ **completely**

deaf 1. adj hearing-impaired, unhearing, hard of hearing ➡ **disabled**
2. adj ➡ **unaware**

death n decease, demise, dying, passing, expiration, loss ➡ **casualty, fate, finish** ⇨ **birth**

debt n liability, obligation, debit, arrears, deficit, indebtedness ➡ **bill**

decay 1. vb deteriorate, disintegrate, crumble, decompose, wear, rot, molder, spoil, putrefy ➡ **corrode, destroy**
2. n deterioration, degeneration, decomposition, spoilage, disrepair, disintegration, corrosion ➡ **damage**

If the word you want is not a main entry above, look below to find it.

daybook ➡ diary
daybreak ➡ morning
daydream ➡ dream
daylight ➡ day
daytime ➡ day
daze ➡ dream, surprise
dazed ➡ dizzy
dazzle ➡ surprise
dazzling ➡ bright, beautiful, striking
deadbeat ➡ loafer
deadlock ➡ tie
deadpan ➡ blank, dry

deafening ➡ loud
deal ➡ agreement, bargain, sale
dealer ➡ seller
deal out ➡ share
dean ➡ principal
dear ➡ expensive, valuable, love
dearly ➡ much
dearth ➡ absence, want
deathless ➡ eternal
deathly ➡ deadly

debacle ➡ disappointment
debase ➡ shame
debate ➡ argue, argument
debit ➡ debt
debonair ➡ suave
debris ➡ trash
debunk ➡ disprove
debut ➡ introduction
decayed ➡ rusty, shabby, bad
decease ➡ death, die
deceased ➡ dead

deceit ➡ dishonesty, pretense
deceitful ➡ dishonest
deceive ➡ betray, cheat, lie
deceiver ➡ liar, hypocrite
decency ➡ kindness, virtue
decent ➡ correct, fair, kind
deception ➡ lie, pretense, trick
deceptive ➡ dishonest, unreliable

decide *vb* settle, resolve, determine, rule, conclude, reconcile, negotiate, mediate, arbitrate, judge, adjudge, convict ➡ **choose**

decision *n* judgment, determination, resolution, ruling, finding, verdict, sentence, decree, declaration ➡ **choice, conclusion**

decorate 1. *vb* adorn, beautify, ornament, embellish, trim, garnish, bedeck, redecorate, refurbish, festoon
2. *vb* ➡ **praise**

decoration 1. *n* adornment, ornamentation, embellishment, redecoration, beautification
2. *n* ornament, garnish, trim, accent, flourish
3. *n* ➡ **prize, award**

decrease 1. *vb* lessen, diminish, abate, decline, wane, subside, ebb, dwindle, taper, shrink, shrivel, reduce, depress, lower, slash, curtail, cut ➡ **condense, weaken, shrink**
2. *n* ➡ **drop**

dedicate *vb* devote, commit, set apart, pledge ➡ **bless**

defeat 1. *vb* conquer, beat, overcome, surmount, overpower, vanquish, best, better, top, break, overthrow, throw, upset, down, whip, crush ➡ **subdue, win**
2. *n* loss, downfall, failure, conquest, destruction, rout, upset, beating, thrashing ⇨ *victory*

defect 1. *n* imperfection, flaw, blemish, shortcoming, drawback, minus ➡ **fault, mistake, spot**
2. *vb* ➡ **leave**

defendant *n* accused, suspect, culprit ➡ **prisoner**

If the word you want is not a main entry above, look below to find it.

decipher ➡ solve, translate, read

decipherable ➡ legible

decisive ➡ conclusive, resolute

decisively ➡ finally

deck ➡ floor, dress

declaim ➡ quote

declaration ➡ announcement, decision

declare ➡ tell, advertise

decline ➡ decrease, drop, refuse, depression

declivity ➡ slant

decode ➡ solve, translate, read

decompose ➡ decay

decomposition ➡ decay

decorative ➡ fancy

decorous ➡ correct, dignified, prim

decorum ➡ behavior

decoy ➡ tempt

decree ➡ act, decision, order

decrepit ➡ old

dedication ➡ loyalty, inscription

deduce ➡ infer

deduct ➡ subtract

deduction ➡ conclusion, reason, subtraction

deed ➡ act, document

deem ➡ believe

deep ➡ broad, profound, ocean

deepness ➡ depth

deface ➡ damage

defame ➡ insult

defective ➡ broken

defector ➡ runaway

defend ➡ protect, verify

defense ➡ protection, justification, alibi

defenseless ➡ vulnerable

---

delay 1. *vb* postpone, defer, put off, deter, stall, procrastinate ➡ **wait, hesitate**
2. *vb* hamper, detain, impede, hinder, retard ➡ **prevent**
3. *n* ➡ **break**

delicate 1. *adj* ➡ **breakable, weak**
2. *adj* ➡ **thin**
3. *adj* sensitive, touchy, ticklish, tricky, sticky ➡ **dangerous, doubtful**

delicious *adj* tasty, delectable, appetizing, luscious, savory, mouth-watering, flavorful, scrumptious ➡ **rich**

delirious *adj* incoherent, hysterical, confused, hallucinating ➡ **frantic, insane**

delivery 1. *n* shipment, transfer, transmission, dispatch, distribution, transportation ➡ **flow**
2. *n* ➡ **birth**
3. *n* ➡ **salvation**
4. *n* enunciation, pronunciation, elocution, diction, presentation, performance

---

If the word you want is not a main entry above, look below to find it.

defer ➡ delay, surrender

deference ➡ respect

deferential ➡ shy, passive

defiance ➡ disobedience, fight

defiant ➡ rebellious

deficiency ➡ absence, want

deficient ➡ inadequate, partial, poor

deficit ➡ debt

defile ➡ dirty

define ➡ describe, specify

definite ➡ certain

definitely ➡ certainly

definition ➡ meaning, clarity

definitive ➡ conclusive, model

deflate ➡ empty, shrink

deflect ➡ distract

deform ➡ damage

defraud ➡ cheat

deft ➡ able

defunct ➡ dead

defy ➡ disobey, rebel, face, dare

degenerate ➡ immoral

degeneration ➡ decay

degrade ➡ condescend

degree ➡ grade

dehydrate ➡ dry

dehydrated ➡ dry

deign ➡ condescend

deist ➡ atheist

deity ➡ god

déjà vu ➡ memory

dejected ➡ sad

dejection ➡ depression

delayed ➡ late

delectable ➡ delicious

delegate ➡ agent, entrust, name

delegation ➡ appointment, committee

delete ➡ erase

deli ➡ restaurant

deliberate ➡ slow, voluntary, think

deliberately ➡ carefully, purposely

delicacy ➡ tact, pastry

delicately ➡ carefully

delight ➡ please, pleasure

delighted ➡ happy

delightful ➡ pleasant, nice

delight in ➡ like

delineate ➡ draw

delinquent ➡ late, negligent, vandal

delirium ➡ hysteria

deliver ➡ bring, take, give, free, save

deliverance ➡ escape, salvation

deliverer ➡ savior

dell ➡ valley

delude ➡ fool

deluge ➡ flood

delusion ➡ illusion

delve ➡ dig, hunt

---

den 1. *n* lair, burrow, nest, hole, warren, covert ➨ **cave**
2. *n* study, office, library, family room, recreation room, rec room, playroom ➨ **room**

density *n* substance, bulk, body, consistency, mass ➨ **weight**

dent 1. *n* indentation, depression, impression, dimple, pit, nick, notch ➨ **hole**
2. *vb* indent, pit, nick, notch ➨ **bend**

department *n* section, division, branch, bureau, agency, chapter, subsidiary, affiliate ➨ **field, business, job, arm**

departure 1. *n* exit, going, leaving, withdrawal, farewell, embarkation, exodus ➨ **escape**
2. *n* deviation, divergence, digression, aberration, irregularity ➨ **change, difference**

depend 1. *vb* trust, rely, count on ➨ **believe**
2. *vb* hang, hinge, rest ➨ **turn**

deploy *vb* position, array, marshal ➨ **arrange**

If the word you want is not a main entry above, look below to find it.

demand ➨ insist, order

demanding ➨ hard

demean
➨ condescend, shame

demeanor
➨ appearance, bearing

demented ➨ insane

demigod ➨ god

demise ➨ death

demolish ➨ destroy

demon ➨ devil

demonic ➨ wicked

demonstrate
➨ explain, verify, protest

demonstration
➨ experiment,
protest, parade, movement

demonstrative
➨ emotional, loving

demoralize
➨ discourage

demur ➨ hesitate

demure ➨ shy

denial ➨ abstinence, rejection

denizen ➨ citizen

denomination
➨ religion

denotation
➨ meaning

denote ➨ mean

denounce ➨ blame

dense ➨ dull, firm, thick

denseness ➨ ignorance

denunciation
➨ complaint

deny ➨ refuse, contradict

depart ➨ leave, die

departed ➨ dead

dependability
➨ loyalty

dependable ➨ reliable

dependency ➨ habit, colony

depict ➨ draw, describe

depiction
➨ description

deplane ➨ leave

deplete ➨ use

deplorable
➨ shameful, unfortunate

deplore ➨ hate, regret

deport ➨ banish

deportation ➨ exile

deportee ➨ exile

deportment ➨ bearing

depose ➨ oust

deposit ➨ put, bank

depository
➨ warehouse, bank

depot ➨ warehouse

depraved ➨ immoral

depravity
➨ immorality

deprecate ➨ ridicule, underestimate

---

depression 1. *n* ➡ **dent**
2. *n* desolation, despair, despondency, dejection ➡ **sorrow, misery**
3. *n* recession, slump, decline, downturn, crash

deprive *vb* withhold, divest, rob ➡ **refuse**

depth 1. *n* deepness, lowness, extent ➡ **measure** ⇨ *height*
2. *n* ➡ **middle**
3. *n* profundity, gravity, insight, profoundness ➡ **wisdom**

descend 1. *vb* swoop, stoop, dip ➡ **fall, decline, sink** ⇨ *ascend*
2. *vb* dismount, land, light, alight, settle, perch
3. *vb* issue, derive, come, spring, arise

describe *vb* characterize, define, depict, represent, recount, detail ➡ **explain, draw**

description *n* portrayal, characterization, account, depiction, portrait, profile ➡ **picture, story**

desert 1. *n* wasteland, wilderness, waste, barrens, badlands ➡ **country, plain**
2. *adj* ➡ **sterile**
3. *vb* ➡ **leave**

deserve *vb* merit, earn, warrant, justify, rate

desire 1. *n* ➡ **ambition**
2. *n* ➡ **hope**
3. *n* passion, lust, infatuation, appetite, urge, hunger, longing, nostalgia, wistfulness, yearning, yen, itch ➡ **love, greed, envy**
4. *vb* ➡ **want, envy**

If the word you want is not a main entry above, look below to find it.

depress ➡ sadden, decrease

depressed ➡ sad, underdeveloped

depressing ➡ bleak, sorry

deprived ➡ poor, underdeveloped

deputy ➡ helper

deranged ➡ insane

derby ➡ race

derelict ➡ abandoned, negligent, guilty, homeless, beggar

deride ➡ ridicule

derision ➡ ridicule

derisive ➡ sarcastic

derivation ➡ source, product

derivative ➡ product

derive ➡ descend, extract

descendant ➡ child

descending ➡ down

descent ➡ drop, slant, ancestry

descry ➡ discover

deserted ➡ abandoned, open

deserter ➡ runaway

desertion ➡ escape

deserts ➡ punishment

deserving ➡ praiseworthy

design ➡ pattern, plan, intend, invent

designate ➡ choose, name

designation ➡ name, appointment

designer ➡ creator

desirable ➡ attractive, pleasant, useful

desk ➡ table

desolate ➡ abandoned, bleak, sadden

desolation ➡ damage, depression

despair ➡ depression

desperado ➡ criminal

desperate ➡ frantic, urgent, useless

destination n end, terminus, terminal, station, address, target

destroy vb wreck, spoil, demolish, ruin, annihilate, damage, devastate, ravage, raze, level, blight ➠ **abolish, break, mutilate** ⇨ *build*

destructive 1. adj ruinous, calamitous, catastrophic, devastating ➠ **violent, dangerous**
2. adj harmful, injurious, adverse, unfavorable, damaging

detail 1. n particular, trait, feature, factor, specific, peculiarity, fact, point
2. vb ➠ **specify, describe**

detour 1. n bypass, diversion, byway, digression, deviation ➠ **departure**
2. vb divert, redirect, skirt, bypass

development 1. n ➠ **growth**
2. n ➠ **invention**
3. n subdivision, project, housing estate

devil n demon, fiend, archfiend

If the word you want is not a main entry above, look below to find it.

despicable ➠ bad

despise ➠ hate

despised ➠ unpopular

despondency ➠ depression

despondent ➠ sad

despot ➠ dictator

despotic ➠ dictatorial

despotism ➠ tyranny

dessicated ➠ dry

destiny ➠ chance, fate, future

destitute ➠ poor

destitution ➠ poverty

destruction ➠ damage, violence, defeat

destructiveness ➠ violence

detach ➠ separate

detached ➠ fair

detachment ➠ division

detain ➠ delay, arrest, jail

detainee ➠ prisoner

detect ➠ discover

detection ➠ discovery

detective ➠ police officer

detention ➠ arrest

deter ➠ delay, prevent

deteriorate ➠ decay, relapse

deteriorated ➠ shabby

deterioration ➠ decay

determination ➠ will, decision

determine ➠ decide, arrange, verify, learn

determined ➠ ambitious, resolute

deterred ➠ disabled

detest ➠ hate

detestable ➠ bad

dethrone ➠ oust

detonate ➠ explode

detonation ➠ bang

detrain ➠ leave

detriment ➠ harm

devastate ➠ destroy, shock

devastating ➠ destructive

devastation ➠ damage

develop ➠ grow, invent, prepare, catch

developing ➠ early

developmental ➠ experimental

deviate ➠ differ, swerve, wander

deviation ➠ change, departure, detour

device ➠ equipment, tool, object, trick

devilish ➠ wicked

devil-may-care ➠ carefree

devilment ➠ mischief

devious ➠ indirect, sly

devise ➠ arrange, invent

devoid ➠ empty

devote ➠ dedicate, concentrate

devoted ➠ faithful, loving

devotee ➠ fan

devotion ➠ love, loyalty, worship

devour ➠ eat

devout ➠ religious

dew ➠ humidity

➠ = synonym cross-reference • ⇨ = antonym cross-reference

dialect n idiom, vernacular, patois, slang, lingo, argot, jargon, cant, creole, pidgin ➡ **accent, language**

diary n journal, chronicle, memoir, datebook, daybook, calendar

dictator n despot, tyrant, autocrat, fascist, totalitarian, authoritarian ➡ **ruler**

dictatorial adj despotic, tyrannical, autocratic, fascist, totalitarian, authoritarian, absolute, arbitrary ➡ **dogmatic**

dictionary n glossary, lexicon, vocabulary, concordance, thesaurus, encyclopedia ➡ **book**

die 1. vb decease, expire, pass away, pass on, perish, succumb, depart, starve ⇨ *live*
2. n ➡ **form**

differ vb vary, contrast, deviate, diverge, disagree ➡ **change**

difference n dissimilarity, contrast, distinction, disparity, variation, variance, discrepancy, irregularity, inequality, nuance, gulf ➡ **departure** ⇨ *similarity*

different 1. adj distinct, other, else, another, separate, dissimilar, unlike, irregular, uneven, unequal ➡ **unique** ⇨ *same, similar*
2. adj diverse, various, assorted, miscellaneous, disparate, eclectic, assorted, varied, heterogeneous, motley ➡ **many**
3. adj ➡ **strange**

differently adv variously, diversely, separately, else, otherwise

dig vb shovel, delve, scoop, excavate, burrow, tunnel, drill, bore, bulldoze, plow, hoe, cultivate, harrow, rake, grub

dignified adj formal, stately, solemn, decorous, ceremonious, lofty, imperious, august ➡ **serious, grand**

If the word you want is not a main entry above, look below to find it.

dexterity ➡ agility

dexterous ➡ able, agile

diabolical ➡ wicked

diacritic ➡ accent

diadem ➡ crown

diagram ➡ pattern, picture, draw

dial ➡ call

dialogue ➡ talk

diameter ➡ width

diamond ➡ field

diaphanous ➡ thin, transparent

dice ➡ cut

dictate ➡ say, order

dictatorship ➡ tyranny

diction ➡ speech, delivery

diet ➡ food

differentiate ➡ distinguish

differently abled ➡ disabled

difficult ➡ hard, intolerable, stubborn

difficulty ➡ trouble, barrier

diffident ➡ shy, reluctant

digest ➡ absorb, learn, summary

digit ➡ number

dignitary ➡ celebrity

dignity ➡ pride, respect, importance

digress ➡ wander

digression ➡ detour, departure

diligence n perseverance, industry, persistence, application, care, carefulness, thoroughness, attentiveness

diligent adj industrious, hardworking, assiduous, tireless, inexhaustible, unflagging, dogged ➡ **patient, careful**

dim adj faint, indistinct, obscure, hazy, blurry, shadowy, murky, foggy ➡ **dark, dull** ⇨ *bright*

dining room n dining hall, eating area, breakfast nook ➡ **room, restaurant**

diplomat n ambassador, consul, emissary, statesman, attaché, envoy, minister, chargé d'affaires ➡ **official**

dirge n lament, requiem, funeral march, elegy, threnody ➡ **hymn**

dirt 1. n earth, soil, loam, humus, turf, topsoil, sand, gravel, grit, land, ground
2. n filth, grime, dust, mud, muck, slime, ooze, slop, sludge, mire ➡ **trash**

dirty 1. adj filthy, grimy, soiled, dingy, grubby, unclean, impure, unsanitary, contaminated, polluted, foul, dusty, squalid ➡ **messy** ⇨ *clean*
2. adj obscene, lewd, pornographic, ribald, vulgar, bawdy, coarse, earthy, salty, risqué, racy ➡ **common**
3. vb soil, stain, sully, pollute, contaminate, infect, defile, tarnish, taint, foul, befoul, smudge, muddy, mess ⇨ *clean*

If the word you want is not a main entry above, look below to find it.

dike ➡ dam, jetty

dilapidated ➡ shabby

dilate ➡ swell

dilatory ➡ slow, negligent

dilemma ➡ problem

dilettante ➡ amateur

dilute ➡ weaken

dimension ➡ measure

diminish ➡ decrease, subtract

diminished ➡ less

diminished by ➡ minus

diminution ➡ subtraction

diminutive ➡ small

dimple ➡ dent

din ➡ noise

dine ➡ eat

diner ➡ restaurant

ding ➡ ring

dingy ➡ dirty, dull

dining hall ➡ dining room

dinnerware ➡ plate

dip ➡ descend, drop, sink, swim

diploma ➡ document

diplomacy ➡ tact

diplomatic ➡ suave

dipper ➡ spoon

dire ➡ awful, urgent

direct ➡ control, lead, order, straight

direction ➡ course, perspective, leadership, order

directions ➡ recipe

directive ➡ order

directly ➡ now, precisely

director ➡ boss

---

disability n handicap, disadvantage, impairment, impediment, affliction, hindrance ➥ **defect**

disabled 1. adj handicapped, physically challenged, differently abled, impaired, incapacitated
2. adj hampered, thwarted, encumbered, deterred, handicapped, disadvantaged, stymied
3. adj ➥ **broken**

disagreement n contention, friction, discord, strife, dissent, dissension, heresy ➥ **argument, contradiction, fight, opposition**

disappear vb vanish, fade, lift, dissipate, dissolve, evaporate, fizzle, disperse, thin ➥ **melt, stop**

disappoint vb let down, fail, discourage, dishearten, dissatisfy, disillusion, frustrate ➥ **sadden**

disappointment 1. n failure, discouragement, dissatisfaction, frustration, disillusionment ➥ **regret**
2. n letdown, failure, disaster, debacle, fiasco, flop, dud (informal)

disaster 1. n catastrophe, calamity, tragedy, casualty, cataclysm, misfortune, pity, evil ➥ **accident, emergency**
2. n ➥ **disappointment**

discard vb throw away, dispose, reject, dump, scrap, junk, jettison ➥ **abandon, shed** ⇨ save

discipline 1. n self-control, self-restraint, willpower, control ➥ **will**
2. n training, regimen, regimentation ➥ **practice, science**
3. n ➥ **field**
4. n ➥ **punishment**
5. vb ➥ **punish**

If the word you want is not a main entry above, look below to find it.

disable ➥ mutilate, paralyze

disadvantage ➥ harm, disability

disadvantaged ➥ disabled, underdeveloped

disagree ➥ argue, differ, object

disagreeable ➥ cross, awful, bad, thankless, uncomfortable

disallow ➥ abolish, forbid

disapproval ➥ opposition

disapprove ➥ object, refuse

disarrange ➥ disturb

disastrous ➥ unfortunate

disband ➥ finish

disbelief ➥ doubt

disbelieve ➥ doubt

disburse ➥ pay

discern ➥ see

discernible ➥ audible, visible

discerning ➥ smart, profound

discernment ➥ wisdom

discharge ➥ fire, explode, shoot, free, relieve, suspension

disciple ➥ student

disclose ➥ reveal, tell

disclosure ➥ discovery

discoloration ➥ scar

discomfit ➥ embarrass

discomfited ➥ uncomfortable

discomfort ➥ pain

disconcert ➥ confuse, disturb, embarrass

discontinue ➥ stop, abandon

discord ➥ disagreement, confusion

discount ➥ bargain, sale, subtraction

discourage 1. *vb* dispirit, dismay, demoralize, intimidate, unnerve, daunt ➡ **disappoint**
2. *vb* dissuade ➡ **prevent**
⇨ *persuade, urge*

discover 1. *vb* detect, unearth, uncover, strike, descry, ferret out ➡ **find, notice**
2. *vb* ➡ **learn**

discovery *n* finding, detection, unearthing, identification, sighting, disclosure ➡ **invention**

disease *n* infection, virus, fever, contagion, blight, syndrome, bug (*informal*), blight ➡ **illness, epidemic**

disguise 1. *n* mask, camouflage, guise, costume, masquerade, makeup ➡ **pretense**
2. *vb* ➡ **hide**

disgust 1. *vb* repel, revolt, offend, nauseate, sicken, appall
2. *n* loathing, revulsion, repugnance, distaste ➡ **hatred**

dishonest *adj* untruthful, untrustworthy, deceitful, crooked, lying, deceptive, corrupt, unprincipled, unscrupulous ➡ **fake, sly, bad**

dishonesty *n* deceit, corruption, fraudulence, vice, crookedness, duplicity, cunning, guile, hypocrisy ➡ **lie, trick**

If the word you want is not a main entry above, look below to find it.

discouragement ➡ disappointment

discourse ➡ speech

discourteous ➡ rude

discourtesy ➡ rudeness

discredit ➡ disprove, shame

discreet ➡ careful

discreetly ➡ carefully

discrepancy ➡ contradiction, difference

discretion ➡ tact

discriminate ➡ distinguish, separate

discrimination ➡ prejudice

discriminatory ➡ prejudiced

discuss ➡ talk

discussion ➡ talk, argument

disdain ➡ hatred, ridicule, hate

disembark ➡ leave

disentangle ➡ comb

disfigure ➡ damage, mutilate

disfigurement ➡ scar

disgrace ➡ shame

disgraceful ➡ awful, shameful

disgusting ➡ bad

dish ➡ bowl, plate, meal

dishcloth ➡ cloth

dishearten ➡ sadden, disappoint

dishevel ➡ disturb

disheveled ➡ messy

dishonor ➡ shame

dishonorable ➡ shameful

dish out ➡ give

dishrag ➡ cloth

disillusion ➡ disappoint

disillusionment ➡ disappointment

disinclined ➡ reluctant

disinfected ➡ sterile

disinformation ➡ lie

disintegrate ➡ decay

disintegration ➡ decay

disinterest ➡ apathy

disinterested ➡ apathetic

disk ➡ circle

dislike ➡ hate, hatred, opposition

disliked ➡ unpopular

dislocate ➡ disturb, hurt

dislodge ➡ move

disloyal ➡ unfaithful

disloyalty ➡ treason

➡ = synonym cross-reference • ⇨ = antonym cross-reference

disobedience *n* defiance, rebellion, insubordination, transgression, waywardness ➡ **revolution**

disobey *vb* defy, disregard, violate, break, misbehave, transgress ➡ **rebel, refuse, fight, sin** ⇨ *obey*

display 1. *n* exhibit, exhibition, presentation, arrangement, array ➡ **show**
2. *n* ➡ **show**
3. *vb* ➡ **show**

disprove *vb* discredit, refute, rebut, invalidate, controvert, expose, debunk ➡ **contradict**

distance 1. *n* stretch, length, interval, gap, way, expanse, extent ➡ **measure**
2. *n* ➡ **background**

distinguish *vb* differentiate, discriminate, identify, recognize ➡ **separate, compare**

If the word you want is not a main entry above, look below to find it.

dismal ➡ bleak, sad

dismay ➡ discourage, fear, shock

dismember ➡ mutilate

dismiss ➡ refuse, fire, relieve

dismissal ➡ rejection

dismount ➡ descend

disobedient ➡ mischievous, rebellious

disorder ➡ confusion, illness, disturb

disorderly ➡ messy, wild

disorient ➡ confuse

disparage ➡ ridicule

disparate ➡ different

disparity ➡ difference

dispatch ➡ delivery, letter, speed, send, kill

dispel ➡ banish

dispense ➡ give, inflict

dispersal ➡ flow

disperse ➡ spread, disappear

dispirit ➡ discourage

displace ➡ disturb

displaced ➡ homeless

displacement ➡ movement

disport ➡ play

dispose ➡ discard, persuade

disposed ➡ likely, ready, vulnerable

disposition ➡ mood, personality, tendency, order

dispossessed ➡ homeless

dispute ➡ argument, argue, contradict, object

disregard ➡ disobey, forget, neglect

disregarded ➡ unnoticed

disrepair ➡ decay

disreputable ➡ shameful, bad

disrespect ➡ rudeness, neglect

disrespectful ➡ rude

disrobe ➡ undress

disrupt ➡ disturb

disruption ➡ disturbance, break

dissatisfaction ➡ disappointment

dissatisfy ➡ disappoint

dissemble ➡ lie

dissembler ➡ hypocrite

dissembling ➡ hypocritical

disseminate ➡ spread

dissemination ➡ flow

dissension ➡ disagreement

dissent ➡ disagreement, object

dissertation ➡ report

dissident ➡ rebel

dissimilar ➡ different

dissimilarity ➡ difference

dissipate ➡ disappear, waste

dissolute ➡ immoral

dissolve ➡ melt, disappear, finish

dissuade ➡ discourage

distant ➡ far, foreign, cool

distaste ➡ disgust

distasteful ➡ thankless, bad

distend ➡ swell, lengthen

distill ➡ concentrate

distinct ➡ different, special, obvious, audible, legible

distinction ➡ difference, excellence

distinctive ➡ special

distinguished ➡ famous

distort 1. *vb* ➡ **bend, damage**
2. *vb* misrepresent, pervert, misconstrue, stretch ➡ **change, lie**

distract *vb* divert, sidetrack, deflect ➡ **bother, disturb**

disturb 1. *vb* disarrange, displace, dislocate, disorder, mess, muss, dishevel, rumple, garble ➡ **move**
2. *vb* interrupt, disrupt, intrude, interfere, impose ➡ **bother, distract**
3. *vb* agitate, upset, perturb, unnerve, unsettle, disconcert, ruffle, jar ➡ **worry, bother**

disturbance *n* commotion, uproar, riot, disruption, fracas, upheaval, turbulence, unrest, rampage ➡ **noise, confusion, protest, violence, fight**

divide 1. *vb* part, split, partition, segment, subdivide, portion, apportion, halve, quarter, zone

➡ **cut, separate, share**
2. *vb* diverge, branch, fork
3. *vb* ➡ **arrange**

divider *n* partition, barrier, screen, curtain, veil ➡ **wall**

division 1. *n* separation, detachment, partition, distribution, divorce, severance, subdivision
2. *n* section, component, chapter, passage, paragraph, scene, episode ➡ **part, share, department**

dizzy *adj* light-headed, giddy, woozy, faint, dazed, tipsy

do 1. *vb* accomplish, achieve, carry out, render ➡ **act, cause, work**
2. *vb* ➡ **solve**
3. *vb* ➡ **satisfy**

dock 1. *n* pier, wharf, quay, landing, slip ➡ **harbor**
2. *vb* moor, land, anchor, berth ➡ **descend** ⇨ *leave*

If the word you want is not a main entry above, look below to find it.

distracted ➡ absentminded

distraught ➡ frantic

distress ➡ misery, sorrow, trouble

distressful ➡ uncomfortable

distressing ➡ pitiful

distribute ➡ spread, share, give

distribution ➡ delivery, division, flow

district ➡ zone

distrust ➡ doubt

distrustful ➡ suspicious

disturbed ➡ anxious

ditch ➡ channel

ditty ➡ song

dive ➡ fall, jump

diverge ➡ differ, divide, swerve, wander

divergence ➡ departure

diverse ➡ different, many

diversely ➡ differently

diversion ➡ detour, entertainment

divert ➡ distract, entertain, detour

divertissement ➡ entertainment

divest ➡ deprive, undress

divination ➡ prediction

divine ➡ holy, heavenly, religious, predict

diviner ➡ prophet

divinity ➡ god

divorce ➡ separate, division

divorced ➡ single

divulge ➡ reveal

docile ➡ gentle, passive, tame

---

doctor 1. *n* physician, M.D., GP, professor, Ph.D.
2. *vb* ➡ **heal**

document *n* record, certificate, form, file, diploma, citation, affidavit, passport, deed, credentials, manuscript ➡ **report, agreement, license, ticket**

dog *n* hound, mongrel, mutt, cur, puppy, canine, whelp

dogmatic *adj* opinionated, doctrinaire, dictatorial, arrogant, overbearing, imperious ➡ **stubborn**

doll *n* dolly, baby doll, figurine, mannequin, action figure ➡ **puppet, toy**

door *n* doorway, entrance, entry, exit, gate, gateway, access, portal, passage, outlet, opening, mouth ➡ **threshold**

doorman *n* doorkeeper, porter, gatekeeper, caretaker, watchman, attendant ➡ **porter, servant**

dose *n* dosage, treatment, teaspoonful ➡ **measure**

doubt 1. *vb* suspect, mistrust, distrust, disbelieve, wonder ➡ **question**
2. *n* uncertainty, suspicion, skepticism, distrust, misgiving, disbelief, doubtfulness, reservation, question, qualm ➡ **suspense**

doubtful *adj* dubious, questionable, uncertain, indefinite, unclear, unsure, skeptical, ambivalent, perplexed, incredulous, vague, tentative ➡ **suspicious, unbelievable, unresolved**

If the word you want is not a main entry above, look below to find it.

doctrinaire ➡ **dogmatic**

doctrine ➡ **belief**

documentation ➡ **proof**

dodder ➡ **limp**

dodge ➡ **avoid, escape, swerve, trick**

dogged ➡ **diligent, stubborn**

dogma ➡ **belief**

doleful ➡ **sad**

dolly ➡ **doll**

dolt ➡ **fool**

domain ➡ **country, field**

domestic ➡ **native, family, tame, servant**

domesticated ➡ **tame**

domicile ➡ **home**

dominant ➡ **predominant**

dominate ➡ **control, excel**

dominion ➡ **country, state, rule**

don ➡ **dress, teacher**

donate ➡ **give**

donation ➡ **gift**

done ➡ **past**

donjon ➡ **castle**

donor ➡ **patron**

doom ➡ **fate**

doorkeeper ➡ **doorman**

doorsill ➡ **threshold**

doorstep ➡ **threshold**

doorway ➡ **door**

do-rag ➡ **scarf**

dormant ➡ **asleep, latent**

dormer ➡ **attic**

dormitory ➡ **bedroom**

dosage ➡ **dose**

dot ➡ **spot**

dote on ➡ **love, pamper**

double ➡ **duplicate, alternate, fold**

double agent ➡ **spy**

double-cross ➡ **betray**

doubter ➡ **skeptic**

doubtfulness ➡ **doubt**

doubting Thomas ➡ **skeptic**

down 1. *adv* downward, downhill, descending
2. *adj* ➡ **sad**
3. *adj* ➡ **broken**
4. *n* ➡ **hill**
5. *vb* ➡ **defeat**
6. *vb* ➡ **drink**

draw 1. *vb* ➡ **pull**
2. *vb* ➡ **earn**
3. *vb* sketch, paint, color, portray, depict, illustrate, picture, trace, delineate, draft, diagram ➡ **describe**
4. *n* ➡ **attraction**
5. *n* ➡ **tie**

dream *n* reverie, daydream, trance, daze, spell, stupor, study, swoon ➡ **hope**

dress 1. *vb* wear, clothe, don, robe, attire, costume, outfit, deck
2. *vb* trim, groom, array ➡ **decorate**
3. *vb* ➡ **bandage**
4. *n* gown, frock, jumper, sheath, skirt, shift, shirtwaist, pinafore, smock, sari, sarong, muumuu ➡ **clothes**

drink 1. *n* beverage, refreshment, alcohol, liquor, spirits ➡ **soda, liquid**
2. *n* sip, glass, swallow, taste, drop, dram, nip, swig, gulp, draft
3. *vb* swallow, gulp, guzzle, quaff, sip, swig, imbibe, down

---

If the word you want is not a main entry above, look below to find it.

dour ➡ bleak

douse ➡ extinguish, wet

dowel ➡ nail

downcast ➡ sad

downfall ➡ defeat, fate

downhearted ➡ sad

downhill ➡ down

downpour ➡ rain

downs ➡ plain

down-to-earth ➡ practical

downturn ➡ drop, depression

downward ➡ down

downy ➡ fuzzy

doze ➡ sleep

dozing ➡ asleep

drab ➡ dull, plain, gray

draft ➡ draw, hire, write, drink, wind

draftee ➡ soldier

drafty ➡ windy

drag ➡ pull, crawl

drain ➡ dry, empty

drained ➡ tired

drainpipe ➡ pipe

dram ➡ drink

drama ➡ emotion, play

dramatic ➡ sensational

dramatization ➡ play

dramatize ➡ exaggerate, act

drape ➡ hang

drastic ➡ excessive

drawback ➡ defect

drawing ➡ picture

drawing room ➡ living room

drawl ➡ accent

drawn ➡ tense

draw near ➡ approach

dread ➡ fear

dreadful ➡ awful, scary

dreamer ➡ idealist

dreaming ➡ asleep

drear ➡ bleak

dreary ➡ bleak, dull

drench ➡ wet

drenched ➡ wet

dresser ➡ chest, table

dressing ➡ bandage

dressing gown ➡ bathrobe

dribble ➡ drop

drift ➡ blow², fly, wander

drifter ➡ loafer

drill ➡ dig, teach, practice, lesson

drinker ➡ drunkard

drip ➡ drop

dripping ➡ wet

---

drive 1. *vb* steer, maneuver, navigate, pilot, ride, propel, jockey ➡ **operate, control**
2. *vb* ➡ **banish**
3. *n* ➡ **trip**
4. *n* ➡ **ambition, energy**

drop 1. *n* droplet, raindrop, teardrop, tear, bead, drip, glob, trickle, dribble ➡ **ball**
2. *n* ➡ **drink**
3. *n* plunge, reduction, decrease, descent, decline, slump, downturn, dip ➡ **fall**
4. *vb* drip, trickle, leak, seep, ooze ➡ **splash**
5. *vb* ➡ **descend, fall, lose, shed**

drug *n* antibiotic, narcotic, sedative, tranquilizer, painkiller, anesthetic, opiate, hallucinogen, antidepressant ➡ **medicine**

drunk *adj* drunken, intoxicated, inebriated, tipsy, besotted

drunkard *n* alcoholic, drinker, inebriate, sot, souse, tippler, lush (*informal*), wino (*informal*)

dry 1. *adj* arid, parched, dehydrated, dessicated, dusty, thirsty ➡ **stale** ⇨ **wet**
2. *adj* ➡ **dull**
3. *adj* droll, wry, deadpan, sardonic ➡ **funny**
4. *adj* ➡ **sour**
5. *vb* wipe, drain
6. *vb* evaporate, dehydrate, wilt, wither, shrivel ➡ **harden**

due 1. *adj* unpaid, payable, outstanding, overdue, receivable
2. *adj* expected, scheduled, anticipated
3. *adv* ➡ **precisely**

If the word you want is not a main entry above, look below to find it.

drivel ➡ **nonsense**
drive out, drive away ➡ **banish**
driver's seat ➡ **wheel**
drizzle ➡ **rain**
drizzly ➡ **wet**
droll ➡ **dry**
drone ➡ **hum**

droop ➡ **bend, weaken**
droopy ➡ **limp**
drop by, drop in ➡ **visit**
drop-kick ➡ **kick**
droplet ➡ **drop**
drown ➡ **choke, flood**
drowsy ➡ **listless**
drudgery ➡ **work**

drum ➡ **barrel, knock**
drunken ➡ **drunk**
dry cleaning ➡ **laundry**
dub ➡ **name**
dubious ➡ **doubtful, suspicious**
duck ➡ **avoid, bend, sink**

duct ➡ **pipe, blood vessel**
duct tape ➡ **adhesive**
dud ➡ **disappointment**
due to ➡ **because**
duel ➡ **fight**
due process ➡ **justice**
duffel bag ➡ **luggage**

dull 1. *adj* uninteresting, boring, tedious, dreary, monotonous, tiresome, prosaic, humdrum, shallow, deadly, dry, drab ➡ **insipid** ⇨ *interesting, lively*
2. *adj* slow, stolid, obtuse, dense, unimaginative, square ➡ **stupid**
3. *adj* blunt, unsharpened ⇨ *sharp*
4. *adj* drab, dim, dingy, faded, lackluster, flat ➡ **bleak, dark, dim** ⇨ *bright*

dumb *adj* mute, speechless, silent, inarticulate, voiceless, wordless, tongue-tied ➡ **quiet**
For the informal use of **dumb** *meaning "not very smart," see* **stupid**.

dumbfounded *adj* astonished, amazed, bewildered, thunderstruck, flabbergasted, surprised

dump 1. *n* landfill, recycling center, trash heap, junkyard
2. *vb* ➡ **discard, empty**

duplicate 1. *n* double, twin, replica, counterpart, equivalent, analogue, parallel ➡ **copy, model**
2. *vb* ➡ **repeat, reproduce**

during *prep* throughout, through

duty 1. *n* responsibility, obligation, trust, charge
2. *n* ➡ **job**
3. *n* ➡ **tax**

If the word you want is not a main entry above, look below to find it.

dullard ➡ boor

dummy ➡ fake, fool, puppet

dunce ➡ fool

dune ➡ hill

dungeon ➡ jail

dunk ➡ sink

duo ➡ pair

dupe ➡ cheat, tool

duplicity ➡ dishonesty

durable ➡ strong, tough, unbreakable, permanent

duration ➡ period

duress ➡ stress

dusk ➡ dark, evening

dusky ➡ dark, gray

dust ➡ dirt, sweep

dustcloth ➡ cloth

dust jacket ➡ wrapper

dusty ➡ dirty, dry

dutiful ➡ good

duvet ➡ blanket

dwarf ➡ midget

dwell ➡ live¹

dwelling ➡ home

dwindle ➡ decrease

dye ➡ paint

dying ➡ death

dynamic ➡ active

dynamo ➡ engine

E

eager *adj* enthusiastic, keen, avid, anxious, ardent, passionate, fervent, exuberant, impatient ➡ **ready, ambitious**

early 1. *adj* initial, original, first, earliest, pioneering, pioneer, primary, inaugural, introductory, preliminary, incipient, embryonic, developing, nascent ⇨ *late*
2. *adj* premature, untimely, precocious, hasty, prompt ➡ **sudden** ⇨ *late*
3. *adj* primitive, primeval, prehistoric, primal, archaic, primordial ➡ **old** ⇨ *modern*

earn 1. *vb* make, collect, realize, profit, net, gross, draw, take (in) ➡ **get, receive, win, pay**
2. *vb* ➡ **deserve**

earth 1. *n* world, globe, nature, creation ➡ **planet, space**
2. *n* ➡ **dirt**

earthquake *n* quake, tremor, tremblor, shock, aftershock ➡ **vibration**

easy *adj* effortless, light, simple, moderate, straightforward ➡ **obvious, plain** ⇨ *hard*

eat 1. *vb* consume, devour, dine, feast, feed, graze, browse, gulp, gobble, wolf, gorge, bolt, prey on
2. *vb* ➡ **corrode**
The words breakfast *and* lunch, *but not* dinner *or* supper, *can also be used as verbs meaning "to eat breakfast or lunch."*

economy 1. *n* thrift, thriftiness, frugality, austerity, prudence, conservation
2. *n* ➡ **brevity**

If the word you want is not a main entry above, look below to find it.

each ➡ all, any

eagerness ➡ enthusiasm, ambition

earlier ➡ before, older

earliest ➡ early

earnest ➡ serious

earnestly ➡ sincerely

earnings ➡ wage

earsplitting ➡ loud

earthenware ➡ pottery

earthworm ➡ worm

earthy ➡ dirty

ease ➡ calm, facilitate, relieve, rest, comfort, freedom, leisure

easygoing ➡ carefree, tolerant

eating area ➡ dining room

eavesdrop ➡ listen, spy

ebb ➡ retreat, decrease

ebony ➡ black, dark

eccentric ➡ strange

eccentricity ➡ oddity

ecclesiastical ➡ religious

echo ➡ answer, reflect, repeat

eclectic ➡ different

eclipse ➡ hide, exceed

economic ➡ financial

economical ➡ efficient, cheap

economics ➡ business

ecosystem ➡ habitat

---

ecstatic *adj* elated, overjoyed, thrilled, blissful, jubilant, exultant, triumphant ► **happy**

edge *n* rim, margin, fringe, brink, boundary, verge, brim, lip, hem, periphery ► **border, circumference, side, shore**

educated *adj* literate, learned, knowledgeable, informed, studious, scholarly, erudite, lettered, well-read, well-informed, well-versed, schooled, bookish ► **smart** ⇨ *ignorant*

education *n* learning, schooling, instruction, teaching, tuition, training, scholarship, erudition ► **study, lesson, knowledge**

effect 1. *n* result, outcome, consequence, upshot, aftermath, issue ► **product**
2. *n* impact, impression, influence
3. *vb* ► **cause**
Be careful not to confuse the verb **effect** *with the verb* **affect**. *See the note at* **affect**.

efficiency *n* productivity, effectiveness, efficacy, proficiency

efficient *adj* proficient, productive, competent, effective, economical, expedient, cost-effective, practical ► **able, useful**

egg 1. *n* ovum, embryo, germ, roe, spawn ► **seed**
2. *vb* ► **urge**

elapse *vb* pass, lapse, slip by, expire

If the word you want is not a main entry above, look below to find it.

ecstasy ► pleasure

Eden ► utopia

edgy ► nervous

edibles ► food

edict ► order

edifice ► building

edit ► correct, write

educate ► teach

educational ► intellectual

educator ► teacher

eerie ► strange

efface ► erase

effective ► efficient, successful

effectively ► practically

effectiveness ► efficiency

effects ► property, luggage

effeminate ► feminine

efficacy ► efficiency, ability

effigy ► statue, god

effort ► work, try

effortless ► easy

effusive ► talkative

eggshell ► shell

egg timer ► clock

ego ► mind, soul

egocentric ► proud

egotism ► pride

egotistic ► proud

Einstein ► genius

either ► any

eject ► exclude, oust

elaborate ► complicated, fancy, exaggerate

elaboration ► exaggeration

elastic ► flexible, rubber band

elastic band ► rubber band

elated ► ecstatic

elbow ► push

elbow grease ► work

elbowroom ► space

elder ► ancestor, older

elderly ► old

elect ► choose

election ► vote, appointment

elective ► course

---

elegance n class, taste, polish, style, grace, splendor, glory, grandeur, sophistication, opulence, luxury ➡ **beauty**

embalm vb preserve, mummify ➡ **keep**

embarrass vb abash, disconcert, rattle, faze, discomfit, fluster, mortify, chagrin ➡ **shame**

embed vb imbed, enclose, insert, inset, wedge, implant, lodge, inlay ➡ **put**

embody vb represent, typify, incorporate, exemplify ➡ **contain**

embrace 1. vb hug, clasp, cuddle, enfold, envelop, squeeze, hold, grip, grasp, clench
2. vb ➡ **adopt**
3. n hug, clasp, handshake, caress, squeeze

emergency n crisis, exigency, extremity ➡ **disaster, trouble, accident**

If the word you want is not a main entry above, look below to find it.

electric ➡ exciting

electricity ➡ energy

electrify ➡ shock

electrifying ➡ exciting

electroplate ➡ plate

elegant ➡ beautiful, grand, fashionable

elegy ➡ dirge

element ➡ matter, part

elemental ➡ basic

elementary ➡ basic

elevate ➡ lift, promote

elevation ➡ height, promotion

elf ➡ fairy

elfin ➡ mischievous

elfish ➡ mischievous

elicit ➡ extract

eligible ➡ able, single

eliminate ➡ abolish, exclude

elite ➡ noble, aristocracy

elocution ➡ delivery

elongate ➡ lengthen

elongated ➡ long

elope ➡ escape

eloquent ➡ articulate

else ➡ different, differently

elsewhere ➡ absent

elucidate ➡ explain

elude ➡ avoid, escape

elusive ➡ inaccessible, sly

elysian fields, Elysium ➡ heaven

emaciated ➡ thin, hungry

e-mail ➡ send

emancipate ➡ free

emancipated ➡ free

emancipation ➡ salvation

embankment ➡ dam

embargo ➡ ban

embark ➡ leave, enter

embarkation ➡ departure

embarrassed ➡ ashamed

embarrassment ➡ shame

embellish ➡ decorate, exaggerate

embellished ➡ fancy

embellishment ➡ decoration, exaggeration

embezzle ➡ steal

embezzlement ➡ theft

embitter ➡ anger

emblem ➡ badge

emboss ➡ print

embroider ➡ sew, exaggerate

embroidery ➡ exaggeration

embryo ➡ egg

embryonic ➡ early

emcee ➡ host

emend ➡ correct

emendation ➡ correction

emerald ➡ green

emerge ➡ appear

emigrant ➡ exile, foreigner

emigrate ➡ move

emigration ➡ movement

emigré ➡ exile, foreigner

eminence ➡ excellence, fame

eminent ➡ famous

emissary ➡ messenger, diplomat

emit ➡ throw

emotion n sentiment, passion, drama, affect ➡ **feeling**

emotional 1. adj moving, poignant, touching, tearful, passionate, impassioned ➡ **pitiful, sad**
2. adj sentimental, demonstrative, sensitive, impetuous, overemotional, maudlin ➡ **temperamental, excited, loving**

emperor n czar, tzar, tsar (Russian), kaiser (German), caliph (Islamic), pharaoh (Egyptian), mikado (Japanese) ➡ **ruler, king**

emphasize vb highlight, feature, stress, accent, accentuate, underscore, underline

employed adj working, occupied, busy, engaged ⇨ **unemployed**

empress n czarina, tzarina, tsarina (Russian), kaiserin (German) ➡ **ruler, queen**

empty 1. adj vacant, unoccupied, uninhabited, bare, austere, blank, void, devoid, hollow, open ➡ **abandoned** ⇨ **full**
2. adj idle, vain, meaningless, hollow
3. vb unload, unpack, unwrap, remove, dump out, pour out, clean out, evacuate, vacate, deflate, drain

enchant vb beguile, entrance, charm, bewitch, hypnotize, mesmerize, spellbind, snow ➡ **fascinate, tempt**

enchantment n charm, spell, allure ➡ **attraction, magic**

encore interj bravo, brava, bravissimo, hurrah ➡ **again**

If the word you want is not a main entry above, look below to find it.

empathy ➡ pity

emphasis ➡ accent

employ ➡ hire, use

employee ➡ servant, worker

employer ➡ boss

employment ➡ profession, use

emporium ➡ market

empower ➡ let

emulate ➡ imitate

enable ➡ let

enact ➡ act, commit

enactment ➡ approval

encephalogram ➡ X ray

enchanted ➡ magic

enchanter ➡ magician

encircle ➡ ring

enclose ➡ ring, embed

enclosure ➡ booth, pen

encompass ➡ ring, concern

encounter ➡ face, fight, meeting, experience

encourage ➡ urge

encouragement ➡ incentive, support

encroach ➡ intrude

encumber ➡ load

encumbered ➡ disabled

encyclopedia ➡ dictionary

end ➡ abolish, finish, back, destination, fate, point, side

endanger ➡ jeopardize

endeavor ➡ try, work

ended ➡ past

endemic ➡ native

ending ➡ finish

endless ➡ eternal, infinite

endlessly ➡ forever

endorse ➡ approve, prefer, sign

➡ = synonym cross-reference • ⇨ = antonym cross-reference

enemy n rival, adversary, antagonist, foe, attacker, assailant ➡ **opponent**

energy 1. n vigor, vitality, life, liveliness, pep, stamina, endurance, vim, drive, get-up-and-go, zip, steam ➡ **strength, excitement**
2. n power, horsepower, pressure, thrust, propulsion, voltage, current, electricity, heat, fuel

engine n motor, machine, generator, turbine, dynamo

enough adj ample, sufficient, adequate, abundant, plentiful, plenty, much

Note that **enough, plenty,** and **much** cannot be used after an or before a singular noun such as supply, amount, quantity, or number. The other words in this list can be used in this way: "an **ample** supply," "a **sufficient** amount," "an **abundant** quantity," "an **adequate** number of items," "a **plentiful** supply."

enter 1. vb penetrate, invade, infiltrate ➡ **go, approach, intrude** ⇨ **leave**
2. vb board, mount, embark, entrain, enplane ⇨ **leave**
3. vb ➡ **join**

If the word you want is not a main entry above, look below to find it.

endow ➡ give

endowment ➡ gift, inheritance

endurance ➡ energy, patience

endure ➡ bear, weather, continue, experience

enduring ➡ permanent

energetic ➡ lively

energize ➡ excite

enfold ➡ embrace

enforce ➡ support

engage ➡ interest, hire

engaged ➡ absorbed, employed, married

engagement ➡ meeting, fight

engaging ➡ interesting

engender ➡ cause

engineer ➡ control, creator

engrave ➡ carve, print

engraving ➡ inscription, print

engross ➡ interest

engrossed ➡ absorbed

engrossing ➡ interesting

engulf ➡ flood, sink

enhance ➡ strengthen, suit

enigma ➡ problem

enigmatic ➡ mysterious, obscure

enjoy ➡ appreciate, like, own

enjoyable ➡ pleasant

enjoyment ➡ pleasure

enlarge ➡ grow, strengthen

enlargement ➡ addition, growth

enlighten ➡ teach

enlightenment ➡ civilization

enlist ➡ join, hire, mobilize

enliven ➡ excite

en masse ➡ together

enmity ➡ opposition

ennui ➡ boredom

enormous ➡ huge

enormously ➡ much

enplane ➡ enter

enrage ➡ anger

enraged ➡ violent

enrich ➡ help

enroll ➡ join, hire

enrollee ➡ member

ensemble ➡ band, choir, suit

enshrine ➡ bury

ensign ➡ flag

enslave ➡ catch

enslavement ➡ slavery

ensnare ➡ catch

ensue ➡ follow, happen

ensuing ➡ consecutive, following

ensure ➡ guarantee, verify

entangle ➡ catch

enterprise ➡ ambition, adventure, business

enterprising ➡ ambitious

entertain 1. *vb* amuse, divert, cheer (up), beguile, regale, enthrall, humor ➡ **please**
2. *vb* host, receive, treat, invite ➡ **welcome**
3. *vb* ➡ **consider**

entertainment *n* diversion, recreation, amusement, divertissement ➡ **pleasure, play, game, program**

enthusiasm *n* passion, zeal, fervor, zest, ardor, eagerness, exuberance, gusto ➡ **pleasure, excitement, ambition**

entrust *vb* commit, confide, consign, delegate, relegate

envy 1. *vb* desire, covet, resent, grudge, begrudge ➡ **want**
2. *n* jealousy, covetousness, resentment, spite, desire, malice ➡ **greed**

epidemic 1. *n* plague, pestilence, outbreak, eruption, rash, pandemic ➡ **disease**
2. *adj* ➡ **contagious**

equal 1. *adj* ➡ **same, fair**
2. *n* peer, fellow, mate, match, compeer ➡ **duplicate**

equipment *n* machinery, apparatus, paraphernalia, device, implement, fixture, gear, tackle, harness, kit, accoutrement, facilities ➡ **tool**

If the word you want is not a main entry above, look below to find it.

entertainer ➡ actor, musician, host

entertaining ➡ interesting

enthrall ➡ fascinate, entertain

enthrone ➡ crown

enthusiast ➡ fan

enthusiastic ➡ eager

entice ➡ tempt, persuade

enticement ➡ attraction

entire ➡ all, complete

entirely ➡ completely

entirety ➡ total

entitle ➡ name, let

entomb ➡ bury

entourage ➡ court, following

entrain ➡ enter

entrance ➡ door, enchant

entranceway ➡ threshold

entrancing ➡ magic

entreat ➡ beg

entrepreneur ➡ tycoon

entry ➡ approach, door, contestant

entryway ➡ hall, threshold

enumerate ➡ list

enunciate ➡ pronounce

enunciation ➡ speech, delivery

envelop ➡ embrace, wrap

envelope ➡ wrapper

envious ➡ jealous

environment ➡ habitat, setting, terrain, nature

envisage ➡ imagine

envision ➡ imagine

envoy ➡ messenger, diplomat

eon ➡ period

épée ➡ sword

ephemeral ➡ temporary

epic ➡ myth

epicure ➡ glutton

epilogue ➡ conclusion

episode ➡ division, event

epistle ➡ letter

epitaph ➡ inscription

epithet ➡ name

epoch ➡ period

epoxy ➡ adhesive

equalize ➡ balance

equatorial ➡ tropical

equestrian ➡ rider

equidistant ➡ parallel

equilibrium ➡ balance

equip ➡ supply

equipped ➡ ready

---

erase *vb* obliterate, delete, scratch, eradicate, expunge, efface ➡ **abolish**

escape 1. *vb* flee, elude, evade, dodge, break out, bolt, elope ➡ **avoid, leave**
2. *n* flight, getaway, evasion, desertion, deliverance, rescue ➡ **departure**

essence *n* core, heart, substance, quintessence, bottom, marrow, root, gist ➡ **basis, middle, soul**

estimate 1. *vb* calculate, evaluate, approximate, reckon, figure, gauge, assess, judge, appraise ➡ **guess**
2. *n* approximation, evaluation, appraisal, assessment, estimation, bid, quotation, quote, comparison ➡ **budget**

eternal *adj* everlasting, endless, unending, perpetual, interminable, infinite, immortal, deathless, undying ➡ **continual, permanent**

If the word you want is not a main entry above, look below to find it.

equitable ➡ fair

equity ➡ justice

equivalent ➡ alike, same, duplicate

equivocate ➡ hesitate, lie

equivocator ➡ liar

era ➡ period

eradicate ➡ abolish, erase, kill

erect ➡ build, lift, vertical

erection ➡ assembly

ergo ➡ therefore

erode ➡ corrode, weaken

err ➡ misunderstand, sin

errand ➡ job

erratic ➡ fickle, periodic, variable, zigzag

erroneous ➡ wrong

error ➡ mistake

ersatz ➡ fake

erudite ➡ educated, profound

erudition ➡ education, knowledge

erupt ➡ explode

eruption ➡ epidemic

escalation ➡ growth

escapade ➡ adventure

escape artist ➡ magician

escapee ➡ runaway

escarpment ➡ cliff

eschew ➡ abstain

escort ➡ accompany, bring, guide, patrol

escutcheon ➡ badge

esoteric ➡ secret

especial ➡ special

especially ➡ chiefly

espionage ➡ spying

espousal ➡ marriage

espouse ➡ adopt, marry

espoused ➡ married

essay ➡ report, try

essayist ➡ writer

essential ➡ necessary, important, necessity

essentially ➡ chiefly, practically

establish ➡ base, verify

establishment ➡ business

estate ➡ property

esteem ➡ respect

esthetics ➡ philosophy

estimable ➡ praiseworthy

estimated ➡ approximate

estimation ➡ estimate, reputation, respect, worth

estuary ➡ bay, river

etch ➡ carve

etching ➡ print

eternally ➡ forever

eternity ➡ future

ethereal ➡ invisible

ethics ➡ philosophy

etiquette ➡ behavior

euphonious ➡ musical

evacuate ➡ empty, leave

evade ➡ avoid, escape

evaluate ➡ estimate, study

evaluation ➡ estimate

evaluator ➡ judge

evaporate ➡ disappear, dry, melt

evasion ➡ escape

evening n nightfall, twilight, dusk, eventide, sundown, sunset
➡ **afternoon, night** ⇨ *morning*

event 1. n incident, occurrence, episode, circumstance, occasion, happening, phenomenon, actuality, fact
2. n milestone, landmark, breakthrough, achievement, experience, adventure ➡ **ceremony, disaster**
3. n ➡ **game**

exaggerate vb overstate, overdo, inflate, embellish, embroider, elaborate, gild, magnify, dramatize

exaggeration n overstatement, hyperbole, embroidery, embellishment, elaboration

examination 1. n exam, test, quiz, final, midterm, take-home, inquest, trial
2. n ➡ **study**

examine 1. vb investigate, scrutinize, inspect, probe, scan
➡ **study, look**
2. vb test, quiz, interrogate ➡ **ask**

example n instance, case, illustration, specimen, sample, representation, representative
➡ **model**

exceed vb outdo, surpass, pass, top, better, best, transcend, outshine, eclipse, outnumber, overstep
➡ **excel**

excel vb dominate, prevail ➡ **exceed**

excellence n perfection, faultlessness, superiority, greatness, distinction, eminence, majesty

---

If the word you want is not a main entry above, look below to find it.

even ➡ level, parallel, straight

evenhandedness ➡ justice

eventide ➡ evening

eventuality ➡ possibility

eventually ➡ finally

ever ➡ regularly

evergreen ➡ pine, tree

everlasting ➡ eternal

evermore ➡ forever

every ➡ all, any

everybody ➡ all

everyday ➡ common

everyone ➡ all

every other ➡ alternate

everything ➡ all

everywhere ➡ about

evict ➡ banish

evidence ➡ proof, knowledge

evident ➡ obvious

evidently ➡ apparently

evil ➡ bad, wicked, crime, disaster, immorality

evoke ➡ extract

evolution ➡ change

evolve ➡ grow

ewer ➡ bottle

exact ➡ careful, correct, literal, extract, inflict

exacting ➡ strict

exactitude ➡ accuracy

exactly ➡ precisely

exactness ➡ accuracy

exaggerated ➡ sensational

exalt ➡ bless, worship

exalted ➡ grand

exam ➡ examination

exasperate ➡ anger

exasperated ➡ angry

excavate ➡ dig

excavation ➡ mine

exceeding ➡ above

excellent ➡ good, model, cool

excellently ➡ well

---

excerpt *n* clause, section, provision, passage, portion, quotation, selection, extract

excessive *adj* extreme, drastic, radical, inordinate, immoderate, intemperate, exorbitant, overabundant ➡ **unnecessary**

excite *vb* stimulate, exhilarate, agitate, thrill, energize, arouse, galvanize, enliven ➡ **fan** ⇨ *calm*

excited *adj* thrilled, exhilarated, hysterical, stimulated ➡ **eager, nervous, frantic, angry, emotional**

excitement *n* agitation, tumult, exhilaration, stimulation, thrill, zest, fever, fireworks ➡ **enthusiasm, energy, confusion, hysteria**

exciting *adj* riveting, gripping, breathtaking, sensational, electric, electrifying, rousing, thrilling, exhilarating ➡ **interesting**

exclude *vb* eliminate, suspend, reject, omit, eject, skip, neglect, ignore, overlook, miss, remove, rid ➡ **banish, bar, forbid, forget**

exercise 1. *n* exertion, training, workout, activity, conditioning
2. *n* ➡ **use**
3. *n* ➡ **lesson**
4. *vb* train, work out, condition
5. *vb* ➡ **use**

exhaustion *n* fatigue, weariness, tiredness, listlessness, prostration

exile 1. *n* expulsion, banishment, deportation, transportation, ostracism
2. *n* refugee, fugitive, emigré, emigrant, deportee, expatriate, outcast, pariah ➡ **foreigner**
3. *vb* ➡ **banish**

If the word you want is not a main entry above, look below to find it.

except ➡ but
exceptional ➡ special
excess ➡ abundance
exchange ➡ trade, change
exchequer ➡ bank
exclaim ➡ say
excluding ➡ but
exclusive ➡ private
exclusively ➡ only
excursion ➡ trip

excuse ➡ apology, alibi, opportunity, pretense, forgive, relieve
execrate ➡ hate
execute ➡ act, kill, hang
execution ➡ behavior
executioner ➡ killer
executive ➡ official
executor ➡ agent
exemplar ➡ model
exemplary ➡ perfect

exemplify ➡ embody, explain
exempt ➡ free
exert ➡ use
exertion ➡ exercise, work
exhalation ➡ breath
exhale ➡ breathe
exhaust ➡ tire, use
exhausted ➡ tired
exhaustive ➡ complete, comprehensive

exhibit ➡ display, show
exhibition ➡ display
exhibition hall ➡ gallery
exhilarate ➡ excite
exhilarated ➡ excited
exhilarating ➡ exciting
exhilaration ➡ excitement
exhort ➡ preach, warn
exigency ➡ emergency

existence *n* being, reality, substance, materiality

expensive *adj* costly, invaluable, precious, dear, high-priced, overpriced, extravagant, upscale
➡ **valuable, rich** ⇨ *cheap*

experience 1. *n* background, training, knowledge, skill, know-how, expertise ➡ **knowledge, wisdom, event**
2. *vb* undergo, encounter, endure, live through ➡ **bear**

experiment 1. *n* trial, test, experimentation, demonstration
➡ **examination, study**
2. *vb* ➡ **try, study**

experimental *adj* test, trial, innovative, developmental, provisional

expert 1. *n* authority, specialist, master, virtuoso, ace, connoisseur
2. *adj* proficient, skilled, masterly, adroit, ace, versed, well-versed
➡ **able, smart**

explain *vb* clarify, interpret, justify, demonstrate, elucidate, illustrate, illuminate, exemplify, expound, show, treat ➡ **solve, describe**

explicit *adj* vivid, realistic, graphic, precise ➡ **straightforward**
⇨ *obscure*

explode *vb* erupt, discharge, detonate, blow up, burst ➡ **break**

If the word you want is not a main entry above, look below to find it.

exist ➡ happen, live[1]

exit ➡ departure, door, leave

exodus ➡ departure

exonerate ➡ forgive

exoneration ➡ forgiveness

exorbitant ➡ excessive

exotic ➡ foreign

expand ➡ grow, spread, swell, strengthen

expanse ➡ distance, space

expansion ➡ addition, growth

expansive ➡ broad

expatriate ➡ banish, exile

expect ➡ anticipate, hope

expectant ➡ optimistic, pregnant

expectation ➡ possibility

expected ➡ due

expecting ➡ pregnant

expedient ➡ efficient

expedite ➡ facilitate

expedition ➡ trip

expeditious ➡ punctual

expeditiously ➡ quickly

expel ➡ banish, oust

expend ➡ pay, use

expenditure ➡ use

expense ➡ price

expenses ➡ budget

experienced ➡ cosmopolitan

experimentation ➡ experiment

expertise ➡ experience, talent

expiate ➡ pay

expiration ➡ death

expire ➡ breathe, die, finish, elapse

explanation ➡ answer, reason, apology

expletive ➡ curse

exploit ➡ adventure, act, use

exploration ➡ hunt, study

explore ➡ hunt, travel

explosion ➡ bang

explosive ➡ dangerous, inflammable

export ➡ send

expose ➡ disprove, reveal, weather

exposed ➡ naked

---

extinguish *vb* put out, quench, douse, smother, stifle ➡ **contain, kill**

extract 1. *vb* remove, withdraw, retract, pluck, extricate, leach ➡ **gather, pull**

2. *vb* elicit, evoke, extort, exact, derive ➡ **get, pull**

3. *n* ➡ **excerpt**

extremist *n* zealot, fanatic, maniac, radical ➡ **rebel**

If the word you want is not a main entry above, look below to find it.

expound ➡ explain

express ➡ say

expression ➡ face, saying, speech, word, sign

expressionless ➡ blank

expressive ➡ meaningful

expressway ➡ highway

expropriate ➡ take

expulsion ➡ exile, suspension

expunge ➡ erase

exquisite ➡ beautiful, perfect

extemporaneous ➡ spontaneous

extend ➡ lengthen, spread, offer, lend

extended ➡ long

extension ➡ addition

extensive ➡ broad, long, general

extent ➡ depth, distance, range, period

exterior ➡ outside

exterminate ➡ abolish, kill

external ➡ outside

extinct ➡ dead

extol ➡ praise

extort ➡ extract

extortion ➡ theft

extra ➡ more, unnecessary

extraction ➡ ancestry

extraneous ➡ unnecessary

extraordinary ➡ special

extravagant ➡ expensive, wasteful

extreme ➡ excessive, last

extremely ➡ much, very

extremity ➡ emergency, limb, foot

extricate ➡ extract, free

exuberance ➡ enthusiasm

exuberant ➡ eager

exude ➡ sweat

exult ➡ boast

exultant ➡ ecstatic

eye ➡ look

eyeglasses ➡ glasses

eyeless ➡ blind

eyesight ➡ sight

eyewitness ➡ observer

F

face 1. *n* features, visage, countenance, expression, profile ➡ **appearance**
2. *n* ➡ **side**
3. *vb* oppose, confront, defy, brave, challenge, encounter ➡ **bear, compete, fight** ⇨ *retreat*

facilitate *vb* ease, expedite, simplify, foster ➡ **help**

factory *n* plant, shop, workshop, mill, assembly plant ➡ **business**

faculty 1. *n* staff, personnel ➡ **teacher**
2. *adj* ➡ **ability**

fair 1. *adj* just, impartial, equal, unbiased, equitable, objective, unprejudiced, neutral nonpartisan, detached, impersonal ➡ **right**

2. *adj* satisfactory, acceptable, adequate, mediocre, decent
3. *adj* clear, sunny, bright, pleasant, mild ➡ **bright** ⇨ *cloudy*
4. *adj* blond, blonde, light, white, ivory, creamy, bleached ➡ **pale**
5. *adj* ➡ **pretty**
6. *n* ➡ **carnival**

fairy *n* elf, pixie, sprite, spirit, brownie, leprechaun

faithful 1. *adj* loyal, true, devoted, steadfast, constant, trusty, trustworthy, resolute, staunch, fast, unfailing, unshaken, committed, tenacious ➡ **reliable, religious** ⇨ *unfaithful*
2. *adj* ➡ **correct**

If the word you want is not a main entry above, look below to find it.

fable ➡ myth, superstition

fabled ➡ legendary

fabric ➡ cloth

fabricate ➡ build, invent, lie

fabrication ➡ pretense, lie, assembly

fabulous ➡ legendary, great

façade ➡ outside

facet ➡ side, part

facetious ➡ funny

facile ➡ suave

facilities ➡ equipment, bathroom

facility ➡ talent

facing ➡ opposite

facsimile ➡ copy

fact ➡ knowledge, detail, event, certainty

faction ➡ party, movement

factor ➡ detail

factual ➡ correct

fad ➡ fashion

fade ➡ disappear, tire, bleach

faded ➡ dull

fail ➡ lose, disappoint

failing ➡ fault

failure ➡ defeat, disappointment, inability

faint ➡ dim, dizzy

fainthearted ➡ cowardly

fairness ➡ justice

fair-skinned ➡ white

faith ➡ belief, religion, hope

faithfully ➡ carefully

faithfulness ➡ loyalty

---

fake 1. *adj* false, artificial, imitation, dummy, ersatz, counterfeit, spurious, phony, bogus, sham, mock ➡ **dishonest** ⇨ *real*
2. *n* phony, counterfeit, forgery, imitation, dummy ➡ **copy**
3. *n* ➡ **cheat**
4. *vb* forge, counterfeit, falsify ➡ **imitate, pretend**

fall 1. *vb* drop, collapse, plunge, topple, tumble, plummet, slump, plump, crumple, subside, slip, lapse, sink, set ➡ **descend, trip, lose**
2. *n* tumble, spill, dive, nosedive ➡ **drop**
3. *n* ➡ **wig**

fame *n* renown, celebrity, glory, eminence, standing, notoriety, popularity, prestige ➡ **reputation, respect**

family 1. *n* relative, relation, kin, people, kindred, lineage, clan, tribe, stock, strain ➡ **ancestry**

2. *adj* familial, domestic, home, homey, household, residential

famous *adj* famed, noted, prominent, renowned, eminent, notorious, celebrated, illustrious, distinguished, well-known, popular, important, great

fan 1. *n* enthusiast, supporter, devotee, aficionado, fanatic, addict, partisan, lover
2. *vb* ventilate, aerate, cool
3. *vb* inflame, incite, excite, stir up, arouse, agitate

fancy 1. *adj* elaborate, ornate, embellished, decorative, ostentatious, flamboyant ➡ **loud, rich**
2. *n* whim, caprice, fantasy, notion, fiction, figment ➡ **illusion, imagination, impulse**
3. *vb* ➡ **imagine**
4. *vb* ➡ **like**

If the word you want is not a main entry above, look below to find it.

faker ➡ hypocrite	false-hearted ➡ unfaithful	famed ➡ famous	fanatic ➡ fan, extremist
fallacious ➡ illogical	falsehood ➡ lie	familial ➡ family	fanciful ➡ imaginary
fallacy ➡ mistake	falsifier ➡ liar	familiar ➡ common	fanny pack ➡ bag
falling-out ➡ argument	falsify ➡ lie, fake	familiarize ➡ introduce	fantasize ➡ imagine
falling star ➡ meteor	falter ➡ hesitate, limp	family room ➡ den	fantastic ➡ nice
false ➡ fake, wrong, unfaithful		famine ➡ hunger	fantasy ➡ fancy
		famished ➡ hungry	

far 1. *adj* distant, remote, faraway, far-flung, removed, outlying, yonder
2. *adv* considerably, incomparably, notably, greatly ➡ **much**
As adverbs, **far** and its synonyms are used with comparative adjectives: "I'm feeling **far** better today." "This hill is **considerably** steeper than I remembered it!"

farm 1. *n* ranch, homestead, plantation, spread, farmstead
2. *vb* till, harvest, garden ➡ **grow**

farmer *n* planter, grower, breeder, rancher, husbandman, sharecropper, farmhand, peasant, yeoman, serf ➡ **worker**

farming 1. *n* agriculture, cultivation, husbandry, horticulture, sharecropping, homesteading, ranching ➡ **rural**
2. *adj* agricultural, agrarian

fascinate *vb* attract, intrigue, captivate, enthrall, charm, appeal ➡ **interest, enchant**

fashion 1. *n* style, trend, fad, craze, rage, mode, vogue, thing
2. *vb* ➡ **make, form, build**

fashionable *adj* stylish, chic, elegant, dapper, dashing, popular, trendy, hot, contemporary, sharp, with-it, smart, in (*informal*) ➡ **suave, cool**

fast 1. *adj* rapid, quick, speedy, swift, fleet, hasty, hurried, prompt, cursory, perfunctory, snap ➡ **sudden** ⇨ *slow*
2. *adj* ➡ **faithful**
3. *adj* ➡ **tight**
4. *adv* ➡ **quickly**

fat 1. *adj* plump, obese, stout, overweight, corpulent, portly, chubby, brawny, husky, heavyset, stocky, pudgy, squat ➡ **big, heavy**
2. *n* oil, lard, shortening, tallow, suet, grease

fate 1. *n* destiny, lot, doom, death, end, ruin, downfall ➡ **future**
2. *n* ➡ **chance**

fatherly *adj* paternal, parental, protective ➡ **masculine** ⇨ *motherly*

If the word you want is not a main entry above, look below to find it.

faraway ➡ far
farce ➡ play
farcical ➡ funny
fare ➡ board, food, price, traveler
far-flung ➡ far
farewell ➡ departure, good-bye

farmhand ➡ farmer, field
farmstead ➡ farm
fascinating ➡ interesting, attractive
fascination ➡ attraction, obsession

fascism ➡ tyranny
fascist ➡ dictator, dictatorial
fashion model ➡ model
fasten ➡ join, close, lock, tie
fastener ➡ clasp

fastidious ➡ choosy
fatal ➡ deadly
fatalistic ➡ pessimistic
fatality ➡ casualty
father ➡ parent
fatherland ➡ country
fathom ➡ know

---

faucet *n* spigot, tap, spout, nozzle, valve, petcock

fault *n* failing, weakness, vice ➥ **defect, guilt, mistake**

favorite 1. *adj* preferred, favored, pet, choice, best-liked, popular
2. *n* darling, pet, precious, ideal ➥ **lover**
3. *n* ➥ **preference**

fear 1. *n* alarm, fright, dread, terror, panic, horror, phobia, anxiety, apprehension, foreboding, dismay, consternation, scare ➥ **worry**
2. *vb* flinch, cower, tremble, quail, quake, dread

feast 1. *n* banquet, fiesta, repast, spread *(informal)* ➥ **meal, party**
2. *vb* ➥ **eat**

feeling 1. *n* sense, sensation, perception, feel, touch ➥ **quality**
2. *n* sensitivity, sentimentality, intuition, instinct, heart, soul, warmth ➥ **emotion, impulse**
3. *n* ➥ **belief**

feminine *adj* female, ladylike, womanly, matronly, effeminate, motherly ⇨ *masculine*

fertile 1. *adj* fruitful, productive, prolific, teeming, fecund, gravid ⇨ *sterile*
2. *adj* ➥ **talented**

If the word you want is not a main entry above, look below to find it.

fatigue ➥ tire, exhaustion

fatigued ➥ tired

fattening ➥ rich

faultless ➥ correct, perfect, infallible, innocent

faultlessness ➥ excellence

faulty ➥ broken

faux pas ➥ mistake

favor ➥ approve, resemble, prefer, gift

favorable ➥ good, successful

favorably ➥ well

favored ➥ favorite

favorite son ➥ candidate

favoritism ➥ prejudice

fawn ➥ flatter, brown

fawning ➥ servile

faze ➥ embarrass

fealty ➥ loyalty

fearful ➥ cowardly, scary, superstitious

fearless ➥ brave

feasible ➥ possible

feasibly ➥ maybe

feat ➥ act

featherbed ➥ blanket

feature ➥ emphasize, detail

features ➥ appearance, face

fecund ➥ fertile

federal ➥ public

federation ➥ union

fee ➥ wage, tax, price

feeble ➥ weak

feed ➥ eat, support, hay

feel ➥ touch, feeling

feign ➥ pretend

feint ➥ tactic

felicity ➥ pleasure

fell ➥ hide

fellow ➥ man, equal, member

fellowship ➥ friendship, award

felon ➥ criminal

felony ➥ crime

female ➥ woman, feminine

fen ➥ swamp

fence ➥ wall

fender-bender ➥ collision

fend off ➥ repel

ferocious ➥ wild

ferret out ➥ discover

fervent ➥ eager

fervor ➥ enthusiasm

festival ➥ carnival, ceremony

festive ➥ happy

festivity ➥ party, mirth

festoon ➥ decorate

few *adj* several, couple, scant, scanty, negligible, sporadic ⇨ **many**
Note that **few** and **couple** are used with a, but **several** is not.

fickle *adj* changeable, untrustworthy, inconstant, mercurial, irresolute, flighty, erratic ➡ **variable, arbitrary, unreliable, unfaithful**

fidget 1. *vb* squirm, twitch, wiggle, wriggle, writhe, stir
2. *vb* ➡ **tinker**

field 1. *n* meadow, pasture, clearing, glade, plot, hayfield, cornfield, wheatfield, farmland ➡ **pen**
2. *n* playing field, athletic field, diamond, gridiron, arena, track, court, stadium, coliseum ➡ **gymnasium**
3. *n* airfield, airport, battlefield, battleground
4. *n* subject, area, sphere, realm, discipline, province, arena, bailiwick, domain, orbit ➡ **department, profession, specialty**

fight 1. *vb* battle, struggle, wrestle, grapple, combat, clash, conflict, war, brawl, feud, duel, skirmish, scrap, strive, resist ➡ **argue, attack, compete, face**
All the terms at **fight** 1 are used as nouns as well as verbs, except for **wrestle, grapple, strive,** and **resist.**
2. *n* battle, engagement, struggle, war, action, strife, conflict, hostilities, warfare, combat, skirmish, confrontation, encounter ➡ **violence, competition, game**
3. *n* altercation, clash, scuffle, tussle, scrap, melee, brawl, feud, duel, showdown, fray, rumble ➡ **argument, disturbance**
4. *n* defiance, resistance, opposition, struggle

If the word you want is not a main entry above, look below to find it.

fetch ➡ bring
fete ➡ party
fetish ➡ obsession
fetter ➡ bond
feud ➡ fight
fever ➡ disease, excitement
feverish ➡ frantic
fewer ➡ less
fiancé ➡ love
fiancée ➡ love

fiasco ➡ disappointment
fib ➡ lie
fibber ➡ liar
fiber ➡ string
fiction ➡ lie, fancy
fictional ➡ imaginary
fictitious ➡ imaginary
fiddle ➡ tinker
fidelity ➡ loyalty
fidgety ➡ nervous

field house ➡ gymnasium
fiend ➡ devil
fiendish ➡ wicked
fierce ➡ wild, sharp, violent, stormy
fiery ➡ burning, wild
fiesta ➡ feast
fighter ➡ soldier
figment ➡ fancy

figure ➡ number, estimate, body, statue
figure out ➡ solve
figurine ➡ doll, statue
filament ➡ string
filch ➡ steal
file ➡ document, row, arrange, walk, sharpen
fill ➡ load, close, occupy
filled ➡ full

---

finally 1. *adv* conclusively, decisively, irrevocably, permanently ➡ **certainly**
2. *adv* eventually, ultimately, lastly

financial *adj* monetary, fiscal, economic, pecuniary, commercial, budgetary ➡ **business**

find *vb* locate, come across, spot, retrieve, stumble across ➡ **discover, recover, learn, notice, get** ⇨ *lose*

finish 1. *vb* complete, end, terminate, conclude, attain, expire, wind up, finalize, clinch, use up, dissolve, disband ➡ **stop, use, climax** ⇨ *start*
2. *n* end, conclusion, ending, finale, completion, termination, culmination, death, fulfillment
3. *n* shine, polish, paint, varnish, shellac, lacquer, stain, wax

finite *adj* limited, measurable, restricted ⇨ *infinite*

fire 1. *n* flame, blaze, conflagration, combustion, campfire, bonfire, pyre, inferno, holocaust ➡ **fireplace**
2. *n* gunfire, shooting, firing, shelling, bombardment
3. *vb* ➡ **shoot**
4. *vb* dismiss, discharge, terminate, lay off, let go, sack (*informal*), can (*informal*) ➡ **oust** ⇨ *hire*

fireplace *n* hearth, chimney, fireside, barbecue ➡ **fire**

fireworks *n* pyrotechnics, illuminations ➡ **excitement**

firm 1. *adj* rigid, hard, solid, stiff, inflexible, steady, compact, dense ➡ **tough, hard, thick**
2. *n* ➡ **business**

If the word you want is not a main entry above, look below to find it.

filly ➡ horse

film ➡ movie, coat, layer

filter ➡ net, clean, sift

filth ➡ dirt

filthy ➡ dirty

fin ➡ limb

final ➡ last, latter, examination

finale ➡ finish

finalize ➡ finish

finance ➡ back, business

finances ➡ budget

financier ➡ tycoon

finding ➡ decision, discovery

find out ➡ learn

fine ➡ good, punish

finer ➡ better

finery ➡ clothes

finesse ➡ tact

finest ➡ best

finger ➡ play

fingerprint ➡ print

finicky ➡ choosy

finished ➡ past

fir ➡ pine

firearm ➡ gun

fireside ➡ fireplace

firewood ➡ wood

firing ➡ fire

firn ➡ snow

first ➡ early, best

first-rate ➡ model

fiscal ➡ financial

fish ➡ hunt

fishpond ➡ lake

fissure ➡ hole

fit¹ 1. *adj* suitable, proper, appropriate, fitting, apt, applicable, pertinent, apposite ➡ **correct, relevant**
2. *adj* ➡ **healthy, able**
3. *vb* ➡ **suit, belong**

fit² 1. *n* seizure, attack, convulsion, spasm, paroxysm, spell ➡ **illness**
2. *n* outburst, tantrum, frenzy, huff, snit, conniption (*informal*) ➡ **hysteria**

fix 1. *vb* repair, mend, patch, restore, renovate, renew, rebuild, overhaul, recondition, service ➡ **adjust, correct, tinker**
2. *vb* ➡ **sterilize**
3. *n* ➡ **trouble**

flag 1. *n* banner, standard, pennant, colors, ensign, jack
2. *vb* ➡ **wave**
3. *vb* ➡ **weaken**
4. *vb* ➡ **cover**

flatter *vb* adulate, fawn, pander, butter up, kowtow to ➡ **praise, suit**

flavor *n* taste, savor, tang, flavoring ➡ **spice**

flexible *adj* bendable, limber, supple, lithe, malleable, elastic, pliable, plastic, soft, resilient, pliant ➡ **limp**

flight 1. *n* flying, gliding, soaring
2. *n* aviation, aeronautics, flying, space flight
3. *n* ➡ **escape**
4. *n* ➡ **floor**

If the word you want is not a main entry above, look below to find it.

fitful ➡ periodic

fitness ➡ health

fitting ➡ fit¹, correct

five o'clock shadow ➡ beard

fixation ➡ obsession

fixed ➡ stationary, tight

fixture ➡ equipment

fizz ➡ foam

fizzle ➡ disappear

flabbergast ➡ surprise

flabbergasted ➡ dumbfounded

flabby ➡ limp

flaccid ➡ limp

flagrant ➡ bald

flair ➡ talent

flake ➡ bit

flamboyant ➡ fancy

flame ➡ fire

flaming ➡ burning

flammable ➡ inflammable

flank ➡ border

flap ➡ wave

flare ➡ burn, light¹

flash ➡ light¹, moment, blink

flashlight ➡ light¹

flashy ➡ loud, bright

flask ➡ bottle

flat ➡ level, prone, dull, insipid, stale, room

flatten ➡ level, iron, trample

flattery ➡ praise

flaunt ➡ advertise

flavorful ➡ delicious

flavoring ➡ herb, flavor

flaw ➡ defect

flawless ➡ perfect, correct

flaxen ➡ yellow

flay ➡ peel

flea market ➡ market

fleck ➡ bit

fledgling ➡ bird

flee ➡ escape, leave

fleece ➡ hide, coat

fleecy ➡ fuzzy

fleet ➡ fast, navy

fleeting ➡ temporary, short

fleshly ➡ physical

flex ➡ bend

flick ➡ lick, movie

flicker ➡ blink

flier ➡ advertisement, pilot

flighty ➡ fickle

---

flood 1. *n* deluge, torrent, inundation, cascade ➨ **rain, storm**
2. *n* river, surge, current, rush, flow, stream, tide ➨ **wave, fountain**
3. *n* barrage, hail, volley, spate, deluge, torrent, storm
4. *vb* inundate, overflow, submerge, drown, engulf, swamp, overwhelm ➨ **flow**

floor 1. *n* flooring, ground, deck, bed, bottom ➨ **base**
2. *n* story, flight, stage, tier, level
3. *vb* ➨ **surprise**

flow 1. *vb* pour, cascade, stream, run, spill, gush, spurt, squirt ➨ **flood**
2. *n* ➨ **flood**
3. *n* distribution, circulation, dissemination, dispersal, spread ➨ **delivery**

flower 1. *n* blossom, bloom, bud, floret, cluster, posy
2. *n* wildflower, perennial, annual, bulb, vine, houseplant ➨ **plant**
3. *vb* ➨ **blossom, prosper**

fly 1. *vb* soar, glide, float, drift, wing, hover, sail, flutter
2. *vb* ➨ **hurry**
3. *n* housefly, horsefly, bluebottle, blackfly, fruit fly ➨ **bug**
4. *n* ➨ **tent**

foam *n* froth, lather, bubbles, suds, head, fizz, spume, scum, spray

fog *n* mist, smog, haze, murk ➨ **cloud, smoke**

fold 1. *n* crease, pleat, tuck, lap, overlap ➨ **wrinkle**
2. *n* ➨ **pen**
3. *vb* crease, pleat, tuck, double, lap, overlap ➨ **wrinkle**

If the word you want is not a main entry above, look below to find it.

flimsy ➨ breakable, thin, unreliable, weak

flinch ➨ jump, fear

fling ➨ throw, binge, adventure

flintlock ➨ gun

flip ➨ turn, rude

flipper ➨ limb

flirt ➨ court

float ➨ fly, blow², swim

flock ➨ herd, crowd, church

floe ➨ glacier

flog ➨ whip

flooring ➨ floor

flop ➨ disappointment

floppy ➨ limp

flora ➨ plant

floret ➨ flower

florid ➨ red

flotilla ➨ navy

flotsam ➨ trash

flounce ➨ strut

flounder ➨ fumble

flourish ➨ prosper, swing, decoration

flout ➨ refuse

flowery ➨ pompous

flowing ➨ liquid

fluctuate ➨ alternate, swing

fluent ➨ articulate

fluffy ➨ fuzzy

fluid ➨ liquid

flurry ➨ snow

flush ➨ blush, level

flushed ➨ red

fluster ➨ embarrass

flutter ➨ wave, fly, shake, rustle

flying ➨ flight

flying machine ➨ airplane

foal ➨ horse

focus ➨ middle, concentrate, clarity

fodder ➨ hay

foe ➨ enemy, opponent

foggy ➨ dim, obscure

foil ➨ sword, prevent, repel

folder ➨ wrapper

foliage ➨ plant

follow 1. *vb* succeed, ensue, supplant, supersede, replace ⇨ *lead, precede*
2. *vb* pursue, chase, trail, track, shadow, hunt, stalk, hound, tail
3. *vb* ➡ **obey**
4. *vb* ➡ **know**

following 1. *adj* succeeding, next, ensuing, subsequent, later, latter ➡ **adjacent**
2. *n* entourage, retinue, coterie, public ➡ **audience, fan**

food *n* nourishment, diet, sustenance, edibles, victuals, refreshment, rations, provisions, cuisine, fare, nutrition, fuel ➡ **board, meal**

fool 1. *n* simpleton, nitwit, idiot, dunce, imbecile, nincompoop, blockhead, moron, oaf, clown, ignoramus, buffoon, dolt, dummy, half-wit, ninny
2. *vb* outsmart, outwit, outfox, delude ➡ **cheat**

foolish *adj* silly, ridiculous, absurd, preposterous, ludicrous, idiotic, crazy, nonsensical, asinine, imbecilic ➡ **funny, stupid** ⇨ *smart*

foot 1. *n* paw, hoof, pad, extremity, claw, talon
2. *n* ➡ **base**
3. *n* ➡ **measure**

forbid *vb* prohibit, ban, disallow, outlaw, censor, gag, boycott, proscribe, sanction ➡ **bar, exclude** ⇨ *let*

force 1. *vb* require, compel, coerce, make, oblige, obligate, impel, constrain, pressure ➡ **insist, order**
2. *n* ➡ **strength**
3. *n* ➡ **army**

If the word you want is not a main entry above, look below to find it.

folio ➡ page
folk ➡ people
folklore ➡ myth
folly ➡ nonsense
fond ➡ loving
fondle ➡ pet
fondness ➡ love
font ➡ source
foolhardy ➡ thoughtless

foolishness ➡ nonsense
footfall ➡ step
foothill ➡ hill
footing ➡ balance, base
footlocker ➡ chest
footpath ➡ path
footprint ➡ print, track
footrace ➡ race
footstep ➡ step

footwear ➡ shoe
for ➡ because, therefore
forage ➡ hunt
foray ➡ attack
forbear ➡ abstain
forbearance ➡ abstinence, pity
forbearing ➡ patient
forceful ➡ certain, strong
fore ➡ front

forearm ➡ arm
forebear ➡ ancestor
foreboding ➡ ominous, fear
forecast ➡ prediction, predict
forefather ➡ ancestor
foregoing ➡ past
foregone conclusion ➡ certainty
foreground ➡ front

➡ = synonym cross-reference • ⇨ = antonym cross-reference

foreign *adj* alien, imported, exotic, remote, distant, nonnative, immigrant ➡ **strange**

foreigner *n* alien, immigrant, émigré, emigrant ➡ **stranger, exile**

foresight 1. *n* foreknowledge, prescience, vision
2. *n* forethought, prudence, anticipation

forest *n* woods, wood, woodland, rainforest, jungle, timberland, grove, thicket, copse

forever *adv* always, eternally, permanently, perpetually, interminably, endlessly, evermore ➡ **regularly**

forget *vb* neglect, omit, overlook, disregard, misremember ➡ **exclude** ⇨ *remember*

forgive *vb* excuse, pardon, absolve, acquit, exonerate, clear, vindicate, condone ⇨ *blame*

forgiveness *n* absolution, pardon, remission, reprieve, exoneration, amnesty, mercy, clemency ➡ **salvation**

form 1. *vb* shape, mold, fashion, pattern ➡ **build, invent, make**
2. *vb* ➡ **appear**
3. *n* mold, die, cast, frame ➡ **structure**
4. *n* ➡ **body**
5. *n* ➡ **document**

If the word you want is not a main entry above, look below to find it.

foreknowledge ➡ foresight

forelimb ➡ arm

foreman ➡ boss

foremost ➡ forward, best, important

forerunner ➡ ancestor

foresee ➡ anticipate, predict

forestall ➡ prevent

foretell ➡ predict

forethought ➡ foresight

forewarn ➡ warn

forewarning ➡ warning

foreword ➡ introduction

forfeit ➡ abandon, surrender

forge ➡ make, fake, furnace

forge ahead ➡ go

forgery ➡ fake

forgetful ➡ absentminded

forgo ➡ abstain

fork ➡ divide, branch

forlorn ➡ sorry, sad

formal ➡ official, dignified, prim

formality ➡ ceremony

formation ➡ order, assembly

former ➡ past

formerly ➡ once, before

formfitting ➡ tight

formidable ➡ strong

formula ➡ recipe

formulate ➡ invent

forsake ➡ leave

forsaken ➡ abandoned

fort ➡ castle

forte ➡ specialty

forth ➡ forward

forthcoming ➡ future

forthright ➡ straightforward, bald

forthwith ➡ soon

fortification ➡ castle

fortify ➡ protect, strengthen

fortitude ➡ courage, strength, patience

fortress ➡ castle

fortuitous ➡ accidental, successful

fortuitously ➡ accidentally

fortunate ➡ lucky, successful

n = noun • *vb* = verb • *adj* = adjective • *adv* = adverb • *prep* = preposition • *conj* = conjunction

forward 1. *adj* front, advance, foremost, progressive
2. *adj* ➡ **rude**
3. *adv* forwards, forth, ahead, onward, onwards ⇨ **backward**
4. *vb* ➡ **send**

fountain 1. *n* spout, geyser, spray, stream, jet, squirt ➡ **well, flood**
2. *n* ➡ **source**

fragrant *adj* pungent, aromatic, savory, perfumed, scented, redolent ➡ **smelly, spicy**

framework 1. *n* frame, shell, hull, skeleton, chassis
2. *n* ➡ **setting**

frantic 1. *adj* frenzied, distraught, overwrought, frenetic, desperate, delirious, feverish ⇨ **calm**

2. *adj* hectic, chaotic, furious ⇨ **calm**

free 1. *vb* release, liberate, emancipate, deliver, discharge, extricate, exempt, loose, loosen, unloose, unloosen ➡ **forgive, open**
2. *adj* independent, liberated, sovereign, self-governing, autonomous, emancipated, unconfined, unrestrained, unfettered, unshackled, loose, exempt
3. *adj* complimentary, gratis, gratuitous
4. *adj* ➡ **generous**

If the word you want is not a main entry above, look below to find it.

fortune ➡ chance, wealth

fortune-telling ➡ prediction

fortune-teller ➡ prophet

forum ➡ court

forwards ➡ forward

fossil fuel ➡ oil

fossilize ➡ harden

foster ➡ adopt, facilitate, support

foster parent ➡ parent

foul ➡ smelly, dirty

found ➡ base

foundation ➡ base, basis, organization

founder ➡ creator

fount ➡ source

fountain pen ➡ pen

fountainhead ➡ source

four-sided ➡ square

foursquare ➡ square

fowl ➡ bird

foyer ➡ hall

fracas ➡ disturbance

fraction ➡ part, number, share

fracture ➡ break

fractured ➡ broken

fragile ➡ breakable, weak

fragment ➡ part, bit

fragmentary ➡ partial

fragrance ➡ smell

frail ➡ weak, mortal

frame ➡ body, form, framework

framer ➡ creator

franchise ➡ license

frank ➡ straightforward

frankly ➡ sincerely

frankness ➡ freedom, honesty

fraternity ➡ organization, friendship

fraternize ➡ mix

fraud ➡ cheat, rascal, theft, pretense

fraudulence ➡ dishonesty

fray ➡ fight

frayed ➡ ragged

freak ➡ monster

freebooter ➡ pirate

➡ = synonym cross-reference • ⇨ = antonym cross-reference

freedom 1. *n* liberty, independence, autonomy, liberation, sovereignty ⇨ *slavery*
2. *n* license, liberty, immunity, frankness, openness, ease, spontaneity ➡ **right**
3. *n* ➡ **leisure**

frequent 1. *adj* regular, recurrent, habitual, incessant, chronic ➡ **continual, usual, many**
2. *vb* visit, haunt, patronize, attend

friction 1. *n* rubbing, abrasion, scraping, resistance, traction, grating, grinding
2. *n* ➡ **fight, disagreement**

friend *n* girlfriend, boyfriend, companion, associate, partner, acquaintance, ally, comrade, pal, chum, playmate, buddy, *amigo* (*Spanish*) ⇨ *enemy, opponent*

friendly *adj* sociable, social, cordial, neighborly, amiable, genial, intimate, close, sweet, warm, convivial, hearty, hospitable ➡ **kind, nice, loving, peaceful** ⇨ *unfriendly*

friendship *n* companionship, amity, company, society, camaraderie, comradeship, fellowship, brotherhood, sisterhood, fraternity ➡ **relationship, link, kindness**

frog *n* bullfrog, spring peeper, tadpole, polliwog

front 1. *n* fore, lead, head, van, vanguard, foreground, bow (*of a boat*), prow (*of a boat*), obverse (*of a coin*) ➡ **beginning** ⇨ *back*
2. *adj* ➡ **forward**

If the word you want is not a main entry above, look below to find it.

freedom fighter ➡ rebel
freely ➡ voluntary
freethinker ➡ atheist
freeway ➡ highway
freeze ➡ harden, cool
freezer ➡ refrigerator
freezing ➡ cold
freight ➡ load
frenetic ➡ active, frantic
frenzied ➡ frantic
frenzy ➡ fit²

frequently ➡ often
fresh ➡ new, rude, clean, cool
freshman ➡ student
freshness ➡ novelty
fret ➡ worry, grieve
friable ➡ breakable
friar ➡ religious
friary ➡ monastery
fridge ➡ refrigerator
friendless ➡ lonely, unpopular
friendliness ➡ kindness

fright ➡ fear
frighten ➡ scare
frightened ➡ afraid
frightening ➡ scary
frightful ➡ scary
frigid ➡ cold
fringe ➡ edge
frippery ➡ trinket
frisk ➡ play
fritter away ➡ waste
frivolity ➡ nonsense
frivolous ➡ arbitrary, trivial

frock ➡ dress
frolic ➡ play, dance
front ➡ forward
frontier ➡ border, country
frontiersman ➡ pioneer
fronting ➡ opposite
front-runner ➡ candidate
frost ➡ ice
frosting ➡ icing
frosty ➡ cold, white
froth ➡ foam

frown 1. *vb, n* scowl, grimace, glare, pout, glower, lower ⇨ *smile*
2. *vb* ➙ **object**

fruit *n* seed, grain, nut, legume, berry ➙ **plant, vegetable**

full 1. *adj* packed, loaded, laden, filled, crowded, stuffed, replete, sated, brimful, crammed, jammed ⇨ *empty*
2. *adj* ➙ **complete**

fumble *vb* bungle, flounder, stumble, wallow, muddle, muff, botch, goof, louse ➙ **try**

function 1. *n* capacity, office, role, part ➙ **duty, job, object, use**
2. *n* ➙ **party**
3. *n* ➙ **behavior**
4. *n* ➙ **sense**
5. *vb* ➙ **operate, act**

fungus 1. *n* mold, mildew, rot, rust, blight
2. *n* mushroom, toadstool, lichen, truffle

funny 1. *adj* laughable, amusing, humorous, witty, hilarious, comical, comic, ridiculous, whimsical, facetious, antic, farcical, zany, ludicrous ➙ **dry, foolish, strange**
2. *adj* ➙ **sick**

furnace *n* heater, boiler, burner, stove, incinerator, kiln, forge

future 1. *n* hereafter, eternity, futurity, *mañana (Spanish)*, tomorrow, morrow, destiny, fate
2. *adj* imminent, impending, pending, forthcoming, upcoming, approaching, prospective, projected

fuzzy *adj* furry, downy, hairy, woolly, shaggy, fluffy, fleecy, velvety, soft

---

If the word you want is not a main entry above, look below to find it.

frugal ➙ cheap, plain

frugality ➙ economy

fruitcake ➙ cake

fruit fly ➙ fly

fruitful ➙ fertile

fruitless ➙ useless

frustrate ➙ prevent, disappoint

frustration ➙ disappointment

fry ➙ cook

fuel ➙ light[1], energy, food

fugitive ➙ runaway, exile

fulcrum ➙ axis

fulfill ➙ keep, satisfy

fulfillment ➙ satisfaction, finish

full-grown ➙ adult

fully ➙ completely

fumbling ➙ clumsy

fume ➙ smoke

fumes ➙ smoke

fuming ➙ violent

fun ➙ pleasure

fund ➙ supply, back

fundamental ➙ necessary, basic

fundamentally ➙ chiefly, practically

funeral march ➙ dirge

funnel ➙ pipe, lead

fur ➙ hair, coat

furious ➙ angry, violent, frantic

furlough ➙ vacation

furnish ➙ give, supply, lend

furrow ➙ channel

furry ➙ fuzzy

further ➙ more

furthermore ➙ more, besides

furtive ➙ sly

furtiveness ➙ secrecy

fury ➙ anger

fuse ➙ melt, unify

fusion ➙ union

fuss ➙ argument, complain

fussy ➙ choosy, cross

futile ➙ useless

futon ➙ bed

futurity ➙ future

➙ = synonym cross-reference • ⇨ = antonym cross-reference

G

gait *n* pace, stride, tread, step, walk, carriage, movement, swagger, strut

gallery 1. *n* art gallery, exhibition hall, salon, showroom, studio, museum
2. *n* ➡ **room, porch**
3. *n* ➡ **audience**

gallows *n* scaffold, gibbet, yardarm

gambling *n* betting, gaming, wagering ➡ **lottery**

game *n* sport, pastime, recreation, contest, match, competition, bout, event, meet, tournament, series ➡ **fight**

garage 1. *n* carport, parking garage
2. *n* service station, gas station, repair shop

gargoyle *n* grotesque, rainspout, waterspout

gasoline *n* gas, petrol (*British*) ➡ **oil**

gather 1. *vb* collect, assemble, accumulate, amass, compile, congregate, convene, meet, rendezvous ➡ **save, pile**
2. *vb* pick, harvest, reap, pluck, garner, glean
3. *vb* ➡ **assume, infer**

If the word you want is not a main entry above, look below to find it.

gadget ➡ object, tool

gag ➡ joke, forbid, quiet, vomit

gaggle ➡ herd

gaiety ➡ mirth

gain ➡ get, take, growth

gal ➡ woman

gala ➡ party, dance

gale ➡ wind, storm

gall ➡ audacity

gallant ➡ brave

gallantry ➡ courage

galley ➡ kitchen

gallop ➡ run

galvanize ➡ excite

gambit ➡ tactic

gamble ➡ bet

gambol ➡ play, dance

game farm, game preserve ➡ zoo

gamin ➡ urchin

gaming ➡ gambling

gamma ray ➡ X ray

gamut ➡ assortment

gang ➡ group

gangplank ➡ bridge

gangway ➡ bridge

gap ➡ hole, break, valley, distance

gape ➡ stare, spread

garb ➡ clothes

garbage ➡ trash

garble ➡ disturb

garden ➡ farm

gargantuan ➡ huge

garish ➡ loud

garland ➡ bouquet, crown, prize

garment bag ➡ luggage

garments ➡ clothes

garner ➡ gather

garnish ➡ decorate, decoration

garret ➡ attic

garrison ➡ castle, troop

garrulous ➡ talkative

gas ➡ smoke, gasoline

gash ➡ cut

gasp ➡ breathe

gas station ➡ garage

gate ➡ door

gatekeeper ➡ doorman

gateway ➡ door

gathering ➡ party, meeting

gauche ➡ clumsy

gaudy ➡ loud

gauge ➡ estimate, measure

gaunt ➡ thin

gauntlet ➡ glove

general 1. *adj* widespread, extensive, comprehensive ➡ **common, usual, universal**
2. *adj* ➡ **approximate**

generosity *n* liberality, bounty, benevolence, philanthropy, charitableness, charity, unselfishness, munificence, largess ➡ **help** ⇨ *greed*

generous 1. *adj* unselfish, charitable, liberal, unsparing, altruistic, kind, free ➡ **noble** ⇨ *selfish*
2. *adj* liberal, handsome, lavish ➡ **abundant, big**

genius 1. *n* prodigy, virtuoso, mastermind, wizard, Einstein (*informal*), wunderkind (*German*), brain (*informal*), whiz (*informal*), rocket scientist (*informal*)

2. *n* ➡ **talent**
3. *n* ➡ **soul**

gentle 1. *adj* light, mild, soft, tender, moderate, temperate ➡ **calm**
2. *adj* ➡ **friendly, kind**
3. *adj* docile, meek, tractable ➡ **tame**

get 1. *vb* obtain, acquire, gain, win, take, procure, earn, score ➡ **catch, receive, seize, find**
2. *vb* ➡ **know**
3. *vb* ➡ **persuade**

ghost *n* spirit, apparition, shade, specter, wraith, spook, phantom ➡ **soul**

giant 1. *n* behemoth, mammoth, titan, leviathan, colossus, Goliath ➡ **monster**
2. *adj* ➡ **big**

If the word you want is not a main entry above, look below to find it.

gauze ➡ bandage

gavel ➡ hammer

gawk ➡ stare

gay ➡ happy, bright

gaze ➡ stare, look

gazette ➡ paper

gear ➡ luggage, equipment

gelatinous ➡ thick

geld ➡ sterilize

gelding ➡ horse

gem ➡ jewel

gemstone ➡ jewel

general store ➡ market

generalize ➡ stereotype

generally ➡ chiefly, usually

generate ➡ cause, reproduce

generator ➡ engine

genesis ➡ beginning

genetic ➡ natural

genial ➡ friendly

geniality ➡ hospitality

genre ➡ type

gentleman ➡ man

gentlemanly ➡ masculine

gentlewoman ➡ woman

gentry ➡ aristocracy

genuflect ➡ bend

genuine ➡ real, sincere

genuinely ➡ really, sincerely

germ ➡ poison, egg

germane ➡ relevant

germ-free ➡ sterile

germinate ➡ grow

gesture ➡ wave, sign

getaway ➡ escape

get-together ➡ visit

get-up-and-go ➡ ambition, energy

gewgaw ➡ trinket

geyser ➡ fountain

ghastly ➡ awful

ghoul ➡ monster

gibber ➡ chatter

gibberish ➡ talk

gibbet ➡ gallows

---

gift 1. *n* present, donation, grant, contribution, endowment, offering, alms, sacrifice, favor, surprise, boon ➡ **inheritance, prize**
2. *n* ➡ **talent**

gifted *adj* precocious, advanced, progressive, mature ➡ **talented, smart**

give 1. *vb* present, donate, grant, endow, bestow, impart, award, confer, bequeath, contribute ➡ **supply** ⇨ *receive*
2. *vb* pass, hand, deliver, convey, render, serve, dish out, hand over, hand in, submit, dispense, distribute, inflict ➡ **offer**
3. *vb* have, hold, stage ➡ **act, play**
4. *vb* ➡ **surrender**
5. *vb* yield, bear, produce, furnish ➡ **make**

glacier *n* iceberg, floe, ice floe, icecap

glass 1. *n* cup, mug, tumbler, goblet, beaker ➡ **container, drink**
2. *n* ➡ **mirror**
3. *n* telescope, binocular, spyglass, magnifying glass, lens, microscope

glasses *n* eyeglasses, spectacles, sunglasses, goggles, bifocals, trifocals, shades, contact lenses, contacts

---

If the word you want is not a main entry above, look below to find it.

gibe ➡ ridicule	gist ➡ subject, essence	glean ➡ gather	glob ➡ drop, lump
giddy ➡ dizzy	give off ➡ throw	glee ➡ pleasure	global ➡ universal
gift wrap ➡ wrap	giver ➡ patron	glee club ➡ choir	globe ➡ earth, ball
gigantic ➡ huge	glad ➡ happy	gleeful ➡ happy	globular ➡ round
giggle ➡ laugh	gladden ➡ please	glen ➡ valley	globule ➡ ball
gild ➡ plate, exaggerate	glade ➡ field	glib ➡ superficial, suave	glockenspiel ➡ xylophone
gimp ➡ limp	gladiator ➡ soldier	glide ➡ fly, slide, dance	gloom ➡ cloud, dark, sorrow
gingerly ➡ carefully	glamorous ➡ beautiful	gliding ➡ flight	gloomy ➡ dark, bleak, sad
gird ➡ ring	glance ➡ look	glimmer ➡ light¹, bit	glorify ➡ worship, bless
girdle ➡ band	glare ➡ light¹, frown	glimpse ➡ view, look, see	glorious ➡ grand
girl ➡ woman, child	glaring ➡ bright, obvious	glint ➡ light¹	glory ➡ elegance, fame
girlfriend ➡ friend, love	glasshouse ➡ greenhouse	glisten ➡ shine	gloss ➡ light¹
girlhood ➡ childhood	glassy ➡ slippery	glistening ➡ shiny	glossary ➡ dictionary
girlish ➡ young	glaze ➡ icing	glitter ➡ light¹	glossy ➡ shiny
girth ➡ width	gleam ➡ shine, light¹	gloat ➡ boast	
	gleaming ➡ shiny		

glove *n* mitten, mitt, gauntlet

glutton *n* gourmand, epicure, pig (*informal*), hog (*informal*)

go 1. *vb* progress, proceed, pass, head, advance, forge ahead ➡ **leave, move, travel** ⇨ *come*
2. *vb* ➡ **act**
3. *vb* ➡ **belong**
4. *vb* ➡ **happen**
5. *n* ➡ **try**

god *n* goddess, deity, divinity, demigod, immortal, idol, icon, effigy

good 1. *adj* fine, excellent, outstanding, choice, admirable, splendid, rave, favorable, hopeful, positive, suitable, proper, capital, tiptop ➡ **fair, great, nice, cool** ⇨ *bad*

2. *adj* honest, honorable, virtuous, worthy, respectable, reputable, moral, righteous, scrupulous ➡ **kind**
3. *adj* obedient, well-behaved, dutiful, well-mannered, respectful, obliging ➡ **polite** ⇨ *rude*
4. *n* ➡ **welfare**

good-bye *interj* farewell, so long, adieu, *adios* (*Spanish*), *au revoir* (*French*), *ciao* (*Italian*), *arrivederci* (*Italian*), *auf Wiedersehen* (*German*), *shalom* (*Hebrew*), *salaam* (*Arabic*), *toodle-oo* (*informal*), cheerio (*informal*) ⇨ *hello*

govern *vb* rule, reign, administer, legislate ➡ **control, lead**

government *n* administration, legislature, congress, senate, parliament, assembly, regime ➡ **rule**

If the word you want is not a main entry above, look below to find it.

glow ➡ light[1], shine, blush, burn

glower ➡ frown

glowing ➡ bright

glue ➡ adhesive, stick

glut ➡ abundance, load

glutinous ➡ thick

gluttonous ➡ greedy

gluttony ➡ greed

gnarled ➡ bent

gnash ➡ grind

gnaw ➡ bite

go back ➡ return

goad ➡ urge

goal ➡ object, base, plan

goatee ➡ beard

gobble ➡ eat

gobbledygook ➡ nonsense

go-between ➡ agent

goblet ➡ glass

goblin ➡ bogeyman

goddess ➡ god

God-fearing ➡ religious

godly ➡ religious

godsend ➡ luck

goggles ➡ glasses

going ➡ departure

gold ➡ yellow

Goliath ➡ giant

gong ➡ bell

good day ➡ hello

good deal ➡ bargain

good-for-nothing ➡ loafer

good-humored ➡ nice

good-looking ➡ pretty

good looks ➡ beauty

good-natured ➡ nice

goodness ➡ virtue

goods ➡ property, product

goodwill ➡ kindness

goof ➡ fumble

goose egg ➡ zero

gore ➡ stick

gorge ➡ canyon, eat

gorgeous ➡ beautiful

gory ➡ bloody

gossamer ➡ thin

gossip ➡ rumor, chatter

gouge ➡ cut

gourmand ➡ glutton

governmental ➡ public

governor ➡ ruler

➡ = synonym cross-reference • ⇨ = antonym cross-reference

grade n class, rank, step, score, standing, position, degree, plateau ➡ **level, state, slant**

grand adj magnificent, superb, majestic, splendid, stately, glorious, grandiose, august, regal, imposing, sumptuous, elegant, exalted, commanding, awe-inspiring, proud ➡ **great, good, rich, dignified**

grateful adj thankful, pleased, appreciative, indebted, obliged, gratified, beholden

gratitude n appreciation, thankfulness, thanks, gratefulness, recognition, acknowledgment

grave 1. n tomb, sepulcher, mausoleum, crypt, vault, catacomb, barrow, pit ➡ **cemetery, monument** 2. adj ➡ **serious**

gray adj, n grey, drab, leaden, dusky, slate, smoky

great 1. adj, interj wonderful, terrific, superb, remarkable, astounding, incredible, spectacular, tremendous, marvelous, fabulous, super, heavenly ➡ **good, grand, nice** 2. adj ➡ **famous** 3. adj ➡ **big**

greed n greediness, selfishness, avarice, gluttony ➡ **desire, envy** ⇨ *generosity*

If the word you want is not a main entry above, look below to find it.

gown ➡ dress

GP ➡ doctor

grab ➡ seize, catch

grace ➡ beauty, class, elegance

gracious ➡ polite

gradual ➡ slow

graduate ➡ promote

graft ➡ join

grain ➡ seed, fruit

grain elevator ➡ warehouse

granary ➡ warehouse

grandeur ➡ elegance

grandiloquent ➡ pompous

grandiose ➡ pompous, grand

grandstand ➡ seat

grant ➡ gift, license, award, give

graph ➡ table

graphic ➡ visible, explicit

grapnel ➡ anchor

grapple ➡ fight

grasp ➡ catch, know, embrace

grasping ➡ greedy

grass ➡ hay, plant

grassland ➡ plain

grate ➡ cut, grind, squeak

gratefulness ➡ gratitude

gratification ➡ satisfaction

gratified ➡ grateful

gratify ➡ please

gratifying ➡ pleasant

grating ➡ hoarse, friction

gratis ➡ free

gratuitous ➡ free, unnecessary

gratuity ➡ tip

graupel ➡ snow

gravel ➡ dirt, rock

gravelly ➡ hoarse

graveyard ➡ cemetery

gravid ➡ pregnant, fertile

gravitate toward ➡ approach

gravity ➡ importance, depth

graze ➡ eat, rub

grease ➡ fat, oil

grease monkey ➡ mechanic

greater ➡ better

greatest ➡ most

greatly ➡ very, far, much

greatness ➡ excellence

greediness ➡ greed

greedy *adj* selfish, possessive, covetous, acquisitive, avaricious, stingy, rapacious, grasping, voracious, insatiable, gluttonous ➙ **jealous, predatory**

green 1. *adj, n* emerald, chartreuse, lime, olive, kelly, pea green, verdant, veridian
2. *adj* ➙ **naive, amateur**
3. *n* ➙ **park**
4. *n* ➙ **vegetable**

greenhouse *n* nursery, conservatory, hothouse, glasshouse, arboretum

grieve *vb* mourn, lament, fret, rue, languish, bewail, pine ➙ **sadden, mope**

grind 1. *vb* crush, pulverize, crumble, powder, mash
2. *vb* ➙ **sharpen**
3. *vb* grate, grit, gnash ➙ **rub**

group 1. *n* gang, bunch, crew, pack, set, class, band, body, cluster, ring, bloc, clique, syndicate, junta ➙ **troop**
2. *n* ➙ **band**

grow 1. *vb* sprout, germinate, develop, expand, increase, mature, ripen, evolve, enlarge, wax, magnify, amplify, heighten, augment, mushroom, multiply ➙ **prosper, blossom, strengthen**
2. *vb* raise, breed, cultivate, nurture, rear ➙ **plant**

growth 1. *n* development, spread, enlargement, expansion, proliferation, escalation, rise, inflation, gain, hike, increment, increase ➙ **progress**
2. *n* lump, tumor, cancer, swelling, cyst, mole, polyp, sarcoma
3. *n* crop, harvest, yield

If the word you want is not a main entry above, look below to find it.

greet ➙ **welcome, receive**

greeting ➙ **welcome**

greetings ➙ **hello**

grey ➙ **gray**

gridiron ➙ **field**

grief ➙ **sorrow, misery**

grievance ➙ **complaint**

grievous ➙ **awful**

grill ➙ **cook, ask**

grim ➙ **bleak, gruesome**

grimace ➙ **frown**

grime ➙ **dirt**

grimy ➙ **dirty**

grin ➙ **smile**

grinding ➙ **friction**

grip ➙ **embrace**

gripe ➙ **complain**

gripping ➙ **exciting**

grisly ➙ **gruesome, ugly**

grit ➙ **dirt, courage, grind**

groan ➙ **cry, complain, grunt**

grocery ➙ **market**

groom ➙ **spouse, comb, dress**

groove ➙ **channel**

grope ➙ **touch**

gross ➙ **obvious, huge, gruesome, earn**

grotesque ➙ **ugly, gargoyle**

grotto ➙ **cave**

grouch ➙ **complain**

grouchy ➙ **cross**

ground ➙ **base, floor, dirt, terrain**

groundless ➙ **superstitious**

grounds ➙ **basis, property, reason**

grove ➙ **forest**

grovel ➙ **crawl**

grower ➙ **farmer**

growl ➙ **bark**

grown-up ➙ **adult**

➙ = synonym cross-reference • ⇨ = antonym cross-reference

gruesome *adj* morbid, gross, sick, sadistic, grisly, macabre, grim ➡ **awful, bad, mean**

grunt *vb, n* groan, snort, oink, croak ➡ **cry**

guarantee 1. *vb* insure, assure, secure, ensure, warrant, certify ➡ **promise**
2. *n* ➡ **promise**

guardian *n* guard, custodian, caretaker, overseer, curator, trustee, keeper, monitor, watchdog ➡ **parent, patrol, guide, boss, savior**

guess *vb* suppose, think, believe, imagine, suspect, reckon, speculate, surmise ➡ **estimate, assume**

guide 1. *n* conductor, escort, leader, usher, shepherd, pilot

2. *n* ➡ **pattern**
3. *vb* ➡ **lead**

guilt *n* fault, blame, responsibility, culpability, liability ➡ **shame**

guilty *adj* culpable, blameworthy, responsible, liable, derelict ⇨ *innocent*

gun *n* firearm, weapon, pistol, revolver, sidearm, handgun, rifle, carbine, shotgun, machine gun, musket, flintlock, muzzle loader, blunderbuss, cannon ➡ **arms**

gymnasium *n* gym, sports center, recreation center, field house

gymnastics *n* acrobatics, tumbling, vaulting, aerobatics, aerobics ➡ **exercise**

If the word you want is not a main entry above, look below to find it.

grub ➡ larva, dig

grubby ➡ dirty

grudge ➡ complaint, envy

grudging ➡ reluctant

gruff ➡ hoarse, abrupt

grumble ➡ complain

grumpy ➡ cross

guard ➡ protect, watch, guardian

guarded ➡ safe, careful

guest ➡ visitor, occupant

guest room ➡ bedroom

guffaw ➡ laugh

guidance ➡ advice, leadership

guideline ➡ rule

guild ➡ union

guile ➡ dishonesty

guiltless ➡ innocent

guise ➡ disguise

gulch ➡ canyon

gulf ➡ bay, difference

gullible ➡ naive

gully ➡ canyon

gulp ➡ drink, eat, breathe

gum band ➡ rubber band

gummy ➡ sticky

gun down ➡ shoot

gunfire ➡ fire

gurney ➡ bed

guru ➡ teacher

gush ➡ flow

gust ➡ wind

gusto ➡ enthusiasm

gut ➡ stomach

guts ➡ courage

gutter ➡ channel

guttural ➡ hoarse

guy ➡ man, rope

guzzle ➡ drink

gym ➡ gymnasium

gymnast ➡ acrobat

gyp ➡ cheat

gypsy ➡ traveler

gyrate ➡ turn

H

habit 1. *n* custom, practice, routine, institution, usage, rule
2. *n* dependency, addiction, instinct, reflex, wont ➡ **tendency**
3. *n* mannerism, affectation, quirk, trait ➡ **oddity**
4. *n* ➡ **clothes**

habitat *n* environment, habitation, ecosystem ➡ **den, house**

hair *n* locks, tresses, mane, fur ➡ **braid, lock, wig, beard, coat**

hall 1. *n* corridor, hallway, passage, passageway, entryway, foyer, vestibule, lobby, lounge, anteroom
2. *n* auditorium, theater, arena, amphitheater ➡ **room, building**

halo *n* nimbus, corona, aurora

hammer 1. *n* clawhammer, mallet, maul, sledgehammer, sledge, ball-peen hammer, gavel ➡ **tool**
2. *vb* ➡ **hit**

handwriting *n* writing, penmanship, script, cursive, longhand, printing, calligraphy ➡ **print**

hang 1. *vb* dangle, drape, suspend, swing, hover ➡ **depend**
2. *vb* lynch, execute ➡ **kill**

If the word you want is not a main entry above, look below to find it.

habitation ➡ home, habitat

habitual ➡ usual, automatic, frequent

habitually ➡ regularly

hack ➡ taxi, cut

hackneyed ➡ trite

haggard ➡ thin

haggle ➡ negotiate

hail ➡ flood, welcome, snow, ice

hailstorm ➡ storm

hairless ➡ bald

hairpiece ➡ wig

hairpin ➡ pin

hairy ➡ fuzzy

hale ➡ healthy

haleness ➡ health

half-wit ➡ fool

hallow ➡ bless

hallowed ➡ holy

hallucinating ➡ delirious

hallucination ➡ illusion

hallucinatory ➡ imaginary

hallucinogen ➡ drug

hallway ➡ hall

halt ➡ stop, limp

halve ➡ divide

ham ➡ actor

hamlet ➡ town

hamper ➡ delay

hampered ➡ disabled

hand ➡ worker, lift, give

handbag ➡ bag

handbook ➡ book

handcuff ➡ bond

hand down ➡ leave

handgun ➡ gun

handicap ➡ disability, bar

handicapped ➡ disabled

hand in ➡ give

handkerchief ➡ scarf

hand over ➡ give

handle ➡ touch, sell, control

handler ➡ agent

handling ➡ treatment

handshake ➡ embrace

handsome ➡ pretty, generous

handy ➡ useful, available, able

hanging ➡ gallows

hanker ➡ want

haphazard ➡ arbitrary

hapless ➡ unfortunate

---

happen *vb* occur, transpire, chance, go, befall, ensue, arise, recur, exist

happy *adj* glad, cheerful, joyful, joyous, merry, gay, jolly, delighted, gleeful, proud, jovial, high, festive, bright ➡ **ecstatic, satisfied, lucky** ⇨ *sad*
Note that **happy**, **glad**, *and* **delighted** *are often used in statements simply to be polite:* *"I'm **happy**/**glad**/**delighted** to meet you."*

harbor *n* port, haven, anchorage ➡ **dock, bay, protection**

hard 1. *adj* stony, rocky, adamant ➡ **firm, tough**
2. *adj* difficult, tough, demanding, strenuous, arduous, rigorous, heavy, rough, trying ⇨ *easy*
3. *adj* harsh, severe, bitter, austere, stark, stern

harden *vb* solidify, freeze, petrify, fossilize, set, temper, dry, calcify, toughen, clot, congeal, jell, thicken, coagulate, congeal, cake
➡ **strengthen**

hardship *n* misfortune, adversity, affliction, need, tribulation, want, complaint, injustice ➡ **trouble, misery, poverty**

harm 1. *n* injury, hurt, loss, impairment, detriment, disadvantage ➡ **abuse, damage**
2. *vb* ➡ **hurt, damage**

harmless 1. *adj* innocuous, inoffensive, unobjectionable ➡ **naive, kind**
2. *adj* ➡ **safe**

hat *n* cap, helmet, headgear, chapeau, bonnet

If the word you want is not a main entry above, look below to find it.

happening ➡ event

happenstance ➡ chance

happiness ➡ pleasure

harangue ➡ yell

harass ➡ bother, abuse

hard of hearing ➡ deaf

hardcover ➡ book

hardhearted ➡ insensitive

hardly ➡ only, seldom

hardwood ➡ tree

hardworking ➡ diligent

hardy ➡ strong, healthy

hark ➡ listen

harmful ➡ dangerous, destructive, unhealthy

harmonious ➡ musical, compatible, unanimous

harmonize ➡ sing, agree

harmony ➡ music, peace, unity, balance, agreement

harness ➡ equipment, control

harrow ➡ dig

harry ➡ attack, trouble

harsh ➡ sharp, hard, rough

harvest ➡ gather, farm, growth

hash ➡ assortment, mess

haste ➡ hurry

hasten ➡ hurry

hastily ➡ quickly

hasty ➡ fast, early

hat pin ➡ pin

hatch ➡ reproduce, invent

hatchet ➡ ax, axe

hate 1. *vb* detest, abhor, despise, deplore, loathe, disdain, dislike, abominate, scorn, execrate ⇨ **love**
2. *n* ➡ **hatred**

hatred *n* hate, abhorrence, aversion, revulsion, loathing, contempt, scorn, malice, hostility, dislike, disdain, antipathy, animosity, malevolence ➡ **prejudice** ⇨ **love**

hay *n* fodder, feed, grass, timothy, alfalfa

headline *n* head, heading, leader, title, header, caption, screamer (*informal*)

heal *vb* cure, remedy, mend, knit, treat, medicate, nurse, doctor
In general, **heal** *refers to the making better or getting better of a sore,*

wound, or injury. **Cure** *usually refers to getting rid of a disease or illness.*

health *n* fitness, condition, shape, vigor, vitality, haleness, wellness, healthfulness ➡ **welfare**

healthy 1. *adj* well, fit, sound, hale, hardy, hearty, vigorous, whole
➡ **better, strong** ⇨ **sick**
2. *adj* healthful, nourishing, nutritious, wholesome

heaven 1. *n* paradise, bliss, nirvana, elysian fields, Elysium, Valhalla
➡ **utopia, pleasure**
2. *n* ➡ **air**

heavenly 1. *adj* divine, sublime, celestial, spiritual ➡ **supernatural**
2. *adj* ➡ **great**

If the word you want is not a main entry above, look below to find it.

hateful ➡ awful

haughtiness ➡ pride

haughty ➡ proud

haul ➡ pull, carry

haunch ➡ back

haunt ➡ frequent

haut monde
➡ aristocracy

have ➡ keep, own, give, need

haven ➡ harbor, protection

havoc ➡ damage

hawk ➡ sell

hayfield ➡ field

hazard ➡ danger, dare, jeopardize

hazardous
➡ dangerous

haze ➡ fog, cloud

hazy ➡ cloudy, dim

head ➡ front, boss, chairperson, bathroom, foam, headline, go

headache ➡ nuisance

header ➡ headline

headgear ➡ hat

heading ➡ headline, name, course

headland ➡ cape

headlong ➡ quickly

headmaster
➡ principal

head-over-heels
➡ upside down

headquarters ➡ base, office

headstrong
➡ stubborn

headway ➡ progress

healing ➡ cure, medicinal

healthful ➡ healthy

healthfulness
➡ health

heap ➡ pile

hear ➡ listen

hearing ➡ tryout, suit

hearing-impaired
➡ deaf

hearken ➡ listen

hearsay ➡ rumor

heart ➡ essence, feeling

heartache ➡ sorrow, misery

heartbreaking
➡ pitiful

hearten ➡ please

heartfelt ➡ sincere

hearth ➡ fireplace

heartily ➡ sincerely

heartless ➡ insensitive

hearty ➡ friendly, healthy

---

heavy 1. *adj* cumbersome, hefty, ponderous, massive, weighty, bulky ➡ **big** ⇨ *light*
2. *adj* ➡ **serious**
3. *adj* ➡ **hard**

hedge *n* hedgerow, shrubbery, bushes

height 1. *n* altitude, elevation, stature, loftiness, tallness ⇨ *depth*
2. *n* ➡ **top**

hello *interj* good day, how do you do?, greetings, hi, *hola (Spanish), bonjour (French), ciao (Italian), shalom (Hebrew),* howdy *(informal),* yo *(informal)* ⇨ *good-bye*

help 1. *vb* assist, aid, serve, wait on, cooperate, collaborate, team up, succor, benefit, improve, enrich, avail ➡ **relieve, support**
2. *n* aid, assistance, cooperation, relief, service ➡ **support, comfort, generosity, welfare**
3. *n* ➡ **worker**

helper *n* assistant, aide, deputy, lieutenant, subordinate ➡ **partner, worker**

herb *n* seasoning, flavoring ➡ **plant, spice**

herd *n* flock, pack, swarm, hive, colony, bevy, brood, school, gaggle, pod ➡ **group, crowd**

hermit *n* recluse, shut-in, ascetic

hesitate *vb* falter, vacillate, balk, pause, demur, equivocate, waver ➡ **stop, delay, wait**

If the word you want is not a main entry above, look below to find it.

heat ➡ **energy**

heated ➡ **warm**

heater ➡ **furnace**

heath ➡ **plain**

heathen ➡ **atheist**

heave ➡ **lift, throw, vomit**

heavens ➡ **space**

heaviness ➡ **weight**

heavyset ➡ **fat**

hectic ➡ **frantic**

hedgerow ➡ **hedge**

heed ➡ **obey, notice**

heedless ➡ **unaware, thoughtless**

heft ➡ **weight**

hefty ➡ **heavy**

heighten ➡ **grow**

heinous ➡ **wicked**

heirloom ➡ **antique**

helm ➡ **wheel**

helmet ➡ **hat**

helmsman ➡ **pilot**

helpful ➡ **useful**

helpless ➡ **weak**

helpmate ➡ **spouse**

hem ➡ **edge**

hem and haw ➡ **stammer**

hence ➡ **therefore**

herald ➡ **welcome, precede**

here ➡ **present**

hereafter ➡ **future**

hereditary ➡ **natural**

heresy ➡ **disagreement**

heritage ➡ **inheritance**

hero ➡ **winner, savior**

heroic ➡ **brave**

heroism ➡ **courage**

hesitant ➡ **reluctant**

heterogeneous ➡ **different**

hew ➡ **cut, carve**

hex ➡ **curse**

hi ➡ **hello**

hiatus ➡ **break**

hibernate ➡ **sleep**

hibernating ➡ **asleep**

hidden ➡ **secret, invisible**

n = noun • *vb* = verb • *adj* = adjective • *adv* = adverb • *prep* = preposition • *interj* = interjection

hide 1. *vb* conceal, disguise, secrete, bury, withhold, hoard, squirrel (away) ⇨ *reveal*
2. *vb* cover (up), camouflage, obscure, eclipse, mask, block, screen, shade, shroud, veil, cloak ➡ **cover**
3. *n* pelt, skin, fleece, fell, rawhide, chamois ➡ **coat**

high 1. *adj* tall, lofty, towering, soaring ➡ **big**
2. *adj* high-pitched, shrill, treble, piping ➡ **loud** ⇨ *low*
3. *adj* ➡ **important**
4. *adj* ➡ **happy**

highway *n* interstate, expressway, freeway, thruway, turnpike, parkway ➡ **road**

hill 1. *n* knoll, mound, hillock, foothill, down, dune, bank, ridge ➡ **pile, mountain, cliff** ⇨ *valley*
2. *n* ➡ **slant**

hire 1. *vb* (*in reference to people*) engage, employ, appoint, enlist, draft, recruit, enroll ⇨ *fire*
2. *vb* (*in reference to things or property*) rent, charter, lease, let, sublet ➡ **lend, borrow**

hit 1. *vb* strike, pound, batter, beat, maul, bash, bump, pelt, smash, smack, swat, hammer, buffet, pat, clobber (*informal*), slug (*informal*), whack (*informal*) ➡ **punch, knock, collide, whip**
2. *n* ➡ **blow**[1]

hoarse *adj* raspy, gruff, grating, throaty, guttural, husky, gravelly ➡ **rough**

If the word you want is not a main entry above, look below to find it.

hidebound ➡ **provincial**

hideous ➡ **ugly**

hiding ➡ **secrecy**

highborn ➡ **noble**

higher than ➡ **above**

highland ➡ **plateau**

highlight ➡ **emphasize**

highly ➡ **well**

high-pitched ➡ **high**

high-priced ➡ **expensive**

high seas ➡ **ocean**

high society ➡ **aristocracy**

high-strung ➡ **tense, nervous**

hijack ➡ **seize**

hike ➡ **walk, growth**

hiker ➡ **pedestrian**

hilarious ➡ **funny**

hilarity ➡ **laughter**

hillock ➡ **hill**

hinder ➡ **prevent, bar, delay**

hindmost ➡ **last**

hindquarters ➡ **back**

hindrance ➡ **barrier, disability**

hinge ➡ **depend, turn, axis**

hint ➡ **suggest, bit, reminder, tip**

hinterland ➡ **country**

hiss ➡ **yell**

historian ➡ **writer**

historic ➡ **memorable**

history ➡ **past, story**

hitch ➡ **knot, trap, tie**

hitchhiker ➡ **rider**

hive ➡ **herd**

hoard ➡ **save, hide, wealth, supply**

hoarder ➡ **miser**

hoary ➡ **old**

hoax ➡ **trick**

hobble ➡ **limp, prevent**

hobby ➡ **pastime**

hobgoblin ➡ **bogeyman**

hobnob ➡ **mix**

hobo ➡ **beggar**

hock ➡ **pawn**

hocus-pocus ➡ **magic**

hole 1. *n* hollow, cavity, pit, crater, abyss, chasm, crevasse ➡ **cave, den, well**

2. *n* puncture, perforation, opening, aperture, vent, crack, cleft, fissure, crevice, split, gap, rupture, leak, pore

holy *adj* sacred, divine, hallowed, blessed, consecrated, sacramental

home 1. *n* house, apartment, condominium, condo (*informal*), dwelling, residence, abode, domicile, habitation, cabin, cottage, bungalow, chalet, mansion, palace, manor, villa, chateau ➡ **den, shack**

2. *n* ➡ **family**

3. *n* ➡ **base**

4. *n* ➡ **hospital**

homeless *adj* vagrant, vagabond, derelict, outcast, stray, lost, displaced, dispossessed

homonym *n* homograph, homophone

honesty *n* candor, frankness, veracity ➡ **truth, virtue**

hope 1. *vb* wish, expect, anticipate, aspire ➡ **believe, want, intend**

2. *n* desire, faith, longing, aspiration, dream ➡ **ambition**

3. *n* ➡ **virtue**

If the word you want is not a main entry above, look below to find it.

hodgepodge ➡ mess

hoe ➡ dig

hog ➡ glutton

hogshead ➡ barrel

hogwash ➡ nonsense

hoi polloi ➡ people

hoist ➡ lift

hola ➡ hello

hold ➡ contain, own, support, embrace, believe, give

holder ➡ owner

holding ➡ supply

holdings ➡ property

holiday ➡ vacation

holier-than-thou ➡ self-righteous

hollow ➡ empty, hole, valley

holm ➡ island

holocaust ➡ fire

homage ➡ respect

home base ➡ base

homecoming ➡ return

homegrown ➡ native

homeland ➡ country

homely ➡ plain

homesick ➡ lonely

homestead ➡ farm

homesteader ➡ pioneer

homesteading ➡ farming

homework ➡ lesson

homey ➡ comfortable, family

homicidal ➡ deadly

homicide ➡ murder

hominid ➡ human being

homogeneity ➡ unity

homograph ➡ homonym

homophone ➡ homonym

hone ➡ sharpen, perfect

honed ➡ sharp

honest ➡ good, sincere

honestly ➡ sincerely

honeyed ➡ rich

honk ➡ blow²

honor ➡ respect, virtue, award, praise, celebrate, keep

honorable ➡ good

hood ➡ top, vandal

hoodlum ➡ vandal

hoodwink ➡ cheat

hoof ➡ foot

hook ➡ lock

hooligan ➡ bully, vandal

hoop ➡ circle, ring

hoot ➡ yell

hop ➡ jump

hopeful ➡ good, optimistic

hopeless ➡ bleak, useless

---

n = noun • *vb* = verb • *adj* = adjective • *adv* = adverb • *prep* = preposition • *conj* = conjunction

horizon n skyline, limit, range
➡ **border**

horse n pony, foal, colt, filly, stallion, mare, steed, mount, gelding

hospital n infirmary, clinic, medical center, rehabilitation center, sanatorium, sanitarium, nursing home, home

hospitality n geniality, cordiality, warmth, amiability, courtesy, welcome ➡ **generosity, kindness**

host 1. n hostess, entertainer, presenter, moderator, master of ceremonies, MC, emcee, chaperon, chaperone
2. n hostess, innkeeper, bartender, barkeep, maitre d'
3. n ➡ **crowd**
4. vb ➡ **entertain**

hot 1. adj scalding, boiling, broiling, roasting, sizzling, sweltering, torrid ➡ **warm, burning, tropical** ⇨ **cold**
2. adj ➡ **spicy**
3. adj ➡ **fashionable**

hotel n inn, motel, hostel, lodge, bed-and-breakfast, resort, spa, retreat

house 1. n ➡ **home**
2. vb accommodate, board, lodge, put up, shelter, quarter, billet

huge adj enormous, immense, gigantic, prodigious, colossal, tremendous, mighty, vast, gross, gargantuan, monstrous, jumbo, mammoth, massive, titanic, humongous (informal) ➡ **big**

If the word you want is not a main entry above, look below to find it.

horde ➡ crowd

horizontal ➡ level, prone

horrible ➡ awful

horrid ➡ ugly

horrify ➡ scare, shock

horrifying ➡ scary

horror ➡ fear

horsefly ➡ fly

horseman ➡ rider

horseplay ➡ play

horsepower ➡ energy

horse race ➡ race

horseshoe ➡ curve

horsewoman ➡ rider

horticulture ➡ farming

hose ➡ pipe

hospitable ➡ friendly

hostage ➡ prisoner

hostel ➡ hotel

hostess ➡ host

hostile ➡ belligerent

hostilities ➡ fight

hostility ➡ opposition, anger, hatred

hothouse ➡ greenhouse

Houdini ➡ magician

hound ➡ dog, bother, follow

hourglass ➡ clock

housebroken ➡ tame

housefly ➡ fly

houseguest ➡ visitor

household ➡ family

householder ➡ occupant

houseplant ➡ flower

house-trained ➡ tame

housing estate ➡ development

hovel ➡ shack

hover ➡ hang, fly

how do you do? ➡ hello

howdy ➡ hello

however ➡ but, anyway

howl ➡ cry, bark, laugh

hub ➡ middle

hubbub ➡ noise

hubris ➡ pride

huddle ➡ snuggle

hue ➡ color

huff ➡ breathe, fit²

hug ➡ embrace

---

hum vb buzz, drone, murmur, whir, purr ➡ **sing**

human being n human, person, individual, being, soul, body, mortal, hominid
➡ **humanity, man, woman, people**

humanity 1. n humankind, mankind, man, society, human race
➡ **people, human being, man, woman**
2. n ➡ **kindness**

Many people object to the words **man** (when used without the or a), and **mankind** in the sense of "humanity," because the word **man** is more frequently used to mean "an adult male person." Because this more common sense (a man, the young man) refers to males and not to females, they feel that the "humanity" sense of **man** and **mankind** also excludes women. It may be more thoughtful to use **humanity**, **humankind**, the phrase the **human race**, or the plural compound **human beings** when you want to refer to humans in general. The "humanity" sense of **man** is very common in the writing of earlier periods.

humble 1. adj meek, modest, unassuming, unpretentious, self-deprecating, self-effacing ➡ **shy** ⇨ **proud**
2. adj ➡ **common**
3. vb ➡ **condescend**

humidity n moisture, dampness, mugginess, wetness, dew ➡ **liquid**

humor 1. n wit, comedy, levity, amusement, jest, jocularity, whimsicality ➡ **irony**
2. n ➡ **mood**
3. vb ➡ **entertain, pamper**

hunger 1. n starvation, famine ➡ **poverty**
2. n ➡ **appetite, desire**

hungry adj starving, starved, famished, ravenous, underfed, malnourished, undernourished, emaciated, wasted

---

If the word you want is not a main entry above, look below to find it.

hull ➡ **framework**

hullabaloo ➡ **noise**

human ➡ **human being, mortal**

humane ➡ **kind**

humanistic ➡ **liberal**

humankind ➡ **humanity**

human-made ➡ **manufactured**

human race ➡ **humanity**

humbug ➡ **cheat**

humdrum ➡ **dull**

humid ➡ **damp, tropical**

humiliate ➡ **insult, shame**

humiliated ➡ **ashamed**

humiliation ➡ **shame**

humongous ➡ **huge**

humorist ➡ **writer, comic**

humorous ➡ **funny**

hump ➡ **bulge**

humus ➡ **dirt**

hunch ➡ **impulse, belief, bend**

hunk ➡ **block, lump**

hunt 1. *vb* fish, shoot, poach, track
➡ **follow**
2. *vb* search, seek, look, investigate, scour, forage, probe, ransack, rummage, delve, explore, prospect, comb, sift
3. *n* search, investigation, pursuit, chase, quest, exploration ➡ **study**

hurry 1. *vb* rush, hasten, hustle, speed, race, hurtle, accelerate, quicken, scurry, sally, dash, zip, whiz, zoom, scamper, scuttle, surge, swarm, pour, stampede, storm
2. *n* rush, haste, scramble, stampede
➡ **speed**

hurt 1. *vb* injure, afflict, damage, wound, bruise, tear, wrench, twist, dislocate ➡ **harm, abuse, hit, insult, punish, break, pull**

2. *vb* smart, sting, burn, irritate, ache, throb ➡ **tingle**

hybrid *n* cross, crossbreed, mongrel
➡ **mixture**

hymn *n* carol, anthem, psalm, chant, motet, oratorio, cantata
➡ **song, dirge**

hypocrite *n* deceiver, faker, dissembler, quack, con artist
➡ **cheat**

hypocritical *adj* insincere, two-faced, dissembling ➡ **self-righteous, dishonest, sly**

hysteria *n* delirium, rage, mania, madness, panic, hysterics
➡ **excitement, confusion, fit**

If the word you want is not a main entry above, look below to find it.

hurdle ➡ barrier, jump

hurl ➡ throw

hurrah ➡ encore

hurricane ➡ storm

hurried ➡ abrupt, fast

hurriedly ➡ quickly

hurtful ➡ sore

hurtle ➡ hurry

husband ➡ man, spouse

husbandman ➡ farmer

husbandry ➡ farming

hush ➡ calm, quiet

hushed ➡ quiet

husk ➡ shell, peel

husky ➡ fat, hoarse

hustle ➡ hurry

hut ➡ shack

hygienic ➡ sterile

hype ➡ advertising

hyperactive ➡ active

hyperbole
➡ exaggeration

hypnotize ➡ enchant

hypocrisy
➡ dishonesty

hypothesis ➡ theory

hypothetical
➡ theoretical, imaginary

hysterical ➡ excited, delirious

hysterics ➡ hysteria

I

ice n frost, hail, sleet, icicle, ice cube, permafrost

ice cream n ice milk, sherbet, sorbet, sundae, spumoni, parfait

icing n frosting, glaze, topping, meringue

idea n thought, concept, impression, inspiration, notion, inkling ➡ **belief, theory, plan, suggestion**

idealist n optimist, romantic, perfectionist, dreamer, visionary

idealistic adj utopian, romantic, visionary ➡ **optimistic, impractical**

ignorance n illiteracy, innocence, simplicity, inexperience, denseness, stupidity, unawareness

ignorant adj illiterate, uneducated, unlearned, unlettered, unschooled, unread ➡ **naive, stupid, unaware** ⇨ *educated*

illegal adj unlawful, illegitimate, illicit, criminal, outlawed, wrongful, prohibited, taboo

illegible adj indecipherable, unreadable, unintelligible ➡ **dim**

illness n sickness, ailment, malady, affliction, disorder, infirmity, complaint ➡ **disease, nausea**

illogical adj irrational, unreasonable, absurd, fallacious, inconsistent, incoherent ➡ **wrong**

If the word you want is not a main entry above, look below to find it.

ICBM ➡ missile

iceberg ➡ glacier

icebox ➡ refrigerator

icecap ➡ glacier

ice cube ➡ ice

ice floe ➡ glacier

ice milk ➡ ice cream

ice storm ➡ storm

icicle ➡ ice

icon ➡ god

icy ➡ cold, slippery

ideal ➡ perfect, model, favorite

identical ➡ same

identification ➡ discovery

identify ➡ name, distinguish

identity ➡ personality, unity

ideology ➡ philosophy

idiom ➡ dialect

idiosyncrasy ➡ oddity

idiosyncratic ➡ unique

idiot ➡ fool

idiotic ➡ foolish

idle ➡ passive, lazy, unemployed, empty, rest

idleness ➡ laziness

idler ➡ loafer

idol ➡ god, statue

idolize ➡ love

ignite ➡ light[1]

ignoble ➡ shameful

ignoramus ➡ fool

ignore ➡ exclude

ill ➡ sick

ill-advised ➡ imprudent

ill at ease ➡ uncomfortable

ill-behaved ➡ mischievous

illegitimate ➡ illegal

illiberal ➡ conservative

illicit ➡ illegal

illiteracy ➡ ignorance

illiterate ➡ ignorant

ill-natured ➡ cross

ill-tempered ➡ cross

illusion n mirage, hallucination, delusion, apparition ➡ **fancy, trick**

imaginary adj unreal, nonexistent, fictional, fictitious, illusory, hypothetical, fanciful, hallucinatory ➡ **legendary** ⇨ *real*

imagination n fancy, ingenuity, creativity, originality, vision, inspiration

imagine 1. vb conceive, picture, see, envision, envisage, visualize, fancy, fantasize ➡ **pretend**
2. vb ➡ **guess, think**

imitate vb copy, mimic, emulate, simulate, parrot, ape, parody, mock, lampoon, satirize, impersonate, caricature

immoral adj unethical, unprincipled, shameless, dissolute, degenerate, depraved, perverted ➡ **bad, wrong**

immorality n sin, depravity, wickedness, evil, iniquity, perversion, perversity

impassable adj closed, obstructed, trackless, pathless, untrodden, impenetrable ➡ **inaccessible**

If the word you want is not a main entry above, look below to find it.

ill-treat ➡ abuse

ill-treatment ➡ abuse

illuminate ➡ light¹, explain

illumination ➡ light¹

illuminations ➡ fireworks

illumine ➡ light¹

illusionist ➡ magician

illusory ➡ imaginary

illustrate ➡ draw, explain

illustration ➡ picture, example

illustrative ➡ visible

illustrious ➡ famous

image ➡ picture, statue, photograph

imaginable ➡ possible

imaginative ➡ talented

imbecile ➡ fool

imbecilic ➡ foolish

imbed ➡ embed

imbibe ➡ drink

imbue ➡ instill

imitation ➡ fake, parody

immaculate ➡ perfect, clean

immature ➡ young, childish

immaturity ➡ childhood

immeasurable ➡ infinite

immediate ➡ sudden, near

immediately ➡ now

immense ➡ huge

immensely ➡ very

immerse ➡ sink, wet

immersed ➡ absorbed

immigrant ➡ foreign, foreigner, pioneer

immigrate ➡ move

immigration ➡ movement

imminent ➡ near, future

immobile ➡ stationary

immobilize ➡ paralyze

immoderate ➡ excessive

immortal ➡ eternal, god

immovable ➡ tight

immune ➡ safe

immunity ➡ freedom

immunize ➡ vaccinate

imp ➡ rascal, urchin

impact ➡ collision, blow¹, effect, collide

impair ➡ damage, weaken

impaired ➡ disabled

impairment ➡ disability, harm

impalpable ➡ invisible

impart ➡ give

impartial ➡ fair

impartiality ➡ justice

impassioned ➡ emotional

impassive ➡ blank

impatient ➡ eager

---

importance *n* significance, consequence, import, moment, value, gravity, weight, stature, dignity ➡ **relevance, worth**

important 1. *adj* significant, principal, chief, major, main, essential, primary, critical, key, paramount, prime, cardinal, foremost, high, weighty ➡ **urgent, necessary, valuable, meaningful, memorable, predominant**
2. *adj* influential, prominent, powerful ➡ **famous**

impossible 1. *adj* inconceivable, unattainable, unthinkable, incomprehensible ➡ **useless, illogical, unbelievable**
2. *adj* insoluble, unsolvable, inexplicable, unexplainable, unaccountable
3. *adj* ➡ **intolerable**

impractical *adj* unrealistic, quixotic, unfeasible ➡ **illogical, idealistic** ⇨ *practical*

improper *adj* inappropriate, unseemly, unbecoming, indecent, indelicate, indecorous, unsuitable, unbefitting, impure ➡ **wrong, bad, shameful**

If the word you want is not a main entry above, look below to find it.

impeach ➡ try

impeccable ➡ perfect, innocent

impede ➡ bar, delay

impediment ➡ barrier, disability

impel ➡ push, force

impending ➡ ominous, future

impenetrable ➡ impassable, thick

imperative ➡ necessary, urgent

imperceptible ➡ invisible

imperfect ➡ partial

imperfection ➡ defect

imperial ➡ noble

imperil ➡ jeopardize

imperious ➡ dignified, dogmatic

impermanent ➡ mortal

impermeable ➡ tight

impersonal ➡ cool, fair

impersonate ➡ act, imitate

impertinence ➡ audacity

impertinent ➡ rude

impetuous ➡ abrupt, emotional

impetus ➡ impulse

impinge ➡ intrude

impish ➡ mischievous

implant ➡ instill, embed, put

implausible ➡ unbelievable

implement ➡ tool, equipment

implicate ➡ blame

implication ➡ meaning

implicit ➡ virtual

implied ➡ virtual

implore ➡ beg

imply ➡ suggest, matter, mean

impolite ➡ rude

import ➡ importance, meaning

importantly ➡ chiefly

imported ➡ foreign

importune ➡ beg

impose ➡ order, inflict, disturb

imposing ➡ grand

imposter ➡ cheat

impotence ➡ inability

impotent ➡ weak, sterile

impound ➡ jail

impoverish ➡ ruin

impoverished ➡ poor, underdeveloped

impoverishment ➡ poverty

impregnable ➡ safe

impress ➡ affect, print

impression ➡ idea, effect, print, track, dent

impressive ➡ awesome, striking

imprint ➡ print, track, signature

imprison ➡ jail

improbable ➡ unbelievable

impromptu ➡ spontaneous

---

imprudent *adj* ill-advised, inadvisable, unwise, rash, indiscreet, overconfident, unsound

impulse 1. *n* whim, fancy, caprice, whimsy, hunch
2. *n* thrust, surge, pulse, pulsation, impetus, shove, momentum

inability *n* incapability, ineptitude, incompetence, incapacity, inefficacy, impotence, powerlessness, failure

inaccessible *adj* unobtainable, unattainable, unreachable, out-of-the-way, elusive, unavailable
➡ **impassable**

inadequate *adj* lacking, deficient, short, sparse, insufficient ➡ **poor**

incentive *n* motivation, motive, encouragement, inspiration, inducement, stimulus, spur, spark
➡ **reason, support**

If the word you want is not a main entry above, look below to find it.

improve ➡ correct, help

improved ➡ better

improvement ➡ repair, progress

improving ➡ better

improvise ➡ invent

impudence ➡ rudeness

impudent ➡ rude

impulsive ➡ spontaneous, arbitrary

impure ➡ improper, dirty

in ➡ fashionable

inaccuracy ➡ mistake

inaccurate ➡ wrong

inactive ➡ passive, unemployed

inadequacy ➡ mediocrity

inadvertent ➡ accidental

inadvertently ➡ accidentally

inadvisable ➡ imprudent

inane ➡ trite

inanimate ➡ dead, unconscious

inappropriate ➡ improper

inarticulate ➡ dumb

inattentive ➡ absentminded, negligent

inaudible ➡ quiet

inaugural ➡ early

inaugurate ➡ start, crown

inauguration ➡ beginning

inauspicious ➡ ominous

inborn ➡ natural

incapability ➡ inability

incapable ➡ incompetent

incapacitate ➡ weaken

incapacitated ➡ disabled

incapacity ➡ inability

incarcerate ➡ jail

incense ➡ anger, smell

incessant ➡ continual, frequent

inch ➡ crawl

inchworm ➡ worm

incident ➡ event

incidental ➡ accidental, circumstantial

incidentally ➡ accidentally

incinerate ➡ burn

incinerator ➡ furnace

incipient ➡ early

incise ➡ carve

incision ➡ cut

incisive ➡ smart

incite ➡ urge, fan

inclement ➡ wet, stormy

inclination ➡ preference, tendency

incline ➡ slant

inclined ➡ likely

include ➡ contain, add

inclusive ➡ comprehensive

incoherent ➡ illogical, delirious

income ➡ wage

incomparable ➡ unique

incomparably ➡ far

➡ = synonym cross-reference • ⇨ = antonym cross-reference

incompetent adj incapable, inept, ineffectual, unqualified, unfit, inefficient, unable ➡ **amateur, clumsy**

inconspicuous adj unnoticeable, unobtrusive, unapparent ➡ **invisible** ⇨ *obvious*

inconvenient adj awkward,

bothersome, troublesome, onerous, irksome, annoying, untimely

indirect adj circuitous, roundabout, twisting, meandering, tortuous, rambling, devious ➡ **circumstantial**

indiscriminate adj aimless, uncritical, promiscuous ➡ **thoughtless, carefree, arbitrary**

If the word you want is not a main entry above, look below to find it.

incompetence
➡ inability

incomplete ➡ partial, unresolved

incompletely ➡ partly

incomprehensible
➡ obscure, impossible

inconceivable
➡ impossible

inconclusive
➡ circumstantial

incongruity
➡ contradiction, irony

inconsiderate
➡ thoughtless

inconsistency
➡ contradiction

inconsistent
➡ illogical, variable

inconstant ➡ fickle

incontrovertible
➡ infallible

inconvenience
➡ nuisance, trouble

incorporate ➡ add, embody

incorrect ➡ wrong

incorrigible ➡ bad

increase ➡ more, growth, strengthen, grow

incredible ➡ great, unbelievable

incredulity ➡ surprise

incredulous
➡ doubtful

increment ➡ growth

inculcate ➡ instill

incur ➡ catch

incurable ➡ deadly

incursion ➡ attack

indebted ➡ grateful

indebtedness ➡ debt

indecent ➡ improper

indecipherable
➡ illegible

indecorous
➡ improper

indeed ➡ certainly, really

indefensible
➡ inexcusable

indefinite ➡ doubtful

indelible
➡ permanent

indelicate ➡ improper

indent ➡ dent

indentation ➡ dent, print

independence
➡ freedom

independent ➡ free

independently
➡ apart

indescribable
➡ unbelievable

indestructible
➡ unbreakable

indeterminate
➡ unresolved

index ➡ sign

indicate ➡ read, mean

indication ➡ sign

indict ➡ try

indictment
➡ complaint

indifference ➡ apathy, neglect

indifferent
➡ apathetic

indigence ➡ poverty

indigenous ➡ native

indigent ➡ poor

indigestion ➡ nausea

indignant ➡ angry

indignation ➡ anger

indignity ➡ insult

indirectly ➡ sideways

indiscernible
➡ invisible

indiscreet
➡ imprudent

indispensable
➡ necessary

indisposed ➡ sick

indistinct ➡ dim

indite ➡ write

individual ➡ human being, private

indivisible
➡ inseparable

indolence ➡ laziness

indolent ➡ lazy

indomitable
➡ invincible

indoor ➡ inside

induce ➡ persuade

inducement
➡ incentive

inexcusable *adj* unforgiveable, unpardonable, unjustifiable, indefensible

infallible *adj* unerring, faultless, irrefutable, authoritative, incontrovertible ➡ **perfect, certain, reliable**

infer *vb* deduce, conclude, gather, judge, reason, ascertain ➡ **assume, mention**

infest *vb* overrun, plague, swarm, beset

infinite *adj* boundless, unbounded, endless, limitless, unlimited, interminable, countless, immeasurable, inexhaustible ➡ **eternal, big** ⇨ *finite*

inflammable *adj* flammable, combustible, burnable, volatile, explosive

inflict *vb* impose, exact, dispense, wreak, mete out ➡ **give**

If the word you want is not a main entry above, look below to find it.

induct ➡ crown

induction ➡ reason

indulge ➡ pamper

indulgent ➡ tolerant

industrialist ➡ tycoon

industrious ➡ lively, ambitious, diligent

industry ➡ diligence, work, business

inebriate ➡ drunkard

inebriated ➡ drunk

ineffective ➡ useless

ineffectual ➡ incompetent, useless

inefficacy ➡ inability

inefficient ➡ incompetent

inept ➡ clumsy, incompetent

ineptitude ➡ inability

inequality ➡ difference

inert ➡ passive, stationary, dead

inescapable ➡ certain

inestimable ➡ valuable

inevitable ➡ certain

inexact ➡ approximate

inexhaustible ➡ infinite, diligent

inexpensive ➡ cheap

inexperience ➡ ignorance

inexperienced ➡ naive, amateur, unprepared

inexpert ➡ amateur

inexplicable ➡ mysterious, obscure, impossible

infamous ➡ bad

infancy ➡ childhood, beginning

infant ➡ baby

infantile ➡ childish

infatuation ➡ love, desire

infect ➡ dirty

infection ➡ disease, poison

infectious ➡ contagious

inference ➡ conclusion

inferential ➡ circumstantial

inferior ➡ cheap, poor, subordinate

inferiority ➡ mediocrity

inferior to ➡ under

inferno ➡ fire

infertile ➡ sterile

infidel ➡ atheist

infiltrate ➡ enter

infinity ➡ space

infirm ➡ weak, sick

infirmary ➡ hospital

infirmity ➡ illness

inflame ➡ fan

inflamed ➡ sore, burning

inflammation ➡ sore

inflate ➡ swell, exaggerate

inflation ➡ growth

inflection ➡ accent

inflexible ➡ firm

influence ➡ affect, effect, persuade

influential ➡ important

inform ➡ tell, introduce, teach

informal ➡ carefree

➡ = synonym cross-reference • ⇨ = antonym cross-reference

inheritance n bequest, legacy, heritage, patrimony, endowment, trust ➡ **gift, acquisition**

innocent 1. adj blameless, guiltless, faultless, sinless, pure, chaste, angelic, impeccable ⇨ **guilty**
2. adj ➡ **naive**

insane adj crazy, mad, crazed, lunatic, psychotic, maniacal, demented, deranged, berserk, paranoid, unbalanced, unhinged, mental (informal) ⇨ **sane**

inscription n engraving, dedication, epitaph, legend, lettering ➡ **signature**

insensitive adj unfeeling, uncaring, tactless, heartless, hardhearted, coldhearted, callous, unsympathetic, cold-blooded ➡ **thoughtless, apathetic, stubborn** ⇨ **thoughtful**

If the word you want is not a main entry above, look below to find it.

information ➡ knowledge

informed ➡ educated

inform on ➡ betray

infraction ➡ crime

infrequent ➡ rare

infrequently ➡ seldom

infringe ➡ intrude

infuriate ➡ anger

infuriated ➡ angry

infuse ➡ instill

ingenious ➡ talented

ingenuity ➡ ability, imagination

ingenuous ➡ naive, straightforward

ingest ➡ take

ingredient ➡ part

inhabit ➡ live[1]

inhabitant ➡ citizen, occupant

inhalation ➡ breath

inhale ➡ breathe, smoke

inherent ➡ natural

inherit ➡ receive

inherited ➡ natural

inhibit ➡ prevent

inhospitable ➡ unfriendly

inhuman ➡ mean

iniquity ➡ immorality

initial ➡ early, sign

initialism ➡ abbreviation

initiate ➡ start

initiation ➡ beginning, introduction

initiative ➡ ambition

inject ➡ instill

injection ➡ medicine

injunction ➡ ban

injure ➡ hurt

injurious ➡ destructive, unhealthy

injury ➡ cut, damage, scar, harm, abuse, casualty

injustice ➡ hardship

inkling ➡ idea

inky ➡ black

inlay ➡ embed

inlet ➡ bay

inmate ➡ prisoner

inn ➡ hotel, restaurant

innate ➡ natural

inner ➡ inside, middle

innermost ➡ inside

innkeeper ➡ host

innocence ➡ virtue, ignorance

innocuous ➡ harmless

innovate ➡ start, change

innovation ➡ invention

innovative ➡ experimental

innovator ➡ creator

innumerable ➡ many

inoculate ➡ vaccinate

inoffensive ➡ harmless

inordinate ➡ excessive

inpatient ➡ patient

inquest ➡ examination

inquire ➡ ask

inquiring ➡ curious

inquiry ➡ question, study

inquisitive ➡ curious

inquisitiveness ➡ interest

insatiable ➡ greedy

inscribe ➡ write, print, carve, sign

inscrutable ➡ obscure

insect ➡ bug

insecure ➡ anxious, unsteady

insensate ➡ unconscious

insensible ➡ unconscious

inseparable *adj* indivisible, unified, united, integrated, integral, joined

inside 1. *adj* interior, internal, inner, indoor, innermost ➡ **middle**
2. *n* ➡ **middle**
Note that **inside** and **interior** *are often used as nouns:* "The **inside** of the house is as beautiful as the outside." "We grew up in the **interior** of the country." **Inside** *may also be used as a preposition* ("I put your things **inside** the suitcase") *or an adverb* ("Greg went **inside** when it started raining").

insipid 1. *adj* bland, tasteless, flat, mild
2. *adj* ➡ **trite, dull**

insist *vb* demand, require, assert ➡ **argue, order, force**

instead *adv* rather, alternatively, alternately, preferably

instill *vb* infuse, suffuse, imbue, inject, interject, implant, inculcate ➡ **teach, give, put**

insult 1. *vb* offend, humiliate, slander, defame, malign, smear, slight, snub, outrage, tease, taunt, scorn ➡ **abuse, hurt, ridicule**
2. *n* affront, offense, indignity, outrage, slander, libel, smear, jeer, put-down (*informal*)

If the word you want is not a main entry above, look below to find it.

insert ➡ put, embed

inset ➡ embed

insight ➡ depth

insightful ➡ smart

insignia ➡ badge, label

insignificant ➡ trivial

insincere ➡ hypocritical

insinuate ➡ suggest

insolence ➡ audacity, rudeness

insolent ➡ rude

insoluble ➡ impossible

inspect ➡ examine, patrol

inspection ➡ look

inspiration ➡ imagination, idea, incentive

inspire ➡ cause, urge

install ➡ put, crown

installation ➡ appointment

instance ➡ example

instant ➡ moment

instantaneous ➡ sudden

instantaneously ➡ quickly

instantly ➡ now

instigate ➡ urge

instinct ➡ habit, feeling, belief

instinctive ➡ automatic, natural

institute ➡ school, college

institution ➡ organization, college, habit

institutionalize ➡ jail

instruct ➡ teach, order

instruction ➡ education

instructions ➡ recipe

instructor ➡ teacher

instrument ➡ tool

instrumentalist ➡ musician

insubordinate ➡ rebellious

insubordination ➡ disobedience

insubstantial ➡ light², thin

insufferable ➡ intolerable

insufficient ➡ inadequate

insular ➡ private, provincial

insulate ➡ separate

insure ➡ guarantee

insurgence ➡ revolution

insurgent ➡ rebel

insurrection ➡ revolution

➡ = synonym cross-reference • ⇨ = antonym cross-reference   119

intellectual *adj* scholarly, scholastic, educational, academic, cerebral, mental ➡ **profound, thoughtful**

intend *vb* mean, propose, plan, aim, design, purpose ➡ **hope, prepare**

interest 1. *n* curiosity, concern, inquisitiveness ➡ **attention**
2. *n* claim, stake, investment ➡ **share**
3. *n* ➡ **pastime**

4. *vb* engage, absorb, preoccupy, engross ➡ **appeal, entertain**

interesting *adj* fascinating, intriguing, stimulating, engrossing, absorbing, engaging, entertaining, provocative, stirring, compelling ➡ **exciting** ⇨ *dull*

interference *n* intervention, intrusion, interruption, prying, meddling

---

If the word you want is not a main entry above, look below to find it.

intact ➡ complete

intake ➡ wage

integer ➡ number

integral ➡ inseparable

integrate ➡ unify, add

integrated ➡ inseparable

integrity ➡ virtue, unity

intellect ➡ mind, wisdom

intelligence ➡ mind, wisdom, spying

intelligent ➡ smart

intelligible ➡ articulate

intemperate ➡ excessive

intense ➡ bright, strong

intensify ➡ strengthen, concentrate

intensity ➡ strength

intent ➡ absorbed, plan, object

intention ➡ object

intentional ➡ voluntary

intentionally ➡ purposely

inter ➡ bury

intercede ➡ negotiate

intercept ➡ seize

interchange ➡ change, trade

intercourse ➡ speech

interfere ➡ meddle, disturb

interfering ➡ meddlesome

interim ➡ temporary

interior ➡ inside, middle

interject ➡ instill

interlace ➡ weave

interlock ➡ join

interlude ➡ break

intermediary ➡ agent

intermediate ➡ middle

interminable ➡ infinite, eternal

interminably ➡ forever

intermingle ➡ mix

intermission ➡ break

intermittent ➡ periodic

intern ➡ page

internal ➡ inside

international ➡ universal

internee ➡ prisoner

interpret ➡ translate, explain

interpretation ➡ translation

interrogate ➡ ask, examine

interrogation ➡ question

interrogative ➡ question

interrupt ➡ disturb

interruption ➡ break, interference

intersection ➡ corner

interstate ➡ highway

intertwine ➡ weave

interval ➡ period, distance

intervene ➡ meddle

intervention ➡ interference

interview ➡ ask, meeting

intimate ➡ friendly, private, near, suggest

intimidate ➡ threaten, discourage

---

intolerable *adj* unbearable, insufferable, difficult, impossible

introduce 1. *vb* present, acquaint, familiarize, inform, apprise
➡ **broach**
2. *vb* preface ➡ **precede, start**

introduction 1. *n* meeting, presentation, debut, initiation, acquaintance ➡ **beginning**
2. *n* preface, foreword, prologue, preamble, prelude, overture, intro (*informal*) ⇨ *conclusion*

intrude *vb* trespass, encroach, infringe, invade, impinge ➡ **enter, meddle, disturb**

invent 1. *vb* devise, design, develop, conceive, formulate, originate, contrive, hatch, improvise, ad-lib
➡ **build, discover, form, make, start**
2. *vb* fabricate, concoct, make up, counterfeit ➡ **lie**

invention 1. *n* creation, contrivance, innovation, development, breakthrough
➡ **discovery, novelty**
2. *n* ➡ **lie**

invincible *adj* unbeatable, unconquerable, invulnerable, indomitable, unmanageable
➡ **strong, safe**

If the word you want is not a main entry above, look below to find it.

intolerance
➡ **prejudice**

intolerant
➡ **prejudiced, mean, provincial**

intoxicated ➡ **drunk**

intractable
➡ **stubborn**

intrepid ➡ **brave**

intricate
➡ **complicated**

intrigue ➡ **fascinate, secret**

intriguing
➡ **interesting, attractive**

intrinsic ➡ **natural**

intro ➡ **introduction**

introductory ➡ **basic, early**

intrusion
➡ **interference**

intrusive
➡ **meddlesome**

intuition ➡ **feeling**

inundate ➡ **flood**

inundation ➡ **flood**

invade ➡ **attack, enter, intrude**

invalid ➡ **weak, patient, wrong**

invalidate ➡ **disprove**

invaluable
➡ **expensive**

invariable ➡ **continual**

invariably ➡ **regularly**

invasion ➡ **attack**

inventive ➡ **talented**

inventor ➡ **creator**

inventory ➡ **supply, list**

inverse ➡ **opposite**

invert ➡ **upset, change**

inverted ➡ **upside down**

invest ➡ **bank, crown**

investigate
➡ **examine, hunt**

investigation ➡ **study, hunt**

investiture
➡ **appointment**

investment ➡ **interest**

invigorate ➡ **renew**

invigorating ➡ **brisk**

---

invisible *adj* imperceptible, indiscernible, undetectable, concealed, hidden, unseen, microscopic, impalpable, ethereal ➡ **supernatural, inconspicuous**

invitation *n* request, bidding, offer, summons ➡ **appeal, suggestion**

iron *vb* press, steam, mangle, flatten

irony *n* sarcasm, satire, incongruity ➡ **parody, humor**

island *n* isle, islet, atoll, key, cay, archipelago, holm

If the word you want is not a main entry above, look below to find it.

invite ➡ call, entertain

inviting ➡ attractive

invoice ➡ bill, charge

invoke ➡ appeal

involuntary ➡ automatic

involve ➡ concern

involved ➡ absorbed, complicated

invulnerable ➡ invincible, safe

iota ➡ bit

irate ➡ angry

ire ➡ anger

irk ➡ bother

irksome ➡ inconvenient

ironic ➡ sarcastic

ironical ➡ sarcastic

irrational ➡ illogical

irrationality ➡ nonsense

irrefutable ➡ infallible

irregular ➡ rough, different, strange, periodic

irregularity ➡ oddity, difference, departure

irrelevant ➡ unnecessary

irresolute ➡ fickle

irresponsible ➡ unreliable, negligent

irreverent ➡ rude

irrevocably ➡ finally

irritable ➡ cross

irritate ➡ hurt, bother

irritated ➡ angry, sore

irritation ➡ nuisance

isle ➡ island

islet ➡ island

isolate ➡ separate

isolated ➡ alone, private

isolation ➡ privacy

issue ➡ subject, effect, descend, print

itch ➡ tingle, desire, want

item ➡ object

itemize ➡ list

itinerant ➡ traveler

itinerary ➡ course

ivory ➡ white, fair

J

jail 1. *n* prison, penitentiary, correctional facility, jailhouse, reformatory, cell, dungeon, brig, stockade, pen (*informal*), slammer (*informal*), clink (*informal*), stir (*informal*), big house (*informal*)
2. *vb* imprison, confine, detain, incarcerate, impound, remand, institutionalize, commit

jealous *adj* envious, resentful, possessive, begrudging ➡ **suspicious, greedy**

jelly *n* jam, preserve, marmalade

jeopardize *vb* risk, endanger, imperil, hazard, threaten

jetty *n* breakwater, dike, sea wall, pier, bulwark ➡ **dam**

jewel *n* gem, gemstone, brilliant, ornament, precious stone, stone, rock ➡ **trinket**

job *n* task, chore, work, duty, errand, assignment, project, mission, labor, living ➡ **profession, function**

join 1. *vb* connect, associate, attach, link, fasten, unite, couple, interlock, anchor, bridge, buckle, clasp, clinch, knit, pair, graft, weld, solder, cement, pin ➡ **tie, unify, marry**
2. *vb* enter, enroll, enlist, register, participate

If the word you want is not a main entry above, look below to find it.

jab ➡ stick, blow[1]

jabber ➡ chatter

jack ➡ flag

jacket ➡ coat, wrapper

jackknife ➡ knife

jaded ➡ bored

jagged ➡ zigzag, rough

jailbird ➡ prisoner

jailhouse ➡ jail

jam ➡ jelly, trouble, push

jammed ➡ full

jangle ➡ ring

jar ➡ container, shake, disturb

jargon ➡ dialect

jaunt ➡ trip

jaunty ➡ lively

javelin ➡ missile

jealousy ➡ envy

jeer ➡ insult, ridicule, yell

jell ➡ harden

jeopardy ➡ danger

jerk ➡ pull, jump

jest ➡ joke, humor

jet ➡ fountain, black

jet set ➡ aristocracy

jettison ➡ discard

jibe ➡ agree

jiffy ➡ moment

jingle ➡ ring

jinx ➡ curse

jittery ➡ nervous

jobholder ➡ worker

jobless ➡ unemployed

jock ➡ athlete

jockey ➡ drive, rider

jocularity ➡ humor

jog ➡ run

John Hancock ➡ signature

joined ➡ inseparable

joining ➡ junction

joint ➡ link, common

jointly ➡ together

joist ➡ beam, board

---

joke 1. *n* prank, practical joke, gag, caper, antic ➡ **trick**
2. *n* jest, wisecrack, pun, witticism, quip, one-liner, bon mot ➡ **story**
3. *vb* jest, quip, banter, spar, kid, tease, josh

judge 1. *n* justice, magistrate, jurist
2. *n* referee, umpire, official, evaluator, reviewer, critic, arbiter
3. *vb* ➡ **decide**
4. *vb* ➡ **estimate, infer**

jump 1. *vb, n* leap, spring, bound, vault, hop, pounce, bounce, jounce, jolt, pop, skip, hurdle, dive, plunge, lunge ➡ **dance**
2. *vb, n* start, flinch, wince, recoil, twitch, jerk, cringe, cower

junction *n* juncture, meeting, convergence, connection, joining ➡ **link, corner**

justice 1. *n* fairness, impartiality, equity, due process, evenhandedness ➡ **honesty, truth, virtue**
2. *n* ➡ **judge**

justification *n* vindication, defense, validation ➡ **basis, reason**

If the word you want is not a main entry above, look below to find it.

joker ➡ comic

jolly ➡ happy

jolt ➡ shock, blow[1], jump

josh ➡ joke

jostle ➡ push

jot ➡ write, bit

jounce ➡ jump

journal ➡ paper, diary

journalist ➡ reporter

journey ➡ trip, travel

jovial ➡ happy

joviality ➡ mirth

joy ➡ pleasure

joyful ➡ happy

joyous ➡ happy

jubilant ➡ ecstatic

jubilee ➡ party

judgment ➡ wisdom, tact, decision

judiciary ➡ court

judicious ➡ careful

jug ➡ bottle

juggle ➡ tinker

juice ➡ liquid

jumble ➡ mess, mix

jumbo ➡ huge

jumper ➡ dress

jumpy ➡ nervous

juncture ➡ junction, corner

jungle ➡ forest, maze

junior ➡ subordinate, student

junior college ➡ college

junk ➡ trash, discard

junkyard ➡ dump

junta ➡ group, party

jurisdiction ➡ rule

jurist ➡ judge

just ➡ fair, only, recently

justify ➡ explain, deserve

jut ➡ swell

juvenile ➡ young, childish, teenager, child

juxtapose ➡ compare

n = noun • *vb* = verb • *adj* = adjective • *adv* = adverb • *prep* = preposition • *conj* = conjunction

K

keep 1. *vb* have, possess, maintain, retain, preserve, sustain ➡ **own**
2. *vb* ➡ **save**
3. *vb* fulfill, honor, respect ➡ **celebrate**
4. *n* ➡ **board**
5. *n* ➡ **castle, tower**

kick 1. *vb* boot, punt, drop-kick, placekick ➡ **hit**
2. *n* ➡ **blow**[1]

kill *vb* murder, slay, assassinate, dispatch, massacre, butcher, execute, slaughter, exterminate, annihilate, eradicate, martyr, sacrifice ➡ **destroy, extinguish, choke**

killer *n* murderer, assassin, slayer, executioner

kind 1. *adj* compassionate, considerate, benevolent, well-meaning, charitable, merciful, kindhearted, tenderhearted, warmhearted, decent, kindly, benign, humane ➡ **friendly, generous, loving, nice, tolerant**
2. *n* ➡ **type**

kindness *n* mercy, charity, compassion, consideration, decency, goodwill, humanity, tenderness, courtesy, thoughtfulness, friendliness ➡ **love, pity**

king *n* monarch, sovereign, maharajah (*India*), rajah (*India*), sultan (*Muslim*), shah (*Iran*), pasha (*Turkey, N. Africa*), khan (*central Asia, China*), sachem (*Native American*) ➡ **ruler, emperor**

kiss *n*, *vb* peck, buss, smooch, smack

kitchen *n* kitchenette, galley, cookhouse, scullery, pantry, larder ➡ **room**

If the word you want is not a main entry above, look below to find it.

kaiser ➡ emperor

kaiserin ➡ empress

keen ➡ sharp, eager, smart

keeper ➡ guardian

keepsake ➡ reminder

keg ➡ barrel

kelly ➡ green

kennel ➡ pen

kernel ➡ seed

kerosene ➡ oil

kettle ➡ pot

key ➡ answer, important, island

khaki ➡ brown

khan ➡ king

kid ➡ joke, child

kidnap ➡ seize

kiln ➡ furnace

kin ➡ family

kindhearted ➡ kind

kindle ➡ light[1]

kindling ➡ wood

kindly ➡ kind, well

kindred ➡ family

kingdom ➡ country

kingly ➡ noble

kink ➡ bend

kinship ➡ relationship

kiosk ➡ booth

kit ➡ equipment

kitchenette ➡ kitchen

knack ➡ talent

knapsack ➡ bag

knave ➡ rascal

knife n blade, jackknife, penknife, dagger, stiletto, scalpel, razor, cleaver ➡ **sword**

knock 1. vb tap, rap, drum, thump, whack ➡ **bang, hit**
2. n tap, rap, thump, patter, pitter-patter ➡ **bang, blow**[1]

knot 1. n tangle, snarl, snag, hitch, splice
2. vb ➡ **tie**

know vb understand, realize, recognize, apprehend, comprehend, see, fathom, grasp, follow, get, penetrate ➡ **remember**

knowledge n fact, information, learning, data, evidence, education, awareness, erudition ➡ **experience, wisdom, education**

If the word you want is not a main entry above, look below to find it.

knead ➡ rub, mix

kneel ➡ bend

knell ➡ ring

knickknack ➡ novelty

knife-edged ➡ sharp

knit ➡ weave, join, heal

knob ➡ bulge

knock out ➡ paralyze

knoll ➡ hill

know-how ➡ experience

knowingly ➡ purposely

knowledgeable ➡ educated

kowtow to ➡ flatter

kudos ➡ praise

n = noun • vb = verb • adj = adjective • adv = adverb • prep = preposition • conj = conjunction

L

label 1. *n* tag, sticker, ticket, tab, marker, insignia, trademark, logo, service mark, brand ➡ **name**
2. *vb* mark, ticket ➡ **name**
3. *vb* ➡ **stereotype**

lag *vb* dawdle, straggle, saunter, plod, trail ➡ **delay, wait**

lake *n* pond, pool, fishpond, lagoon, loch, reservoir

lame 1. *adj* crippled, limping
2. *adj* ➡ **poor**

language *n* tongue, lingua franca ➡ **accent, dialect, speech**

larva *n* grub, maggot, caterpillar ➡ **worm**

last 1. *adj* latest, final, ultimate, extreme, concluding, closing, terminal, hindmost, outermost ➡ **latter**
2. *vb* ➡ **continue**

If the word you want is not a main entry above, look below to find it.

labor ➡ work, job

laborer ➡ worker

labyrinth ➡ maze

lace ➡ string, tie

lacerate ➡ cut

laceration ➡ cut

lack ➡ need, want, absence

lackadaisical ➡ slow

lacking ➡ inadequate

lackluster ➡ dull

laconic ➡ short

lacquer ➡ finish

lad ➡ man

laden ➡ full

ladle ➡ spoon

lady ➡ woman, noble

ladylike ➡ feminine

lagoon ➡ bay, lake

laid-back ➡ carefree

lair ➡ den

lamasery ➡ monastery

lameness ➡ limp

lament ➡ grieve, regret, complaint, dirge

lamentable ➡ unfortunate

laminate ➡ plate

lamp ➡ light[1]

lampoon ➡ imitate

lance ➡ stick, missile

land ➡ property, country, dirt, terrain, descend, leave, dock

landfill ➡ dump

landing ➡ dock

landlady ➡ owner

landlord ➡ owner

landmark ➡ event

landowner ➡ owner

landscape ➡ country, nature, terrain, background

landslide ➡ avalanche

lane ➡ road, path

languid ➡ listless

languish ➡ grieve

languor ➡ laziness

languorous ➡ listless

lank ➡ thin

lanky ➡ thin

lantern ➡ light[1]

lap ➡ fold, lick

lapse ➡ relapse, fall, elapse

larceny ➡ theft

lard ➡ fat

larder ➡ closet, kitchen

large ➡ big

largess ➡ generosity

lariat ➡ rope

lark ➡ adventure

lash ➡ tie, whip

lass ➡ woman

lassitude ➡ laziness

lasso ➡ rope

lasting ➡ permanent

lastly ➡ finally

---

late 1. *adj* overdue, tardy, belated, delayed, delinquent ⇨ **early, punctual**
2. *adj* ➡ **new**
3. *adj* ➡ **dead**
4. *adv* behind, behindhand, belatedly, tardily

latent *adj* potential, dormant, undeveloped, unrealized, underlying

latter *adj* second, final ➡ **last, following**

laugh *vb, n* giggle, chuckle, snicker, roar, guffaw, snigger, titter, cackle, howl, shriek ➡ **smile**

laughter *n* hilarity, merriment, levity ➡ **laugh, ridicule, mirth**

laundry *n* wash, washing, cleaning, dry cleaning

layer *n* stratum, tier, sheet, level, film, membrane ➡ **coat**

laziness *n* indolence, sloth, lethargy, listlessness, idleness, torpor, languor, lassitude

lazy *adj* indolent, idle, shiftless, slothful, apathetic ➡ **listless** ⇨ **ambitious**

lead 1. *vb* guide, direct, conduct, usher, steer, take, send, show, funnel ➡ **bring** ⇨ **follow**
2. *vb* direct, manage, supervise, administer, run, preside, oversee, chair, officiate ➡ **control, govern, command** ⇨ **follow**
3. *n* ➡ **front**

leadership *n* supervision, management, guidance, administration, direction ➡ **rule**

If the word you want is not a main entry above, look below to find it.

latch ➡ lock

lately ➡ recently

later ➡ following

latest ➡ last, new

lather ➡ foam

latrine ➡ bathroom

latter-day ➡ modern

latterly ➡ recently

laud ➡ praise, worship

laudable ➡ praiseworthy

laughable ➡ funny

launch ➡ shoot, throw, start

launder ➡ clean

laurel ➡ prize

lavatory ➡ bathroom, sink

lavender ➡ purple

lavish ➡ generous, rich, wasteful

law ➡ rule, act

lawbreaker ➡ criminal

law court ➡ court

lawful ➡ legal

lawlessness ➡ confusion

lawsuit ➡ suit

lawyer ➡ adviser

lax ➡ negligent

lay ➡ put

layabout ➡ loafer

layer cake ➡ cake

lay off ➡ fire

layout ➡ order

lay to rest ➡ bury

laze ➡ rest

lazybones ➡ loafer

leach ➡ extract

leaden ➡ gray

leader ➡ boss, ruler, official, guide, headline

leading ➡ best

leaf ➡ page

leaflet ➡ pamphlet

league ➡ union, party

leak ➡ drop, hole

lean ➡ slant, thin

leaning ➡ tendency

leap ➡ jump

learn 1. *vb* ascertain, realize, discover, determine, see, find, find out
2. *vb* memorize, absorb, assimilate, master, digest ➡ **study, remember, practice**

least *adj* smallest, tiniest, minutest, slightest, minimal, minimum, merest ⇨ *best*

leave 1. *vb* depart, exit, embark, withdraw, desert, abandon, vacate, evacuate, forsake, quit, maroon, strand, set out, set off, flee, defect ➡ **go, move** ⇨ *enter, wait*
2. *vb* disembark, detrain, deplane, land ➡ **descend** ⇨ *enter*
3. *vb* will, bequeath, bestow, hand down ➡ **give**
4. *n* ➡ **vacation**

legal *adj* lawful, legitimate, permissible, statutory, prescribed, allowable, licit, constitutional, sanctioned, valid ➡ **official** ⇨ *illegal*

legendary *adj* mythical, mythological, fabulous, fabled, apocryphal, traditional, proverbial ➡ **imaginary**

legible *adj* readable, decipherable, distinct, clear, neat

leisure *n* freedom, relaxation, recreation, repose, ease ➡ **vacation**

lend *vb* loan, advance, furnish, extend ➡ **give, hire**

lengthen *vb* stretch, extend, prolong, elongate, protract, distend, amplify ⇨ *shrink, condense*

less 1. *adj* fewer, smaller, diminished, reduced, lower ⇨ *more*
2. *prep* ➡ **minus**

lesson *n* class, teaching, drill, exercise, homework, assignment ➡ **education**

If the word you want is not a main entry above, look below to find it.

learned ➡ **smart, educated**

learner ➡ **student**

learning ➡ **knowledge, education**

lease ➡ **agreement, hire**

leash ➡ **rope, prevent**

leaving ➡ **departure**

lecher ➡ **rascal**

lecture ➡ **speech, teach**

lecturer ➡ **speaker, teacher**

ledge ➡ **shelf**

leery ➡ **suspicious**

leftover ➡ **unnecessary**

left-wing ➡ **liberal**

leg ➡ **limb**

legacy ➡ **inheritance**

legal pad ➡ **notepad**

legalize ➡ **approve**

legend ➡ **myth, inscription**

legion ➡ **crowd, army**

legislate ➡ **govern**

legislation ➡ **act**

legislature ➡ **government**

legitimate ➡ **legal, official, real**

legume ➡ **fruit**

leisurely ➡ **slow**

leitmotif ➡ **chorus**

lemon ➡ **yellow**

length ➡ **distance**

lengthy ➡ **long**

lenient ➡ **tolerant**

lens ➡ **glass**

leprechaun ➡ **fairy**

lessen ➡ **decrease, relieve**

less than ➡ **under**

➡ = synonym cross-reference • ⇨ = antonym cross-reference

let 1. *vb* allow, permit, authorize, license, tolerate, enable, entitle, qualify, empower ➡ **agree**
⇨ *prevent*
2. *vb* ➡ **hire**

letter *n* message, card, postcard, note, epistle, missive, memorandum, memo, reminder, dispatch ➡ **mail**

letter carrier *n* mail carrier, mailman, postman, postmaster, postmistress ➡ **messenger**

level 1. *adj* flat, smooth, even, flush, parallel, trim ➡ **straight**
2. *adj* plane, horizontal, flat ➡ **low**
3. *n* ➡ **grade, layer, floor**
4. *vb* ➡ **destroy**
5. *vb* even, smooth, flatten, grade, plane ➡ **straighten**

liar *n* fibber, storyteller, deceiver, prevaricator, perjurer, falsifier, equivocator ➡ **cheat**

liberal 1. *adj* ➡ **generous**
2. *adj* progressive, broadminded, radical, left-wing, reformist, humanistic ➡ **tolerant**
⇨ *conservative*

license 1. *n* permit, registration, copyright, franchise, charter, patent, grant ➡ **document**
2. *n* ➡ **permission, freedom, right**
3. *vb* ➡ **let**

lick 1. *vb* lap, tongue, flick
2. *n* ➡ **blow¹**
3. *n* ➡ **bit**

lie 1. *n* falsehood, fib, untruth, fiction, story, tale, fabrication, invention, deception, disinformation, misrepresentation, concoction, canard ➡ **pretense, dishonesty** ⇨ *truth*
2. *vb* deceive, fib, prevaricate, falsify, mislead, dissemble, misstate, equivocate, fabricate ➡ **invent, pretend**
3. *vb* rest, recline, repose, sprawl, loll

If the word you want is not a main entry above, look below to find it.

let down ➡ disappoint
letdown ➡ disappointment
let go ➡ fire
lethal ➡ deadly
lethargic ➡ listless
lethargy ➡ laziness
lettered ➡ educated
lettering ➡ inscription

letters ➡ literature
levee ➡ dam
lever ➡ lift
leviathan ➡ giant
levity ➡ humor, laughter
levy ➡ tax
lewd ➡ dirty
lexicon ➡ dictionary

liability ➡ guilt, debt
liable ➡ likely, guilty
liaison ➡ agent
libel ➡ insult
liberality ➡ generosity
liberate ➡ free
liberated ➡ free
liberation ➡ freedom, salvation

libertine ➡ rascal
liberty ➡ freedom
library ➡ den
libretto ➡ book
licensed ➡ official
lichen ➡ fungus
licit ➡ legal
lid ➡ top
lieutenant ➡ helper

life 1. *n* being, animation, vitality, breath, sentience, consciousness, living ➡ **existence**
2. *n* lifetime, longevity, span, career
3. *n* ➡ **energy**

lift 1. *vb* raise, elevate, hoist, boost, heave, uplift, rear, erect, pry, lever
2. *vb* ➡ **stop**
3. *vb* ➡ **disappear**
4. *n* boost, hand

light[1] 1. *n* radiance, illumination, luminosity, brilliance, brightness, glare, glow, sheen, glimmer, shine, gleam, luster, gloss, glitter, twinkle, sparkle, glint
2. *n* ➡ **day**
3. *n* lamp, lightbulb, bulb, streetlight, lantern, chandelier, flashlight, torch
4. *n* ray, beam, beacon, flash, flare, signal, spark
5. *adj* ➡ **bright**
6. *adj* ➡ **fair**

7. *vb* illuminate, light up, illumine, brighten, lighten
8. *vb* ignite, kindle, strike, fuel ➡ **burn**

light[2] 1. *adj* lightweight, underweight, slight, slender, scant, sparse, buoyant, weightless, insubstantial ⇨ *heavy*
2. *adj* ➡ **gentle**
3. *adj* ➡ **easy**
4. *vb* ➡ **descend**

like 1. *vb* enjoy, be fond of, care for, relish, fancy, delight in ➡ **love, appreciate**
2. *adj* ➡ **alike, same**

likely 1. *adj* liable, prone, apt, inclined, disposed
2. *adj* probable, apparent ➡ **possible**

limb 1. *n* bough, offshoot ➡ **branch, stick**
2. *n* member, appendage, extremity, arm, leg, wing, pinion, flipper, fin

---

If the word you want is not a main entry above, look below to find it.

lifeless ➡ dead, passive

lifesaver ➡ savior

lifetime ➡ life

lightbulb ➡ light[1]

lighten ➡ light[1], relieve, bleach

light-headed ➡ dizzy

lighthearted ➡ carefree

lightweight ➡ light[2]

likelihood ➡ possibility

liken ➡ compare

likeness ➡ similarity, photograph, copy, statue

likewise ➡ alike

lilac ➡ purple

Lilliputian ➡ small

limber ➡ flexible, agile, limp

lime ➡ green

limit ➡ contain, horizon

limitation ➡ term

limited ➡ finite

limitless ➡ infinite, universal

limo ➡ taxi

limousine ➡ taxi

---

limp 1. *vb* shuffle, stagger, hobble, totter, dodder, falter ➡ **walk**
2. *n* falter, halt, lameness, shuffle, gimp
3. *adj* flaccid, droopy, floppy, flabby, limber, slack ➡ **flexible**

link 1. *n* connection, association, contact, bond, correlation, attachment, tie, joint, affinity, affiliation, bridge, junction ➡ **union**
2. *vb* ➡ **join**

liquid 1. *n* fluid, juice, sap, water, liquor ➡ **humidity**
2. *adj* fluid, flowing, molten, aqueous, watery ➡ **wet, damp**

list 1. *n* catalog, program, schedule, agenda, outline, menu, roster, inventory ➡ **table**
2. *vb* itemize, record, catalogue, inventory, register, tabulate, enumerate ➡ **specify**
3. *vb* ➡ **slant**

listen *vb* hear, hearken, hark, overhear, eavesdrop, attend

listless *adj* lethargic, sluggish, drowsy, languid, languorous ➡ **tired, lazy, passive, dull, slow** ⇨ *active*

literal 1. *adj* word-for-word, verbatim, exact ➡ **correct**
2. *adj* ➡ **real**

literature *n* letters, writing, belles lettres

live[1] 1. *vb* exist, be, thrive, subsist, breathe ➡ **experience**
2. *vb* survive, outlive, outlast, persevere, persist ➡ **continue** ⇨ *die*
3. *vb* reside, dwell, stay, abide, inhabit, lodge, room, sojourn ➡ **occupy**

live[2] *adj* ➡ **lively, alive, active**

lively *adj* vital, energetic, vivacious, vigorous, industrious, spry, zestful, playful, spirited, sprightly, jaunty, brisk, zippy ➡ **active, alive** ⇨ *dull*

livestock *n* cattle, animals

living room *n* sitting room, drawing room, parlor, salon, lounge ➡ **room**

If the word you want is not a main entry above, look below to find it.

limpid ➡ transparent

limping ➡ lame

line ➡ rope, string, row

lineage ➡ ancestry, family

linear ➡ straight

lineup ➡ ballot

linger ➡ wait

lingo ➡ dialect

lingua franca ➡ language

lip ➡ edge

liquefy ➡ melt

liquor ➡ drink, liquid

listeners ➡ audience

listlessness ➡ exhaustion, laziness

literally ➡ really

literate ➡ educated

lithe ➡ flexible

lithograph ➡ print

litigant ➡ party

litigation ➡ suit

litter ➡ trash, mess, bed

little ➡ small

liturgical ➡ religious

livelihood ➡ support, profession

liveliness ➡ energy, activity

live through ➡ experience

livid ➡ angry, sore

living ➡ alive, life, job

lizard ➡ reptile

load 1. *n* burden, cargo, freight, shipment ➤ **weight**
2. *n* ➤ **abundance**
3. *vb* fill, pack, encumber, burden, stuff, cram, glut, stock, stow

loafer 1. *n* idler, layabout, slacker, sluggard, lazybones (*informal*), malingerer, ne'er-do-well, good-for-nothing (*informal*), drifter, deadbeat
2. *n* ➤ **shoe**

loan 1. *n* credit, advance, mortgage, rental, accommodation, allowance
2. *vb* ➤ **lend**

lock 1. *vb* fasten, latch, bolt, bar, secure ➤ **close**
2. *n* latch, catch, hook, bolt, padlock ➤ **clasp**
3. *n* tuft, ringlet, curl, tress, shock ➤ **braid, hair**

lonely *adj* lonesome, homesick, solitary, friendless, outcast ➤ **alone, sad**

long 1. *adj* lengthy, tall, extended, elongated, outstretched, extensive ➤ **big** ⇨ *short*
2. *adj* lengthy, protracted, unending, long-winded, sustained
3. *vb* ➤ **want**

look 1. *vb* watch, glance, observe, witness, view, regard, spy, sight, eye, survey, peek ➤ **see, stare, examine**
2. *vb* seem, appear ➤ **resemble**
3. *vb* ➤ **hunt**
4. *n* glance, peek, view, gaze, glimpse, scrutiny, inspection
5. *n* ➤ **appearance**

If the word you want is not a main entry above, look below to find it.

loaded ➤ full
loaf ➤ bread, rest
loam ➤ dirt
loath ➤ reluctant
loathe ➤ hate
loathing ➤ hatred, disgust
loathsome ➤ ugly
lobby ➤ hall, party
local ➤ native, near
locale ➤ place
locality ➤ place
locate ➤ find, base, place
location ➤ place

loch ➤ lake
locker ➤ closet, cupboard, chest
locks ➤ hair
locomotion ➤ movement
locution ➤ speech, word
lodge ➤ house, hotel, live[1], embed
lodging ➤ room
loft ➤ attic
loftiness ➤ height
lofty ➤ high, dignified
log ➤ wood
logic ➤ reason

logical ➤ valid
logician ➤ philosopher
logo ➤ label
loiter ➤ wait
loll ➤ lie
lone ➤ alone, only
lonesome ➤ lonely
longevity ➤ life
longhand ➤ handwriting
longing ➤ hope, desire
long-suffering ➤ patient
long-winded ➤ long, talkative

look forward to ➤ anticipate
looking glass ➤ mirror
look like ➤ resemble
lookout ➤ patrol, watch
looks ➤ appearance
loom ➤ approach, tower
loop ➤ round, circle, ring
loose ➤ free
loosen ➤ free
loot ➤ booty, pillage
looting ➤ theft

---

lose 1. *vb* misplace, mislay, drop, miss ➡ **forget** ⇨ *find*
2. *vb* succumb, fall, fail ➡ **surrender** ⇨ *win*

lost 1. *adj* missing, mislaid, misplaced ➡ **absent**
2. *adj* ➡ **homeless**

lottery *n* raffle, pool, sweepstakes, wager ➡ **gambling**

loud 1. *adj* noisy, resounding, deafening, thunderous, earsplitting, piercing, resonant, strident, shrill ➡ **audible, high** ⇨ *quiet*
2. *adj* boisterous, rowdy, rambunctious, raucous, vociferous, clamorous, obstreperous, stentorian, cacophonous, uproarious ➡ **rude**
3. *adj* garish, flashy, gaudy, showy, ostentatious, tacky ➡ **bright, fancy**

love 1. *vb* adore, cherish, admire, worship, idolize, dote on, revere ➡ **like, court** ⇨ *hate*
2. *n* affection, devotion, fondness, passion, tenderness, adoration, attachment, infatuation ➡ **kindness, desire, virtue** ⇨ *hate*
3. *n* ➡ lover, beloved, darling, dear, sweetheart, girlfriend, boyfriend, fiancé, fiancée
4. *n* ➡ **zero** (*in tennis*)

loving *adj* affectionate, caring, devoted, tender, attentive, demonstrative, amorous, romantic, passionate, adoring, ardent, fond ➡ **friendly, eager**

low 1. *adj* squat, level, low-lying, low-hanging ➡ **short**
2. *adj* low-pitched, bass, baritone
3. *adj* ➡ **quiet**
4. *adj* ➡ **mean**
5. *adj* ➡ **sad**

loyalty *n* allegiance, fidelity, faithfulness, devotion, fealty, dependability, dedication, patriotism

---

If the word you want is not a main entry above, look below to find it.

lope ➡ run

loquacious ➡ talkative

lord ➡ ruler, noble

lore ➡ myth, superstition

loss ➡ defeat, death, harm

lot ➡ chance, number, property, abundance, fate

lotion ➡ medicine

lounge ➡ bar, hall, living room, rest

louse ➡ fumble

lousy ➡ bad

lout ➡ boor

loveliness ➡ beauty

lovely ➡ pretty

lover ➡ love

lower ➡ less, subordinate, decrease, frown

lowering ➡ cloudy

lower than ➡ under

lowest ➡ worst

low-hanging ➡ low

lowland ➡ valley

low-lying ➡ low

lowness ➡ depth

low-pitched ➡ low

low-priced ➡ cheap

loyal ➡ faithful, patriotic

LPN ➡ nurse

luck *n* windfall, godsend, opportunity, break, success ➡ **chance**

lucky *adj* fortunate, auspicious, serendipitous, providential ➡ **accidental, magic**

luggage *n* baggage, suitcase, trunk, duffel bag, overnight bag, garment bag, valise, gear, effects ➡ **bag**

lump *n* mass, glob, clot, clump, chunk, hunk, blob, tuft ➡ **bulge, growth, pile**

If the word you want is not a main entry above, look below to find it.

lube ➡ oil

lubricate ➡ oil

lucid ➡ articulate, sane, transparent

lucidity ➡ reason, clarity

ludicrous ➡ foolish, funny, strange

lug ➡ carry

lukewarm ➡ warm

lull ➡ break, calm

lullaby ➡ song

lumber ➡ board, wood, walk

luminary ➡ celebrity

luminosity ➡ light¹

luminous ➡ bright

lummox ➡ boor

lunacy ➡ nonsense

lunatic ➡ insane

luncheonette ➡ restaurant

lunchtime ➡ afternoon

lunge ➡ jump

lurch ➡ trip, swing

lure ➡ tempt, attraction

lurid ➡ sensational

lurk ➡ sneak

luscious ➡ delicious, rich

lush ➡ rich, tropical, drunkard

lust ➡ desire

luster ➡ light¹

lustrous ➡ shiny

luxurious ➡ rich

luxury ➡ wealth, elegance

lying ➡ dishonest

lying (down) ➡ prone

lyric ➡ song, poem

lyrical ➡ musical

M

magic 1. *adj* enchanted, charmed, magical, mystical, occult, bewitching, entrancing, spellbinding ➡ **lucky, mysterious**
2. *n* sorcery, witchcraft, wizardry, enchantment, hocus-pocus, voodoo

magician 1. *n* conjurer, enchanter, sorcerer, wizard, witch, warlock, shaman, medicine man ➡ **prophet**
2. *n* illusionist, prestidigitator, escape artist, Houdini

mail 1. *n* post, correspondence, communication ➡ **letter, package**
2. *vb* ➡ **send**

make 1. *vb* create, make up, manufacture, produce, fashion, model, compose, constitute, forge, strike ➡ **build, form, invent**
2. *vb* ➡ **force**
3. *vb* ➡ **earn**
4. *n* brand, model, brand name ➡ **type**

If the word you want is not a main entry above, look below to find it.

macabre ➡ gruesome

machine ➡ tool, engine

machine gun ➡ gun

machine-made ➡ manufactured

machinery ➡ equipment

machinist ➡ mechanic

macho ➡ masculine

mad ➡ angry, insane

madden ➡ anger

made ➡ manufactured

madness ➡ hysteria, nonsense

madrigal ➡ song

magazine ➡ paper, warehouse

magenta ➡ purple

maggot ➡ larva

magical ➡ magic

magistrate ➡ judge

magnanimous ➡ noble

magnate ➡ tycoon

magnetic ➡ attractive

magnetism ➡ personality

magnificent ➡ grand, beautiful

magnify ➡ strengthen, grow, exaggerate

magnifying glass ➡ glass

magnitude ➡ size

magnum opus ➡ masterpiece

maharajah ➡ king

maharani ➡ queen

maiden ➡ woman

mail carrier ➡ letter carrier

mailman ➡ letter carrier

maim ➡ mutilate

main ➡ important

mainly ➡ chiefly

mainstay ➡ anchor, support

maintain ➡ keep, save, own, support, argue

maintenance ➡ support

maitre d' ➡ host

majestic ➡ grand

majesty ➡ excellence

major ➡ important, course

majority ➡ most, maturity

makeshift ➡ temporary

makeup ➡ disguise

malady ➡ illness

male ➡ man, masculine

malefactor ➡ criminal

malevolence ➡ hatred

malevolent ➡ wicked, ominous

malfunctioning ➡ broken

malice ➡ hatred, envy

malicious ➡ mean

malign ➡ insult

malignant ➡ mean, deadly

malingerer ➡ loafer

mall ➡ market

malleable ➡ flexible

man *n* gentleman, boy, guy, fellow, husband, male, chap, lad ➡ **human being, humanity, adult**

manufactured *vb* made, machine-made, manmade, mass-produced, synthetic, artificial, human-made

many 1. *adj* numerous, various, countless, manifold, diverse, multiple, innumerable, sundry, myriad ➡ **different** ⇨ *few*
2. *n* ➡ **abundance**

market 1. *n* supermarket, store, shop, grocery, mall, shopping mall, marketplace, mart, general store, bazaar, emporium, flea market
2. *vb* ➡ **sell**

marriage 1. *n* wedding, nuptials, espousal ➡ **union**
2. *n* matrimony, wedlock

married *adj* wed, wedded, espoused, attached, betrothed, engaged ⇨ *single*

marry *vb* wed, espouse ➡ **join**

If the word you want is not a main entry above, look below to find it.

mallet ➡ hammer, bat

malnourished ➡ hungry

maltreat ➡ abuse

mammoth ➡ giant, huge

manacle ➡ bond

manage ➡ control, afford, lead

manageable ➡ tame

management ➡ leadership

manager ➡ boss

mañana ➡ future

mandarin orange ➡ orange

mandate ➡ order

mandatory ➡ necessary

mane ➡ hair

maneuver ➡ movement, tactic, drive

mangle ➡ mutilate, iron

mangy ➡ shabby

manhood ➡ maturity

mania ➡ obsession, hysteria

maniac ➡ extremist

maniacal ➡ insane

manifest ➡ show

manifestation ➡ sign

manifold ➡ many

manikin ➡ midget

manipulate ➡ touch, tinker

mankind ➡ humanity

manly ➡ masculine

manmade ➡ manufactured

mannequin ➡ model, doll, puppet

manner ➡ method, type, bearing

mannerism ➡ habit

manners ➡ behavior

manor ➡ home

mansion ➡ home

manslaughter ➡ murder

mantel ➡ shelf

mantelpiece ➡ shelf

mantle ➡ wrap, coat

manual ➡ book

manufacture ➡ make, assembly

manufacturing ➡ business

manuscript ➡ book, document

map ➡ plan

mar ➡ damage

marathon ➡ race

marauder ➡ pirate

march ➡ walk, parade, movement, border

mare ➡ horse

margin ➡ edge

marimba ➡ xylophone

marine ➡ nautical

mariner ➡ sailor

marionette ➡ puppet

maritime ➡ nautical

mark ➡ spot, signature, tick, label, scar

marked ➡ obvious

marker ➡ pen, monument, label

marketing ➡ sale

marketplace ➡ market

marmalade ➡ jelly

maroon ➡ red, leave

marrow ➡ essence

masculine *adj* male, manly, virile, macho, gentlemanly, fatherly
⇨ *feminine*

masterpiece *n* masterwork, showpiece, classic, magnum opus (*Latin*), pièce de résistance (*French*), monument

mathematics *n* computation, calculation, math ➡ **science**

matter 1. *n* substance, material, body, element, constituent, stuff
2. *n* ➡ **subject**
3. *n* ➡ **business**
4. *n* ➡ **trouble**
5. *vb* count, signify, imply ➡ **mean**

maturity *n* adulthood, majority, womanhood, manhood

maybe *adv* perhaps, possibly, conceivably, feasibly, perchance
➡ **probably**
All of these words express uncertainty about something. **Maybe** *and* **perhaps** *are very close synonyms and it usually makes no difference which one you use.* **Possibly** *stresses the uncertainty more than* **maybe**. **Conceivably** *and* **feasibly** *suggest even greater uncertainty.* **Perchance** *is a more formal and less common synonym.*

If the word you want is not a main entry above, look below to find it.

marsh ➡ swamp

marshal ➡ police officer, mobilize, deploy

marshland ➡ swamp

mart ➡ market

martial ➡ military

martyr ➡ kill

marvel ➡ miracle

marvelous ➡ great

mash ➡ grind

mask ➡ disguise, hide

masking tape ➡ adhesive

masquerade ➡ disguise

mass ➡ size, density, weight, measure, lump, pile

massacre ➡ kill, murder

massage ➡ rub

massive ➡ heavy, huge

mass media ➡ media

mass-produced ➡ manufactured

master ➡ learn, expert, principal, owner

masterly ➡ expert

mastermind ➡ genius

master of ceremonies ➡ host

masterwork ➡ masterpiece

mastery ➡ victory, rule

mat ➡ cushion, rug

match ➡ game, agree, resemble, compare, equal

matching ➡ same

matchless ➡ unique

mate ➡ equal, spouse

material ➡ cloth, matter, real

materiality ➡ existence

materialize ➡ appear

matériel ➡ arms, ammunition

maternal ➡ motherly

math ➡ mathematics

matriarch ➡ ancestor

matrimony ➡ marriage

matron ➡ woman

matronly ➡ feminine

matter-of-fact ➡ practical

mattress ➡ bed

mature ➡ adult, old, gifted, grow

maudlin ➡ emotional

maul ➡ hit, hammer

mausoleum ➡ grave, monument

mauve ➡ purple

maxim ➡ saying

maximum ➡ most

mayhem ➡ confusion, mess, damage

---

n = noun • *vb* = verb • *adj* = adjective • *adv* = adverb • *prep* = preposition • *pl* = plural

maze *n* labyrinth, network, morass, jungle, tangle ➡ **net, mess, confusion**

meal *n* refreshment, repast, bite, snack, picnic, banquet, dish ➡ **feast, food, board**

mean 1. *adj* cruel, vicious, malicious, merciless, savage, malignant, ruthless, brutal, low, cold-blooded, inhuman, relentless, pitiless, unkind ➡ **violent, revengeful**
2. *adj* small-minded, petty, selfish, intolerant ➡ **prejudiced, greedy** ⇨ *tolerant*
3. *adj* ➡ **middle**
4. *n* ➡ **average**
5. *vb* signify, indicate, symbolize, connote, denote, imply, spell ➡ **matter, intend, suggest**

meaning *n* sense, denotation, connotation, definition, significance, implication, import

meaningful *adj* significant, telling, pregnant, expressive ➡ **important**

measure 1. *n* dimension, distance, capacity, weight, volume, mass, amount ➡ **number, size, speed**
2. *n* rule, gauge, scale, standard, criterion, benchmark, yardstick, touchstone
3. *n* ➡ **rhythm**
4. *vb* weigh, gauge, rule, time

mechanic *n* repairman, machinist, technician, grease monkey (*informal*)

meddle *vb* interfere, intervene, intrude, pry, snoop, tamper

meddlesome *adj* intrusive, obtrusive, interfering, meddling, pushy ➡ **curious**

media *n, pl* mass media, communications

medicinal *adj* medical, therapeutic, healing, curative, remedial, pharmaceutical

---

If the word you want is not a main entry above, look below to find it.

MC ➡ host
M.D. ➡ doctor
meadow ➡ field
meager ➡ small, trivial
mealy-mouthed ➡ servile
meander ➡ wander, bend

meandering ➡ zigzag, indirect
meanest ➡ worst
meaningless ➡ empty
means ➡ tool, wealth
measurable ➡ finite
mechanical ➡ automatic
mechanism ➡ tool

mechanized ➡ automatic
medal ➡ award
medalist ➡ winner
medallion ➡ badge
meddling ➡ meddlesome, interference
median ➡ average, middle

mediate ➡ negotiate, decide
medic ➡ nurse
medical ➡ medicinal
medical center ➡ hospital
medicate ➡ heal
medication ➡ medicine

medicine 1. *n* medication, prescription, pill, tablet, capsule, ointment, lotion, injection, shot, vaccine ➡ **cure, drug**
2. *n* medical science, medical profession, healing ➡ **science**

mediocrity *n* inferiority, inadequacy, ordinariness

meditate *vb* ponder, contemplate, muse, reflect, speculate ➡ **think, consider**

meeting 1. *n* appointment, engagement, date, rendezvous, tryst, encounter, confrontation, run-in, brush
2. *n* conference, assembly, gathering, reunion, convention, council, interview, session ➡ **talk**

3. *n* ➡ **introduction**
4. *n* ➡ **junction**

melt *vb* dissolve, thaw, liquefy, fuse, evaporate, soften ➡ **disappear**

member 1. *n* affiliate, constituent, fellow, enrollee, colleague, participant ➡ **partner**
2. *n* ➡ **limb**

memorable *adj* unforgettable, momentous, historic, notable, monumental ➡ **important**

memory *n* recollection, reminiscence, recall, remembrance, déjà vu

mention 1. *vb* refer to, touch on, infer, allude, state, name, specify ➡ **say, suggest, broach**
2. *n* ➡ **remark**

If the word you want is not a main entry above, look below to find it.

medicine man ➡ magician

mediocre ➡ cheap, average, fair

meditative ➡ thoughtful

medium ➡ average, setting, tool, prophet

medley ➡ assortment

meek ➡ humble, shy, gentle

meet ➡ touch, gather, obey, game

megalopolis ➡ town

melancholy ➡ sad, sorrow

melee ➡ fight

mellow ➡ carefree

melodious ➡ musical

melodrama ➡ play

melodramatic ➡ sensational

melody ➡ song, music

membrane ➡ layer

memento ➡ reminder

memo ➡ letter

memoir ➡ diary

memo pad ➡ notepad

memorandum ➡ letter

memorial ➡ reminder, monument

memorial park ➡ cemetery

memorialize ➡ remember

memorize ➡ learn

menace ➡ danger, threaten

menacing ➡ ominous

menagerie ➡ zoo

mend ➡ fix, repair, heal, sew

men's room ➡ bathroom

mental ➡ insane, intellectual

mental health ➡ reason

mentor ➡ teacher

menu ➡ list

mercenary ➡ soldier

merchandise ➡ product

merchant ➡ seller

merciful ➡ kind

merciless ➡ mean

mercurial ➡ fickle

mercy ➡ kindness, pity, forgiveness

mess 1. *n* jumble, tangle, litter, clutter, mayhem, hodgepodge, muddle, hash ➡ **confusion**
2. *vb* ➡ **disturb, dirty**
3. *vb* ➡ **tinker**

messenger *n* courier, carrier, runner, envoy, ambassador, emissary

messy *adj* untidy, disorderly, sloppy, slovenly, disheveled, bedraggled, unkempt ➡ **dirty** ⇨ *neat*

meteor *n* meteorite, shooting star, falling star, comet, asteroid

method *n* approach, procedure, process, technique, system, routine, manner, way ➡ **plan**

middle 1. *n* center, core, midpoint, hub, nucleus, focus, midst, interior, inside, soul, depth ➡ **essence**
2. *adj* central, inner, interior, median, mean, midmost, intermediate ➡ **inside, average**

midget *n* dwarf, pygmy, manikin

military 1. *adj* armed, militant, combative, warlike, martial, militaristic, bellicose, soldierly
2. *n* ➡ **army**

If the word you want is not a main entry above, look below to find it.

mere ➡ trivial

merely ➡ only

merest ➡ least

merge ➡ mix, unify

merger ➡ union

meringue ➡ icing

merit ➡ worth, deserve

meritorious ➡ praiseworthy

merriment ➡ mirth, laughter

merry ➡ happy

merrymaking ➡ party

mesa ➡ mountain, plateau

mesh ➡ net

mesmerize ➡ enchant

message ➡ announcement, letter

metamorphosis ➡ change

metaphysics ➡ philosophy

meteoric ➡ sudden

meteorite ➡ meteor

mete out ➡ inflict, share

meter ➡ rhythm

meticulous ➡ careful

meticulously ➡ carefully

métier ➡ specialty

metropolis ➡ town

metropolitan ➡ urban

mettle ➡ courage

microscope ➡ glass

microscopic ➡ invisible

microwave ➡ cook

midday ➡ day, afternoon

middleman ➡ agent

midmost ➡ middle

midnight ➡ night

midpoint ➡ middle, average

midriff ➡ stomach

midsection ➡ stomach

midshipman ➡ sailor

midst ➡ middle

midterm ➡ examination

mien ➡ bearing, appearance

might ➡ strength

mighty ➡ strong, huge

migrant ➡ traveler

migrate ➡ move

migration ➡ movement

mikado ➡ emperor

mild ➡ gentle, fair, insipid, warm

mildew ➡ fungus

mild-tempered ➡ patient

milestone ➡ event

milieu ➡ setting

militant ➡ belligerent, military

militaristic ➡ military

militia ➡ army

milky ➡ white

mill ➡ factory

millionaire ➡ tycoon

mimic ➡ imitate

minaret ➡ tower

mince ➡ cut

---

mind 1. *n* brain, intellect, intelligence, psyche, consciousness, subconscious, ego ➡ **soul, wisdom**
2. *n* ➡ **belief**
3. *vb* ➡ **protect**
4. *vb* ➡ **obey**

mine 1. *n* quarry, pit, excavation, tunnel ➡ **hole**
2. *n* ➡ **supply**

minister 1. *n* preacher, pastor, rector, chaplain, clergyman, clergywoman, clergy, cleric ➡ **priest, religious**
2. *n* ➡ **diplomat**

minus 1. *prep* less, without, diminished by
2. *n* ➡ **defect**

miracle *n* wonder, marvel, phenomenon, rarity, oddity, portent

mirror 1. *n* looking glass, glass, reflector
2. *vb* ➡ **reflect**

mirth *n* merriment, joviality, festivity, gaiety ➡ **humor, pleasure, laughter**

mischief *n* misconduct, misbehavior, devilment, tomfoolery, rascality, shenanigans (*informal*) ➡ **trouble**

mischievous *adj* naughty, disobedient, unruly, wayward, spoiled, ill-behaved, impish, elfish, elfin ➡ **rude, rebellious, bad** ⇨ *good*

miser *n* skinflint, penny-pincher, scrooge, niggard, cheapskate, tightwad, hoarder, misanthrope

misery *n* suffering, agony, anguish, distress, grief, pain, torment, torture, heartache ➡ **hardship, sorrow**

If the word you want is not a main entry above, look below to find it.

mindfully ➡ carefully

mingle ➡ mix

miniature ➡ small, model

minimal ➡ least

minimum ➡ least

minion ➡ servant

minor ➡ trivial, child, course

minority ➡ childhood

minstrel ➡ musician

minstrelsy ➡ music

minute ➡ small, trivial, moment

minutest ➡ least

miraculous ➡ awesome

mirage ➡ illusion

mire ➡ swamp, dirt, catch

misanthrope ➡ miser, skeptic

misapprehension ➡ misunderstanding

misbehave ➡ disobey

misbehavior ➡ mischief

miscalculation ➡ mistake

miscellaneous ➡ different

miscellany ➡ assortment, mixture

misconception ➡ misunderstanding

misconduct ➡ mischief

misconstrue ➡ misunderstand, distort

misdeed ➡ crime

misdemeanor ➡ crime

miserable ➡ sad, bad

miserly ➡ cheap

misfortune ➡ hardship, disaster

misgiving ➡ doubt

mishap ➡ accident

misinterpret ➡ misunderstand

misjudge ➡ misunderstand

mislaid ➡ lost

mislay ➡ lose

mislead ➡ lie

misleading ➡ unreliable

missile 1. *n* projectile, arrow, dart, lance, spear, javelin, bullet, shell, bolt, slug
2. *n* rocket, torpedo, ICBM

mistake 1. *n* error, slip, blunder, oversight, faux pas, inaccuracy, fallacy, miscalculation, blooper (*informal*), boo-boo (*informal*) ► **fault, defect, misunderstanding**
2. *vb* ► **misunderstand**

misunderstand *vb* misinterpret, misjudge, misconstrue, mistake, err

misunderstanding 1. *n* misapprehension, misconception, confusion ► **mistake**
2. *n* ► **argument**

mix 1. *vb* combine, blend, merge, mingle, compound, consolidate, stir, whip, beat, knead, roll, churn, jumble, scramble, shuffle ► **join**
2. *vb* associate, mingle, intermingle, socialize, fraternize, consort, hobnob (*informal*) ► **join**
3. *n* ► **assortment**

mixture *n* combination, blend, composite, compound, solution, amalgam, amalgamation, potpourri, miscellany, concoction ► **mess, hybrid**

mobilize *vb* muster, enlist, marshal, summon, rally ► **gather**

model 1. *n* paragon, ideal, archetype, exemplar, paradigm, nonpareil, standard, prototype, original ► **example**
2. *n* miniature, representation, reduction, mock-up ► **copy, duplicate**
3. *n* ► **make, pattern**
4. *n* subject, sitter, fashion model, poser, mannequin
5. *vb* ► **make**
6. *vb* pose, sit ► **show**
7. *adj* classic, outstanding, first-rate, excellent, authoritative, typical, archetypal, definitive ► **perfect**

If the word you want is not a main entry above, look below to find it.

misplace ► lose

misplaced ► lost

misremember ► forget

misrepresent ► distort

misrepresentation ► lie, pretense

miss ► lose, exclude

misshapen ► bent

missing ► absent, lost

mission ► job, committee, church

missive ► letter

misspend ► waste

misstate ► lie

mist ► fog, cloud

mistaken ► wrong

mistreat ► abuse

mistreatment ► abuse

mistress ► owner

mistrust ► doubt

misty ► wet

misuse ► abuse, waste

mitigate ► relieve

mitt ► glove

mitten ► glove

mixer ► dance

moan ► cry, complain

moat ► channel

mob ► crowd

mobile ► portable

mobility ► movement

mock ► imitate, ridicule, fake

mockery ► ridicule

mock-up ► model

mode ► fashion

---

modern 1. *adj* contemporary, current, up-to-date, stylish, recent, modernistic, newfangled, space-age, state-of-the-art, latter-day ➡ **new**
2. Modern *adj* ➡ **art**

moment 1. *n* instant, point, minute, second, twinkling, wink, jiffy, flash, trice, time ➡ **period**
2. *n* ➡ **importance**

monastery *n* abbey, convent, nunnery, cloister, priory, friary, lamasery, ashram

money *n* cash, currency, coin, revenue, capital, specie ➡ **wealth, property**

monopoly *n* trust, syndicate, cartel, corner, consortium, ownership

monster *n* beast, ogre, ghoul, brute, savage, freak, monstrosity ➡ **animal**

monument 1. *n* marker, shrine, mausoleum, memorial, tribute ➡ **reminder, statue**
2. *n* ➡ **masterpiece**

mood *n* humor, morale, temper, temperament, disposition, spirits, vein ➡ **state, setting**

mope *vb* sulk, pout, brood ➡ **worry, grieve**

If the word you want is not a main entry above, look below to find it.

moderate ➡ easy, gentle, slow, conservative, negotiate

moderation ➡ abstinence

moderator ➡ host

modernistic ➡ modern

modernity ➡ novelty

modest ➡ humble, average

modesty ➡ virtue

modicum ➡ bit

modification ➡ change

modify ➡ change, adjust, soften

moist ➡ damp

moisten ➡ wet

moisture ➡ humidity

mold ➡ form, fungus

molder ➡ decay

moldy ➡ stale, bad

mole ➡ growth

molecule ➡ atom

molest ➡ abuse

mollify ➡ pacify

molt ➡ shed

molten ➡ liquid

momentarily ➡ soon

momentary ➡ temporary

momentous ➡ memorable

momentum ➡ progress, impulse

monarch ➡ king, queen

monetary ➡ financial

moneyed ➡ rich

mongrel ➡ dog, hybrid

monitor ➡ guardian

monk ➡ religious

monogram ➡ signature

monotonous ➡ dull

monotony ➡ boredom

monsoon ➡ storm

monstrosity ➡ monster

monstrous ➡ huge

monumental ➡ memorable

mooch ➡ borrow

moody ➡ temperamental, sad

moor ➡ dock, plain

mooring ➡ anchor

mop ➡ sweep

moral ➡ good

morale ➡ mood

morality ➡ virtue

moralize ➡ preach

morass ➡ maze

morbid ➡ gruesome

more 1. *adj* additional, extra, added, further, supplementary, another, new ⇨ *less*
2. *adv* additionally, furthermore, still, yet, better, preferably, sooner, rather
3. *n* increase, supplement, extra, surplus

morning *n* a.m., daybreak, dawn, sunrise, sunup, morn ➡ **day** ⇨ *evening*

mortal 1. *adj* human, transient, frail, impermanent, perishable ➡ **temporary** ⇨ *eternal*
2. *adj* ➡ **deadly**
3. *n* ➡ **human being**

most 1. *adj* maximum, utmost, greatest
2. *n* majority, maximum, bulk, preponderance
3. *adv* ➡ **very, best**

motherly *adj* maternal, parental, protective ➡ **feminine** ⇨ *fatherly*

mountain *n* mount, peak, ridge, summit, butte, mesa ➡ **hill, cliff** ⇨ *valley*

move 1. *vb* shift, remove, budge, dislodge ➡ **carry, push**
2. *vb* transfer, relocate, migrate, emigrate, immigrate ➡ **leave, go, travel**
3. *vb* ➡ **affect**
4. *vb* ➡ **suggest**

If the word you want is not a main entry above, look below to find it.

moreover ➡ besides

more than ➡ above

morn ➡ morning

moron ➡ fool

morose ➡ pessimistic

morrow ➡ future

morsel ➡ bite

mortgage ➡ loan, pawn

mortified ➡ ashamed

mortify ➡ embarrass

mosque ➡ church

mostly ➡ chiefly

motel ➡ hotel

motet ➡ hymn

mother ➡ parent

motherland ➡ country

motif ➡ pattern, chorus

motion ➡ movement, activity, wave

motionless ➡ stationary, passive, dead

motivate ➡ cause

motivation ➡ incentive

motive ➡ reason, incentive

motley ➡ different

motor ➡ engine

motorcade ➡ parade

motorcyclist ➡ rider

motorized ➡ automatic

mottled ➡ speckled

motto ➡ saying

mound ➡ pile, hill

mount ➡ ascend, enter, mountain, horse

mourn ➡ grieve

mournful ➡ pitiful

mouth ➡ door

mouthful ➡ bite

mouth-watering ➡ delicious

movable ➡ portable

---

movement 1. *n* locomotion, motion, progress, shift, mobility, play, maneuver ➡ **activity, speed**
2. *n* campaign, crusade, march, faction, demonstration ➡ **cause**
3. *n* migration, immigration, emigration, transition, displacement, removal, transfer, transmission, conveyance
4. *n* ➡ **gait**

movie *n* film, picture, show, video, flick (*informal*) ➡ **play**

movies *n* pictures, cinema, silver screen

much 1. *adv* greatly, enormously, extremely, dearly ➡ **very, far**
2. *adj* ➡ **enough, abundant**
3. *n* ➡ **abundance**

mumble *vb* murmur, mutter, whisper, breathe, sigh ➡ **complain, say, talk, stammer**

murder 1. *n* homicide, manslaughter, assassination, bloodshed, massacre, slaughter, slaying, carnage, annihilation ➡ **crime**
2. *vb* ➡ **kill**

music *n* harmony, melody, minstrelsy ➡ **song**

musical 1. *adj* harmonious, melodious, tuneful, lyrical, symphonic, rhythmical, euphonious, assonant
2. *adj* ➡ **talented**
3. *n* ➡ **play**

If the word you want is not a main entry above, look below to find it.

moving ➡ emotional

mow ➡ cut

mucilage ➡ adhesive

muck ➡ dirt

mud ➡ dirt

muddle ➡ fumble, mess

muddy ➡ dirty

mudslide ➡ avalanche

muff ➡ fumble

muffle ➡ quiet

muffler ➡ wrap

mug ➡ glass, attack

mugginess ➡ humidity

muggy ➡ damp, tropical

mulish ➡ stubborn

multiple ➡ many

multiply ➡ reproduce, grow

multitude ➡ crowd

mum ➡ quiet

mummify ➡ embalm, bury

munch ➡ bite

municipal ➡ public, urban

municipality ➡ town

munificence ➡ generosity

munitions ➡ ammunition

murderer ➡ killer

murderous ➡ deadly

murk ➡ fog

murky ➡ dark, dim

murmur ➡ mumble, hum, rustle

muscle ➡ strength

muscular ➡ strong

muse ➡ meditate

museum ➡ gallery

mushroom ➡ fungus, grow

musician *n* composer, player, instrumentalist, performer, entertainer, minstrel, troubadour, bard ➡ **singer, artist**

mutilate *vb* maim, disfigure, dismember, mangle, disable ➡ **hurt, destroy**

mysterious *adj* puzzling, enigmatic, perplexing, baffling, inexplicable, uncanny, mystic, mystical ➡ **magic, strange, obscure**

myth *n* legend, fable, epic, lore, folklore, tradition, mythology ➡ **story, superstition**

If the word you want is not a main entry above, look below to find it.

musket ➡ gun

muss ➡ disturb

must ➡ need, necessity

muster ➡ mobilize

musty ➡ stale, trite

mutable ➡ variable

mutate ➡ change

mutation ➡ change

mute ➡ dumb, quiet

mutineer ➡ rebel

mutinous ➡ rebellious

mutiny ➡ treason, rebel

mutt ➡ dog

mutter ➡ mumble

mutual ➡ common

mutually ➡ together

muumuu ➡ dress

muzzle ➡ quiet

muzzle loader ➡ gun

myriad ➡ many

mystery ➡ secret, problem, play

mystic ➡ mysterious

mystical ➡ magic, mysterious, supernatural

mystify ➡ confuse

mythical ➡ legendary

mythological ➡ legendary

mythology ➡ myth, religion

N

nail 1. *n* spike, brad, stud, tack, bolt, rivet, screw, peg, dowel ➡ **pin**
2. *vb* pin, tack, screw, bolt, rivet ➡ **join**

naive *adj* unsophisticated, inexperienced, simple, innocent, artless, ingenuous, trusting, green, gullible, credulous ➡ **unaware, amateur, harmless**

naked *adj* undressed, nude, exposed, unclothed, unclad, bare, stripped, bald

> Some people consider **nude** to be a more polite word than **naked** when referring to the unclothed human body. **Nude** is the term regularly used in reference to works of art showing unclothed figures.

name 1. *n* appellation, proper name, surname, designation, nickname, epithet, title, heading ➡ **label**
2. *n* ➡ **reputation**
3. *n* ➡ **celebrity**
4. *vb* christen, nickname, call, dub, designate, entitle, title, label, identify
5. *vb* ➡ **mention**
6. *vb* appoint, delegate, nominate, assign ➡ **choose**

narrow *adj* snug, thin, slender, constricted, close, slim ➡ **small** ⇨ **broad**

native 1. *adj* indigenous, aboriginal, endemic, original, domestic, local, homegrown ➡ **natural**
2. *n* ➡ **citizen**

natural 1. *adj* organic, pure, unprocessed, raw, uncooked ➡ **plain, normal**
2. *adj* inborn, inherent, instinctive, innate, hereditary, inherited, congenital, genetic, intrinsic ➡ **native**

nature 1. *n* environment, outdoors, out-of-doors, landscape ➡ **earth**
2. *n* ➡ **type**
3. *n* ➡ **personality**

If the word you want is not a main entry above, look below to find it.

nab ➡ arrest

nag ➡ bother, complain

nah ➡ no

nameless ➡ anonymous

nap ➡ sleep

napping ➡ asleep, unprepared

narcissism ➡ pride

narcotic ➡ drug

narrate ➡ tell

narration ➡ story

narrative ➡ story

narrow-minded ➡ provincial

nascent ➡ early

nasty ➡ bad

nation ➡ country

national ➡ citizen

national park ➡ park

nationalistic ➡ patriotic

nativity ➡ birth

naturally ➡ regularly

---

n = noun • *vb* = verb • *adj* = adjective • *adv* = adverb • *prep* = preposition • *conj* = conjunction

nausea n indigestion, queasiness, vomiting, sickness, qualm ➡ **illness**

nautical adj maritime, marine, naval, sailing, boating, yachting, seagoing

navy 1. n fleet, flotilla, armada, naval forces ➡ **army**
2. adj ➡ **blue**

near 1. adj close, nearby, immediate, intimate, imminent, local
➡ **adjacent, about, approximate**
2. adj ➡ **future**
3. prep ➡ **beside**
4. vb ➡ **approach**

neat adj tidy, trim, orderly, organized, shipshape, precise, spruce
➡ **clean, prim, legible** ⇨ messy

necessary adj essential, indispensable, basic, required, requisite, fundamental, mandatory, compulsory, obligatory, imperative
➡ **important**

necessity n requirement, essential, staple, requisite, prerequisite, qualification, must, need ➡ **reason**

need 1. vb require, lack ➡ **want**
2. vb must, should, ought, have
3. n ➡ **necessity, reason**
4. n ➡ **hardship, poverty**

neglect 1. n indifference, disregard, disrespect
2. vb ➡ **forget, exclude**

negligent adj neglectful, inattentive, lax, remiss, derelict, delinquent, slack, dilatory, irresponsible ➡ **thoughtless, absent-minded**

negotiate vb mediate, moderate, bargain, referee, confer, transact, haggle, parley, intercede, arbitrate
➡ **decide**

neighborhood n community, block, vicinity, quarter, precinct, ward, borough ➡ **place, zone**

If the word you want is not a main entry above, look below to find it.

naught ➡ zero

naughty ➡ bad, mischievous

nauseate ➡ disgust

nauseated ➡ sick

nauseating ➡ bad

nauseous ➡ sick

naval ➡ nautical

naval forces ➡ navy

navel orange ➡ orange

navigate ➡ drive, pilot

navigator ➡ pilot

nay ➡ no

nearby ➡ near, about

nearly ➡ about, practically

nearness ➡ presence

nebulous ➡ obscure

neck ➡ cape

necktie ➡ tie

needle ➡ bother

needless ➡ unnecessary

needy ➡ poor

ne'er-do-well ➡ loafer

nefarious ➡ bad

negative ➡ no, pessimistic

neglected ➡ abandoned

neglectful ➡ negligent

negligee ➡ bathrobe

negligible ➡ trivial, few

neighbor ➡ border

neighboring ➡ adjacent

neighborly ➡ friendly

➡ = synonym cross-reference • ⇨ = antonym cross-reference

nervous *adj* restless, fidgety, shaky, edgy, uptight, skittish, self-conscious, jittery, jumpy, high-strung ➡ **afraid, anxious, cowardly**

net 1. *n* screen, mesh, web, webbing, network, sieve, filter, sifter
2. *vb* ➡ **earn**

new 1. *adj* fresh, original, recent, late, latest, novel, brand-new, trendy, up-to-date, unused, unspoiled, pristine, virgin, untouched ➡ **modern** ⇨ **old**
2. *adj* ➡ **more**

nice 1. *adj* agreeable, delightful, fantastic ➡ **good, great, pleasant**
2. *adj* good-natured, charming, pleasant, agreeable, affable, good-humored ➡ **thoughtful, polite, friendly, kind**
3. *adj* ➡ **careful**
   Nice *is a very general word to describe someone or something you like, but it is not very specific. Be careful not to overuse it. Often a stronger or more specific synonym is better.*

night *n* nighttime, p.m., bedtime, midnight, dark ➡ **evening** ⇨ *day*

no *interj* nay, negative, nope (*informal*), nah (*informal*) ⇨ *yes*

If the word you want is not a main entry above, look below to find it.

neophyte ➡ amateur

nerve ➡ audacity, courage

nervousness ➡ confusion

nest ➡ den

nestle ➡ snuggle

network ➡ net, maze

neuter ➡ sterilize

neutral ➡ fair

neutralize ➡ balance

névé ➡ snow

nevertheless ➡ anyway, but

newborn ➡ baby

newcomer ➡ stranger

newfangled ➡ modern

newly ➡ recently

newness ➡ novelty

news ➡ announcement

newscaster ➡ reporter

newsman ➡ reporter

newspaper ➡ paper

newspaperman ➡ reporter

newspaperwoman ➡ reporter

newsprint ➡ paper

newswoman ➡ reporter

next ➡ adjacent, following

next door ➡ adjacent

next to ➡ beside

nib ➡ pen

nibble ➡ bite

niche ➡ bay

nick ➡ cut, dent

nickname ➡ name, pseudonym

niggard ➡ miser

niggardly ➡ cheap

nightclub ➡ bar

nightcrawler ➡ worm

nightfall ➡ evening

nighttime ➡ night

nil ➡ zero

nimble ➡ agile

nimbleness ➡ agility

nimbus ➡ halo

nincompoop ➡ fool

ninny ➡ fool

nip ➡ squeeze, drink, bite

nippy ➡ cool

nirvana ➡ heaven

nitwit ➡ fool

noble 1. *adj* royal, aristocratic, highborn, patrician, titled, blue-blooded, princely, kingly, regal, imperial, elite
2. *adj* worthy, generous, magnanimous, courtly, chivalrous, chivalric ➡ **grand, good**
3. *n* nobleman, noblewoman, aristocrat, peer, lord, lady

noise *n* sound, din, uproar, clamor, racket, hubbub, tumult, commotion, pandemonium, hullabaloo, peal ➡ **bang, cry, peep**

nonsense 1. *n* foolishness, stupidity, absurdity, irrationality, madness, lunacy, senselessness, silliness, folly, frivolity

2. *n* poppycock, balderdash, twaddle, gobbledygook, drivel, buncombe, bunk, claptrap, baloney, hogwash

normal *adj* typical, average, natural, standard, conventional ➡ **common, usual**

nose *n* nostril, snout, proboscis, beak, bill, trunk

notepad *n* pad, memo pad, tablet, notebook, steno pad, legal pad ➡ **paper**

notice 1. *vb* observe, note, perceive ➡ **discover, look, see**
2. *n* attention, observation, regard, heed, note, publicity ➡ **warning**
3. *n* ➡ **advertisement, announcement, reminder**

If the word you want is not a main entry above, look below to find it.

nobility ➡ aristocracy
nobleman ➡ noble
noblewoman ➡ noble
nod ➡ sleep
noiseless ➡ quiet
noisy ➡ loud
nomad ➡ traveler
nom de plume ➡ pseudonym
nominate ➡ name
nomination ➡ appointment
nominee ➡ candidate
nonattendance ➡ absence

nonbeliever ➡ skeptic, atheist
nonchalance ➡ apathy
nonchalant ➡ carefree, apathetic
none ➡ zero
nonetheless ➡ anyway
nonexistent ➡ imaginary
nonnative ➡ foreign
nonpareil ➡ model
nonpartisan ➡ fair
nonprofessional ➡ amateur

nonsensical ➡ foolish
nonstop ➡ continual
nonviolent ➡ peaceful
nook ➡ bay
nope ➡ no
nor'easter ➡ storm
norm ➡ average
normally ➡ usually
nosedive ➡ fall
nosegay ➡ bouquet
nostalgia ➡ desire
nostril ➡ nose
nosy ➡ curious

notable ➡ memorable, celebrity
notably ➡ chiefly, far
notch ➡ cut, dent
note ➡ notice, letter
notebook ➡ notepad
noted ➡ famous
notepaper ➡ paper
noteworthy ➡ special
nothing ➡ zero
noticeable ➡ obvious
notification ➡ announcement
notify ➡ tell

novelty 1. *n* newness, originality, freshness, uniqueness, modernity ➡ **invention**
2. *n* oddity, curiosity, knickknack, curio ➡ **trinket**

now *adv* immediately, straightaway, directly, right away, instantly ➡ **quickly, soon**

nuisance *n* annoyance, inconvenience, irritation, bother, pain, pest, headache, vexation ➡ **trouble**

number 1. *n* numeral, figure, digit, cipher, integer, fraction
2. *n* amount, quantity, batch, lot, bunch, bundle ➡ **group, assortment**
3. *n* ➡ **act**
Number and **batch** *usually refer to plural nouns:* "*a number of mistakes,*" "*a batch of cookies.*" **Amount** *is usually used with nouns that are not plural:* "*a small amount of sunshine,*" "*a tiny amount of water.*"

nurse 1. *n* RN, LPN, medic, orderly
2. *vb* ➡ **heal**

If the word you want is not a main entry above, look below to find it.

notion ➡ belief, idea, fancy

notoriety ➡ fame

notorious ➡ famous

notwithstanding ➡ anyway

nought ➡ zero

nourish ➡ support

nourishing ➡ healthy

nourishment ➡ food

novel ➡ new

novelist ➡ writer

novice ➡ amateur

noxious ➡ deadly, unhealthy

nozzle ➡ faucet

nuance ➡ difference

nucleus ➡ middle

nude ➡ naked

nudge ➡ push

nugget ➡ pile

nullify ➡ abolish

numb ➡ paralyze

numeral ➡ number

numerical ➡ consecutive

numerous ➡ many

nun ➡ religious

nunnery ➡ monastery

nuptials ➡ marriage

nursery ➡ bedroom, greenhouse

nursing home ➡ hospital

nurture ➡ grow, support

nut ➡ seed, fruit

nutrition ➡ food

nutritious ➡ healthy

nuzzle ➡ snuggle

O

obey *vb* comply, mind, follow, heed, behave, adhere, observe, meet ⇨ **disobey**

object 1. *vb* protest, disagree, dissent, oppose, dispute, disapprove, frown ➡ **argue, complain, contradict** ⇨ *agree*
2. *n* thing, article, item, gadget, device
3. *n* objective, purpose, aim, goal, sake, target, intention, intent, ambition

obscure 1. *adj* ➡ **dim, dark**
2. *adj* ambiguous, cryptic, enigmatic, inscrutable, unclear, inexplicable, abstruse, vague, incomprehensible, foggy, cloudy,

nebulous ➡ **mysterious** ⇨ *obvious, explicit*
3. *vb* ➡ **hide**

observer *n* spectator, witness, eyewitness, viewer, onlooker, bystander

obsession *n* fixation, fascination, preoccupation, compulsion, mania, fetish ➡ **desire**

obvious *adj* clear, evident, apparent, transparent, noticeable, overt, glaring, blatant, gross, conspicuous, prominent, palpable, pronounced, marked, distinct, patent ➡ **bald, easy, plain** ⇨ *obscure*

If the word you want is not a main entry above, look below to find it.

oaf ➡ fool, boor

oar ➡ paddle

oath ➡ promise, curse

obdurate ➡ stubborn

obedient ➡ good

obelisk ➡ tower

obese ➡ fat

objection ➡ complaint

objectionable ➡ bad

objective ➡ object, fair, real

obligate ➡ force

obligation ➡ duty, debt

obligatory ➡ necessary

oblige ➡ force

obliged ➡ grateful

obliging ➡ good

oblique ➡ zigzag

obliquely ➡ sideways

obliterate ➡ erase, abolish

oblivious ➡ unaware, absentminded

obnoxious ➡ bad

obscene ➡ dirty

obsequious ➡ servile

observable ➡ visible

observation ➡ remark, notice

observe ➡ look, see, notice, celebrate, obey

obsolete ➡ old

obstacle ➡ barrier

obstinate ➡ stubborn, wild

obstreperous ➡ loud

obstruct ➡ bar, close

obstructed ➡ impassable

obstruction ➡ barrier

obtain ➡ get

obtrusive ➡ meddlesome

obtuse ➡ unaware, dull

obverse ➡ front

obviously ➡ apparently

➡ = synonym cross-reference • ⇨ = antonym cross-reference   153

occupant n resident, tenant, renter, householder, inhabitant, guest

occupy vb fill, pervade, take up ➡ **live, own, seize**

ocean n sea, deep, high seas, seven seas

oddity n peculiarity, abnormality, irregularity, idiosyncrasy, eccentricity, aberration, anomaly ➡ **novelty, miracle**

offer 1. vb propose, present, tender, bid, proffer, extend, suggest, quote ➡ **give, sell**
2. n ➡ **suggestion, invitation**

office 1. n workplace, headquarters ➡ **den**
2. n ➡ **function**

official 1. adj authentic, authorized, legitimate, approved, licensed, valid, formal ➡ **real, correct**
2. n leader, administrator, executive, bureaucrat, civil servant, public servant ➡ **boss, judge**

often adv frequently, repeatedly, oftentimes, recurrently ➡ **regularly, usually** ⇨ *seldom*

oil 1. n petroleum, kerosene, crude oil, fossil fuel ➡ **gasoline**
2. n ➡ **fat**
3. vb grease, lubricate, lube (*informal*)

old 1. adj elderly, aged, venerable, mature, senior, hoary, seasoned ⇨ *young*
2. adj ancient, old-fashioned, antique, archaic, antiquated, obsolete, outdated ⇨ *new*
3. adj worn, used, rundown, worn-out, secondhand, decrepit ➡ **shabby, ragged**

older adj elder, senior, prior, earlier

If the word you want is not a main entry above, look below to find it.

occasion ➡ opportunity, event, party

occasional ➡ periodic, rare

occasionally ➡ seldom

occult ➡ magic, supernatural

occupation ➡ profession

occupied ➡ employed

occur ➡ happen

occurrence ➡ event, presence

odd ➡ strange

odious ➡ awful

odor ➡ smell

odorous ➡ smelly

odyssey ➡ trip

offend ➡ insult, disgust, sin

offender ➡ criminal

offense ➡ crime, insult, attack

offensive ➡ bad, attack

offering ➡ gift

officer ➡ police, soldier

office-seeker ➡ candidate

officiate ➡ lead

offset ➡ balance

offshoot ➡ branch, limb, product

offspring ➡ child

oftentimes ➡ often

ogle ➡ stare

ogre ➡ monster

oink ➡ grunt

ointment ➡ medicine

OK ➡ yes

okay ➡ yes

okey-dokey ➡ yes

old-fashioned ➡ old

old wives' tale ➡ superstition

olive ➡ green

ominous *adj* foreboding, threatening, baleful, menacing, malevolent, sinister, impending, inauspicious, unfavorable ➡ **bad**

once *adv* previously, formerly ➡ **before**

only 1. *adv* just, barely, hardly, scarcely, merely, simply, exclusively
2. *adj* single, sole, solitary, unique, one, lone

open 1. *adj* ajar, uncovered, unfastened, unlocked, accessible, unobstructed, unsealed
2. *adj* spacious, deserted, clear ➡ **empty**
3. *vb* unfasten, undo, unbolt, untie, free, clear ➡ **separate**
4. *vb* ➡ **start**

operate *vb* function, perform, run ➡ **drive, act, work, use**

opponent *n* rival, competitor, opposition, challenger, antagonist, adversary, foe, competition ➡ **contestant, enemy** ⇨ *friend*

opportunity *n* chance, occasion, excuse, opening, situation ➡ **luck**

opposite 1. *adj* opposing, contradictory, contrary, conflicting, inverse, converse, reverse, contrasting, antithetical, counter ➡ **different**
2. *adj* facing, opposed, fronting, confronting
3. *n* reverse, contrary, converse, antithesis, inverse
4. *prep* facing, across from, against, opposed to, versus

opposition 1. *n* disapproval, dislike, aversion, antagonism, hostility, antipathy, enmity ➡ **disagreement, fight** ⇨ *support*
2. *n* ➡ **opponent**

If the word you want is not a main entry above, look below to find it.

omen ➡ **warning, sign**

omit ➡ **forget, exclude**

on ➡ **above**

on account of ➡ **because**

once more ➡ **again**

one ➡ **only**

one-liner ➡ **joke**

onerous ➡ **inconvenient**

one-sided ➡ **prejudiced**

on hand ➡ **present**

ongoing ➡ **continual**

onlooker ➡ **observer, audience**

onset ➡ **beginning, attack**

onslaught ➡ **attack**

onward ➡ **forward**

onwards ➡ **forward**

ooze ➡ **dirt, drop**

opaque ➡ **dark**

open fire ➡ **shoot**

opening ➡ **hole, break, opportunity, door**

openness ➡ **freedom, truth**

operation ➡ **behavior, use, attack**

opiate ➡ **drug**

opinion ➡ **belief**

opinionated ➡ **stubborn, dogmatic**

oppose ➡ **object, face**

opposed ➡ **opposite**

opposing ➡ **opposite**

---

optimistic adj hopeful, confident, cheerful, sanguine, expectant, bullish ➡ **idealistic, certain** ⇨ *pessimistic*

orange 1. adj, n tangerine, apricot, peach, coral, salmon
2. n navel orange, Seville orange, mandarin orange, tangerine, clementine, tangelo ➡ **fruit, tree**

order 1. vb command, direct, instruct, decree, bid, dictate, impose, prescribe, ordain, mandate ➡ **ask, tell, insist, force**
2. vb ➡ **arrange, straighten**
3. n arrangement, formation, organization, layout, disposition, alignment, placement, sequence, succession, system ➡ **plan**
4. n decree, command, commandment, demand, ultimatum, direction, directive, charge, mandate, edict, behest, writ
5. n ➡ **religion**

organization 1. n association, corporation, institution, foundation, society, club, fraternity, sorority ➡ **business, union, group**
2. n ➡ **order**

If the word you want is not a main entry above, look below to find it.

oppress ➡ abuse, sadden

oppression ➡ tyranny

oppressive ➡ bleak, sharp

opt ➡ choose

optical ➡ visible

optimist ➡ idealist

optimum ➡ best

option ➡ choice

optional ➡ voluntary, unnecessary

opulence ➡ wealth, elegance

opulent ➡ rich

opus ➡ work

oracle ➡ prophet

oral ➡ spoken

oration ➡ speech

orator ➡ speaker

oratorio ➡ hymn

orb ➡ ball

orbit ➡ circle, field

orchestra ➡ band

orchestration ➡ score

ordain ➡ order, bless

ordeal ➡ shock, trouble

orderly ➡ neat, nurse

ordinance ➡ act

ordinarily ➡ usually

ordinariness ➡ mediocrity

ordinary ➡ common, usual

ordination ➡ appointment

ordnance ➡ arms

organic ➡ natural, alive

organism ➡ animal, plant

organize ➡ arrange

organized ➡ neat

orient ➡ arrange, adjust

orientate ➡ arrange

orientation ➡ perspective

origin ➡ beginning, cause, source

original ➡ new, early, model, native

originality ➡ novelty, imagination

originate ➡ start, invent

originator ➡ creator

ornament ➡ jewel, decoration, decorate

ornamentation ➡ decoration

ornate ➡ rich, fancy

ornery ➡ stubborn

orthodox ➡ religious, conservative

orthodoxy ➡ religion

oscillate ➡ alternate, swing

oscillation ➡ vibration

ostentatious ➡ loud, fancy

ostracism ➡ exile

ostracize ➡ banish

other ➡ different

otherwise ➡ differently

ought ➡ need

oust *vb* eject, remove, expel, depose, dethrone, unseat ➡ **fire, banish**

outside 1. *n* exterior, surface, façade 2. *adj* exterior, external, outer, outermost, outward, outdoor, alfresco 3. *adv* outdoors, out-of-doors, out, alfresco

If the word you want is not a main entry above, look below to find it.

out ➡ outside

outbreak ➡ epidemic

outburst ➡ fit[2]

outcast ➡ exile, lonely, homeless

out cold ➡ unconscious

outcome ➡ effect, score

outcry ➡ complaint

outdated ➡ old

outdo ➡ exceed

outdoor ➡ outside

outdoors ➡ outside, nature

outer ➡ outside

outer space ➡ space

outermost ➡ outside, last

outfit ➡ dress, suit, business, supply

outfox ➡ fool

outgrowth ➡ shoot, product

outing ➡ trip

outlandish ➡ strange

outlast ➡ live[1]

outlaw ➡ criminal, forbid

outlawed ➡ illegal

outlay ➡ price

outlet ➡ door

outline ➡ circumference, summary, list, plan

outlive ➡ live[1]

outlook ➡ view

outlying ➡ far

outmoded ➡ unpopular

outnumber ➡ exceed

out-of-doors ➡ outside, nature

out of order ➡ broken

out-of-the-way ➡ inaccessible

out-of-towner ➡ stranger

out-of-work ➡ unemployed

outpatient ➡ patient

output ➡ productivity

outrage ➡ insult, anger

outrageous ➡ awful

outright ➡ bald, perfect, unconditional

outrun ➡ catch

outset ➡ beginning

outshine ➡ exceed

outsider ➡ stranger

outsmart ➡ fool

outspoken ➡ straightforward

outstanding ➡ good, special, model, due

outstretched ➡ long

outstrip ➡ catch

outward ➡ outside

outwit ➡ fool

oval ➡ round

over ➡ above, again, past

overabundant ➡ excessive

overbearing ➡ dogmatic

overcast ➡ dark, cloudy

overcoat ➡ coat

overcome ➡ defeat, win, weather

overconfident ➡ imprudent

overdo ➡ exaggerate

overdue ➡ late, due

overemotional ➡ emotional

overflow ➡ flood

overgrown ➡ wild

overhaul ➡ fix

overhead ➡ above

overhear ➡ listen

overjoyed ➡ ecstatic

overlap ➡ fold

overlay ➡ plate

overlook ➡ forget, exclude, tower

overlooked ➡ unnoticed

overnight bag ➡ luggage

overpass ➡ bridge

overpower ➡ defeat

overpriced ➡ expensive

overrule ➡ abolish

overrun ➡ wild, infest

overseas ➡ abroad

oversee ➡ lead

overseer ➡ guardian

oversight ➡ mistake

overspread ➡ cover

overstate ➡ exaggerate

overstatement ➡ exaggeration

overstep ➡ exceed

overt ➡ obvious

overtake ➡ catch

overthrow ➡ victory, defeat

overture ➡ introduction

overturn ➡ upset

overused ➡ trite

overweight ➡ fat

overwhelm ➡ flood, shock

overwrought ➡ frantic

ovum ➡ egg

own 1. *vb* possess, hold, have, retain, maintain, enjoy, occupy
➡ **keep**
2. *vb* ➡ **admit**
3. *adj* ➡ **private**

owner *n* proprietor, buyer, possessor, holder, master, mistress, landowner, landlord, landlady

If the word you want is not a main entry above, look below to find it.

ownership
➡ **possession, monopoly**

oxbow ➡ **curve**
oxidize ➡ **corrode**

oxygen ➡ **air**

oxymoron
➡ **contradiction**

P

pacify *vb* appease, placate, soothe, mollify ➡ **calm, satisfy**

package 1. *n* parcel, packet, bundle, pack ➡ **container, mail**
2. *vb* ➡ **wrap**

paddle 1. *n* oar, scull, sweep
2. *vb* row, scull, pole
3. *vb* ➡ **punish, hit, whip**
4. *vb* ➡ **swim**

page 1. *n* sheet, leaf, folio
2. *n* intern ➡ **servant**
3. *vb* ➡ **call**

pain 1. *n* suffering, discomfort, ache, pang, soreness, twinge, stitch, spasm, cramp, sting
2. *n* ➡ **misery**
3. *n* ➡ **nuisance**

paint 1. *n* pigment, dye, stain, tint ➡ **color, finish**
2. *vb* ➡ **draw**

pair 1. *n* couple, duo, twosome, twins, brace (*of animals*), yoke (*of oxen*), span (*of horses*) ➡ **team**
2. *vb* ➡ **join**

pale 1. *adj* pallid, pasty, wan, sallow, ashen, chalky ➡ **white, fair**
2. *vb* ➡ **bleach**

pamper *vb* coddle, spoil, indulge, dote on, humor, baby, patronize ➡ **please**

pamphlet *n* booklet, brochure, leaflet, tract ➡ **book**

If the word you want is not a main entry above, look below to find it.

pace ➡ speed, step, gait

pacific ➡ peaceful

pacifist ➡ peaceful

pack ➡ bag, package, load, group, herd, carry

packed ➡ full, thick

packet ➡ package

pact ➡ agreement

pad ➡ cushion, notepad, foot, protect

padding ➡ cushion

paddock ➡ pen

padlock ➡ lock

pageant ➡ play

pail ➡ container

painful ➡ sore, uncomfortable

painkiller ➡ drug

pains ➡ work

painstaking ➡ careful

painter ➡ artist, rope

painting ➡ picture

pal ➡ friend

palace ➡ castle, home

palisade ➡ cliff, wall, barrier

pall ➡ cloud

pallet ➡ cushion

palliate ➡ soften

pallid ➡ pale

palpable ➡ real, obvious

paltry ➡ poor, small, trivial

pan ➡ pot

panache ➡ class

pandemic ➡ epidemic

pandemonium ➡ noise

pander ➡ flatter

panel ➡ committee

pang ➡ pain

panhandler ➡ beggar

panic ➡ fear, hysteria

panorama ➡ view

pant ➡ breathe

pantry ➡ kitchen, closet

➡ = synonym cross-reference • ⇨ = antonym cross-reference

paper 1. *n* stationery, notepaper, writing paper, newsprint, crepe paper, tissue, wax paper, tar paper, parchment, vellum
2. *n* ➡ **document, report**
3. *n* newspaper, magazine, journal, periodical, tabloid, gazette, daily, weekly

parade 1. *n* procession, march, demonstration, cavalcade, motorcade
2. *vb* ➡ **walk, strut**
3. *vb* ➡ **advertise**

parallel 1. *adj* equidistant, collateral, aligned, even, alongside, abreast ➡ **level**
2. *adj* ➡ **alike**
3. *n* ➡ **duplicate, similarity**
4. *vb* ➡ **compare**

paralyze *vb* disable, cripple, immobilize, numb, stun, knock out

parent *n* father, mother, foster parent, stepparent ➡ **ancestor, guardian**

park 1. *n* green, common, square, playground, recreational area
2. *n* national park, state park, reserve, preserve, reservation, refuge ➡ **zoo**
3. *vb* ➡ **put**

parody 1. *n* imitation, satire, caricature, burlesque ➡ **irony**
2. *vb* ➡ **imitate**

part 1. *n* piece, section, portion, segment, fragment, fraction, share, element, facet, aspect, component, ingredient, content ➡ **bit, block, division** ⇨ *total*
2. *vb* ➡ **divide, separate**
3. *n* ➡ **role, function**

If the word you want is not a main entry above, look below to find it.

paparazzo, paparazzi ➡ photographer

paperback ➡ book

par ➡ average

paradigm ➡ model

paradise ➡ heaven, utopia

paradox ➡ contradiction

paragon ➡ model

paragraph ➡ division

paramount ➡ important

paranoid ➡ suspicious, insane

paranormal ➡ supernatural

parapet ➡ wall

paraphernalia ➡ equipment

paraphrase ➡ summary, translation, quote, translate

parboil ➡ boil

parcel ➡ package

parched ➡ dry

parchment ➡ paper

pardon ➡ forgive, forgiveness

pare ➡ peel

parental ➡ motherly, fatherly

parfait ➡ ice cream

pariah ➡ exile

parish ➡ church

parishioners ➡ church

parka ➡ coat

parking garage ➡ garage

parkway ➡ highway

parley ➡ negotiate, talk

parliament ➡ government

parlor ➡ living room

parochial ➡ provincial

paroxysm ➡ fit²

parrot ➡ imitate, quote

parry ➡ repel

partial 1. *adj* incomplete, unfinished, fragmentary, deficient, imperfect ⇨ *complete*
2. *adj* ➡ **prejudiced**

partly *adv* partially, partway, somewhat, incompletely, slightly

partner 1. *n* associate, co-worker, confederate, accomplice, accessory, sidekick ➡ **helper**
2. *n* ➡ **friend**
3. *n* ➡ **love, spouse**

party 1. *n* celebration, festivity, gathering, reception, soiree, fete, occasion, gala, function, revelry, jubilee, merrymaking ➡ **feast**
2. *n* faction, bloc, league, lobby, junta, cabal ➡ **organization, group**
3. *n* participant, litigant, principal ➡ **member, contestant**
4. *vb* ➡ **celebrate**

passive 1. *adj* idle, inactive, inert, lifeless, motionless, sedentary
➡ **listless, lazy, slow** ⇨ *active*
2. *adj* resigned, submissive, docile, deferential, compliant, yielding
➡ **patient**

past 1. *adj* former, preceding, foregoing, prior, previous, antecedent ➡ **old**
2. *adj* finished, over, ended, through, done
3. *n* history, antiquity, yesterday, yesteryear, yore
4. *prep* beyond, through, behind, over, after

pastime *n* activity, pursuit, interest, hobby, avocation, venture ➡ **game**

pastry *n* baked goods, delicacy, Danish, pie, tart, shortbread, cookie
➡ **cake, bread**

If the word you want is not a main entry above, look below to find it.

partiality
➡ preference, prejudice

partially ➡ partly

participant
➡ contestant, member, party

participate ➡ join

particle ➡ bit

particular ➡ special, careful, choosy, detail

particularize ➡ specify

particularly ➡ chiefly

partisan ➡ fan, prejudiced

partition ➡ wall, division, divider, divide

partnership
➡ business, union

partway ➡ partly

pasha ➡ king

pass ➡ exceed, go, throw, give, catch, elapse, ticket

passage ➡ hall, door, approval, excerpt, division, trip, travel

passageway ➡ hall

pass away ➡ die

passenger ➡ rider

passerby ➡ pedestrian

passing ➡ death

passion ➡ love, desire, enthusiasm, emotion

passionate
➡ emotional, loving, eager

pass on ➡ die

passport ➡ document, ticket

paste ➡ stick, adhesive

pastor ➡ minister

pastoral ➡ rural

pastry chef ➡ cook

pasture ➡ field

pasty ➡ pale

pat ➡ pet, hit

patch ➡ fix, repair

patent ➡ license, obvious

patently ➡ apparently

paternal ➡ fatherly

---

path *n* pathway, footpath, trail, track, lane, walk, walkway, runway, shortcut ➡ **road, course**

patience *n* tolerance, understanding, fortitude, stoicism, endurance, perserverance, persistence

patient 1. *adj* understanding, forbearing, mild-tempered, long-suffering ➡ **tolerant, calm, passive**
2. *adj* persistent, perservering, steadfast, assiduous ➡ **diligent**
3. *n* subject, victim, sufferer, convalescent, invalid, outpatient, inpatient

patriotic *adj* loyal, zealous, nationalistic, chauvinistic ➡ **faithful**

patrol 1. *n* scout, lookout, sentinel, sentry, escort, vanguard, picket, watch ➡ **guardian**
2. *vb* police, inspect, cruise, reconnoiter, scout ➡ **protect**

patron 1. *n* sponsor, benefactor, philanthropist, supporter, contributor, donor, subscriber, giver
2. *n* client, customer, buyer, shopper, regular ➡ **audience**

pattern 1. *n* design, motif, configuration ➡ **structure, plan**
2. *n* model, blueprint, template, diagram, guide, sketch
3. *vb* ➡ **form**

pawn 1. *vb* hock, pledge, mortgage ➡ **sell**
2. *n* ➡ **tool**

pay 1. *vb* compensate, recompense, spend, reward, tip, remunerate, settle, disburse, expend, atone, expiate ➡ **give, earn, refund**
2. *n* ➡ **wage**

peace *n* harmony, concord, repose, amity, reconciliation ➡ **agreement, calm, truce**

peaceful 1. *adj* ➡ **calm**
2. *adj* peaceable, pacific, amicable, nonviolent, pacifist, conciliatory ➡ **friendly**

If the word you want is not a main entry above, look below to find it.

pathetic ➡ pitiful

pathless ➡ impassable

pathway ➡ path

patio ➡ porch, court

patois ➡ dialect

patriarch ➡ ancestor

patrician ➡ noble

patrimony ➡ inheritance

patriotism ➡ loyalty

patrolman ➡ police officer

patrolwoman ➡ police officer

patronize ➡ frequent, condescend, pamper

patrons ➡ audience

patter ➡ talk, knock, rustle

paucity ➡ want

paunch ➡ stomach

pauper ➡ beggar

pause ➡ stop, hesitate, break

pave ➡ cover

pavilion ➡ tent

paw ➡ foot, touch

payable ➡ due

pay for ➡ afford, buy

payment ➡ price

peaceable ➡ peaceful

peacefulness ➡ calm

peach ➡ orange

pea green ➡ green

peak ➡ top, mountain, climax, bill

peal ➡ ring, noise

---

pedestrian 1. *n* walker, hiker, passerby, rover, stroller, straggler
2. *adj* ➡ **common, poor**

peel 1. *vb* skin, pare, strip, scale, husk, shuck, flay ➡ **cut**
2. *n* skin, rind, bark ➡ **shell**

peep *n* squeak, chirp, cheep, squawk, clink, tinkle, click, ping, pop, plink, plunk ➡ **noise, bang**

pen 1. *n* corral, fold, pound, paddock, enclosure, coop, cage, sty, stall, kennel ➡ **barn, field, jail**
2. *n* ballpoint, marker, fountain pen, quill, nib
3. *vb* ➡ **write**

pension *n* benefit, support, annuity, Social Security ➡ **wage**

people 1. *n* citizenry, populace, public, population, society, civilization, community, folk, hoi polloi (*Greek*), bourgeoisie (*French*) ➡ **human being, humanity, citizen**
2. *n* ➡ **family**

perfect 1. *adj* ideal, flawless, faultless, impeccable, unblemished, immaculate, exquisite, exemplary, model ➡ **correct, infallible**
2. *adj* pure, sheer, outright ➡ **complete**
3. *vb* polish, hone, amend ➡ **fix, correct**

If the word you want is not a main entry above, look below to find it.

pearl ➡ ball

peasant ➡ farmer

pebble ➡ rock

peck ➡ abundance, stick, kiss

peculiar ➡ strange, special

peculiarity ➡ oddity, detail

pecuniary ➡ financial

peddle ➡ sell

peddler ➡ seller

pedestal ➡ post

peek ➡ look

peer ➡ stare, equal, noble

peerless ➡ unique

peevish ➡ cross

peg ➡ nail

peignoir ➡ bathrobe

pellet ➡ ball

pelt ➡ hit, hide

penalize ➡ punish

penalty ➡ punishment

penance ➡ punishment

penchant ➡ tendency

pending ➡ future, unresolved

penetrate ➡ enter, stick, know

penetrating ➡ profound

peninsula ➡ cape

penitent ➡ sorry

penitentiary ➡ jail

penknife ➡ knife

penmanship ➡ handwriting

pen name ➡ pseudonym

pennant ➡ flag

penniless ➡ poor

penny-pinching ➡ cheap

penny-pincher ➡ miser

pensive ➡ thoughtful

penurious ➡ cheap

penury ➡ poverty

pep ➡ energy

peppery ➡ spicy

perceivable ➡ visible

perceive ➡ see, notice, read

percent ➡ share

percentage ➡ share

perceptible ➡ audible, visible

perception ➡ sight, wisdom, feeling

perceptive ➡ smart

perch ➡ descend, seat

perchance ➡ maybe

perennial ➡ flower, permanent

perfection ➡ excellence

perfectionist ➡ idealist

perfectly ➡ certainly

---

period 1. *n* interval, term, span, spell, duration, extent, stretch, streak, cycle, bout, season, phase, stage, time, shift, watch, tour, stint ➡ **round, moment**
2. *n* age, eon, era, epoch, date

periodic *adj* intermittent, cyclic, cyclical, recurrent, spasmodic, sporadic, fitful, erratic, irregular, occasional ➡ **alternate, frequent**

permanent *adj* durable, lasting, enduring, abiding, perennial, persistent, indelible ➡ **continual, eternal, stationary** ⇨ *temporary*

permission *n* consent, authorization, authority, approval, license, sanction ➡ **support**

personality 1. *n* character, disposition, temperament, temper, nature, identity
2. *n* charisma, charm, presence, allure, magnetism ➡ **bearing, attraction**
3. *n* ➡ **celebrity**

perspective *n* point of view, viewpoint, standpoint, orientation, direction, angle, position, attitude, side ➡ **view**

persuade *vb* convince, satisfy, influence, induce, dispose, coax, sway, get, wheedle, cajole, entice, prevail, snow ➡ **urge, tempt** ⇨ *discourage*

If the word you want is not a main entry above, look below to find it.

perfidious ➡ unfaithful

perforate ➡ stick

perforation ➡ hole

perform ➡ act, operate, play

performance ➡ act, behavior, delivery, program

performer ➡ actor, musician

perfume ➡ smell

perfumed ➡ fragrant

perfunctory ➡ fast, superficial

perhaps ➡ maybe

peril ➡ danger

perilous ➡ dangerous

perimeter ➡ circumference, circle

periodical ➡ paper

periphery ➡ edge, circumference, circle

perish ➡ die

perishable ➡ mortal

periwig ➡ wig

perjurer ➡ liar

perk ➡ tip

permafrost ➡ ice

permanently ➡ forever, finally

permissible ➡ legal

permissive ➡ tolerant

permit ➡ let, ticket, license

perpendicular ➡ vertical, steep

perpetrate ➡ commit

perpetrator ➡ criminal

perpetual ➡ eternal

perpetually ➡ forever

perplex ➡ confuse

perplexed ➡ doubtful

perplexing ➡ mysterious

perplexity ➡ confusion

perquisite ➡ tip

persecute ➡ abuse

perseverance ➡ diligence, patience

persevere ➡ continue, live¹

persevering ➡ patient

persist ➡ continue, live¹

persistence ➡ diligence, patience

persistent ➡ patient, continual, permanent

person ➡ human being

personage ➡ celebrity

personal ➡ private

personnel ➡ faculty

perspiration ➡ sweat

perspire ➡ sweat

---

pessimistic *adj* cynical, negative, glum, sullen, morose, fatalistic ➡ **bleak, sad** ⇨ *optimistic*

pet 1. *vb* pat, caress, fondle, stroke, tickle ➡ **rub**
2. *adj*, *n* ➡ **favorite**

philosopher *n* thinker, sage, logician, scholar

philosophy *n* metaphysics, theory, thought, ideology, esthetics, ethics ➡ **knowledge, wisdom, belief**

photograph *n* photo, snapshot, image, slide, print, likeness ➡ **picture, X ray**

photographer *n* camerman, cinematographer, paparazzo (*Italian*; *plural*: paparazzi), shutterbug (*informal*) ➡ **artist**

physical *adj* bodily, corporal, corporeal, fleshly ➡ **real**

picture 1. *n* portrait, image, drawing, painting, illustration, representation, diagram, sketch, cartoon, poster, work, plate, print ➡ **description, photograph, X ray**
2. *n* ➡ **movie**
3. *vb* ➡ **imagine**
4. *vb* ➡ **draw**

If the word you want is not a main entry above, look below to find it.

pert ➡ rude

pertain ➡ belong, concern

pertinaceous ➡ stubborn

pertinence ➡ relevance

pertinent ➡ relevant, fit[1]

perturb ➡ disturb, scare

peruse ➡ read

pervade ➡ occupy

perverse ➡ stubborn

perversion ➡ immorality

perversity ➡ immorality

pervert ➡ debase, distort

perverted ➡ immoral

pessimist ➡ skeptic

pest ➡ nuisance, bug

pester ➡ bother

pestilence ➡ epidemic

petcock ➡ faucet

petition ➡ appeal, ask

petrified ➡ afraid

petrify ➡ scare, harden

petrol ➡ gasoline

petroleum ➡ oil

petty ➡ trivial, mean

petulant ➡ temperamental, cross

pew ➡ seat

phantom ➡ ghost

pharaoh ➡ emperor

pharmaceutical ➡ medicinal

phase ➡ state, period

Ph.D. ➡ doctor

phenomenal ➡ special

phenomenon ➡ event, miracle

philanthropist ➡ patron

philanthropy ➡ generosity

Philistine ➡ boor

philosophical ➡ theoretical, profound

phobia ➡ fear

phone ➡ call

phony ➡ fake

photo ➡ photograph

photocopy ➡ reproduce, print, copy

phrase ➡ saying, say

physically challenged ➡ disabled

physician ➡ doctor

physics ➡ science

physique ➡ body

piazza ➡ court, porch

pick ➡ choose, gather, choice

pickax ➡ ax, axe

picket ➡ post, patrol, protest

pickle ➡ trouble

pick up ➡ continue

picky ➡ choosy

picnic ➡ meal

pictorial ➡ scenic

pictures ➡ movies

picturesque ➡ scenic

➡ = synonym cross-reference • ⇨ = antonym cross-reference

pile 1. *n* heap, stack, mound, hill, lump, wad, clump, mass, nugget ➡ **bulk, assortment**
2. *vb* heap, stack ➡ **gather**
3. *n* ➡ **post**

pillage 1. *vb* plunder, ransack, sack, loot ➡ **steal, attack**
2. *n* ➡ **theft, booty**

pilot 1. *n* aviator, flier, airman, aeronaut
2. *n* helmsman, navigator, coxswain, steersman
3. *vb* sail, navigate ➡ **lead, guide, drive**

pin 1. *n* safety pin, straight pin, bobby pin, hairpin, hat pin, cotter pin, brooch, tiepin, clip ➡ **nail**
2. *vb* attach ➡ **join, nail**

pine 1. *n* fir, evergreen ➡ **tree**
2. *vb* ➡ **grieve**
3. *vb* ➡ **want**

pioneer 1. *n* settler, homesteader, backwoodsman, frontiersman, immigrant, colonist, colonizer
2. *n* ➡ **creator**
3. *adj* ➡ **early**

pipe *n* tube, drainpipe, waterpipe, duct, conduit, pipeline, tubing, hose, funnel ➡ **channel**

pirate 1. *n* buccaneer, privateer, freebooter, corsair, plunderer, marauder ➡ **criminal, vandal**
2. *vb* ➡ **steal**

pitiful *adj* pathetic, piteous, pitiable, mournful, woeful, distressing, heartbreaking ➡ **sad, sorry, poor, unfortunate, emotional**

If the word you want is not a main entry above, look below to find it.

piddling ➡ trivial

pidgin ➡ dialect

pie ➡ pastry

piebald ➡ speckled

piece ➡ part, bit, block

pièce de résistance ➡ masterpiece

pier ➡ dock, jetty, post

pierce ➡ stick

piercing ➡ loud

pig ➡ glutton

pigeonhole ➡ stereotype

pigheaded ➡ stubborn

pigment ➡ paint

pigtail ➡ braid

pilfer ➡ steal

pilgrim ➡ traveler

pilgrimage ➡ trip

pill ➡ medicine

pillar ➡ post, support

pillow ➡ cushion

pinafore ➡ dress

pinch ➡ squeeze, steal, trouble, bit

ping ➡ peep

pinion ➡ limb

pink ➡ red

pinnacle ➡ top, tower

pioneering ➡ early

pious ➡ religious

pip ➡ seed

pipeline ➡ pipe

piping ➡ high

piquant ➡ spicy

pirouette ➡ dance

pistol ➡ gun

pit ➡ dent, hole, grave, mine, seed

pitch ➡ throw, advertise, swing, slant, advertisement

pitch-black ➡ black, dark

pitcher ➡ bottle

piteous ➡ pitiful

pitfall ➡ trap

pitiable ➡ pitiful

---

pity 1. *n* sympathy, compassion, empathy, mercy, forbearance, ruth, clemency, condolence, commiseration ➡ **kindness, comfort**
2. *vb* sympathize, commiserate, comfort
3. *n* ➡ **disaster**

place 1. *n* location, position, situation, locale, site, spot, locality, region, vicinity ➡ **space, zone**
2. *vb* locate, situate, assign, store ➡ **put**
3. *vb* ➡ **arrange**
4. *n* ➡ **house**
5. *n* ➡ **profession**

plain 1. *adj* simple, uncomplicated, unadorned, unvarnished, frugal, severe, austere, stark ➡ **common, humble, natural, naked** ⇨ *complicated*
2. *adj* unattractive, homely, drab, unlovely ➡ **ugly** ⇨ *pretty*
3. *adj* ➡ **obvious, straightforward**
4. *n* prairie, range, grassland, savanna, heath, moor, tundra, downs ➡ **field, plateau**

plan 1. *n* design, project, plot, schematic, outline, map ➡ **table**
2. *n* aim, intent, goal, purpose, strategy, scheme, plot, conspiracy, program, policy, platform, plank, provision ➡ **method, recipe**
3. *vb* plot, scheme, conspire, contrive, connive, chart, map, outline ➡ **arrange, prepare, intend**

planet *n* heavenly body, celestial body, satellite ➡ **earth, space**

plant 1. *n* shrub, weed, grass, bush, shrub, vegetation, flora, foliage, organism ➡ **flower, tree, herb, vegetable, fruit**
2. *n* ➡ **factory**
3. *vb* seed, sow, pot, transplant, propagate, set, broadcast, scatter ➡ **grow**
4. *vb* ➡ **put**

plate 1. *n* dish, platter, saucer, dinnerware, china ➡ **bowl, tray**
2. *n* ➡ **picture**
3. *n* ➡ **base**
4. *vb* laminate, overlay, gild, electroplate ➡ **cover**

If the word you want is not a main entry above, look below to find it.

pitiless ➡ mean	placate ➡ pacify	plague ➡ epidemic, infest, bother	plank ➡ board, wood, plan
pitter-patter ➡ knock	place-kick ➡ kick		
pivot ➡ axis, turn	placement ➡ order	plainly ➡ apparently	plantation ➡ farm
pixie ➡ fairy	placid ➡ calm	plait ➡ braid, weave	planter ➡ farmer
pizzeria ➡ restaurant	plagiarize ➡ steal	plane ➡ airplane, level, side	plastic ➡ flexible

---

plateau 1. *n* tableland, table, mesa, steppe, upland, highland ➡ **plain**
2. *n* ➡ **grade**

platform 1. *n* stage, dais, pulpit, rostrum, stand, riser
2. *n* ➡ **plan**

play 1. *vb* frisk, sport, disport, romp, frolic, gambol, recreate
2. *vb* ➡ **compete**
3. *vb* perform, finger, bow, strum ➡ **practice, blow²**
4. *vb* ➡ **act**
5. *vb* run, show, present, air, broadcast
6. *n* recreation, horseplay, clowning ➡ **pleasure, entertainment**
7. *n* drama, dramatization, skit, pageant, tragedy, melodrama, comedy, farce, musical, mystery ➡ **program, movie**
8. *n* ➡ **movement**

pleasant 1. *adj* pleasurable, gratifying, agreeable, pleasing, enjoyable, congenial, satisfying, appealing, desirable, delightful, sweet ➡ **happy**
2. *adj* ➡ **nice, friendly**
3. *adj* ➡ **fair**

please *vb* delight, gratify, gladden, content, hearten ➡ **satisfy, entertain, pamper**

pleasure *n* amusement, joy, happiness, fun, delight, glee, enjoyment, pride, ecstasy, bliss, rapture, content, felicity ➡ **satisfaction, entertainment, play** ⇨ *pain*

If the word you want is not a main entry above, look below to find it.

platitude ➡ cliché

platter ➡ plate, tray

plausibility ➡ possibility

plausible ➡ possible

plausibly ➡ probably

player ➡ actor, musician, athlete, contestant

playful ➡ lively

playground ➡ park

playing field ➡ field

playmate ➡ friend

playroom ➡ den

plaything ➡ toy

playwright ➡ writer

plaza ➡ court

plea ➡ appeal

plead ➡ argue, beg

pleased ➡ grateful

pleasing ➡ pleasant

pleasurable ➡ pleasant

pleat ➡ fold

plebeian ➡ common

pledge ➡ promise, dedicate, pawn

plenteous ➡ abundant

plentiful ➡ abundant, enough

plenty ➡ abundance, enough

plethora ➡ abundance

pliable ➡ flexible

pliant ➡ flexible

plight ➡ trouble

plink ➡ peep

plod ➡ walk, lag

plot ➡ plan, property, field, story

plow ➡ dig

ploy ➡ trick

pluck ➡ pull, gather, extract

plucky ➡ brave

plug ➡ close, repair, advertise, advertisement, top

plum ➡ purple

plumb ➡ vertical

plummet ➡ fall

plump ➡ fat, fall

plunder ➡ booty, pillage

plunderer ➡ pirate

plunge ➡ fall, drop, jump, stick, swim

plunk ➡ peep

plus ➡ besides, advantage

ply ➡ act

pocket 1. *n* pouch, sac ➡ **bag**
2. *vb* ➡ **steal**

poem *n* verse, poetry, lyric, rhyme
➡ **stanza, song, work**

point 1. *n* end, tip, spike, tine
➡ **top, thorn**
2. *n* ➡ **cape**
3. *n* ➡ **subject**
4. *n* ➡ **detail**
5. *n* ➡ **moment**

poison 1. *n* venom, toxin, bane,
infection, virus, germ
2. *vb* ➡ **kill**

police 1. *n* authorities, officer
➡ **police officer**
2. *vb* ➡ **patrol**

police officer *n* policeman,
policewoman, cop (*informal*),

patrolman, patrolwoman, constable,
sheriff, marshal, detective

polite *adj* courteous, well-mannered,
civil, chivalrous, gracious
➡ **friendly, thoughtful, nice, prim**
⇨ **rude**

pompous *adj* grandiloquent,
flowery, grandiose, bombastic,
pretentious, turgid, condescending
➡ **proud**

poor 1. *adj* needy, penniless,
destitute, broke, impoverished,
deprived, indigent, poverty-stricken
⇨ **rich**
2. *adj* pitiful, sorry, paltry, inferior,
shoddy, deficient, pedestrian, tawdry,
unsatisfactory, inadequate,
worthless, wretched, abject, lame

If the word you want is not a main entry above, look below to find it.

p.m. ➡ **night,
afternoon**

poach ➡ **boil, hunt,
steal**

pocketbook ➡ **bag,
wallet**

pod ➡ **shell, herd**

poet ➡ **writer**

poetry ➡ **poem**

poignant ➡ **emotional**

pointed ➡ **sharp**

pointer ➡ **tip**

pointless
➡ **unnecessary**

point of view
➡ **perspective**

pointy ➡ **sharp**

poise ➡ **balance, tact**

poised ➡ **calm**

poisonous ➡ **deadly**

poke ➡ **push, stick,
blow**[1]

poker-faced ➡ **blank**

polar ➡ **cold**

pole ➡ **bar, bat, paddle**

poleax ➡ **ax, axe**

policeman ➡ **police
officer**

policewoman
➡ **police officer**

policy ➡ **plan**

polish ➡ **shine, finish,
perfect, class,
elegance, civilization**

politic ➡ **careful**

poll ➡ **vote, study**

polliwog ➡ **frog**

pollute ➡ **dirty, debase**

polluted ➡ **dirty**

polyp ➡ **growth**

pomp ➡ **ceremony**

pond ➡ **lake**

ponder ➡ **meditate**

ponderous ➡ **heavy**

pontiff ➡ **priest**

pony ➡ **horse**

pool ➡ **lake, lottery**

pop ➡ **bang, peep,
soda, jump**

pope ➡ **priest**

poppycock
➡ **nonsense**

populace ➡ **people**

popular ➡ **common,
fashionable, famous,
favorite**

popularity ➡ **fame**

population ➡ **people**

---

porch n veranda, stoop, piazza, patio, breezeway, portico, gallery

portable adj movable, transportable, mobile ⇨ **stationary**

porter n redcap, skycap, bellboy, bellhop, baggage carrier ➡ **doorman**

possession 1. n ownership, custody, title, proprietorship, receipt ➡ **control, rule**
2. n ➡ **property, acquisition**
3. n ➡ **colony**

possibility n probability, likelihood, chance, plausibility, prospect, expectation, eventuality, potential, potentiality

possible adj plausible, conceivable, believable, credible, feasible, potential, reasonable, imaginable, practicable, viable ➡ **likely**

post 1. n pillar, column, pedestal, stud, upright, picket, stanchion, pier, pile
2. n ➡ **profession**
3. n ➡ **mail**
4. n ➡ **base**
5. vb ➡ **send**

posture n pose, stance, carriage, bearing, attitude

pot 1. n pan, saucepan, kettle, teakettle, teapot, coffeepot, vat, cauldron ➡ **bowl, container**
2. vb ➡ **plant**

pottery n ceramics, porcelain, china, earthenware, stoneware, terra cotta

---

If the word you want is not a main entry above, look below to find it.

porcelain ➡ pottery

pore ➡ hole

pore over ➡ study

pornographic ➡ dirty

port ➡ harbor

portal ➡ door

portend ➡ predict

portent ➡ miracle

portico ➡ porch

portion ➡ part, excerpt, divide

portly ➡ fat

portrait ➡ picture, description

portray ➡ act, draw

portrayal ➡ description, role

pose ➡ posture, model, act

poser ➡ model

posh ➡ rich

position ➡ place, put, deploy, grade, profession, reputation, perspective

positive ➡ certain, good

positively ➡ certainly

possess ➡ own, keep

possessive ➡ greedy, jealous

possessor ➡ owner

possibly ➡ maybe

postcard ➡ letter

poster ➡ picture, advertisement

posterior ➡ back

postlude ➡ conclusion

postman ➡ letter carrier

postmaster ➡ letter carrier

postmistress ➡ letter carrier

postpone ➡ delay

postscript ➡ conclusion

postulate ➡ assume

posy ➡ bouquet, flower

potency ➡ strength

potent ➡ strong

potentate ➡ ruler

potential ➡ possible, latent, possibility

potentiality ➡ possibility

potpourri ➡ mixture, assortment

potter ➡ tinker

n = noun • vb = verb • adj = adjective • adv = adverb • prep = preposition • conj = conjunction

poverty n destitution, want, need, penury, indigence, privation, impoverishment ➡ **hardship**

practical 1. adj matter-of-fact, down-to-earth, realistic, reasonable, rational, sensible, unsentimental ➡ **able** ⇨ *impractical*
2. adj ➡ **useful, efficient**
3. adj ➡ **virtual**

practically adv virtually, effectively, essentially, fundamentally, nearly, basically, principally ➡ **about**

practice 1. vb rehearse, drill, train ➡ **study, learn**
2. vb ➡ **use**
3. n rehearsal, repetition, preparation ➡ **discipline**
4. n ➡ **habit**

praise 1. n applause, acclaim, compliment, approval, adulation, acclamation, kudos, congratulations, flattery ➡ **respect**
2. vb commend, extol, acclaim, laud, compliment, honor, decorate, congratulate, toast, rave ➡ **celebrate, clap, flatter, worship**

praiseworthy adj commendable, laudable, deserving, creditable, estimable, worthy, meritorious

preach vb exhort, sermonize, moralize, proclaim ➡ **teach**

precede vb preface, herald, antedate, introduce ⇨ *follow*

precisely adv exactly, directly, right, due ➡ **correctly, carefully**

If the word you want is not a main entry above, look below to find it.

pouch ➡ bag, pocket

pounce ➡ jump

pound ➡ hit, pen

pour ➡ flow, rain, hurry

pour out ➡ empty

pout ➡ frown, mope

poverty-stricken ➡ poor

powder ➡ grind, snow

powder blue ➡ blue

power ➡ strength, energy, ability, right

powerful ➡ strong, important

powerless ➡ weak

powerlessness ➡ inability

practicable ➡ possible

practical joke ➡ joke

pragmatic ➡ useful

prairie ➡ plain

prank ➡ joke

prate ➡ chatter

prattle ➡ chatter, talk

pray ➡ appeal

prayer ➡ worship

preacher ➡ minister, speaker

preamble ➡ introduction

precarious ➡ unsteady, dangerous

precaution ➡ protection

preceding ➡ before, past

precept ➡ rule

precinct ➡ neighborhood

precious ➡ valuable, expensive, favorite

precious stone ➡ jewel

precipice ➡ cliff

precipitate ➡ sudden, rain

precipitation ➡ rain

precipitous ➡ steep

précis ➡ summary

precise ➡ correct, careful, neat, punctual, explicit

precision ➡ accuracy

precocious ➡ gifted, early

---

predatory *adj* voracious, rapacious, ravenous, bloodthirsty, carnivorous ➡ **greedy**

predict *vb* forecast, foretell, prophesy, prognosticate, project, divine, tell, foresee, augur, portend, presage ➡ **anticipate**

prediction 1. *n* forecast, prognostication
2. *n* prophecy, divination, fortune-telling, augury

predominant *adj* dominant, preeminent, prevalent, prevailing ➡ **important**

prefer *vb* favor, endorse, advocate ➡ **choose, like, want**

preference *n* favorite, partiality, predilection, inclination, proclivity ➡ **choice, tendency**

pregnant 1. *adj* expecting, expectant, with child, gravid
2. *adj* ➡ **meaningful**

prejudice *n* intolerance, bigotry, bias, partiality, predisposition, predilection, favoritism, discrimination, racism, sexism, chauvinism, ageism ➡ **hatred**

prejudiced *adj* biased, unfair, unjust, partial, one-sided, partisan, predisposed, bigoted, intolerant, discriminatory

prepare *vb* develop, provide, ready, plan, adapt, prime, process, refine ➡ **arrange, cook, make, invent**

presence 1. *n* proximity, nearness, closeness ⇨ *absence*
2. *n* attendance, occurrence ➡ **existence** ⇨ *absence*
3. *n* ➡ **bearing, personality**

If the word you want is not a main entry above, look below to find it.

predecessor ➡ ancestor

predicament ➡ trouble

predicate ➡ base

predilection ➡ prejudice, preference

predisposed ➡ prejudiced, ready

predisposition ➡ prejudice

predominantly ➡ chiefly

preeminent ➡ best, predominant

preface ➡ introduction, introduce, precede

preferable ➡ better

preferably ➡ more, instead

preferment ➡ promotion

preferred ➡ favorite

prehistoric ➡ early

preliminary ➡ early

prelude ➡ introduction

premature ➡ early

premier ➡ ruler

premise ➡ theory

premises ➡ property

premium ➡ best, prize

premonition ➡ warning

preoccupation ➡ obsession

preoccupied ➡ absorbed, absentminded

preoccupy ➡ interest

preparation ➡ practice

preparatory school ➡ school

prepared ➡ ready

preponderance ➡ most

preposterous ➡ foolish

prerequisite ➡ necessity

prerogative ➡ right

presage ➡ predict

prescience ➡ foresight

prescribe ➡ order, suggest

prescribed ➡ legal

prescription ➡ medicine, recipe

present 1. *adj* here, on hand
➡ **near** ⇨ *absent*
2. *vb* ➡ **give, offer**
3. *vb* ➡ **introduce**
4. *vb* ➡ **play, show**
5. *n* ➡ **gift**

pretend *vb* feign, affect, simulate, profess ➡ **act, assume, imagine, lie, fake**

pretense 1. *n* affectation, deceit, deception, fabrication, trickery, misrepresentation, fraud ➡ **act, lie, disguise, dishonesty**
2. *n* excuse, pretext, subterfuge ➡ **trick**

pretty *adj* lovely, handsome, attractive, good-looking, fair, becoming, comely, striking ➡ **beautiful, cute** ⇨ *ugly*

prevent *vb* avert, hinder, forestall, check, restrain, thwart, foil, frustrate, deter, inhibit, stunt, hobble, leash ➡ **stop, block, discourage, contain** ⇨ *let*

prey 1. *n* quarry, victim, target
2. *vb* ➡ **eat**
3. *vb* ➡ **cheat**

price *n* charge, expense, cost, fare, payment, amount, fee, consideration, outlay ➡ **worth, bill**

pride 1. *n* self-respect, self-esteem, dignity, self-confidence ➡ **respect**
2. *n* vanity, conceit, arrogance, vainglory, egotism, hubris, narcissism, haughtiness
3. *n* ➡ **pleasure**

priest *n* vicar, bishop, cardinal, pope, pontiff, rabbi ➡ **minister, religious**

If the word you want is not a main entry above, look below to find it.

presentation ➡ **display, introduction, program, delivery**

presenter ➡ **host**

presently ➡ **soon**

preservation ➡ **salvation**

preserve ➡ **save, keep, embalm, park, jelly**

preside ➡ **lead**

president ➡ **ruler**

press ➡ **push, squeeze, iron, urge**

pressing ➡ **urgent**

pressure ➡ **weight, energy, stress, force**

prestidigitator ➡ **magician**

prestige ➡ **fame, respect**

presumably ➡ **apparently, probably**

presume ➡ **assume, dare**

presumption ➡ **theory**

presumptuous ➡ **rude**

presuppose ➡ **assume**

pretentious ➡ **pompous, proud**

preternatural ➡ **supernatural**

pretext ➡ **pretense**

prettiness ➡ **beauty**

prevail ➡ **win, excel, persuade**

prevailing ➡ **predominant**

prevalent ➡ **predominant, common**

prevaricate ➡ **lie**

prevaricator ➡ **liar**

previous ➡ **past**

previously ➡ **once, before**

priceless ➡ **valuable**

prick ➡ **stick**

prickle ➡ **tingle**

---

prim *adj* proper, formal, stiff, wooden, stilted, decorous ➡ **correct, neat, polite**

primitive 1. *adj* ➡ **basic**
2. *adj* ➡ **early**
3. *adj* uncivilized, simple, crude, rough, rustic, unsophisticated, untamed, aboriginal, pristine

principal 1. *adj* ➡ **important**
2. *n* headmaster, master, administrator, superintendent, dean ➡ **boss**
3. *n* ➡ **party**

print 1. *vb* publish, issue, reprint ➡ **write**
2. *vb* imprint, impress, engrave, stamp, emboss, inscribe
3. *n* etching, engraving, woodcut, lithograph, photocopy ➡ **photograph, picture**
4. *n* impression, imprint, indentation, fingerprint, footprint ➡ **track**

5. *n* text, printing, type, typescript, writing

prisoner *n* captive, inmate, detainee, internee, slave, hostage, jailbird (*informal*)

privacy *n* solitude, seclusion, isolation, retirement, withdrawal, confinement, quarantine, segregation ➡ **secrecy**

private 1. *adj* secluded, isolated, remote, withdrawn, insular, quarantined
2. *adj* personal, individual, intimate, own ⇨ **public**
3. *adj* exclusive, restricted, reserved, special ⇨ **public**
4. *adj* ➡ **secret**

prize 1. *n* reward, premium, bonus, trophy, garland, laurel, winnings, purse ➡ **award, gift, booty**
2. *vb* ➡ **appreciate, respect**

If the word you want is not a main entry above, look below to find it.

primal ➡ early

primarily ➡ chiefly

primary ➡ basic, important, early

prime ➡ best, important, top, prepare

prime minister ➡ ruler

primeval ➡ early

primordial ➡ early

prince ➡ ruler

princely ➡ noble

principally ➡ chiefly, practically

principle ➡ rule, belief, cause, virtue

printing ➡ print, handwriting

prior ➡ past, older, religious

prior to ➡ before

prioress ➡ religious

priory ➡ monastery

prison ➡ jail

pristine ➡ clean, new, primitive

privateer ➡ pirate

privation ➡ poverty

privilege ➡ right

prized ➡ valuable

prizewinner ➡ winner

---

probably *adv* presumably, apparently, plausibly, seemingly ➡ **maybe**

Note that **probably** and its synonyms also express a degree of uncertainty about something, but not as much as **maybe** and its synonyms.

problem 1. *n* mystery, puzzle, riddle, dilemma, enigma, ambiguity, conundrum ➡ **contradiction, question**
2. *n* ➡ **trouble**

product 1. *n* merchandise, commodity, goods, wares
2. *n* by product, outgrowth, derivative, derivation, offshoot, spin off ➡ **answer, effect**

productivity *n* turnout, output, production, volume ➡ **growth, efficiency**

profession *n* occupation, employment, appointment, vocation, avocation, calling, career, livelihood, post, position, situation, place, craft, trade ➡ **job, field, business, specialty**

profound *adj* deep, sage, sagacious, intellectual, philosophical, penetrating, discerning, erudite, cerebral ➡ **smart, thoughtful, serious**

If the word you want is not a main entry above, look below to find it.

probability ➡ **possibility**

probable ➡ **likely**

probe ➡ **stick, hunt, study, examine**

proboscis ➡ **nose**

procedure ➡ **method**

proceed ➡ **go, continue**

process ➡ **method, prepare**

procession ➡ **parade**

proclaim ➡ **advertise, preach**

proclamation ➡ **announcement**

proclivity ➡ **tendency, preference**

procrastinate ➡ **delay**

procreate ➡ **reproduce**

procure ➡ **get**

procurement ➡ **acquisition**

prod ➡ **push, urge**

prodigal ➡ **wasteful, abundant**

prodigious ➡ **huge**

prodigy ➡ **genius**

produce ➡ **make, cause, give, show, vegetable**

production ➡ **program,** assembly, productivity

productive ➡ **successful, efficient, fertile**

profanity ➡ **curse**

profess ➡ **pretend, tell**

professor ➡ **teacher, doctor**

proffer ➡ **offer**

proficiency ➡ **ability, efficiency**

proficient ➡ **able, expert, efficient**

profile ➡ **face, description**

profit ➡ **advantage, wage, earn**

profitable ➡ **useful**

profligate ➡ **wasteful**

profoundness ➡ **depth**

profundity ➡ **depth**

profuse ➡ **abundant, thick, rich**

profusion ➡ **abundance**

progenitor ➡ **ancestor**

progeny ➡ **child**

prognosticate ➡ **predict**

prognostication ➡ **prediction**

---

program 1. *n* performance, concert, recital, show, production, broadcast, telecast, presentation, series ➡ **play, movie, entertainment**
2. *n* ➡ **list**
3. *n* ➡ **plan, course**

progress 1. *n* improvement, progression, headway, advance, advancement, momentum ➡ **movement, growth, success**
2. *vb* ➡ **go**

promise 1. *n* oath, vow, word, pledge, assurance, commitment, covenant, guarantee
2. *vb* swear, pledge, vow, assure, warrant ➡ **guarantee**

promote 1. *vb* raise, advance, elevate, graduate, upgrade

2. *vb* ➡ **back, support**
3. *vb* ➡ **advertise**

promotion 1. *n* advancement, preferment, elevation, raise
2. *n* ➡ **advertisement, advertising**

prone 1. *adj* ➡ **likely**
2. *adj* prostrate, flat, supine, recumbent, lying (down), reclining, horizontal
3. *adj* ➡ **vulnerable**

pronounce *vb* enunciate, articulate, utter, vocalize ➡ **say, tell**

proof *n* evidence, testimony, verification, certification, documentation, data, corroboration, confirmation, substantiation, authentication

---

If the word you want is not a main entry above, look below to find it.

progression
➡ progress

progressive ➡ forward, gifted, consecutive, liberal

prohibit ➡ forbid

prohibited ➡ illegal

prohibition ➡ ban

project ➡ plan, job, development, shoot, throw, swell, predict

projected ➡ future

projectile ➡ missile

projection ➡ branch

proliferate
➡ reproduce

proliferation
➡ growth

prolific ➡ fertile

prologue
➡ introduction

prolong ➡ lengthen

prom ➡ dance

prominence ➡ accent

prominent ➡ famous, obvious, important

promiscuous
➡ indiscriminate

promised land
➡ utopia

promontory ➡ cape, cliff

prompt ➡ early, fast, punctual, reminder, cause, urge

promptly ➡ quickly

pronounced
➡ obvious

pronouncement
➡ announcement

pronunciation
➡ accent, delivery

prop ➡ support

propaganda
➡ advertising

propagate
➡ reproduce, plant

propel ➡ shoot, throw, drive

propensity ➡ tendency

proper ➡ fit[1], correct, prim, good, special

properly ➡ well, correctly

proper name ➡ name

property 1. *n* possessions, belongings, effects, goods, assets, holdings, capital, things, stuff ➡ **wealth, acquisition**
2. *n* land, lot, estate, yard, grounds, premises, plot, tract
3. *n* ➡ **quality**

prophet *n* seer, soothsayer, oracle, clairvoyant, medium, fortune teller, astrologer, diviner ➡ **magician**

prosper *vb* flourish, thrive, succeed, benefit, flower ➡ **blossom, grow, excel**

protect 1. *vb* defend, guard, shield, safeguard, fortify, watch, mind, tend ➡ **save, patrol** ⇨ *attack*
2. *vb* shelter, cover, cushion, pad

protection 1. *n* security, safety, defense, caution, precaution, care, safeguard ➡ **support**

2. *n* shelter, refuge, cover, retreat, harbor, haven, sanctuary, asylum, shield, buffer

protest 1. *n* demonstration, strike, sit-in, teach-in, rally ➡ **complaint**
2. *vb* demonstrate, picket, strike, walk out ➡ **complain, object**
3. *vb* ➡ **complain, object, argue**

proud 1. *adj* egotistic, conceited, vain, arrogant, egocentric, haughty, smug, superior, pretentious ➡ **pompous** ⇨ *humble*
2. *adj* ➡ **grand**
3. *adj* ➡ **happy**

provincial 1. *adj* ➡ **rural**
2. *adj* narrow-minded, unsophisticated, parochial, unpolished, intolerant, insular, hidebound ➡ **naive, primitive, mean**

If the word you want is not a main entry above, look below to find it.

prophecy ➡ prediction

prophesy ➡ predict

proportion ➡ balance, size, share

proposal ➡ suggestion

propose ➡ offer, suggest, intend

proposition ➡ suggestion

proprietor ➡ owner

proprietorship ➡ possession

propulsion ➡ energy

prosaic ➡ dull

proscribe ➡ forbid

proscription ➡ ban

prosecute ➡ try

prospect ➡ view, possibility, hunt

prospective ➡ future

prosperity ➡ wealth, welfare, success

prosperous ➡ rich

prostrate ➡ prone

prostration ➡ exhaustion

protected ➡ safe

protective ➡ motherly, fatherly

protector ➡ savior

protocol ➡ ceremony

prototype ➡ model

protract ➡ lengthen

protracted ➡ long

protrude ➡ swell

protrusion ➡ bulge

protuberance ➡ bulge

prove ➡ verify

proverb ➡ saying

proverbial ➡ legendary

provide ➡ supply, prepare

providential ➡ lucky

province ➡ state, field

provision ➡ plan, supply, excerpt

provisional ➡ temporary, experimental

provisions ➡ food

---

pseudonym *n* pen name, alias, stage name, nom de plume, nickname, sobriquet

public 1. *adj* civic, civil, governmental, communal, municipal, federal, social
➡ **common** ⇨ *private*
2. *n* ➡ **people**
3. *n* ➡ **following**

pull 1. *vb* tow, drag, haul, draw, tug, yank, jerk, pluck, attract, bring, tighten, strain ➡ **extract** ⇨ *push*
2. *vb* sprain, strain ➡ **hurt**
3. *n* tug, yank, drag, jerk, wrench
➡ **attraction**

punch 1. *vb* slap, belt, pummel, box
➡ **hit**
2. *n* ➡ **blow**¹

punctual *adj* timely, prompt, precise, expeditious, punctilious ⇨ *late*

punish *vb* discipline, penalize, sentence, correct, fine ➡ **abuse, hurt, hit, scold, whip**

punishment *n* penalty, sentence, penance, deserts, retribution, consequence, discipline ➡ **abuse**

puppet 1. *n* marionette, dummy, mannequin ➡ **doll**
2. *n* ➡ **tool**

If the word you want is not a main entry above, look below to find it.

provocative
➡ interesting

provoke ➡ anger, dare, urge

prow ➡ front

prowess ➡ talent

prowl ➡ sneak

proximity ➡ presence

prudence ➡ foresight, economy

prudent ➡ careful, cheap

prudently ➡ carefully

prune ➡ cut, condense

pry ➡ lift, meddle, spy

prying ➡ curious, interference

psalm ➡ hymn

pseudonymous
➡ anonymous

psyche ➡ mind, soul

psychic
➡ supernatural

psychology ➡ science

psychotic ➡ insane

pub ➡ bar

puberty ➡ childhood

public assistance
➡ welfare

publication ➡ book

publicity
➡ advertising, notice

publicize ➡ advertise

public servant
➡ official

publish ➡ print, write

pucker ➡ wrinkle

pudgy ➡ fat

puerile ➡ childish

puff ➡ wind, smoke, breathe

puff up ➡ swell

pugnacious
➡ belligerent

puke ➡ vomit

pulchritude ➡ beauty

pull out ➡ retreat

pulpit ➡ platform

pulsar ➡ star

pulsate ➡ shake

pulsation ➡ impulse

pulse ➡ rhythm, impulse

pulverize ➡ grind

pummel ➡ punch

pun ➡ joke

punctilious
➡ punctual

puncture ➡ hole, stick

pungent ➡ fragrant, spicy

punk ➡ vandal

punt ➡ kick

puny ➡ weak

pupil ➡ student

puppy ➡ dog

purple *adj, n* violet, magenta, lilac, mauve, plum, lavender

purposely *adv* deliberately, purposefully, intentionally, consciously, knowingly, willfully ⇨ *accidentally*

push 1. *vb* press, shove, impel, thrust, jostle, nudge, elbow, shoulder, shove, slide, thrust, prod, poke, ram, jam, wedge ➡ **move, force** ⇨ *pull*
2. *vb* ➡ **urge**
3. *n* ➡ **blow, impulse**

put *vb* set, lay, park, deposit, plant, position, implant, install, insert ➡ **place**

If the word you want is not a main entry above, look below to find it.

purchase ➡ acquisition, sale, buy

pure ➡ innocent, perfect, natural, real

purify ➡ clean

purity ➡ virtue

purloin ➡ steal

purpose ➡ reason, object, plan, use, intend

purposefully ➡ purposely

purr ➡ hum

purse ➡ bag, wallet, prize

pursue ➡ follow

pursuit ➡ pastime, hunt

pushy ➡ meddlesome

put-down ➡ insult

put off ➡ delay

put out ➡ extinguish

putrefy ➡ decay

putrid ➡ smelly, bad

putter ➡ tinker

put up ➡ house

puzzle ➡ problem, confuse

puzzlement ➡ confusion

puzzle out ➡ solve

puzzling ➡ mysterious

pygmy ➡ midget

pyre ➡ fire

pyrotechnics ➡ fireworks

Q

quality *n* property, characteristic, character, trait, attribute, air, atmosphere, texture, tone ➡ **class, feeling**

queen *n* monarch, sovereign, maharani *(India)*, rani *(India)*, sultana *(Muslim)* ➡ **ruler, empress**

question 1. *n* query, inquiry, interrogation, interrogative ➡ **problem** ⇨ *answer*
2. *n* ➡ **doubt**
3. *n* ➡ **subject**
4. *vb* ➡ **ask**

quickly *adv* speedily, hastily, hurriedly, fast, rapidly, expeditiously, instantaneously, promptly, headlong ➡ **now, soon**

quiet 1. *adj* silent, still, hushed, noiseless, soundless, inaudible, mute, mum, speechless ➡ **low** ⇨ *loud*
2. *n* ➡ **calm**
3. *vb* hush, silence, soften, mute, muffle, stifle, muzzle, gag

quote 1. *vb* cite, repeat, parrot, paraphrase, recite, declaim, render ➡ **mention, say, tell**
2. *n* ➡ **estimate**

If the word you want is not a main entry above, look below to find it.

quack ➡ cheat, hypocrite

quad ➡ court

quadrangle ➡ square, court

quadrilateral ➡ square

quaff ➡ drink

quagmire ➡ swamp

quail ➡ fear, retreat

quaint ➡ strange, cute

quake ➡ shake, fear, vibration, earthquake

qualification ➡ necessity, term

qualified ➡ able, ready

qualify ➡ let, soften

qualm ➡ doubt, nausea

quandary ➡ trouble

quantity ➡ number, size

quarantine ➡ privacy, separate

quarantined ➡ private

quarrel ➡ argue, argument

quarrelsome ➡ unfriendly

quarry ➡ prey, mine

quarter ➡ term, zone, neighborhood, divide, house

quash ➡ subdue, contain

quaver ➡ vibration, shake

quay ➡ dock

queasiness ➡ nausea

queasy ➡ sick

queer ➡ strange, suspicious

quell ➡ contain

quench ➡ extinguish, contain, satisfy

query ➡ question, ask

quest ➡ hunt

questionable ➡ doubtful

queue ➡ braid, row

quibble ➡ argue

quick ➡ fast, agile, smart, alive

quicken ➡ hurry

quill ➡ pen

quilt ➡ blanket

quintessence ➡ essence

quip ➡ joke

quirk ➡ habit

quit ➡ abandon, leave, surrender

quite ➡ completely, very

quiver ➡ shake, vibration

quixotic ➡ impractical

quiz ➡ examination, examine, ask

quota ➡ share

quotation ➡ excerpt, estimate

---

n = noun • *vb* = verb • *adj* = adjective • *adv* = adverb • *prep* = preposition • *conj* = conjunction

R

race 1. *n* run, dash, sprint, relay, marathon, footrace, horse race, steeplechase, derby ➡ **game**
2. *vb* ➡ **run, hurry**
3. *n* ➡ **type**
4. *n* ➡ **humanity**

ragged *adj* tattered, frayed, threadbare, torn, rent ➡ **old, shabby**

rain 1. *n* precipitation, shower, downpour, drizzle, cloudburst, torrent ➡ **storm**

2. *vb* pour, drizzle, sprinkle, shower, teem, precipitate

range 1. *n* extent, scope, spread, reach, compass, sweep, spectrum ➡ **assortment, space, horizon**
2. *n* ➡ **plain**
3. *vb* ➡ **wander**
4. *vb* ➡ **spread**

rare *adj* uncommon, scarce, infrequent, occasional ➡ **special, valuable**

If the word you want is not a main entry above, look below to find it.

rabbi ➡ priest

racetrack ➡ course

rack ➡ shelf

racket ➡ noise

racy ➡ dirty

radiance ➡ light[1]

radiant ➡ bright

radiate ➡ shine, throw

radiation ➡ X ray

radical ➡ excessive, liberal, extremist

radiograph ➡ X ray

raffle ➡ lottery

rafter ➡ beam, board

rag ➡ cloth

ragamuffin ➡ urchin

rage ➡ anger, hysteria, fashion

raging ➡ rough, wild

raid ➡ attack

rail ➡ bar

raincoat ➡ coat

raindrop ➡ drop

rainforest ➡ forest

rainspout ➡ gargoyle

rainstorm ➡ storm

rainy ➡ wet, stormy

raise ➡ lift, grow, adopt, build, broach, promote, promotion

raison d'être ➡ basis

rajah ➡ king

rake ➡ dig, rascal

rally ➡ mobilize, protest

ram ➡ push

ramble ➡ wander, chatter

rambling ➡ indirect

rambunctious ➡ loud

ramp ➡ channel

rampage ➡ disturbance

rampant ➡ wild

rampart ➡ wall

ranch ➡ farm

rancher ➡ farmer

ranching ➡ farming

rancid ➡ sour, smelly, bad

random ➡ arbitrary

R & R ➡ vacation

range ➡ plain

rani ➡ queen

rank ➡ grade, row, arrange, smelly

rankle ➡ bother

ransack ➡ pillage, hunt

ransom ➡ recover

rant ➡ yell

rap ➡ knock, talk

rapacious ➡ greedy, predatory

rapid ➡ fast, sharp

rapidity ➡ speed

rapidly ➡ quickly

rapier ➡ sword

rapport ➡ relationship

rapture ➡ pleasure

rarely ➡ seldom

rarity ➡ miracle

---

rascal *n* scoundrel, villain, knave, wretch, scamp, imp, sneak, charlatan, fraud, swindler, rogue, rake, libertine, lecher ➡ **bully, criminal**

read 1. *vb* peruse, skim, scan, browse ➡ **study**
2. *vb* comprehend, decipher, decode, perceive
3. *vb* indicate, register, record ➡ **show**

ready 1. *adj* prepared, set, qualified, ripe, equipped ➡ **available**
2. *adj* willing, disposed, predisposed ➡ **eager, likely**
3. *vb* ➡ **prepare**

real 1. *adj* actual, material, tangible, substantive, concrete, objective, solid, true, palpable ➡ **physical** ⇨ *imaginary*
2. *adj* actual, genuine, authentic, bona fide, veritable, literal, legitimate, pure ➡ **natural** ⇨ *fake*

really 1. *adv* actually, genuinely, literally, indeed, veritably ➡ **certainly**
2. *adv* ➡ **very**

reason 1. *n* purpose, cause, motive, explanation, call, grounds, need, rationale ➡ **necessity, incentive, justification**
2. *n* logic, reasoning, thinking, induction, deduction, analysis ➡ **wisdom**
3. *vb* ➡ **think, infer**
4. *n* sanity, mental health, lucidity, saneness

If the word you want is not a main entry above, look below to find it.

rascality ➡ **mischief**

rash ➡ **thoughtless, imprudent, epidemic**

rasp ➡ **squeak**

raspy ➡ **hoarse**

rate ➡ **speed, deserve**

rather ➡ **very, more, instead**

ratification ➡ **approval**

ratify ➡ **approve**

ratio ➡ **share**

ration ➡ **share, budget**

rational ➡ **practical, sane**

rationale ➡ **reason**

rations ➡ **food**

rattle ➡ **embarrass, bang**

raucous ➡ **loud**

ravage ➡ **destroy, attack**

rave ➡ **yell, praise, good**

raven ➡ **black**

ravenous ➡ **hungry, predatory**

ravine ➡ **canyon**

ravishing ➡ **beautiful**

raw ➡ **natural, cold, sore**

rawhide ➡ **hide**

ray ➡ **light¹**

raze ➡ **destroy**

razor ➡ **knife**

reach ➡ **come, touch, range**

react ➡ **answer**

reaction ➡ **answer**

reactionary ➡ **conservative**

readable ➡ **legible**

readers ➡ **audience**

reading ➡ **tryout**

realign ➡ **straighten**

realistic ➡ **practical, explicit**

reality ➡ **existence, certainty**

realize ➡ **learn, know, earn**

realm ➡ **country, field**

reap ➡ **cut, gather**

reappear ➡ **return**

reappearance ➡ **return**

rear ➡ **back, adopt, grow, lift, tower**

rearend ➡ **back, collide**

rearward ➡ **backward**

rebel 1. *vb* revolt, mutiny, resist, defy ➡ **face, dare**
2. *n* revolutionary, insurgent, mutineer, subversive, dissident, freedom fighter, traitor, turncoat ➡ **extremist**

rebellious *adj* disobedient, mutinous, defiant, insubordinate, seditious

receive 1. *vb* accept, admit, take, inherit, greet ➡ **get** ⇨ *give, refuse*
2. *vb* ➡ **welcome, entertain**

recently *adv* lately, newly, just, latterly

recipe *n* formula, directions, instructions, prescription ➡ **plan**

recover *vb* regain, retrieve, recoup, reclaim, redeem, ransom ➡ **find, save**

If the word you want is not a main entry above, look below to find it.

reasonable ➡ practical, sane, possible, cheap

reasoning ➡ reason

reassure ➡ comfort

reawaken ➡ renew

reawakening ➡ revival

rebate ➡ refund

rebellion ➡ revolution, disobedience

rebirth ➡ revival

rebound ➡ reflect, return

rebuff ➡ rejection, refuse

rebuild ➡ fix

rebuke ➡ scold

rebut ➡ disprove

recall ➡ remember, memory

recapitulate ➡ repeat

recede ➡ retreat

receipt ➡ ticket, possession

receivable ➡ due

recent ➡ new, modern

receptacle ➡ container

reception ➡ welcome, party, treatment

recess ➡ break, vacation, bay

recession ➡ depression

reciprocate ➡ alternate, answer

reciprocation ➡ answer

recital ➡ program

recite ➡ quote, tell

reckless ➡ thoughtless, wasteful

reckon ➡ guess, estimate

reckoning ➡ score, addition

reclaim ➡ recover

recline ➡ lie

reclining ➡ prone

recluse ➡ hermit

recognition ➡ gratitude

recognize ➡ remember, distinguish, know

recoil ➡ retreat, jump

recollect ➡ remember

recollection ➡ memory

recommence ➡ continue

recommend ➡ suggest, approve

recommendation ➡ advice, suggestion

recompense ➡ pay

reconcile ➡ correct, decide

reconciliation ➡ peace

recondition ➡ fix

reconnoiter ➡ patrol

record ➡ document, list, write, read

recount ➡ describe, repeat

recoup ➡ recover

recourse ➡ choice

recovery ➡ return, cure

recreate ➡ play

recreation ➡ game, leisure, entertainment, play

recreational area ➡ park

recreation center ➡ gymnasium

recreation room ➡ den

rec room ➡ den

recruit ➡ soldier, hire

rectangle ➡ square

rectangular ➡ square

rectification ➡ correction

rectify ➡ correct

rectilinear ➡ square

rector ➡ minister

recumbent ➡ prone

➡ = synonym cross-reference • ⇨ = antonym cross-reference

red 1. *adj, n* pink, scarlet, crimson, maroon, vermilion, carmine, ruby, rose
2. *adj* ruddy, rosy, flushed, florid, blushing

reflect 1. *vb* echo, mirror, ricochet, rebound, bounce
2. *vb* ➡ **consider, meditate**

refrigerator *n* icebox, fridge, freezer, cooler

refund 1. *vb* reimburse, repay, remit, compensate ➡ **pay**

2. *n* reimbursement, repayment, compensation, rebate

refuse 1. *vb* deny, reject, decline, dismiss, disapprove, spurn, repudiate, rebuff, snub, scorn, flout ➡ **deprive, repel**
2. *n* ➡ **trash**

regret 1. *vb* repent, apologize, bewail, bemoan, lament, deplore, rue ➡ **grieve**
2. *n* compunction, repentance ➡ **disappointment, sorrow, shame**

If the word you want is not a main entry above, look below to find it.

recuperate ➡ rest

recuperation ➡ cure

recur ➡ repeat, return, happen

recurrence ➡ return, relapse

recurrent ➡ frequent, periodic

recurrently ➡ often

recycling center ➡ dump

redcap ➡ porter

redden ➡ blush

redecorate ➡ decorate

redecoration ➡ decoration

redeem ➡ balance, recover

redeemer ➡ savior

redemption ➡ salvation

redirect ➡ detour

redo ➡ repeat

redolent ➡ fragrant

redress ➡ correct

reduce ➡ decrease

reduced ➡ less

reduction ➡ subtraction, drop, bargain, model

redundant ➡ unnecessary, talkative

reduplicate ➡ repeat

reek ➡ smell

reel ➡ swing

reestablish ➡ renew

referee ➡ judge, negotiate

referendum ➡ vote

refer to ➡ mention, concern, use

refill ➡ renew

refine ➡ prepare

refinement ➡ class, civilization

reflective ➡ thoughtful

reflector ➡ mirror

reflex ➡ automatic, habit

reform ➡ correct

reformatory ➡ jail

reformist ➡ liberal

refrain ➡ abstain, chorus, stanza

refresh ➡ renew

refreshment ➡ meal, food, drink

refrigerate ➡ cool

refuge ➡ protection, park

refugee ➡ exile

refurbish ➡ decorate

refusal ➡ rejection

refute ➡ contradict, disprove

regain ➡ recover

regal ➡ noble, grand

regale ➡ entertain

regard ➡ look, notice, respect, concern

regarding ➡ about

regardless ➡ anyway

regime ➡ government

regimen ➡ discipline

regimentation ➡ discipline

region ➡ zone, place

register ➡ read, join, list, table, cash register

registration ➡ license

regress ➡ relapse

regression ➡ relapse

regressive ➡ backward

regressively ➡ backward

regrets ➡ apology

regrettable ➡ unfortunate

---

regularly *adv* constantly, invariably, always, ever, continually, habitually, routinely, religiously, naturally, typically ➡ **often, usually, forever**

rejection *n* refusal, rebuff, denial, dismissal, renunciation, repudiation, veto

relapse 1. *vb* regress, backslide, revert, deteriorate, lapse, retrogress, worsen
2. *n* regression, reversion, recurrence, reverse, setback

relationship *n* relation, kinship, affinity, rapport, compatibility ➡ **link, friendship**

relevance *n* connection, bearing, significance, pertinence ➡ **importance**

relevant *adj* pertinent, germane, apposite, applicable, apropos, related, relative ➡ **fit**

reliable *adj* dependable, trustworthy, responsible, reputable, unimpeachable, solid, conscientious, sure, surefire ➡ **faithful, able, indisputable**

relieve 1. *vb* alleviate, ease, soothe, lessen, lighten, mitigate, allay ➡ **help, please**
2. *vb* dismiss, replace, discharge, substitute, excuse ➡ **free**

religion 1. *n* faith, mythology, theology, religiosity, spirituality, orthodoxy ➡ **belief, philosophy**
2. *n* denomination, sect, order, cult

If the word you want is not a main entry above, look below to find it.

regular ➡ usual, frequent, straight, patron

regulate ➡ adjust, control

regulation ➡ rule

regurgitate ➡ vomit

rehabilitation ➡ cure

rehabilitation center ➡ hospital

rehash ➡ repeat

rehearsal ➡ practice

rehearse ➡ practice, repeat

reign ➡ govern

reimburse ➡ refund

reimbursement ➡ refund, return

rein ➡ rope

reinforce ➡ strengthen

reinforcement ➡ support

reins ➡ wheel

reiterate ➡ repeat

reject ➡ refuse, exclude, discard

rejected ➡ abandoned

rejoice ➡ celebrate

rejoinder ➡ answer

rejuvenate ➡ renew

rejuvenation ➡ revival

rekindle ➡ renew

relate ➡ tell, belong

related ➡ relevant

relating to ➡ about

relation ➡ family, relationship

relative ➡ family, relevant

relax ➡ calm, rest

relaxation ➡ comfort, leisure, rest

relaxed ➡ calm

relay ➡ race, broadcast

release ➡ free

relegate ➡ entrust

relent ➡ surrender

relentless ➡ continual, mean

relic ➡ antique

relief ➡ help

➡ = synonym cross-reference • ⇨ = antonym cross-reference

religious 1. *adj* devout, pious, spiritual, orthodox, godly, reverent, God-fearing, reverential, churchgoing ➡ **faithful**
2. *adj* sacred, divine, ecclesiastical, clerical, liturgical, theological ➡ **holy**
3. *n* monk, friar, brother, abbot, prior, nun, sister, abbess, prioress ➡ **priest, minister**

reluctant *adj* hesitant, unwilling, grudging, disinclined, loath, averse, diffident, squeamish

remainder *n* remains, rest, remnant, residue, balance, surplus

remark 1. *n* comment, statement, mention, observation, commentary, utterance ➡ **saying**

2. *vb* ➡ **say**
3. *vb* ➡ **see**

remember *vb* recall, recollect, reminisce, remind, recognize, commemorate, memorialize ➡ **know, learn** ⇨ *forget*

reminder 1. *n* hint, cue, notice, prompt ➡ **warning, letter**
2. *n* souvenir, memento, token, remembrance, keepsake, memorial

renew 1. *vb* restore, revive, rejuvenate, refresh, reawaken, invigorate, reestablish, rekindle, update ➡ **continue**
2. *vb* refill, replenish, replace, restock
3. *vb* ➡ **fix**

If the word you want is not a main entry above, look below to find it.

religiosity ➡ religion

religiously ➡ regularly

relinquish ➡ surrender

relish ➡ like, appreciate, spice

relocate ➡ move

rely ➡ depend

remain ➡ wait, continue

remains ➡ remainder, body

remand ➡ jail

remarkable ➡ great, special

remedial ➡ medicinal

remedy ➡ cure, correction, heal, correct

remembrance ➡ reminder, memory

remind ➡ remember

reminisce ➡ remember

reminiscence ➡ memory

remiss ➡ negligent

remission ➡ forgiveness

remit ➡ refund

remnant ➡ remainder, cloth

remorse ➡ shame

remorseful ➡ sorry

remote ➡ far, foreign, private, cool

removal ➡ suspension, movement

remove ➡ move, subtract, exclude, oust, empty, extract, shed

removed ➡ far

remunerate ➡ pay

renaissance ➡ revival

rend ➡ rip

render ➡ quote, translate, give, act, do

rendezvous ➡ meeting, gather

rendition ➡ translation

renegade ➡ runaway

renewal ➡ revival

renounce ➡ abstain, abandon

renovate ➡ fix

renovation ➡ repair

renown ➡ fame

renowned ➡ famous

rent ➡ hire, borrow, ragged, rip

rental ➡ loan

renter ➡ occupant

renunciation ➡ rejection, surrender

repair 1. *n* adjustment, improvement, renovation, restoration, patch, plug, mend, service, servicing ➡ **correction**
2. *vb* ➡ **fix**

repeat 1. *vb* redo, replicate, duplicate, reduplicate ➡ **reproduce**
2. *vb* recur, reoccur
3. *vb* reiterate, restate, recapitulate, echo, rehearse, rehash, recount ➡ **quote**

repel 1. *vb* repulse, foil, ward off, stave off, fend off, withstand, parry ➡ **refuse**
2. *vb* ➡ **disgust**

report 1. *n* essay, paper, composition, theme, treatise, thesis, dissertation, article ➡ **announcement, speech, story, study**

2. *n* ➡ **bang**
3. *vb* ➡ **tell**

reporter *n* journalist, correspondent, newspaperman, newspaperwoman, newsman, newswoman, newscaster, anchor ➡ **writer**
Note that **reporters** *and other newspeople are referred to as a group as* the press, the media, *and the* fourth estate.

reproduce 1. *vb* copy, duplicate, photocopy, clone ➡ **imitate**
2. *vb* procreate, breed, propagate, multiply, proliferate, generate, beget, spawn, hatch

reptile *n* reptilian, amphibian, lizard ➡ **snake, animal**

If the word you want is not a main entry above, look below to find it.

reoccur ➡ repeat, return

reoccurrence ➡ return

repairman ➡ mechanic

repair shop ➡ garage

reparation ➡ correction

repast ➡ meal, feast

repay ➡ refund, revenge

repayment ➡ refund, return, revenge

repeal ➡ abolish

repeatedly ➡ often

repellent ➡ ugly

repent ➡ regret

repentance ➡ regret

repentant ➡ sorry

repetition ➡ practice

repetitious ➡ talkative

replace ➡ renew, change, relieve, follow

replacement ➡ alternate

replenish ➡ renew

replete ➡ full

replica ➡ duplicate

replicate ➡ repeat

reply ➡ answer

repose ➡ peace, sleep, leisure, rest, comfort, lie

repository ➡ bank

represent ➡ describe, embody

representation ➡ picture, model, example

representative ➡ example, agent

repress ➡ abuse, contain

repression ➡ tyranny

reprieve ➡ forgiveness

reprimand ➡ scold

reprint ➡ print

reproach ➡ scold, complaint

reproduction ➡ copy

reprove ➡ scold

reptilian ➡ reptile

---

reputation n status, position, repute, estimation, character, name

resemble vb look like, take after, match, approximate, favor, correspond

resolute adj strong-minded, determined, resolved, steadfast, unwavering, staunch, unyielding, adamant, uncompromising, assured, decisive ➡ **brave, faithful, stubborn**

respect 1. n admiration, honor, reverence, dignity, homage, esteem, regard, estimation, deference, courtesy, awe, wonder, prestige ➡ **pride**
2. vb esteem, admire, revere, value, prize, cherish ➡ **appreciate**
3. vb ➡ **keep**

rest 1. vb relax, repose, unwind, recuperate, lounge, loaf, laze, idle, vegetate (*informal*) ➡ **sleep, lie**
2. vb ➡ **depend**
3. n relaxation, repose, ease ➡ **sleep, break, vacation**
4. n ➡ **remainder**

If the word you want is not a main entry above, look below to find it.

republic ➡ country

repudiate ➡ refuse

repudiation ➡ rejection

repugnance ➡ disgust

repugnant ➡ ugly

repulse ➡ repel

repulsive ➡ ugly, bad

reputable ➡ good, reliable

repute ➡ reputation

reputedly ➡ apparently

request ➡ ask, appeal, invitation

requiem ➡ dirge

require ➡ force, need, insist

required ➡ necessary

requirement ➡ necessity

requisite ➡ necessary, necessity

requite ➡ revenge

rescind ➡ abolish

rescue ➡ save, escape

rescuer ➡ savior

research ➡ study

resemblance ➡ similarity

resent ➡ envy

resentful ➡ jealous

resentment ➡ envy

reservation ➡ park, doubt, term

reserve ➡ park, supply

reserved ➡ shy, private, cool

reservoir ➡ well, lake, supply

reside ➡ live[1]

residence ➡ home

resident ➡ citizen, occupant

residential ➡ family

residue ➡ remainder

resign ➡ surrender, abandon

resignation ➡ surrender

resigned ➡ passive

resilient ➡ tough, flexible

resist ➡ rebel, fight

resistance ➡ fight, friction

resistant ➡ unbreakable

resolution ➡ will, answer, decision, clarity

resolve ➡ decide, solve, will

resolved ➡ resolute

resonant ➡ loud

resort ➡ hotel

resort to ➡ use

resound ➡ ring

resounding ➡ loud

resource ➡ support

resourceful ➡ ambitious

resources ➡ budget

respectable ➡ correct, good

respectful ➡ good

respective ➡ special

respiration ➡ breath

respire ➡ breathe

respite ➡ break, vacation

resplendent ➡ rich

respond ➡ answer

response ➡ answer

responsibility ➡ duty, guilt

responsible ➡ reliable, guilty

restate ➡ repeat

restaurant *n* café, inn, deli, diner, cafeteria, tavern, luncheonette, bistro, pizzeria, canteen, tearoom, coffeehouse

retreat 1. *vb* withdraw, retire, recede, ebb, back out, back down, recoil, shrink, quail, pull out ➡ **abandon, leave**
2. *n* ➡ **protection**
3. *n* ➡ **hotel**

return 1. *vb* come back, go back, revisit, recur, reoccur, resurface, reappear, rebound ➡ **renew**
2. *n* arrival, homecoming, reappearance, recurrence, reoccurrence, resurgence
3. *n* recovery, restoration, restitution, reimbursement, repayment
4. *n* ➡ **wage**

reveal 1. *vb* disclose, divulge, confess, bare, betray ➡ **discover** ⇨ *hide*
2. *vb* expose, uncover, unveil, unearth ➡ **show**

revenge 1. *n* vengeance, retaliation, repayment, compensation, satisfaction, vindication
2. *vb* avenge, retaliate, repay, requite, vindicate

revengeful *adj* vindictive, vengeful, avenging, retaliatory, spiteful ➡ **mean**

If the word you want is not a main entry above, look below to find it.

restful ➡ comfortable

resting ➡ asleep

restitution ➡ return

restless ➡ nervous

restock ➡ renew

restoration ➡ repair, return

restore ➡ fix, renew

restrain ➡ prevent, contain

restraint ➡ bond

restrict ➡ bar

restricted ➡ finite, private

restriction ➡ ban, term

restroom ➡ bathroom

result ➡ effect, answer

resume ➡ continue

resurface ➡ return

resurgence ➡ return

resurrection ➡ revival

retail ➡ sell

retain ➡ keep, own

retainer ➡ servant

retaliate ➡ revenge

retaliation ➡ revenge

retaliatory ➡ revengeful

retard ➡ delay

retch ➡ vomit

retinue ➡ court, following

retire ➡ retreat

retirement ➡ privacy

retiring ➡ shy

retort ➡ answer

retract ➡ extract

retribution ➡ punishment

retrieve ➡ recover, find

retrograde ➡ backward

retrogress ➡ relapse

reunion ➡ meeting

revel ➡ celebrate

revelation ➡ announcement

revelry ➡ party

revenue ➡ money, wage

revere ➡ respect, love, worship

reverence ➡ respect, worship

reverent ➡ religious

reverential ➡ religious

reverie ➡ dream

reverse ➡ back, opposite, relapse, change

reversed ➡ backward, upside down

reversion ➡ relapse

revert ➡ relapse

revival *n* rebirth, renaissance, resurrection, renewal, reawakening, rejuvenation, revitalization

revolution 1. *n* rebellion, revolt, insurrection, uprising, coup, coup d'état, insurgence
➡ **treason, disturbance**
2. *n* ➡ **change**
3. *n* ➡ **circle**

rhythm *n* beat, cadence, meter, tempo, time, measure, swing, pulse

rich 1. *adj* wealthy, affluent, prosperous, well-to-do, moneyed, well-off, comfortable, posh
➡ **successful** ⇨ *poor*
2. *adj* opulent, resplendent, ornate, lavish, lush, luxurious, profuse
➡ **grand, fashionable, expensive, fancy**
3. *adj* sweet, sugary, creamy, buttery, fattening, luscious, succulent,

cloying, saccharine, honeyed
➡ **delicious**
4. *n* ➡ **aristocracy**

rider 1. *n* passenger, hitchhiker, cyclist, bicyclist, motorcyclist
2. *n* jockey, equestrian, horseman, horsewoman
3. *n* ➡ **addition**

ridicule 1. *n* derision, mockery, scorn, disdain ➡ **laughter**
2. *vb* jeer, belittle, deprecate, disparage, mock, deride, scoff, gibe
➡ **insult**

right 1. *n* power, privilege, prerogative, authority, license
➡ **freedom**
2. *adj* ➡ **correct, fit, fair** ⇨ *wrong*
3. *adv* ➡ **correctly**
4. *adv* ➡ **soon**
5. *adv* ➡ **precisely**

If the word you want is not a main entry above, look below to find it.

review ➡ study
reviewer ➡ judge
revile ➡ curse
revise ➡ correct
revision ➡ correction
revisit ➡ return
revitalization
➡ revival
revive ➡ renew
revoke ➡ abolish
revolt ➡ revolution, rebel, disgust

revolting ➡ ugly
revolutionary ➡ rebel
revolve ➡ turn
revolver ➡ gun
revulsion ➡ hatred, disgust
reward ➡ prize, pay, tip
rhetorical
➡ theoretical
rhetorician ➡ speaker
rhyme ➡ poem
rhythmical ➡ musical

rib ➡ bar
ribald ➡ dirty
ribbon ➡ band, award
ribcage ➡ chest
ribs ➡ chest
riches ➡ wealth
rickety ➡ weak
ricochet ➡ reflect
rid ➡ exclude
riddle ➡ problem, stick
ride ➡ drive
ridge ➡ mountain, hill

ridiculous ➡ foolish, funny
rifle ➡ steal, gun
rift ➡ break
rig ➡ supply, tinker
right away ➡ now
righteous ➡ good
right-wing
➡ conservative
rigid ➡ firm
rigorous ➡ hard, strict
rile ➡ anger

ring 1. *n* hoop, circlet ➡ **band, circle**
2. *n* chime, knell, toll, peal, clang, jingle, jangle, tinkle, clang, tintinnabulation ➡ **noise**
3. *n* ➡ **group**
4. *vb* circle, encircle, encompass, surround, enclose, loop, gird
5. *vb* resound, peal, knell, chime, toll, jingle, jangle, clang, bong, ding, sound, tinkle
6. *vb* ➡ **call**

rip 1. *vb* tear, rend, shred ➡ **cut, separate**
2. *n* tear, rent ➡ **hole, cut**

river 1. *n* stream, creek, brook, rivulet, tributary, estuary
2. *n* ➡ **flood**
Both **creek** and **brook** are *widely used terms for a small stream. Both*

words often refer to streams of the same size, but some people use **brook** *to refer to a stream smaller than one they would call a* **creek**.

road *n* street, avenue, boulevard, thoroughfare, artery, roadway, lane, alley ➡ **highway, path**

rock 1. *n* stone, pebble, boulder, gravel, cobblestone ➡ **jewel**
2. *vb* ➡ **swing**

role *n* character, part, portrayal, bit ➡ **function**

room 1. *n* chamber, apartment, salon, suite, lodging, flat, gallery ➡ **living room, kitchen, bedroom, dining room, bathroom, den, basement, hall, attic**
2. *n* ➡ **space**
3. *vb* ➡ **live¹**

If the word you want is not a main entry above, look below to find it.

rim ➡ edge
rind ➡ peel
ringlet ➡ lock
rinse ➡ clean, wet, cleaning
riot ➡ disturbance
ripe ➡ ready, adult
ripen ➡ grow
riposte ➡ answer
ripple ➡ wave, rustle
rise ➡ ascend, climb, appear, tower, slant, growth
riser ➡ platform

risk ➡ danger, bet, dare, jeopardize
risky ➡ dangerous
risqué ➡ dirty
rite ➡ ceremony
ritual ➡ ceremony
rival ➡ enemy, opponent, competitive, compete
rivalry ➡ competition
rivet ➡ nail
riveting ➡ exciting
rivulet ➡ river
RN ➡ nurse

roadblock ➡ barrier
roadway ➡ road
roam ➡ wander, travel
roar ➡ laugh, cry
roast ➡ cook
roasting ➡ hot
rob ➡ steal, deprive
robber ➡ criminal
robbery ➡ theft
robe ➡ bathrobe, dress
robust ➡ strong
rocket ➡ missile
rocket scientist ➡ genius

rockslide ➡ avalanche
rocky ➡ hard
rod ➡ bar
roe ➡ egg
Roentgen ray ➡ X ray
rogue ➡ rascal
roll ➡ bread, swing, mix
roller ➡ wheel, wave
romance ➡ court
romantic ➡ loving, idealistic, idealist
romp ➡ play, dance
roomy ➡ comfortable

---

rope n line, lasso, lariat, cable, wire, guy, painter, tether, leash, rein, strap ➡ **string**

rough 1. adj coarse, uneven, rugged, irregular, bumpy, jagged, crumpled, rumpled, harsh, scratchy ➡ **hoarse**
2. adj choppy, raging, ruffled, wild ➡ **stormy**
3. adj ➡ **rude, primitive**
4. adj ➡ **hard**
5. adj ➡ **approximate**

round 1. adj circular, spherical, cylindrical, oval, globular, rotund
2. adv ➡ **about**
3. n circuit, cycle, loop, beat, turn ➡ **period**

row 1. n line, string, file, rank, column, chain, queue, series, sequence
2. n ➡ **argument**
3. vb ➡ **paddle**

rub 1. vb scrape, chafe, graze, skim, brush, abrade, scuff, scratch ➡ **grind**
2. vb knead, massage, smooth, stroke ➡ **touch, pet**
3. vb daub, smear, spread, slather, anoint, dab, swab

rubber band n elastic, elastic band, gum band

rude adj impolite, insolent, discourteous, ungracious, impertinent, impudent, fresh, uncouth, crude, coarse, crass, bold, brash, presumptuous, audacious, sassy, forward, surly, pert, flip, disrespectful, irreverent, cheeky ➡ **abrupt, cross, thoughtless** ⇨ *polite*

rudeness n discourtesy, insolence, vulgarity, impudence, disrespect, crudity, crudeness, coarseness, boorishness

If the word you want is not a main entry above, look below to find it.

roost ➡ seat	rotten ➡ bad	routinely ➡ regularly	rubble ➡ trash
root ➡ base, essence, clap	rotund ➡ round	rove ➡ wander	ruby ➡ red
rose ➡ red	roughly ➡ about	rover ➡ pedestrian	ruddy ➡ red
roster ➡ list	roundabout ➡ indirect	rowdy ➡ loud, bully	rudiment ➡ basis
rostrum ➡ platform	rouse ➡ wake	royal ➡ noble	rudimentary ➡ basic
rosy ➡ red	rousing ➡ exciting	royal blue ➡ blue	rue ➡ grieve, regret
rot ➡ decay, corrode, fungus	rout ➡ defeat	royal household ➡ court	ruffian ➡ bully
rotate ➡ turn	route ➡ course	rubbing ➡ friction	ruffle ➡ disturb
	routine ➡ habit, method, act, average	rubbish ➡ trash	ruffled ➡ rough

rug 1. *n* carpet, mat, carpeting, runner
2. *n* ➡ **wig**

ruin 1. *vb* ➡ **destroy**
2. *vb* impoverish, bankrupt, beggar
3. *n* ➡ **damage**
4. *n* ➡ **fate**

rule 1. *n* law, regulation, custom, principle, axiom, guideline, code, precept, canon, ultimatum ➡ **act, habit**
2. *n* command, control, authority, mastery, sway, sovereignty, charge, government, jurisdiction, dominion ➡ **leadership**
3. *n* ➡ **measure**
4. *vb* ➡ **govern**
5. *vb* ➡ **decide**

ruler *n* potentate, prince, lord, governor, leader, president, premier, prime minister ➡ **king, queen, emperor, empress, dictator**

rumor *n* gossip, hearsay, scandal, talk

run 1. *vb* jog, trot, dash, sprint, bolt, dart, streak, gallop, lope, canter ➡ **hurry, race**
2. *vb* ➡ **escape, leave**
3. *vb* ➡ **lead**
4. *vb* ➡ **operate**
5. *vb* ➡ **play**
6. *vb* ➡ **flow**
7. *n* ➡ **race**

runaway *n* fugitive, deserter, escapee, renegade, defector, truant, absentee

rural *adj* rustic, pastoral, provincial, backwoods ➡ **farming** ⇨ *urban*

rustle 1. *n* whisper, swish, ripple, crackle, patter, stir
2. *vb* whisper, swish, crackle, sigh, murmur, shuffle, flutter

rusty *adj* corroded, decayed ➡ **old**

If the word you want is not a main entry above, look below to find it.

rugged ➡ rough, tough, unbreakable

ruinous ➡ destructive

ruling ➡ decision

rumble ➡ bang, fight

rummage ➡ hunt

rump ➡ back

rumple ➡ wrinkle, disturb

rumpled ➡ rough

rundown ➡ old, summary

rung ➡ step

run-in ➡ meeting

runner ➡ messenger, shoot, rug

runway ➡ path

rupture ➡ break, hole

ruse ➡ trick

rush ➡ hurry, flood

rust ➡ corrode, fungus

rustic ➡ rural, primitive

rut ➡ channel

ruth ➡ pity

ruthless ➡ mean

S

sad *adj* unhappy, miserable, depressed, gloomy, dismal, melancholy, blue, downhearted, downcast, dejected, despondent, doleful, forlorn, moody, down, low, bad, glum ➡ **lonely, pitiful, sorry, thoughtful, pessimistic** ⇨ *happy*

sadden *vb* dishearten, disappoint, grieve, sorrow, oppress, depress, desolate

safe 1. *adj* secure, protected, harmless, snug, guarded, impregnable, invulnerable, immune ➡ **invincible** ⇨ *dangerous*
2. *n* vault, strongbox, chest, coffer, treasury, safe-deposit box ➡ **cash register**

sailor *n* seaman, mariner, seafarer, boatman, yachtsman, midshipman ➡ **soldier**

sale 1. *n* deal, transaction, purchase, marketing, auction ➡ **trade**
2. *n* bargain, deal, clearance, closeout, discount

salty 1. *adj* briny, brackish, saline
2. *adj* ➡ **dirty**

salvation *n* redemption, deliverance, preservation, liberation, emancipation, delivery ➡ **forgiveness, escape**

If the word you want is not a main entry above, look below to find it.

sabbatical ➡ vacation

saber ➡ sword

sable ➡ black, dark

sabotage ➡ damage, weaken

sac ➡ pocket

saccharine ➡ rich

sachem ➡ king

sack ➡ bag, base, pillage, attack, fire

sacramental ➡ holy

sacred ➡ holy, religious

sacrifice ➡ surrender, kill, gift

sadistic ➡ gruesome

sadness ➡ sorrow

safe-deposit box ➡ safe

safeguard ➡ protect, protection

safety ➡ protection

safety pin ➡ pin

saffron ➡ yellow

sag ➡ slant, weaken

saga ➡ story

sagacious ➡ profound

sagacity ➡ wisdom

sage ➡ philosopher, herb, profound

sail ➡ blow², fly, travel, pilot

sailing ➡ nautical

sake ➡ object

salaam ➡ good-bye

salary ➡ wage

salesman ➡ seller

salesperson ➡ seller

sales slip ➡ ticket

saleswoman ➡ seller

saline ➡ salty

sallow ➡ pale

sally ➡ attack, hurry

salmon ➡ orange

salon ➡ gallery, living room, room

saloon ➡ bar

salutation ➡ welcome

salute ➡ wave, welcome

salvage ➡ save

salver ➡ tray

same *adj* identical, equal, equivalent, corresponding, matching, uniform, consistent, like ➡ **alike** ⇨ *different*

sane *adj* rational, sensible, reasonable, lucid, balanced, sound ⇨ *insane*

sarcastic *adj* scornful, snide, ironic, ironical, satiric, satirical, sardonic, caustic, derisive

satisfaction 1. *n* gratification, fulfillment, contentment ➡ **pleasure** 2. *n* ➡ **revenge**

satisfied *adj* content, contented, self-satisfied, complacent ➡ **happy**

satisfy 1. *vb* appease, slake, quench, sate, satiate ➡ **please, relieve, pacify** 2. *vb* ➡ **persuade** 3. *vb* suffice, serve, do, fulfill, answer

save 1. *vb* keep, preserve, conserve, maintain, hoard, stockpile, stash ➡ **gather** ⇨ *discard, abolish, waste* 2. *vb* rescue, deliver, salvage, spare ➡ **free, protect** 3. *vb* ➡ **bank** 4. *prep* ➡ **but**

savior *n* rescuer, deliverer, protector, hero, champion, redeemer, lifesaver ➡ **guardian**

If the word you want is not a main entry above, look below to find it.

sameness ➡ unity

sample ➡ example, try

sampling ➡ study

sanatorium ➡ hospital

sanctify ➡ bless, worship

sanctimonious ➡ self-righteous

sanction ➡ approve, forbid, permission, ban

sanctioned ➡ legal

sanctuary ➡ protection

sand ➡ dirt

sandy ➡ yellow

saneness ➡ reason

sanguine ➡ optimistic

sanitarium ➡ hospital

sanitary ➡ sterile

sanity ➡ reason

sap ➡ liquid, tire

sapling ➡ tree

sarcasm ➡ irony

sarcoma ➡ growth

sardonic ➡ sarcastic, dry

sari ➡ dress

sarong ➡ dress

sash ➡ band, scarf

sashay ➡ strut

sassy ➡ rude

satchel ➡ bag

sate ➡ satisfy

sated ➡ full

satellite ➡ colony, planet

satiate ➡ satisfy

satiny ➡ shiny

satire ➡ irony, parody

satiric ➡ sarcastic

satirical ➡ sarcastic

satirize ➡ imitate

satisfactorily ➡ well, correctly

satisfactory ➡ fair

satisfying ➡ pleasant

saturate ➡ wet

saturated ➡ wet

saucepan ➡ pot

saucer ➡ plate

saunter ➡ wander, lag

sauté ➡ cook

savage ➡ wild, mean, violent, monster, vandal

savagery ➡ violence

savanna ➡ plain

savings and loan ➡ bank

savings bank ➡ bank

savoir faire ➡ tact

savor ➡ spice, flavor, appreciate

savory ➡ delicious, fragrant

saw ➡ saying

➡ = synonym cross-reference • ⇨ = antonym cross-reference

say *vb* state, speak, remark, exclaim, phrase, verbalize, express, signify, air, vent, dictate ➡ **talk, tell, pronounce, reveal**

saying *n* expression, motto, proverb, maxim, adage, aphorism, axiom, slogan, byword, saw, phrase ➡ **remark, cliché**

scar 1. *n* blemish, cicatrix, injury, disfigurement, mark, discoloration
2. *vb* ➡ **damage**

scare 1. *vb* frighten, alarm, startle, terrify, petrify, shock, horrify, perturb, unnerve, cow ➡ **threaten**
2. *n* ➡ **fear**

scarf *n* sash, bandanna, veil, ascot, handkerchief, do-rag ➡ **wrap**

scary *adj* frightening, frightful, dreadful, terrifying, terrible, horrifying, unnerving, appalling, fearful, awesome

scenic *adj* picturesque, pictorial, spectacular, striking ➡ **pretty**

school 1. *n* academy, institute ➡ **college**
2. *vb* ➡ **teach**
3. *n* ➡ **herd**

science *n* discipline, technique ➡ **education, knowledge**

scold *vb* rebuke, admonish, reprimand, chastise, chide, castigate, berate, reproach, upbraid, reprove ➡ **punish, blame** ⇨ *praise*

scaffold ➡ gallows
scalding ➡ hot
scale ➡ climb, measure, peel, coat
scalpel ➡ knife
scamp ➡ rascal
scamper ➡ dance, hurry
scan ➡ read, examine
scandal ➡ rumor
scandalous ➡ sensational, shameful
scant ➡ few, light[2]
scanty ➡ small, few

scarce ➡ rare
scarcely ➡ only, seldom
scarcity ➡ want
scared ➡ afraid
scarlet ➡ red
scatter ➡ spread, plant
scatterbrained ➡ absentminded
scenario ➡ story
scene ➡ view, division
scenery ➡ view, setting
scent ➡ smell
scented ➡ fragrant

schedule ➡ list, table, arrange
scheduled ➡ due
schematic ➡ plan
scheme ➡ plan
scheming ➡ sly
schism ➡ break
scholar ➡ student, teacher, philosopher
scholarly ➡ intellectual, educated
scholarship ➡ education, award
scholastic ➡ intellectual

schoolboy ➡ student
schoolchild ➡ student
schooled ➡ educated
schoolgirl ➡ student
schooling ➡ education
schoolmaster ➡ teacher
schoolmistress ➡ teacher
scimitar ➡ sword
scoff ➡ ridicule
scoop ➡ spoon, dig, catch
scope ➡ space, range

score 1. *n* count, tally, reckoning, outcome ➡ **grade**
2. *n* transcription, arrangement, composition, orchestration
vb ➡ **get, add, win**

seat *n* chair, bench, sofa, couch, settee, stool, pew, bleachers, grandstand, stands, perch, roost

secrecy *n* stealth, hiding, confidence, subterfuge, furtiveness ➡ **privacy**

secret 1. *adj* hidden, arcane, cryptic, esoteric ➡ **mysterious, anonymous**
2. *adj* clandestine, confidential, classified, top secret, private, covert, undercover, surreptitious, underground ➡ **sly**
3. *n* mystery, confidence, intrigue ➡ **problem**

If the word you want is not a main entry above, look below to find it.

scorch ➡ burn

scorn ➡ hatred, hate, ridicule, refuse, insult

scornful ➡ sarcastic

Scotch® tape ➡ adhesive

scoundrel ➡ rascal

scour ➡ clean, shine, hunt

scourge ➡ whip

scout ➡ patrol

scowl ➡ frown

scramble ➡ mix, hurry, climb

scrap ➡ fight, bite, bit, discard

scrape ➡ clean, rub, cut, damage

scraping ➡ friction

scratch ➡ cut, rub, damage, erase

scratchy ➡ rough

scrawl ➡ write

scrawny ➡ thin

scream ➡ yell, cry

screamer ➡ headline

screech ➡ yell, cry, squeak

screen ➡ divider, net, hide, sift

screening ➡ tryout

screenwriter ➡ writer

screw ➡ nail, turn

scribble ➡ write

script ➡ handwriting, book

scriptwriter ➡ writer

scrooge ➡ miser

scrounge ➡ borrow

scrub ➡ clean, brush, cleaning

scruffy ➡ shabby

scrumptious ➡ delicious

scrupulous ➡ careful, good

scrutinize ➡ examine

scrutiny ➡ look

scuff ➡ rub

scuffle ➡ fight

scull ➡ paddle

scullery ➡ kitchen

sculpt ➡ carve

sculptor ➡ artist

sculpture ➡ statue, carve

scum ➡ foam

scurry ➡ hurry

scuttle ➡ hurry, abandon

sea ➡ ocean

seafarer ➡ sailor

seagoing ➡ nautical

seagull ➡ bird

seal ➡ close, signature

sealed ➡ tight

seam ➡ band

seaman ➡ sailor

sear ➡ burn

search ➡ hunt

seashore ➡ shore

seaside ➡ shore

season ➡ period, weather

seasoned ➡ old

seasoning ➡ spice, herb

sea wall ➡ jetty

seclude ➡ separate

secluded ➡ private

seclusion ➡ privacy

second ➡ moment, latter

secondary ➡ subordinate

secondhand ➡ old

second-rate ➡ cheap

secret agent ➡ spy

secrete ➡ hide, sweat

secretive ➡ sly

sect ➡ religion

section ➡ part, excerpt, division, department

➡ = synonym cross-reference • ⇨ = antonym cross-reference

see 1. *vb* behold, discern, observe, perceive, notice, glimpse, spot, remark ➡ **look**
2. *vb* ➡ **know, learn**
3. *vb* ➡ **imagine**

seed 1. *n* kernel, grain, pit, pip, nut, bulb ➡ **egg, fruit**
2. *vb* ➡ **plant**

seize *vb* take, grab, snatch, clutch, wrest, abduct, kidnap, hijack, skyjack, carjack, occupy, intercept, tackle ➡ **catch, get**

seldom *adv* rarely, occasionally, infrequently, sometimes, scarcely, hardly, barely ⇨ *often*

self-righteous *adj* sanctimonious, holier-than-thou, unctuous ➡ **hypocritical**

sell *vb* carry, stock, retail, handle, trade (in), market, peddle, vend, barter, hawk ➡ **offer**

seller *n* salesperson, salesman, saleswoman, dealer, merchant, vendor, tradesman, shopkeeper, peddler, trader, supplier, wholesaler ➡ **agent**

send 1. *vb* dispatch, transmit, mail, post, e-mail, forward, convey, ship, transfer, export ➡ **spread, broadcast**
2. *vb* ➡ **lead**
3. *vb* ➡ **throw**

If the word you want is not a main entry above, look below to find it.

secure ➡ safe, guarantee, lock, tie

security ➡ protection

sedate ➡ serious

sedative ➡ drug

sedentary ➡ passive

sedition ➡ treason

seditious ➡ rebellious

seduce ➡ tempt

seduction ➡ attraction

seedling ➡ tree

seedy ➡ shabby

seek ➡ hunt

seem ➡ act, look

seemingly ➡ apparently, probably

seemly ➡ correct

seep ➡ drop

seer ➡ prophet

seethe ➡ boil

see-through ➡ transparent

segment ➡ part, divide

segregate ➡ separate

segregation ➡ privacy

seizure ➡ arrest, fit²

select ➡ choose, special

selection ➡ choice, assortment, excerpt, appointment

self-acting ➡ automatic

self-confidence ➡ pride, certainty

self-confident ➡ certain

self-conscious ➡ nervous

self-control ➡ discipline

self-denial ➡ abstinence

self-deprecating ➡ humble

self-effacing ➡ humble

self-esteem ➡ pride

self-governing ➡ free

selfish ➡ greedy, mean

selfishness ➡ greed

self-possessed ➡ calm

self-respect ➡ pride

self-restraint ➡ abstinence, discipline

self-satisfied ➡ satisfied

self-starting ➡ automatic

semester ➡ term

seminar ➡ course

senate ➡ government

senior ➡ old, older, student

---

n = noun • vb = verb • adj = adjective • adv = adverb • prep = preposition • conj = conjunction

sensational 1. *adj* scandalous, shocking, lurid, dramatic, melodramatic, vulgar, exaggerated
2. *adj* ➡ **exciting, awesome**

sense 1. *n* sensation, function, capability ➡ **feeling, ability**
2. *n* ➡ **wisdom**
3. *n* ➡ **meaning**

separate 1. *vb* part, sever, undo, detach, cleave, sunder ➡ **divide, rip, share, open**
2. *vb* isolate, insulate, segregate, discriminate, sequester, quarantine, seclude ➡ **distinguish**
3. *vb* divorce, split up, break up
4. *adj* ➡ **different**

serious 1. *adj* solemn, grave, somber, earnest, sedate, sober, heavy ➡ **important, profound, dignified**
2. *adj* ➡ **sincere**

servant *n* retainer, domestic, employee, minion, attendant, subordinate ➡ **helper**

servile *adj* obsequious, submissive, subservient, slavish, fawning, sycophantic, spineless, mealy-mouthed, abject ➡ **passive, humble**

setting *n* environment, surroundings, framework, background, context, backdrop, scenery, climate, ambiance, mood, medium, milieu

---

If the word you want is not a main entry above, look below to find it.

sensation ➡ **feeling, sense**

senseless ➡ **unconscious**

senselessness ➡ **nonsense**

sensible ➡ **practical, sane**

sensitive ➡ **sore, thoughtful, delicate, emotional, temperamental**

sensitivity ➡ **feeling**

sentence ➡ **punish, punishment, decision**

sentience ➡ **life**

sentiment ➡ **emotion, belief**

sentimental ➡ **emotional**

sentimentality ➡ **feeling**

sentinel ➡ **patrol**

sentry ➡ **patrol**

separately ➡ **apart, differently**

separation ➡ **division**

sepulcher ➡ **grave, cemetery**

sequence ➡ **order, row**

sequential ➡ **consecutive**

sequester ➡ **separate**

seraph ➡ **angel**

serendipitous ➡ **lucky**

serendipity ➡ **chance**

serene ➡ **calm**

serenity ➡ **calm**

serf ➡ **farmer**

serfdom ➡ **slavery**

serial ➡ **consecutive**

series ➡ **row, assortment, program, game**

sermon ➡ **speech**

sermonize ➡ **preach**

serpent ➡ **snake**

serve ➡ **help, satisfy, act, give**

service ➡ **ceremony, army, tray, help, repair, fix**

serviceman ➡ **soldier**

service mark ➡ **label**

service station ➡ **garage**

servicewoman ➡ **soldier**

servicing ➡ **repair**

servitude ➡ **slavery**

session ➡ **meeting**

set ➡ **put, group, harden, plant, fall, ready, usual**

set apart ➡ **dedicate**

setback ➡ **relapse, accident**

set off ➡ **leave**

set out ➡ **leave**

settee ➡ **seat**

---

sew *vb* stitch, mend, embroider, baste, tailor ➡ **weave**

shabby *adj* dilapidated, deteriorated, broken-down, decayed, scruffy, seedy, mangy ➡ **old, ragged, sorry**

shack *n* cabin, hut, shanty, hovel, shed ➡ **house**

shake 1. *vb* vibrate, tremble, shudder, shiver, quiver, quake, quaver, flutter, wobble, wag, waggle, pulsate, throb, jar ➡ **tingle**
2. *vb* ➡ **spread**
3. *n* ➡ **vibration**

shame 1. *n* disgrace, dishonor, discredit, humiliation, remorse, regret, contrition, embarrassment, chagrin ➡ **guilt**
2. *vb* humiliate, dishonor, disgrace, debase, abase, demean, discredit ➡ **embarrass**

shameful *adj* disgraceful, contemptible, scandalous, shocking, disreputable, dishonorable, ignoble, deplorable ➡ **improper, bad**

share 1. *n* division, percentage, allowance, allotment, stake, quota, ration, proportion, fraction, percent, ratio ➡ **part, interest**
2. *vb* distribute, apportion, split (up), deal out, ration, mete out ➡ **divide, budget**

sharp 1. *adj* keen, acute, honed, pointed, pointy, sharp-edged, knife-edged
2. *adj* ➡ **smart**
3. *adj* acute, abrupt, rapid ➡ **sudden**
4. *adj* ➡ **steep**
5. *adj* severe, biting, caustic, bitter, harsh, cutting, fierce, brutal, oppressive
6. *adj* ➡ **spicy, sour**
7. *adj* ➡ **smelly**
8. *adj* ➡ **fashionable**

If the word you want is not a main entry above, look below to find it.

settle ➡ decide, pay, descend

settlement ➡ town, colony

settler ➡ pioneer

set up ➡ arrange

seven seas ➡ ocean

sever ➡ separate

several ➡ few

severance ➡ division

severe ➡ sharp, hard, plain, strict

severity ➡ strength

Seville orange ➡ orange

shackle ➡ bond

shade ➡ dark, color, bit, ghost, hide

shades ➡ glasses

shadow ➡ dark, cloud, follow

shadowy ➡ dim

shady ➡ dark, suspicious

shaft ➡ bar, well, channel

shaggy ➡ fuzzy

shah ➡ king

shaky ➡ unsteady, nervous

shallow ➡ superficial, dull

shalom ➡ good-bye, hello

sham ➡ fake

shaman ➡ magician

shamed ➡ ashamed

shameless ➡ immoral

Shangri-la ➡ utopia

shanty ➡ shack

shape ➡ form, structure, health

sharecropper ➡ farmer

sharecropping ➡ farming

shared ➡ common

sharp-edged ➡ sharp

sharpen *vb* whet, hone, file, grind, strop

shed 1. *n* ➡ **shack, barn, building**
2. *vb* remove, take off, cast off, drop, molt, slough ➡ **discard**

shelf *n* rack, counter, stand, ledge, mantel, mantelpiece

shell 1. *n* husk, pod, casing, sheath, carapace, eggshell ➡ **peel**
2. *n* ➡ **framework**
3. *n* ➡ **missile**
4. *vb* ➡ **shoot**

shine 1. *vb* radiate, beam, sparkle, gleam, glow, shimmer, glisten, twinkle
2. *vb* polish, burnish, buff, wax, scour ➡ **clean, finish**
3. *n* ➡ **light**[1]

shiny *adj* lustrous, gleaming, glossy, sleek, glistening, sparkling, silky, satiny ➡ **bright**

shock 1. *vb* astound, appall, dismay, devastate, overwhelm, stun, electrify, stagger, awe, horrify ➡ **surprise, scare**
2. *n* ➡ **blow**[1], **vibration**
3. *n* ➡ **earthquake**
4. *n* blow, upset, jolt, ordeal, trauma ➡ **surprise**
5. *n* ➡ **lock**

shoe *n* boot, footwear

shoot 1. *vb* fire, discharge, open fire, blast, gun down, shell, propel, launch, project
2. *vb* ➡ **hunt, kill**
3. *n* sprout, bud, runner, twig, outgrowth ➡ **stick**

If the word you want is not a main entry above, look below to find it.

sharpness ➡ clarity	shelling ➡ fire	shiftless ➡ lazy	shocking ➡ sensational, shameful
shatter ➡ break	shells ➡ ammunition	shifty ➡ sly	
shattered ➡ broken	shelter ➡ protect, protection, house, building	shimmer ➡ shine	shoddy ➡ cheap, poor
shave ➡ cut		ship ➡ boat, send	shooting ➡ fire
shawl ➡ wrap		shipment ➡ load, delivery	shooting star ➡ meteor
shear ➡ cut	shenanigans ➡ mischief		
sheath ➡ dress, shell	shepherd ➡ guide	shipshape ➡ neat	shop ➡ market, factory, buy
sheathe ➡ wrap	sherbet ➡ ice cream	shirk ➡ avoid	shopkeeper ➡ seller
sheen ➡ light[1]	sheriff ➡ police officer	shirtwaist ➡ dress	shoplift ➡ steal
sheer ➡ steep, perfect, thin, transparent	shield ➡ protect, protection, badge	shiver ➡ shake	shoplifting ➡ theft
sheet ➡ layer, page, blanket	shift ➡ move, change, swerve, movement, period, dress	shock absorber ➡ cushion	shopper ➡ patron
shellac ➡ finish			shopping mall ➡ market

shore n beach, coast, seashore, seaside, strand, bank ➡ **edge**

short 1. adj slight, low, undersized, skimpy, brief ➡ **small** ⇨ **long**
2. adj brief, concise, compact, succinct, abbreviated, terse, laconic, abridged, fleeting, transient, short-lived ➡ **fast, temporary**
3. adj ➡ **abrupt**
4. adj ➡ **inadequate**

show 1. vb display, exhibit, present, manifest, produce ➡ **reveal, advertise, model**
2. vb ➡ **lead**
3. vb ➡ **explain, verify**
4. n spectacle, display ➡ **play, movie, program**

shrink 1. vb contract, shrivel, deflate, constrict ➡ **condense, decrease** ⇨ **grow, lengthen**
2. vb ➡ **retreat**

shy adj bashful, timid, meek, retiring, diffident, reserved, demure, deferential, timorous, tentative ➡ **humble**

sick 1. adj ill, ailing, sickly, unwell, unhealthy, nauseous, nauseated, queasy, infirm, indisposed, funny ➡ **weak** ⇨ **healthy**
2. adj ➡ **gruesome**

side 1. n surface, face, end, facet, plane ➡ **edge**
2. n ➡ **perspective**
3. n ➡ **team**

If the word you want is not a main entry above, look below to find it.

shortage ➡ want

shortbread ➡ pastry

shortcoming ➡ defect

shortcut ➡ path

shorten ➡ condense

shortening ➡ abbreviation, fat

short-lived ➡ short

shortly ➡ soon

shot ➡ medicine, try

shotgun ➡ gun

should ➡ need

shoulder ➡ push, bear

shout ➡ yell, cry

shove ➡ push, impulse

shovel ➡ dig

showdown ➡ fight

shower ➡ rain, cleaning

showery ➡ wet

show off ➡ boast

showpiece ➡ masterpiece

showroom ➡ gallery

show up ➡ appear

showy ➡ loud

shred ➡ cut, rip, bit

shrewd ➡ sly, smart

shriek ➡ yell, cry, laugh

shrill ➡ loud, high

shrine ➡ monument

shrivel ➡ shrink, decrease, dry

shroud ➡ blanket, wrap, hide

shrub ➡ plant

shrubbery ➡ hedge, brush

shuck ➡ peel

shudder ➡ shake

shuffle ➡ limp, rustle, mix

shun ➡ avoid, abstain

shut ➡ close

shut-eye ➡ sleep

shut-in ➡ hermit

shutterbug ➡ photographer

shyster ➡ cheat

sicken ➡ disgust

sickening ➡ bad

sickly ➡ sick

sickness ➡ illness, nausea

sidearm ➡ gun

sideboard ➡ cupboard

sideburns ➡ beard

sidekick ➡ partner

sidestep ➡ avoid

sideswipe ➡ collide

sidetrack ➡ distract

sideways *adv* broadside, obliquely, askance, indirectly

sift 1. *vb* strain, filter, screen, winnow, sort
2. *vb* ➠ **hunt**

sight 1. *n* vision, eyesight, perception ➠ **sense**
2. *n* ➠ **view**
3. *vb* ➠ **look**

sign 1. *n* symbol, signal, token, omen, clue, index, indication, manifestation, symptom, gesture, expression ➠ **track, warning**
2. *vb* autograph, inscribe, endorse, countersign, initial ➠ **write**

signature *n* autograph, John Hancock, seal, monogram, mark, stamp, imprint

similarity *n* likeness, resemblance, correspondence, parallel, similitude, affinity, congruity, analogy, comparison

simultaneous *adj* concurrent, coincident, coinciding, synchronized, synchronous, contemporary, contemporaneous

sin 1. *vb* err, offend, transgress, trespass ➠ **disobey**
2. *n* ➠ **crime, immorality**

sincere *adj* genuine, honest, heartfelt, wholehearted, true, trustworthy, serious, straight ➠ **straightforward**

sincerely *adv* truly, honestly, earnestly, genuinely, heartily, frankly

sing *vb* chant, harmonize, vocalize, croon, warble, chirp ➠ **hum**

singer *n* vocalist, chorister, soloist, songster, cantor ➠ **choir, musician**

If the word you want is not a main entry above, look below to find it.

siesta ➠ sleep

sieve ➠ net

sifter ➠ net

sigh ➠ mumble, rustle

sighting ➠ discovery

sightless ➠ blind

signal ➠ sign, warning, wave, bell, light[1]

significance ➠ importance, meaning, relevance

significant ➠ important, meaningful

signify ➠ mean, matter, say

silence ➠ quiet, calm

silent ➠ dumb, quiet

silhouette ➠ circumference

silky ➠ shiny

sill ➠ threshold

silliness ➠ nonsense

silly ➠ foolish

silo ➠ warehouse

silver screen ➠ movies

silvery ➠ white

similar ➠ alike, compatible

similarly ➠ alike

similitude ➠ similarity

simmer ➠ boil

simple ➠ plain, easy, naive, primitive

simple-minded ➠ stupid

simpleton ➠ fool

simplicity ➠ clarity, ignorance

simplify ➠ facilitate

simply ➠ only

simulate ➠ imitate, pretend

simultaneously ➠ together

since ➠ because

sincerity ➠ truth

sinful ➠ bad

singe ➠ burn

---

single 1. *adj* ➡ **only**
2. *adj* alone, unmarried, unwed, unattached, eligible, divorced ⇨ *married*

sink 1. *vb* submerge, submerse, swamp, engulf, immerse, duck, dunk, dip ➡ **descend, fall, flood**
2. *n* washbasin, basin, lavatory, washstand ➡ **bowl**

size *n* magnitude, mass, volume, bulk, quantity, proportion, capacity

skeptic *n* cynic, pessimist, doubter, doubting Thomas

slant 1. *vb* tilt, lean, list, incline, slope, bank, sag, pitch, cant ➡ **bend**
2. *n* slope, incline, climb, ascent, rise, descent, declivity, grade, hill

slavery *n* bondage, servitude, enslavement, serfdom, subjugation, vassalage ⇨ *freedom*

sleep 1. *vb* slumber, doze, snooze, nod, nap, hibernate ➡ **rest**
2. *n* slumber, doze, rest, repose, siesta, nap, catnap, shut-eye (*informal*)

If the word you want is not a main entry above, look below to find it.

single-handed ➡ alone

singular ➡ unique

sinister ➡ ominous

sinless ➡ innocent

sip ➡ drink

sister ➡ religious

sisterhood ➡ friendship

sit ➡ model

site ➡ place

sit-in ➡ protest

sitter ➡ model

sitting room ➡ living room

situate ➡ place, base

situation ➡ place, state, opportunity, profession

sizzling ➡ hot

skate ➡ slide

skeleton ➡ framework, body

skeptical ➡ doubtful

skepticism ➡ doubt

sketch ➡ picture, pattern, act, draw

skid ➡ slide

skill ➡ talent, art, experience

skilled ➡ expert

skillful ➡ able

skim ➡ read, slide, rub

skimpy ➡ small, short

skin ➡ peel, hide

skin-deep ➡ superficial

skinflint ➡ miser

skinny ➡ thin

skintight ➡ tight

skip ➡ exclude, jump

skipper ➡ boss

skirmish ➡ fight

skirt ➡ dress, border, detour

skit ➡ act, play

skittish ➡ nervous

skulk ➡ sneak

sky ➡ air

sky blue ➡ blue

skycap ➡ porter

skyjack ➡ seize

skyline ➡ horizon

skyscraper ➡ tower

slab ➡ block

slack ➡ limp, negligent

slacker ➡ loafer

slake ➡ satisfy

slam ➡ close

slammer ➡ jail

slander ➡ insult

slang ➡ dialect

slap ➡ punch, blow¹

slash ➡ cut, decrease

slat ➡ board

slate ➡ gray, ballot

slather ➡ rub

slaughter ➡ kill, murder

slave ➡ servant, prisoner, work

slavish ➡ servile

slay ➡ kill

slayer ➡ killer

slaying ➡ murder

sled ➡ vehicle

sledge ➡ hammer

sledgehammer ➡ hammer

sleek ➡ shiny

sleeping ➡ asleep

sleepless ➡ awake

sleepy ➡ tired

---

slide 1. *vb* glide, skim, coast, skid, slip, skate ➡ **push**
2. *n* ➡ **channel**
3. *n* ➡ **photograph**
4. *n* ➡ **avalanche**

slippery *adj* smooth, slick, glassy, icy, waxy, soapy

slow 1. *adj* leisurely, gradual, sluggish, deliberate, moderate, torpid ⇨ *fast*
2. *adj* dilatory, lackadaisical ➡ **passive, lazy, listless**
3. *adj* ➡ **dull, stupid**

sly 1. *adj* devious, crafty, cunning, shrewd, subtle, tricky, sneaky, wily, slick, shifty, artful, scheming, underhanded ➡ **dishonest**
2. *adj* secretive, furtive, sneaky, surreptitious, stealthy, elusive ➡ **private**

small 1. *adj* little, tiny, miniature, minute, diminutive, Lilliputian, compact ➡ **trivial** ⇨ *big*
2. *adj* scanty, meager, slight, spare, skimpy, stingy, paltry ➡ **inadequate**

smart 1. *adj* intelligent, clever, bright, wise, learned, brilliant, keen, acute, quick, alert, apt, astute, perceptive, insightful, discerning, incisive, canny, shrewd ➡ **precocious, educated, profound** ⇨ *foolish, stupid*
2. *adj* ➡ **fashionable**
3. *vb* ➡ **hurt**
In general, **smart**, **clever**, *and* **bright**, *which all suggest quickness in learning, are more often applied to young people than are* **intelligent**, **wise**, *and* **learned**, *which suggest the wisdom that comes from experience, education, and age.*

If the word you want is not a main entry above, look below to find it.

sleet ➡ ice

slender ➡ thin, narrow, light[2]

slew ➡ abundance

slice ➡ cut, block

slick ➡ slippery, sly

slight ➡ small, thin, short, light[2], insult

slightest ➡ least

slightly ➡ partly

slim ➡ thin, narrow

slime ➡ dirt

sling ➡ throw

slink ➡ sneak

slip ➡ mistake, trip, dock, ticket, slide, fall

slip by ➡ elapse

slit ➡ cut

slither ➡ crawl

slogan ➡ saying

slop ➡ dirt

slope ➡ slant

sloppy ➡ messy

slosh ➡ splash

sloth ➡ laziness

slothful ➡ lazy

slouch ➡ bend

slough ➡ shed

slovenly ➡ messy

sludge ➡ dirt

slug ➡ hit, missile

sluggard ➡ loafer

sluggish ➡ slow, listless

sluice ➡ channel

slumber ➡ sleep

slumbering ➡ asleep

slump ➡ depression, fall, drop, bend

slush ➡ snow

slushy ➡ wet

smack ➡ hit, kiss, blow[1]

smaller ➡ less

smallest ➡ least

small-minded ➡ mean

smash ➡ break, hit, collide

smear ➡ rub, insult

---

smell 1. *n* scent, odor, aroma, fragrance, perfume, incense, bouquet, stench
2. *vb, n* sniff, whiff, scent ➡ **sense**
3. *vb, n* stink, reek

smelly *adj* odorous, rancid, rank, foul, putrid, acrid, sharp, strong ➡ **fragrant**

smile *vb, n* beam, grin, smirk, sneer ➡ **laugh** ⇨ *frown*

smoke 1. *n* vapor, fumes, gas, steam ➡ **fog**
2. *vb* smolder, fume ➡ **burn**
3. *vb* inhale, puff

snake *n* serpent, viper ➡ **reptile**

sneak 1. *vb* creep, slink, prowl, skulk, steal, tiptoe, lurk
2. *n* ➡ **rascal**

snow 1. *n* snowfall, snowstorm, blizzard, flurry ➡ **storm**
2. *n* snowflake, powder, slush, hail, graupel, névé, firn
3. *vb* ➡ **enchant, persuade**

snuggle *vb* cuddle, nuzzle, nestle, huddle

soda *n* pop, soda pop, soft drink, cola, Coke (*trademark*), tonic ➡ **drink**

If the word you want is not a main entry above, look below to find it.

smirk ➡ smile

smock ➡ dress

smog ➡ fog

smoky ➡ gray

smolder ➡ smoke

smoldering ➡ burning

smooch ➡ kiss

smooth ➡ level, slippery, suave, rub

smother ➡ extinguish, choke

smudge ➡ spot, dirty

smug ➡ proud

snack ➡ meal

snag ➡ knot, catch

snap ➡ break, bite, clasp, fast

snapshot ➡ photograph

snare ➡ trap, catch

snarl ➡ bark, knot

snatch ➡ seize, steal, bit

sneaky ➡ sly

sneer ➡ smile

snicker ➡ laugh

snide ➡ sarcastic

sniff ➡ smell

snigger ➡ laugh

snip ➡ cut

snippet ➡ bit

snit ➡ fit²

snoop ➡ meddle, spy

snooze ➡ sleep

snort ➡ grunt

snout ➡ nose

snowfall ➡ snow

snowflake ➡ snow

snowstorm ➡ snow, storm

snow-white ➡ white

snowy ➡ white, wet

snub ➡ refuse, insult

snug ➡ safe, comfortable, warm, narrow, tight

so ➡ therefore

soak ➡ wet, cleaning, absorb

soaked ➡ wet

soapy ➡ slippery

soar ➡ fly

soaring ➡ high, flight

sob ➡ cry

sober ➡ serious

sobriquet ➡ pseudonym

sociable ➡ friendly

social ➡ friendly, public, dance

socialize ➡ mix

Social Security ➡ pension

society ➡ humanity, people, friendship, organization, aristocracy

sociology ➡ science

soda pop ➡ soda

sodden ➡ wet

sofa ➡ seat

soften 1. *vb* ➡ **melt**
2. *vb* modify, assuage, temper, qualify, appease, palliate ➡ **change, quiet**

soldier *n* fighter, warrior, volunteer, conscript, draftee, recruit, cadet, veteran, officer, serviceman, servicewoman, combatant, mercenary, soldier of fortune, gladiator ➡ **army, troop**

solve *vb* figure out, puzzle out, resolve, decode, decipher, answer, do, work (out), unravel, unscramble ➡ **explain**

song *n* tune, melody, lyric, theme, ballad, lullaby, ditty, madrigal ➡ **hymn, poem, music**

soon *adv* presently, shortly, forthwith, momentarily, anon ➡ **quickly, now**

sore 1. *adj* painful, sensitive, tender, raw, hurtful, irritated, inflamed, bruised, livid
2. *adj* ➡ **angry**
3. *n* boil, abscess, ulcer, inflammation, welt, swelling ➡ **cut, pain**

sorrow 1. *n* grief, sadness, regret, anguish, melancholy, distress, gloom, woe, heartache ➡ **misery, depression**
2. *vb* ➡ **sadden**

If the word you want is not a main entry above, look below to find it.

soft ➡ gentle, flexible, fuzzy

soft drink ➡ soda

soggy ➡ wet

soil ➡ dirt, dirty

soiled ➡ dirty

soiree ➡ party

sojourn ➡ live¹, visit

solace ➡ comfort

solder ➡ join

soldier of fortune ➡ soldier

soldierly ➡ military

sole ➡ only

solemn ➡ serious, dignified

solemnity ➡ ceremony

solemnize ➡ celebrate

solicit ➡ beg

solicitous ➡ thoughtful

solid ➡ firm, strong, reliable, real

solidify ➡ harden

solitary ➡ alone, only, lonely

solitude ➡ privacy

solo ➡ alone

soloist ➡ singer

so long ➡ good-bye

solution ➡ answer, mixture

somber ➡ serious, bleak, dark

some ➡ any

sometimes ➡ seldom

somewhat ➡ partly

somnolent ➡ asleep

son ➡ child

songbird ➡ bird

songster ➡ singer

sooner ➡ more

soothe ➡ relieve, pacify, calm

soothsayer ➡ prophet

sophisticated ➡ cosmopolitan, complicated

sophistication ➡ elegance

sophomore ➡ student

sophomoric ➡ childish

sop up ➡ absorb

sorbet ➡ ice cream

sorcerer ➡ magician

sorcery ➡ magic

soreness ➡ pain

sorority ➡ organization

sorrowful ➡ sorry

➡ = synonym cross-reference • ⇨ = antonym cross-reference   **207**

sorry 1. *adj* sorrowful, repentant, apologetic, contrite, penitent, remorseful ➡ **sad**
2. *adj* forlorn, wretched, depressing ➡ **sad, pitiful**
3. *adj* ➡ **poor**

soul 1. *n* spirit, psyche, essence, genius, ego ➡ **mind, ghost**
2. *n* ➡ **human being**
3. *n* ➡ **feeling**
4. *n* ➡ **middle**

sour *adj* tart, bitter, rancid, acidic, sharp, acid, tangy, dry ⇨ *sweet*

source 1. *n* origin, derivation, birthplace, cradle, fountain, fountainhead, font, fount, well, wellspring
2. *n* ➡ **beginning, cause**

space 1. *n* universe, cosmos, heavens, outer space, infinity, void ➡ **air**
2. *n* room, area, scope, range, expanse, territory, elbowroom

speaker *n* lecturer, orator, speechmaker, rhetorician, preacher, talker

special 1. *adj* distinct, particular, specific, especial, distinctive, respective, proper, certain ➡ **unique**
2. *adj* select, choice, extraordinary, exceptional, unusual, peculiar, remarkable, noteworthy, phenomenal, outstanding ➡ **rare, striking, strange**

specialty *n* speciality, forte, métier, specialization ➡ **talent, field, profession**

If the word you want is not a main entry above, look below to find it.

sort ➡ type, arrange, sift

sortie ➡ attack

sot ➡ drunkard

sound ➡ noise, valid, healthy, sane, strong, blow², ring

soundless ➡ quiet

sous-chef ➡ cook

souse ➡ drunkard

souvenir ➡ reminder

sovereign ➡ king, queen, free

sovereignty ➡ freedom, rule

sow ➡ plant

spa ➡ hotel

space-age ➡ modern

space flight ➡ flight

spacey ➡ absentminded

spacious ➡ open, comfortable

span ➡ period, life, bridge, width, pair, team

spank ➡ whip

spar ➡ joke

spare ➡ save, small, thin

spark ➡ light¹, incentive, start

sparkle ➡ shine, light¹

sparkling ➡ shiny

sparse ➡ light², inadequate

spasm ➡ pain, fit²

spasmodic ➡ periodic

spat ➡ argument

spate ➡ flood

spatter ➡ splash

spawn ➡ reproduce, egg

spay ➡ sterilize

speak ➡ say, talk

speak to ➡ approach

spear ➡ stick, missile

specialist ➡ expert

speciality ➡ specialty

specialization ➡ specialty

specie ➡ money

species ➡ type

specify *vb* stipulate, define, particularize, detail ➡ **name, mention, list**

speckled *adj* spotted, mottled, variegated, dappled, piebald

speech 1. *n* voice, communication, discourse, intercourse, utterance, articulation, diction, locution, enunciation, expression ➡ **talk, language, remark, accent, dialect** 2. *n* lecture, talk, sermon, address, report, oration

speed 1. *n* velocity, acceleration, swiftness, pace, rate, tempo, rapidity,

celerity, dispatch ➡ **hurry** 2. *vb* ➡ **hurry**

spice 1. *n* seasoning, zest, savor, relish ➡ **herb** 2. *n* ➡ **excitement**

spicy *adj* zesty, piquant, tangy, tart, sharp, hot, pungent, peppery

splash *vb, n* splatter, sprinkle, squirt, spray, spatter, slosh ➡ **drop, wet**

spoken *adj* verbal, oral, voiced, stated, unwritten, vocal

spontaneous *adj* impromptu, impulsive, unplanned, extemporaneous, casual ➡ **automatic, voluntary**

If the word you want is not a main entry above, look below to find it.

specific ➡ special, detail

specimen ➡ example

speck ➡ spot

spectacle ➡ show, view

spectacles ➡ glasses

spectacular ➡ great, scenic

spectator ➡ observer

spectators ➡ audience

specter ➡ ghost

spectrum ➡ range

speculate ➡ guess, meditate

speculation ➡ theory

speculative ➡ theoretical

speechless ➡ dumb, quiet

speechmaker ➡ speaker

speedily ➡ quickly

speedy ➡ fast

spell ➡ period, curse, enchantment, dream, fit², mean

spellbind ➡ enchant

spellbinding ➡ magic

spend ➡ pay

spendthrift ➡ wasteful

sphere ➡ ball, field

spherical ➡ round

spider ➡ bug

spigot ➡ faucet

spike ➡ nail, point

spill ➡ flow, fall

spin ➡ turn, trip

spine ➡ thorn

spineless ➡ servile

spinoff ➡ product

spire ➡ tower

spirit ➡ courage, soul, angel, ghost, fairy

spirited ➡ active, lively

spirits ➡ mood, drink

spiritual ➡ religious, heavenly

spirituality ➡ religion

spit ➡ cape

spite ➡ envy

spiteful ➡ revengeful

splatter ➡ splash

splendid ➡ grand, good

splendidly ➡ well

splendor ➡ elegance

splice ➡ knot

splinter ➡ break

split ➡ hole, divide, break

split up ➡ separate, share

spoil ➡ decay, destroy, pamper

spoilage ➡ decay

spoiled ➡ stale, mischievous, bad

spoils ➡ booty

spokesperson ➡ agent

sponsor ➡ patron, back

spontaneity ➡ freedom

spook ➡ ghost, spy

---

spoon *n* ladle, scoop, dipper, tablespoon, teaspoon

spot 1. *n* speck, dot, mark, taint, stain, blot, blemish, blotch, smudge
2. *n* ➡ **place**
3. *n* ➡ **trouble**
4. *vb* ➡ **find, see**

spouse *n* mate, partner, husband, wife, bride, groom, consort, helpmate

spread 1. *vb* distribute, disseminate, disperse, circulate, strew, shake, sprinkle, scatter ➡ **send, broadcast**
2. *vb* extend, stretch, range, unfold, expand, widen, gape, yawn
3. *vb* ➡ **cover**
4. *vb* ➡ **rub**
5. *n* ➡ **growth**
6. *n* ➡ **range**

7. *n* ➡ **farm**
8. *n* ➡ **feast**
9. *n* ➡ **flow**

spy 1. *n* agent, counterspy, secret agent, double agent, spook (*informal*)
2. *vb* eavesdrop, pry, snoop
3. *vb* ➡ **look**

spying *n* espionage, surveillance, intelligence, counterespionage, counterintelligence

square 1. *adj* foursquare, four-sided, quadrilateral
2. *adj* ➡ **dull**
3. *n* box, rectangle, quadrilateral, quadrangle
4. *n* ➡ **court, park**

If the word you want is not a main entry above, look below to find it.

spoor ➡ track

sporadic ➡ few, periodic

sport ➡ game, play

sport coat ➡ coat

sport jacket ➡ coat

sports center ➡ gymnasium

sportsman ➡ athlete

sportswoman ➡ athlete

spotless ➡ clean

spotted ➡ speckled

spout ➡ fountain, faucet

sprain ➡ pull

sprawl ➡ lie, trip

spray ➡ foam, bouquet, fountain, splash

spreadable ➡ contagious

spreadsheet ➡ table

spree ➡ binge, adventure

sprightly ➡ lively, agile

spring ➡ jump, descend, well

spring peeper ➡ frog

sprinkle ➡ wet, rain, splash, spread

sprint ➡ run, race

sprite ➡ angel, fairy

sprout ➡ grow, shoot

spruce ➡ neat

spry ➡ lively, agile

spryness ➡ agility

spume ➡ foam

spumoni ➡ ice cream

spur ➡ urge, incentive

spurious ➡ fake

spurn ➡ refuse

spurt ➡ flow

sputter ➡ stammer

spyglass ➡ glass

squabble ➡ argue, argument

squad ➡ troop, team

squalid ➡ dirty

squall ➡ storm, yell

squander ➡ waste

squash ➡ trample, break

squat ➡ low, fat, bend

squawk ➡ peep, cry, complain

squeak 1. *vb* creak, screech, squeal, rasp, grate
2. *n* ➡ **peep**

squeeze 1. *vb* pinch, clasp ➡ **embrace**
2. *vb* compress, wring, press ➡ **tighten**
3. *n* pinch, nip, tweak ➡ **embrace**

stage 1. *n* ➡ **platform, floor**
2. *n* theater, boards
3. *n* ➡ **state, period**
4. *vb* ➡ **act, give**

stale 1. *adj* moldy, spoiled, wilted, flat, musty ➡ **dry, bad**
2. *adj* ➡ **trite**

stammer 1. *n* stutter, stammering
2. *vb* stutter, hem and haw, sputter ➡ **mumble**

stanza *n* verse, canto, strophe, stave, refrain, strain ➡ **poem**

star 1. *n* sun
2. *n* ➡ **celebrity, actor**

stare *vb* gaze, peer, gape, ogle, gawk ➡ **look**

start 1. *vb* begin, commence, initiate, cause, activate, launch, originate, stem, inaugurate, introduce, innovate, open, trigger, touch off, spark ➡ **continue** ⇨ *finish, stop*
2. *n* ➡ **beginning**
3. *vb* ➡ **jump**

If the word you want is not a main entry above, look below to find it.

squeal ➡ cry, squeak
squeamish ➡ reluctant
squirm ➡ crawl, fidget
squirrel (away) ➡ hide
squirt ➡ flow, splash, fountain
squish ➡ trample
stab ➡ stick, blow¹, try
stability ➡ balance
stabilize ➡ balance
stable ➡ stationary, barn
stack ➡ pile
stadium ➡ field
staff ➡ stick, faculty

stage name ➡ pseudonym
stagecoach ➡ wagon
stagger ➡ limp, shock
stagnant ➡ stationary, stuffy, dead
stain ➡ spot, dirty, finish, paint
stair ➡ step
stake ➡ bar, share, bet, interest
statement ➡ tie
stalk ➡ stick, follow
stall ➡ booth, pen, barn, delay
stallion ➡ horse

stalwart ➡ brave, strong
stamina ➡ energy
stammering ➡ stammer
stamp ➡ print, signature, trample
stampede ➡ hurry
stance ➡ posture
stanchion ➡ post
stand ➡ bear, booth, platform, shelf, table
standdown ➡ truce
standard ➡ normal, average, model, measure, flag

standing ➡ fame, grade
standoff ➡ tie
standpoint ➡ perspective
stands ➡ seat
staple ➡ necessity, basic
stark ➡ plain, hard, completely
startle ➡ surprise, scare
starvation ➡ hunger
starve ➡ die
starved ➡ hungry
starving ➡ hungry
stash ➡ save

state 1. *n* condition, circumstance, situation, status, stage, phase ➡ **grade**
2. *n* territory, province, dominion, commonwealth ➡ **country, colony, zone**
3. *vb* ➡ **mention, say, tell**

stationary *adj* fixed, immobile, permanent, motionless, steady, stable, still, stock-still, inert, stagnant ⇨ *portable*

statue *n* sculpture, statuette, figure, figurine, bust, bronze, likeness, image, effigy, idol, statuary ➡ **monument**

steal 1. *vb* rob, swipe, snatch, shoplift, purloin, embezzle, burglarize, rifle, poach, pinch, pilfer, pocket, plagiarize, pirate, filch ➡ **take, seize, pillage**

2. *vb* ➡ **sneak**
3. *n* ➡ **bargain**

steep 1. *adj* sheer, abrupt, precipitous, sharp, perpendicular, vertical, uphill
2. *vb* ➡ **wet**

step 1. *n* footstep, stride, pace, tread, footfall
2. *n* ➡ **gait**
3. *n* ➡ **act**
4. *n* rung, tread, stair ➡ **grade**
5. *vb* ➡ **walk, dance**

stereotype 1. *n* convention, generalization, categorization, characterization ➡ **cliché**
2. *vb* categorize, pigeonhole, characterize, label, generalize

---

If the word you want is not a main entry above, look below to find it.

stated ➡ spoken

state-of-the-art ➡ modern

stately ➡ grand, dignified

statement ➡ remark, announcement, bill

state park ➡ park

statesman ➡ diplomat

station ➡ base, destination

stationery ➡ paper

statuary ➡ statue

statuette ➡ statue

stature ➡ height, importance

status ➡ reputation, state

statute ➡ act

statutory ➡ legal

staunch ➡ resolute, faithful

stave ➡ stick, stanza

stave off ➡ repel

stay ➡ live[1], wait, anchor, visit, support

stay with ➡ visit

steadfast ➡ faithful, resolute, patient

steady ➡ balance, firm, stationary, continual

stealing ➡ theft

stealth ➡ secrecy

stealthy ➡ sly

steam ➡ cook, iron, smoke, energy

steed ➡ horse

steeple ➡ tower

steeplechase ➡ race

steer ➡ lead, drive

steering wheel ➡ wheel

steersman ➡ pilot

stem ➡ stick, start, stop

stench ➡ smell

steno pad ➡ notepad

stentorian ➡ loud

stepparent ➡ parent

steppe ➡ plateau

sterile 1. *adj* antiseptic, sterilized, disinfected, sanitary, hygienic, germ-free ➡ **clean**
2. *adj* infertile, childless, barren, impotent ⇨ *fertile*
3. *adj* waste, desert, arid, barren ➡ **abandoned, empty**

sterilize 1. *vb* ➡ **clean**
2. *vb* spay, neuter, fix, geld, castrate

stick 1. *vb* poke, jab, probe, stab, plunge, pierce, prick, spear, puncture, lance, gore, peck, penetrate, perforate, riddle ➡ **hit**
2. *vb* adhere, cohere, glue, paste, tape, cling, cleave ➡ **join**
3. *n* branch, limb, twig, stem, stalk, staff, stave, wand, cane, club, baton ➡ **bar, bat**

sticky 1. *adj* adhesive, gummy, tacky, viscid, viscous
2. *adj* ➡ **damp**
3. *adj* ➡ **delicate**

stomach 1. *n* abdomen, midsection, paunch, belly, tummy, gut, midriff
2. *vb* ➡ **bear**
3. *n* ➡ **courage**

stop 1. *vb* halt, pause, cease, terminate, brake, arrest, check, stem, discontinue, lift ➡ **finish** ⇨ *start*
2. *vb* ➡ **prevent, bar**
3. *vb* ➡ **close**

If the word you want is not a main entry above, look below to find it.

sterilized ➡ sterile

stern ➡ strict, hard, back

stew ➡ cook, boil, worry

sticker ➡ label

sticks ➡ country

stiff ➡ firm, thick, prim

stiffen ➡ tighten

stifle ➡ choke, extinguish, quiet

stifling ➡ stuffy

stiletto ➡ knife

still ➡ quiet, more, dead, stationary, anyway

stillness ➡ calm

stilted ➡ prim

stimulate ➡ excite

stimulated ➡ excited

stimulating ➡ interesting

stimulation ➡ excitement

stimulus ➡ cause, incentive

sting ➡ hurt, pain

stingy ➡ cheap, greedy, small

stink ➡ smell

stint ➡ period

stipend ➡ wage

stipulate ➡ specify

stipulation ➡ term

stir ➡ mix, fidget, rustle, jail

stir up ➡ fan

stirring ➡ interesting

stitch ➡ sew, pain

stock ➡ sell, supply, load, family, trite

stockade ➡ wall, jail

stockpile ➡ supply, save

stockroom ➡ warehouse

stock-still ➡ stationary

stocky ➡ big, fat

stodgy ➡ stuffy

stoicism ➡ patience

stole ➡ wrap

stolid ➡ dull

stomp ➡ trample

stone ➡ rock, jewel

stoneware ➡ pottery

stony ➡ hard

stooge ➡ tool

stool ➡ seat

stoop ➡ descend, bend, condescend, porch

stopgap ➡ temporary

stopper ➡ top

stopwatch ➡ clock

store ➡ market, place, supply

storehouse ➡ warehouse

storeroom ➡ closet

---

storm 1. *n* tempest, gale, rainstorm, snowstorm, blizzard, hailstorm, ice storm, hurricane, typhoon, cyclone, monsoon, tornado, nor'easter, squall ➡ **rain, wind, snow**
2. *n* ➡ **flood**
3. *vb* ➡ **attack**
4. *vb* ➡ **hurry**

stormy *adj* rainy, blustery, inclement, tempestuous, turbulent, tumultuous, wild, fierce, violent ➡ **wet, windy**

story 1. *n* narrative, account, history, saga, chronicle, tale, narration, anecdote, yarn, plot, scenario, version ➡ **report, myth, joke, description**
2. *n* ➡ **lie**
3. *n* ➡ **floor**

straight 1. *adj* direct, undeviating, even, unbent, regular, linear, true ➡ **level, vertical** ⇨ *bent, zigzag*
2. *adj* ➡ **sincere**

straighten 1. *vb* unbend, untwist, order, arrange, align, realign ➡ **level** ⇨ *bend*
2. *vb* ➡ **comb**

straightforward 1. *adj* frank, outspoken, plain, candid, forthright, ingenuous, blunt, vocal ➡ **sincere, explicit**
2. *adj* ➡ **easy**

strange 1. *adj* unfamiliar, unusual, unknown, unaccustomed, outlandish ➡ **foreign, new** ⇨ *common*
2. *adj* odd, peculiar, curious, abnormal, eccentric, quaint, queer, weird, eerie, bizarre, unnatural, ludicrous, different, irregular ➡ **mysterious, funny**

stranger *n* newcomer, outsider, out-of-towner ➡ **foreigner**

strength *n* power, force, might, potency, muscle, fortitude, intensity, vehemence, violence, severity ➡ **ability, energy**

If the word you want is not a main entry above, look below to find it.

storm cellar ➡ **basement**

storyteller ➡ **liar**

stout ➡ **big, tough, fat**

stove ➡ **furnace**

stow ➡ **load**

straggle ➡ **lag**

straggler ➡ **pedestrian**

straightaway ➡ **now**

straight pin ➡ **pin**

strain ➡ **hurt, pull, work, sift, stress, chorus, stanza, type, family**

strait ➡ **trouble**

strand ➡ **leave, string, shore**

strangle ➡ **choke**

strap ➡ **string, rope, tie**

strategem ➡ **trick, tactic**

strategy ➡ **plan**

stratosphere ➡ **air**

stratum ➡ **layer**

stray ➡ **wander, homeless, arbitrary**

streak ➡ **band, period, tendency, run**

stream ➡ **river, fountain, flow, flood**

street ➡ **road**

streetlight ➡ **light**[1]

strengthen 1. *vb* intensify, magnify, amplify, increase, expand, enhance, enlarge, boost, augment, swell ➡ **grow**
2. *vb* fortify, brace, buttress, reinforce ➡ **harden, support**

stress 1. *n* pressure, tension, strain, duress ➡ **worry**
2. *n* ➡ **accent**
3. *vb* ➡ **emphasize**

strict *adj* stern, stringent, austere, severe, rigorous, exacting, unyielding, uncompromising

striking *adj* conspicuous, impressive, dazzling, stunning, unusual ➡ **obvious, special, attractive, pretty, scenic**

string 1. *n* cord, line, twine, thread, lace, strap, yarn, fiber, filament, strand, tendril ➡ **rope**
2. *n* ➡ **row**
3. *n* ➡ **team**

strong 1. *adj* powerful, mighty, almighty, hardy, stalwart, robust, muscular, vigorous, athletic, virile, burly ➡ **tough, invincible, healthy** ⇨ **weak**
2. *adj* solid, sturdy, durable, sound, substantial ➡ **tough**
3. *adj* potent, powerful, formidable, violent, forceful, intense
4. *adj* ➡ **smelly**

structure 1. *n* composition, arrangement, shape, form ➡ **pattern**
2. *n* ➡ **building**
3. *vb* ➡ **arrange**

strut 1. *vb* parade, swagger, sashay, flounce ➡ **walk**
2. *n* ➡ **gait**

stubborn *adj* obstinate, headstrong, pertinaceous, dogged, opinionated, obdurate, tenacious, pigheaded, unrelenting, unruly, intractable, difficult, perverse, unmanageable, mulish, ornery ➡ **resolute, dogmatic, wild**

If the word you want is not a main entry above, look below to find it.

strenuous ➡ active, hard

stretch ➡ distance, period, spread, lengthen, distort

stretched ➡ tense

stretcher ➡ bed

strew ➡ spread

stride ➡ step, gait, walk

strident ➡ loud

strife ➡ fight, disagreement

strike ➡ hit, blow[1], attack, protest, discover, light[1], make

stringent ➡ strict

strip ➡ bar, band, peel, undress

stripe ➡ bar, band

stripped ➡ naked

strive ➡ fight, try, work

stroke ➡ blow[1], pet, rub

stroll ➡ walk

stroller ➡ pedestrian

strongbox ➡ safe

stronghold ➡ castle

strong-minded ➡ resolute

strop ➡ sharpen

strophe ➡ stanza

struggle ➡ fight, try, work

strum ➡ play

stubble ➡ beard

stud ➡ nail, beam, post

➡ = synonym cross-reference • ⇨ = antonym cross-reference   **215**

student n pupil, learner, scholar, disciple, schoolchild, schoolgirl, schoolboy, freshman, sophomore, junior, senior, undergraduate, trainee, apprentice

study 1. vb analyze, evaluate, think through, pore over, review, research, criticize, survey, poll, canvass ➡ **examine, consider, learn, read**
2. n examination, analysis, investigation, inquiry, exploration, survey, poll, census, sampling, probe
3. n ➡ **report**
4. n ➡ **den**
5. n ➡ **dream**

stuffy 1. adj close, stifling, airless, suffocating, claustrophic, stagnant
2. adj congested, clogged
3. adj stodgy, conservative, conventional ➡ **dull**

stupid adj ignorant, unintelligent, dumb (*informal*), vacuous ➡ **foolish, dull, thoughtless** ⇨ *smart*
Some people consider it rude to use **dumb** *in reference to people. When you are writing, it might be better to use one of the other more specific synonyms.*

suave adj urbane, debonair, diplomatic, cultured, charming, smooth, glib, facile ➡ **fashionable**

subdue vb subjugate, suppress, quash ➡ **defeat, contain**

subject 1. n theme, topic, question, substance, matter, thesis, gist, point, text, issue ➡ **field**
2. n ➡ **course**
3. n ➡ **model, patient**
4. n ➡ **citizen**
5. vb ➡ **control**

If the word you want is not a main entry above, look below to find it.

studio ➡ gallery

studious ➡ careful, educated

stuff ➡ matter, property, load

stuffed ➡ full

stumble ➡ trip, fumble

stumble across ➡ find

stump ➡ confuse

stun ➡ shock, paralyze

stunned ➡ unconscious

stunning ➡ beautiful, striking

stunt ➡ trick, prevent

stupidity ➡ ignorance, nonsense

stupor ➡ dream

sturdy ➡ tough, strong

stutter ➡ stammer

sty ➡ pen

style ➡ type, class, fashion, elegance

stylish ➡ fashionable, modern

stymie ➡ confuse

stymied ➡ disabled

subcommittee ➡ committee

subconscious ➡ mind

subdivide ➡ divide

subdivision ➡ division, development

subject to ➡ under

subjective ➡ arbitrary

subjugate ➡ subdue

subjugation ➡ slavery, victory

sublet ➡ hire

sublime ➡ heavenly

submerge ➡ flood, sink

submerse ➡ sink

submission ➡ surrender

submissive ➡ passive, servile

submit ➡ surrender, give, suggest

subordinate 1. *adj* inferior, secondary, auxiliary, junior, lower ➡ **under**
2. *n* ➡ **helper, servant**

subtract *vb* deduct, remove, withhold, diminish ➡ **decrease** ⇨ *add*

subtraction *n* deduction, reduction, diminution, discount ⇨ *addition*

success *n* accomplishment, achievement, attainment, progress, prosperity ➡ **victory, luck**

successful 1. *adj* fortunate, accomplished ➡ **rich, famous**
2. *adj* effective, fortuitous, favorable, productive, victorious, triumphant, auspicious

sudden *adj* immediate, abrupt, swift, meteoric, precipitate, instantaneous, unexpected, unforeseen ➡ **sudden, sharp, early**

suggest 1. *vb* recommend, urge, propose, advise, counsel, move, submit, prescribe ➡ **offer**
2. *vb* imply, hint, intimate, insinuate

suggestion 1. *n* proposal, proposition, offer, recommendation ➡ **advice, idea, tip**
2. *n* ➡ **bit**

If the word you want is not a main entry above, look below to find it.

subordinate to ➡ **under**

subscriber ➡ **patron**

subsequent ➡ **following**

subservient ➡ **servile**

subside ➡ **decrease, fall**

subsidiary ➡ **department**

subsist ➡ **live¹**

substance ➡ **matter, essence, existence, density, weight, subject, support**

substantial ➡ **big, strong**

substantially ➡ **chiefly**

substantiate ➡ **verify**

substantiation ➡ **proof**

substantive ➡ **real**

substitute ➡ **change, trade, relieve, alternate**

substitution ➡ **trade**

subterfuge ➡ **pretense, trick, secrecy**

subterranean ➡ **underground**

subtle ➡ **sly, complicated, smart**

suburb ➡ **town**

subversive ➡ **rebel**

subvert ➡ **weaken**

succeed ➡ **prosper, win, follow**

succeeding ➡ **following**

succession ➡ **order**

successive ➡ **consecutive**

succinct ➡ **short**

succinctness ➡ **brevity**

succor ➡ **support, comfort, help**

succulent ➡ **rich**

succumb ➡ **surrender, lose, die**

suck up ➡ **absorb**

suds ➡ **foam**

sue ➡ **appeal, try**

suet ➡ **fat**

suffer ➡ **bear**

sufferer ➡ **patient**

suffering ➡ **pain, misery**

suffice ➡ **satisfy**

sufficient ➡ **enough**

suffocate ➡ **choke**

suffocating ➡ **stuffy**

suffuse ➡ **instill**

sugary ➡ **rich**

---

suit 1. *vb* fit, become, befit, enhance, flatter, agree with, complement
2. *n* outfit, ensemble, uniform, costume ➡ **clothes**
3. *n* lawsuit, litigation, action, hearing, case

summary *n* outline, synopsis, abstract, paraphrase, condensation, abridgment, digest, précis, rundown ➡ **essence**

superficial *adj* cursory, perfunctory, shallow, surface, skin-deep, cosmetic, uncritical, glib ➡ **trivial, trite**

supernatural *adj* preternatural, superhuman, paranormal, unearthly, occult, mystical, psychic ➡ **invisible, heavenly**

superstition *n* old wives' tale, fable, lore ➡ **myth, belief**

superstitious 1. *adj* credulous, fearful
2. *adj* unfounded, groundless

supply 1. *n* stock, store, stockpile, inventory, reserve, hoard, cache, mine, holding, account, fund, reservoir
2. *vb* provide, equip, outfit, furnish, provision, rig ➡ **give, sell**

If the word you want is not a main entry above, look below to find it.

suitable ➡ fit[1], able, good

suitcase ➡ luggage

suite ➡ room

sulk ➡ mope

sulky ➡ temperamental

sullen ➡ pessimistic, cross

sully ➡ dirty

sultan ➡ king

sultana ➡ queen

sultry ➡ damp, tropical

sum ➡ total, add, all

summation ➡ addition

summit ➡ top, mountain

summon ➡ call, mobilize

summons ➡ invitation

sumptuous ➡ grand

sun ➡ star

sundae ➡ ice cream

sunder ➡ separate

sundial ➡ clock

sundown ➡ evening

sundry ➡ many

sunglasses ➡ glasses

sunken ➡ underground

sunny ➡ bright, fair

sunrise ➡ morning

sunset ➡ evening

sunup ➡ morning

super ➡ great

superb ➡ grand, great

superfluous ➡ unnecessary

superhuman ➡ supernatural

superintendent ➡ principal

supersede ➡ follow

superior ➡ better, proud, boss

superiority ➡ excellence, advantage

superlative ➡ best

supermarket ➡ market

superstar ➡ celebrity

supervise ➡ lead

supervision ➡ leadership

supervisor ➡ boss

supine ➡ prone

supplant ➡ follow

supple ➡ flexible, agile

supplement ➡ add, more, addition

supplementary ➡ more

supplicate ➡ appeal

supplier ➡ seller

support 1. *vb* bear, hold (up), bolster (up), brace, sustain, prop (up), buttress, carry, nourish, nurture, feed, promote, foster ➡ **strengthen**
2. *vb* uphold, sustain, maintain, champion, enforce ➡ **back, help, approve**
3. *vb* ➡ **afford**
4. *n* backing, encouragement, assistance, succor, maintenance, livelihood, subsistence, upkeep, resource ➡ **help, protection, approval, permission, incentive, pension** ⇨ *opposition*
5. *n* mainstay, pillar, backer, champion ➡ **patron, fan**
6. *n* brace, prop, buttress, stay, bolster, truss, reinforcement ➡ **base, basis**

surprise 1. *vb* startle, amaze, astonish, daze, dazzle, bedazzle, flabbergast, throw, floor ➡ **shock**
2. *n* amazement, astonishment, wonder, incredulity ➡ **shock**
3. *n* ➡ **gift**

surrender 1. *vb* yield, concede, submit, resign, relinquish, sacrifice, acquiesce, capitulate, quit, give (in), bow, accede, defer, succumb, relent ➡ **lose, abandon**
2. *n* submission, capitulation, resignation, acquiescence, concession, abdication, renunciation, forfeit, sacrifice

---

If the word you want is not a main entry above, look below to find it.

supporter ➡ **fan, patron**

suppose ➡ **guess**

supposedly ➡ **apparently**

supposition ➡ **theory**

suppress ➡ **subdue, contain, abuse**

supreme ➡ **best**

sure ➡ **certain, reliable**

surefire ➡ **reliable**

surely ➡ **certainly**

sure thing ➡ **certainty**

surf ➡ **wave**

surface ➡ **outside, top, side, appear, cover, superficial**

surge ➡ **wave, flood, impulse, hurry**

surly ➡ **rude, cross**

surmise ➡ **assume, guess, theory**

surmount ➡ **defeat, tower**

surname ➡ **name**

surpass ➡ **exceed**

surplus ➡ **remainder, abundance, more, unnecessary**

surprised ➡ **dumbfounded**

surreptitious ➡ **sly, secret**

surrogate ➡ **alternate**

surround ➡ **ring**

surroundings ➡ **setting**

surveillance ➡ **watch, spying**

survey ➡ **look, study, tower**

survive ➡ **live¹**

suspense *n* uncertainty, apprehension, anticipation
➡ **doubt, fear**

suspension 1. *n* ➡ **break**
2. *n* expulsion, banishment, discharge, removal ➡ **exile**

suspicious 1. *adj* distrustful, wary, leery, paranoid, apprehensive
➡ **jealous**
2. *adj* suspect, queer, shady, dubious
➡ **doubtful, strange**

swamp 1. *n* marsh, bog, marshland, bottomland, bayou, fen, quagmire, mire
2. *vb* ➡ **flood, sink**

sweat 1. *vb* perspire, swelter, secrete, exude
2. *n* perspiration, body odor, B.O.

sweep 1. *vb* wipe, whisk, brush, swish, dust, mop, vacuum ➡ **clean**
2. *n* ➡ **range**
3. *n* ➡ **paddle**

swell 1. *vb* bulge, distend, protrude, project, jut, balloon, dilate, expand, inflate, puff up
2. *vb* ➡ **strengthen**
3. *n* ➡ **wave**

swerve *vb* veer, shift, diverge, deviate, dodge ➡ **turn**

If the word you want is not a main entry above, look below to find it.

susceptible
➡ vulnerable

suspect ➡ guess, doubt, suspicious, defendant

suspend ➡ hang, exclude

suspicion ➡ doubt, belief

sustain ➡ support, keep

sustained ➡ long

sustenance ➡ food

swab ➡ rub

swaddle ➡ wrap

swagger ➡ boast, gait, strut

swallow ➡ drink, take, contain

swap ➡ trade, change

swarm ➡ herd, crowd, hurry, infest

swarthy ➡ dark

swat ➡ hit, blow[1]

swathe ➡ wrap, bandage

sway ➡ swing, wave, affect, persuade, rule

swear ➡ promise, testify, curse

sweepstakes ➡ lottery

sweet ➡ rich, pleasant, friendly

sweetheart ➡ love

swelling ➡ bulge, growth, sore

swelter ➡ sweat

sweltering ➡ hot

swift ➡ fast, sudden

swiftness ➡ speed

swig ➡ drink

swim 1. *vb* float, paddle, bathe
2. *n* dip, plunge, swimming, bathing

swing 1. *vb* sway, rock, oscillate,
vibrate, fluctuate, undulate, wave,
roll, wobble, pitch, lurch, reel,
waddle ➡ turn

2. *vb* wave, brandish, flourish,
wield, whirl, twirl
3. *vb* ➡ hang
4. *n* ➡ rhythm, music

sword *n* rapier, cutlass, foil, épée,
saber, broadsword, scimitar ➡ knife

If the word you want is not a main entry above, look below to find it.

swimming ➡ swim

swindle ➡ cheat

swindler ➡ cheat,
rascal

swipe ➡ steal

swirl ➡ turn

swish ➡ rustle, sweep

switch ➡ trade,
change, alternate,
whip

swivel ➡ turn, axis

swoon ➡ dream

swoop ➡ descend

sycophantic ➡ servile

syllable ➡ word

symbol ➡ sign

symbolize ➡ mean

symmetry ➡ balance

sympathetic
➡ thoughtful

sympathize ➡ pity

sympathy ➡ pity,
agreement

symphonic ➡ musical

symptom ➡ sign

synagogue ➡ church

synchronized
➡ simultaneous

synchronous
➡ simultaneous

syndicate ➡ group,
monopoly

syndrome ➡ disease

synopsis ➡ summary

synthetic
➡ manufactured

syrupy ➡ thick

system ➡ method,
order

systematize ➡ arrange

T

table 1. *n* desk, stand, counter, bar, dresser
2. *n* chart, graph, spreadsheet, timetable, schedule, table of contents, catalog, register, appendix ➡ **plan**
3. *n* ➡ **plateau**

tact *n* judgment, poise, diplomacy, savoir faire, discretion, delicacy, circumspection, finesse

tactic *n* strategem, maneuver, gambit, feint ➡ **plan, trick**

take 1. *vb* convey, deliver, transport ➡ **carry, bring, lead**
2. *vb* ➡ **get, receive**
3. *vb* confiscate, appropriate, expropriate, commandeer, usurp, gain ➡ **seize, catch**
4. *vb* ingest, swallow ➡ **eat, drink**
5. *vb* ➡ **bear**

6. *vb* ➡ **choose**
7. *vb* take in ➡ **earn**

talent *n* gift, aptitude, genius, skill, expertise, flair, knack, prowess, adroitness, facility ➡ **ability, agility, specialty, art**

talented *adj* gifted, artistic, musical, creative, inventive, versatile, imaginative, ingenious, fertile ➡ **able**

talk 1. *vb* speak, converse, discuss, chat, communicate, confer, consult, parley, rap ➡ **argue, chatter, say, tell**
2. *n* conversation, discussion, dialogue, consultation, word, chat, chitchat, patter, prattle, gibberish ➡ **speech, rumor, meeting**

talkative *adj* voluble, loquacious, verbose, garrulous, long-winded, effusive, chatty

---

If the word you want is not a main entry above, look below to find it.

tab ➡ bill, label

tableland ➡ plateau

tablespoon ➡ spoon

tablet ➡ medicine, notepad

tabloid ➡ paper

taboo ➡ illegal

tabulate ➡ list

tabulating ➡ addition

tack ➡ nail

tackle ➡ equipment, try, seize

tacky ➡ sticky, loud

tactful ➡ thoughtful

tactless ➡ insensitive

tadpole ➡ frog

tag ➡ label

tail ➡ follow, back

tailor ➡ adjust, sew

taint ➡ dirty, spot

take after ➡ resemble

take-home ➡ examination

take in ➡ adopt, take

take off ➡ shed

take on ➡ try

takeover ➡ acquisition

take prisoner ➡ arrest

take up ➡ occupy

tale ➡ story, lie

talker ➡ speaker

tall ➡ high, long

tallness ➡ height

tallow ➡ fat

tally ➡ add, bill, score, vote

n = noun • *vb* = verb • *adj* = adjective • *adv* = adverb • *prep* = preposition • *conj* = conjunction

tame 1. *adj* housebroken, house-trained, trained, manageable, domestic, domesticated, docile, broken ➡ **gentle**
2. *vb* ➡ **control**

tax 1. *n* duty, tariff, toll, levy, fee, assessment, tribute
2. *vb* ➡ **tire**

taxi *n* cab, taxicab, limousine, limo, hack ➡ **vehicle**

teach *vb* instruct, educate, train, school, tutor, coach, lecture, inform, drill, enlighten ➡ **explain, preach**

teacher *n* instructor, educator, schoolmaster, schoolmistress, scholar, tutor, mentor, guru, professor, lecturer, academic, don, coach ➡ **adviser, faculty**

team 1. *n* squad, company, unit, crew, side ➡ **group**
2. *n* (*in reference to horses, mules, or oxen*) pair, span, yoke, string, tandem

teenager *n* adolescent, teen, youth, juvenile ➡ **child**

If the word you want is not a main entry above, look below to find it.

talon ➡ foot

tamper ➡ tinker, meddle

tan ➡ brown, dark

tandem ➡ team

tang ➡ flavor, bit

tangelo ➡ orange

tangent ➡ adjacent

tangerine ➡ orange

tangible ➡ real

tangle ➡ knot, mess, maze, bend

tangy ➡ spicy, sour

tank ➡ container

tantalize ➡ tempt

tantrum ➡ fit²

tap ➡ knock, faucet

tape ➡ adhesive, band, stick

taper ➡ decrease

tardily ➡ late

tardy ➡ late

target ➡ object, prey, destination

tariff ➡ tax

tarnish ➡ corrode, dirty

tarp ➡ tent

tar paper ➡ paper

tarpaulin ➡ tent

tarry ➡ wait

tart ➡ sour, spicy, pastry

task ➡ job

taste ➡ bite, drink, flavor, elegance, try

tasteless ➡ insipid

tasty ➡ delicious

tattered ➡ ragged

tattle ➡ tell, chatter

taunt ➡ insult

taupe ➡ brown

taut ➡ tense

tavern ➡ bar, restaurant

tawdry ➡ poor

tawny ➡ brown

taxicab ➡ taxi

teach-in ➡ protest

teaching ➡ education, lesson

teakettle ➡ pot

team up ➡ help

teapot ➡ pot

tear ➡ drop, hurt, rip

teardrop ➡ drop

tearful ➡ emotional

tearoom ➡ restaurant

tease ➡ bother, insult, joke, comb

teaspoon ➡ spoon

teaspoonful ➡ dose

teatime ➡ afternoon

technician ➡ mechanic

technique ➡ art, method

tedious ➡ dull

tedium ➡ boredom

teem ➡ rain

teeming ➡ fertile

teen ➡ teenager

telecast ➡ broadcast, program

telephone ➡ call

telescope ➡ glass, condense

televise ➡ broadcast

---

tell *vb* report, narrate, relate, recite, declare, inform, announce, disclose, communicate, convey, notify, state, profess, pronounce, tattle ➡ **say, talk, order, warn, testify, predict**

temperamental *adj* moody, touchy, volatile, sensitive, testy, petulant, sulky ➡ **fickle, emotional**

temporary *adj* transitory, fleeting, momentary, ephemeral, provisional, stopgap, makeshift, interim, acting ➡ **short** ⇨ *permanent*

tempt *vb* entice, tantalize, lure, seduce, decoy, bait ➡ **persuade**

tendency *n* disposition, propensity, trend, proclivity, penchant, streak, inclination, leaning, bias ➡ **habit, preference**

tense 1. *adj* taut, stretched, drawn ➡ **firm, tight**
2. *adj* high-strung, agitated ➡ **anxious, nervous**
3. *vb* ➡ **tighten**

tent *n* pavilion, canopy, tarp, tarpaulin, fly ➡ **protection**

term 1. *n* ➡ **word**
2. *n* semester, trimester, quarter, tenure ➡ **period**
3. *n* qualification, limitation, condition, restriction, stipulation, reservation, clause

terrain *n* ground, land, territory, landscape, environment, topography

---

If the word you want is not a main entry above, look below to find it.

tell on ➡ betray

telling ➡ meaningful, valid

temerity ➡ audacity

temper ➡ personality, anger, mood, harden, soften

temperament ➡ personality, mood

temperance ➡ abstinence

temperate ➡ gentle

tempest ➡ wind, storm

tempestuous ➡ stormy

template ➡ pattern

temple ➡ church

tempo ➡ speed, rhythm

temptation ➡ attraction

tenacious ➡ stubborn, faithful

tenant ➡ occupant

tend ➡ protect

tender ➡ gentle, offer, loving, sore

tenderhearted ➡ kind

tenderness ➡ love, kindness

tendril ➡ string

tension ➡ stress

tentative ➡ doubtful, shy

tenure ➡ term

tepid ➡ warm

terminal ➡ base, destination, deadly, last

terminally ➡ deadly

terminate ➡ finish, stop, fire

termination ➡ finish

terminus ➡ destination

terra cotta ➡ pottery

terrarium ➡ zoo

terrible ➡ awful, scary

terribly ➡ very

terrific ➡ great, awesome

terrified ➡ afraid

terrify ➡ scare

terrifying ➡ scary

territory ➡ space, terrain, state

terror ➡ fear

terrorize ➡ threaten

terse ➡ short

terseness ➡ brevity

---

n = noun • *vb* = verb • *adj* = adjective • *adv* = adverb • *prep* = preposition • *conj* = conjunction

testify *vb* affirm, swear, certify, vouch, attest ➡ **tell**

thankless 1. *adj* ➡ **thoughtless**
2. *adj* unappreciated, unrewarded, unrewarding, disagreeable, distasteful ➡ **useless**

theft *n* robbery, burglary, stealing, larceny, thievery, fraud, extortion, shoplifting, looting, pillage, embezzlement ➡ **crime**

theoretical *adj* hypothetical, academic, abstract, philosophical, rhetorical, speculative, conjectural

theory *n* hypothesis, conjecture, speculation, supposition, premise, presumption, assumption, surmise ➡ **idea, reason, philosophy**

therefore *adv* consequently, hence, accordingly, thus, ergo, wherefore, for, so

thick 1. *adj* dense, compact, close, condensed, packed, impenetrable, profuse ⇨ **thin**
2. *adj* stiff, firm, viscous, syrupy, gelatinous, glutinous, viscid
3. *adj* ➡ **broad**

thin 1. *adj* flimsy, slim, slender, sheer, delicate, diaphanous, insubstantial, gossamer ➡ **weak** ⇨ **thick, heavy**
2. *adj* ➡ **narrow**
3. *adj* slender, slim, lean, slight, skinny, scrawny, lanky, lank, wiry, spare, gaunt, haggard, emaciated ⇨ **big, tough**
4. *vb* ➡ **weaken, disappear**

think 1. *vb* reason, deliberate, cogitate ➡ **consider, meditate, believe**
2. *vb* ➡ **guess**

If the word you want is not a main entry above, look below to find it.

test ➡ examination, experiment, try, examine, experimental

testament ➡ will

testimony ➡ proof

testy ➡ temperamental, cross

tether ➡ tie, rope

text ➡ book, print, subject

textile ➡ cloth

texture ➡ quality

thank ➡ appreciate

thankful ➡ grateful

thankfulness ➡ gratitude

thanks ➡ gratitude

thaw ➡ melt

theater ➡ stage, hall

theme ➡ subject, report, song, chorus

theme park ➡ carnival

theological ➡ religious

theology ➡ religion

therapeutic ➡ medicinal

therapy ➡ cure

thesaurus ➡ dictionary

thesis ➡ report, subject

thespian ➡ actor

thicken ➡ concentrate, harden

thicket ➡ brush, forest

thief ➡ criminal

thievery ➡ theft

thing ➡ object, fashion

things ➡ property

think through ➡ study

thinker ➡ philosopher

thinking ➡ reason

thirst ➡ appetite

thirsty ➡ dry

➡ = synonym cross-reference • ⇨ = antonym cross-reference

thorn *n* briar, brier, bramble, barb, spine ➡ **point**

thoughtful 1. *adj* considerate, sympathetic, tactful, solicitous, sensitive ➡ **friendly, polite, kind, nice** ➪ *thoughtless*
2. *adj* meditative, contemplative, pensive, reflective, wistful ➡ **sad, absorbed, intellectual**

thoughtless *adj* inconsiderate, careless, reckless, wanton, heedless, rash, foolhardy, ungrateful, thankless, unappreciative ➡ **rude, abrupt, indiscriminate, negligent** ➪ *thoughtful*

threaten 1. *vb* intimidate, menace, torment, bully, terrorize ➡ **scare**
2. *vb* ➡ **jeopardize**

threshold 1. *n* sill, doorsill, doorstep, entryway, entranceway ➡ **door, porch**
2. *n* ➡ **beginning**

through 1. *prep* among, around, between ➡ **past**
2. *prep* ➡ **during**
3. *adj* ➡ **past**

throw 1. *vb* pitch, toss, hurl, fling, cast, pass, heave, chuck, sling
2. *vb* project, propel, launch, catapult, emit, radiate, send, give off ➡ **shoot**
3. *vb* ➡ **confuse, surprise**
4. *vb* ➡ **defeat**
5. *n* toss, pitch, pass, cast

If the word you want is not a main entry above, look below to find it.

thorax ➡ **chest**

thorough ➡ **complete, comprehensive, careful**

thoroughfare ➡ **road**

thoroughly ➡ **completely, well, carefully**

thoroughness ➡ **diligence**

though ➡ **but**

thought ➡ **idea, philosophy, attention**

thoughtfulness ➡ **kindness**

thrash ➡ **whip**

thrashing ➡ **defeat**

thread ➡ **string, bend**

threadbare ➡ **ragged**

threat ➡ **danger, warning**

threatening ➡ **ominous**

threnody ➡ **dirge**

thrift ➡ **economy**

thriftiness ➡ **economy**

thrifty ➡ **cheap**

thrill ➡ **excitement, excite**

thrilled ➡ **ecstatic, excited**

thrilling ➡ **exciting**

thrive ➡ **prosper, live¹**

throaty ➡ **hoarse**

throb ➡ **shake, hurt**

throng ➡ **crowd**

throughout ➡ **during**

throw away ➡ **discard**

throw up ➡ **vomit**

thrust ➡ **impulse, energy, push**

thruway ➡ **highway**

thud ➡ **bang**

thug ➡ **vandal**

thump ➡ **knock**

thunder ➡ **bang, yell**

thunderous ➡ **loud**

thunderstruck ➡ **dumbfounded**

thus ➡ **therefore**

thwack ➡ **blow¹**

thwart ➡ **prevent, bar**

thwarted ➡ **disabled**

tiara ➡ **crown**

---

tick 1. *n* ticktock, beat, click, clack 2. *n* check, check mark, mark, x, cross

ticket 1. *n* pass, admission, voucher, permit, visa, passport, receipt, sales slip, slip 2. *n* ➡ **ballot** 3. *n, vb* ➡ **label**

tie 1. *vb* fasten, secure, knot, bind, lash, tether, hitch, lace, strap ➡ **join, link** 2. *n* necktie, bow tie, cravat, ascot 3. *n* draw, deadlock, stalemate, standoff

tight 1. *adj* fast, unyielding, immovable, fixed ➡ **tense, firm, stationary** 2. *adj* sealed, airtight, watertight, impermeable 3. *adj* snug, close-fitting, skintight, formfitting, constricting 4. *adj* ➡ **cheap**

tighten *vb* stiffen, tense, clench, contract, squeeze ➡ **pull**

tingle *vb* prickle, itch, creep ➡ **hurt, shake**

tinker 1. *vb* putter, fiddle, dabble, mess, potter, twiddle, fidget, toy ➡ **fix** 2. *vb* tamper, juggle, rig, manipulate, fiddle ➡ **change**

tip 1. *n* ➡ **top, point** 2. *n* pointer, suggestion, hint ➡ **advice** 3. *n* gratuity, bonus, perk, perquisite, reward ➡ **wage** 4. *vb* ➡ **pay** 5. *vb* ➡ **upset** 6. *vb* ➡ **warn**

If the word you want is not a main entry above, look below to find it.

tickle ➡ **pet**

ticklish ➡ **delicate**

ticktock ➡ **tick**

tidal wave ➡ **wave**

tide ➡ **flood**

tidings ➡ **announcement**

tidy ➡ **neat, clean**

tiepin ➡ **pin**

tier ➡ **layer, floor**

tiff ➡ **argument**

tight-fisted ➡ **cheap**

tightwad ➡ **miser**

till ➡ **until, farm, cash register**

tiller ➡ **wheel**

tilt ➡ **slant**

timber ➡ **wood, board, beam**

timberland ➡ **forest**

time ➡ **moment, period, rhythm, measure**

timely ➡ **punctual**

timepiece ➡ **clock**

timer ➡ **clock**

timetable ➡ **table**

timid ➡ **shy, cowardly**

timorous ➡ **shy, cowardly, afraid**

timothy ➡ **hay**

tine ➡ **point**

tinge ➡ **color**

tiniest ➡ **least**

tinkle ➡ **ring, peep**

tint ➡ **color, paint**

tintinnabulation ➡ **ring**

tiny ➡ **small**

tippler ➡ **drunkard**

tipsy ➡ **drunk, dizzy**

tiptoe ➡ **sneak**

tiptop ➡ **good**

➡ = synonym cross-reference • ⇨ = antonym cross-reference

tire 1. *vb* exhaust, fatigue, tax, sap, fade, weary, bore ➡ **weaken**
2. *n* ➡ **wheel**

tired 1. *adj* exhausted, weary, worn out, sleepy, fatigued, listless, drained, dead
2. *adj* ➡ **trite**

together 1. *adv* jointly, mutually, collectively, en masse, cooperatively ⇨ *apart*
2. *adv* simultaneously, concurrently, contemporaneously

tolerant *adj* permissive, lenient, indulgent, easygoing ➡ **liberal, kind, patient**

tool 1. *n* instrument, utensil, machine, appliance, gadget, implement, device, mechanism, apparatus, means, vehicle, medium ➡ **equipment, hammer**
2. *n* instrument, pawn, puppet, stooge, dupe, victim

top 1. *n* peak, summit, pinnacle, apex, apogee, zenith, crest, tip, surface, climax, acme, prime, ultimate ⇨ *base*
2. *n* cover, lid, cap, hood, stopper, cork, plug, bung
3. *adj* ➡ **best**
4. *vb* ➡ **defeat, exceed**

total 1. *n* sum, whole, aggregate, amount, totality, entirety ➡ **all** ⇨ *part*
2. *adj* ➡ **all, complete**
3. *vb* ➡ **add**

If the word you want is not a main entry above, look below to find it.

tiredness ➡ exhaustion	toilet ➡ bathroom	tonic ➡ soda	torn ➡ ragged
tireless ➡ diligent	token ➡ sign, reminder	too ➡ besides, very	tornado ➡ storm
tiresome ➡ dull	tolerance ➡ patience	toodle-oo ➡ good-bye	torpedo ➡ missile
tissue ➡ paper	tolerate ➡ bear, let	toot ➡ blow²	torpid ➡ slow
titan ➡ giant	toll ➡ tax, ring	topic ➡ subject	torpor ➡ laziness
titanic ➡ huge	tomahawk ➡ ax, axe	topography ➡ terrain	torrent ➡ rain, flood
title ➡ name, possession, headline	tomb ➡ grave	topping ➡ icing	torrid ➡ hot, tropical
titled ➡ noble	tome ➡ book	topple ➡ fall, upset	torso ➡ body
titter ➡ laugh	tomfoolery ➡ mischief	top secret ➡ secret	torte ➡ cake
to ➡ until	tomorrow ➡ future	topsoil ➡ dirt	tortilla ➡ bread
toadstool ➡ fungus	ton ➡ abundance	topsy-turvy ➡ upside down	tortuous ➡ indirect
toast ➡ praise	tone ➡ color, quality	torch ➡ light¹	torture ➡ misery, abuse
toddler ➡ baby	tongue ➡ language, lick	torment ➡ abuse, threaten, misery	toss ➡ throw
toil ➡ work	tongue-tied ➡ dumb	tormentor ➡ bully	tot ➡ baby

touch 1. *vb* feel, handle, caress, manipulate, paw, clutch, grope ➡ **rub**
2. *vb* contact, meet, reach ➡ **border**
3. *vb* ➡ **concern**
4. *n* ➡ **feeling, sense**
5. *n* ➡ **bit**

tough 1. *adj* sturdy, durable, stout, unbreakable, rugged, resilient, firm ➡ **strong**
2. *adj* ➡ **hard**
3. *n* ➡ **bully, vandal**

tower 1. *n* spire, steeple, turret, belfry, campanile, keep, minaret, pinnacle, obelisk, skyscraper
2. *vb* overlook, survey, loom, rise, rear, surmount

town *n* city, village, municipality, township, hamlet, community, borough, suburb, metropolis, megalopolis, settlement ➡ **neighborhood**

toy 1. *n* plaything, amusement ➡ **trinket, pastime, game**
2. *vb* ➡ **tinker**

track 1. *n* ➡ **path, course, field**
2. *n* trail, footprint, print, impression, imprint, spoor, sign, trace
3. *vb* ➡ **follow, hunt**

trade 1. *vb* exchange, swap, barter, switch, substitute, interchange, traffic, trade in ➡ **sell, change**
2. *n* exchange, swap, switch, substitution ➡ **sale**
3. *n* ➡ **business, profession**

If the word you want is not a main entry above, look below to find it.

totalitarian ➡ dictator, dictatorial

totalitarianism ➡ tyranny

totality ➡ all, total

totally ➡ completely

tote ➡ bag, carry

tote bag ➡ bag

totter ➡ limp

touching ➡ about, emotional

touch off ➡ start

touch on ➡ mention

touchstone ➡ measure

touchy ➡ temperamental, delicate

toughen ➡ harden

toupee ➡ wig

tour ➡ trip, travel, period

touring ➡ abroad

tourist ➡ traveler, visitor

tournament ➡ game

tow ➡ pull

towering ➡ high

township ➡ town

toxic ➡ deadly, unhealthy

toxin ➡ poison

trace ➡ bit, draw, track

trackless ➡ impassable

tract ➡ property, pamphlet

tractable ➡ gentle

traction ➡ friction

trademark ➡ label

trader ➡ seller

tradesman ➡ seller

tradition ➡ myth, ceremony

traditional ➡ legendary, conservative

traffic ➡ business, trade, travel

tragedy ➡ disaster, play

tragic ➡ unfortunate

trail ➡ path, track, course, follow, lag

➡ = synonym cross-reference • ⇨ = antonym cross-reference

trample *vb* tramp, stamp, stomp, tread, flatten, squash, squish, crush

translate *vb* convert, interpret, decipher, decode, paraphrase, render, transcribe, transliterate, paraphrase, transform

translation *n* rendition, paraphrase, adaptation, interpretation, version, transliteration

transparent 1. *adj* clear, see-through, sheer, diaphanous, limpid, lucid, crystalline, translucent
2. *adj* ➡ **obvious**

trap 1. *n* pitfall, snare, catch, hitch ➡ **trick**
2. *vb* ➡ **catch**

trash *n* garbage, rubbish, refuse, waste, debris, litter, rubble, flotsam, wreckage, junk

travel 1. *vb* journey, voyage, tour, cruise, trek, commute, explore, traverse, roam, visit, sail ➡ **go, wander**
2. *n* passage, transportation, traffic, transit ➡ **trip**

traveler *n* tourist, voyager, wayfarer, commuter, fare, pilgrim, wanderer, itinerant, gypsy, vagabond, migrant, nomad ➡ **rider**

If the word you want is not a main entry above, look below to find it.

train ➡ teach, practice, exercise

trained ➡ tame

trainee ➡ student

training ➡ education, experience, discipline, exercise

traipse ➡ walk

trait ➡ quality, detail, habit

traitor ➡ rebel

traitorous ➡ unfaithful

trajectory ➡ curve

tramp ➡ beggar, trample, walk

trance ➡ dream

tranquil ➡ calm

tranquilizer ➡ drug

tranquillity ➡ calm

transact ➡ negotiate

transaction ➡ business, sale

transcend ➡ exceed

transcribe ➡ write, translate

transcription ➡ score

transfer ➡ move, carry, send, movement, delivery

transform ➡ change, translate

transformation ➡ change

transgress ➡ disobey, sin

transgression ➡ crime, disobedience

transient ➡ short, mortal

transit ➡ travel

transition ➡ movement, change

transitory ➡ temporary

transliterate ➡ translate

transliteration ➡ translation

translucent ➡ transparent

transmissible ➡ contagious

transmission ➡ movement, delivery

transmit ➡ broadcast, send

transmittable ➡ contagious

transparency ➡ clarity

transpire ➡ happen

transplant ➡ plant

transport ➡ carry, take, vehicle

transportable ➡ portable

transportation ➡ vehicle, travel, delivery, exile

transpose ➡ change

trapeze artist ➡ acrobat

trash heap ➡ dump

trauma ➡ shock

travail ➡ work

traveling ➡ abroad

---

tray *n* platter, service, salver, trencher ➡ **plate**

treason *n* treachery, disloyalty, betrayal, mutiny, sedition ➡ **revolution, crime**

treatment 1. *n* care, handling, usage, reception, approach 2. *n* ➡ **cure, dose**

tree *n* sapling, seedling, hardwood, conifer, evergreen ➡ **wood, plant**

trick 1. *n* stunt, illusion, hoax, artifice, ploy, ruse, device, strategem, deception, subterfuge, wile, dodge ➡ **joke, trap, pretense** 2. *vb* ➡ **cheat, betray**

trinket *n* bauble, frippery, gewgaw, trifle, bead ➡ **jewel, novelty**

trip 1. *n* journey, voyage, tour, excursion, expedition, cruise, passage, drive, travel, jaunt, outing, spin, pilgrimage, odyssey 2. *vb* stumble, slip, lurch, sprawl ➡ **fall** 3. *vb* ➡ **dance**

trite *adj* insipid, banal, uninteresting, unexciting, vapid, inane, hackneyed, clichéd, stale, musty, overused, tired, stock ➡ **superficial**

trivial *adj* petty, trifling, unimportant, negligible, frivolous, paltry, piddling, insignificant, meager, small, minute, minor, mere ➡ **superficial**

If the word you want is not a main entry above, look below to find it.

traverse ➡ travel

treacherous ➡ dangerous, unfaithful

treachery ➡ treason

tread ➡ gait, step, trample

treasure ➡ appreciate, wealth

treasury ➡ safe, bank

treat ➡ heal, entertain, explain

treatise ➡ report

treaty ➡ agreement

treble ➡ high

trek ➡ travel, walk

tremble ➡ shake, fear, vibration

tremblor ➡ earthquake

tremendous ➡ huge, great

tremor ➡ vibration, earthquake

trench ➡ channel

trench coat ➡ coat

trencher ➡ tray

trend ➡ tendency, fashion

trendy ➡ fashionable, new

trespass ➡ crime, sin, intrude

tress ➡ lock

tresses ➡ hair

trial ➡ try, tryout, experiment, examination, experimental

tribe ➡ family

tribulation ➡ hardship

tribunal ➡ court

tributary ➡ river, branch

tribute ➡ monument, tax

trice ➡ moment

trickery ➡ pretense

trickle ➡ drop

tricky ➡ sly, delicate

trifle ➡ trinket, bit

trifling ➡ trivial

trifocals ➡ glasses

trigger ➡ start

trim ➡ neat, level, cut, decorate, dress, decoration

trimester ➡ term

triumph ➡ victory, win

triumphant ➡ successful, ecstatic

➡ = synonym cross-reference • ⇨ = antonym cross-reference   231

troop *n* troupe, company, squad, unit, corps, garrison ➡ **band, group, crowd, soldier, army**

tropical *adj* tropic, sultry, torrid, humid, muggy, equatorial, lush ➡ **hot**

trouble 1. *n* difficulty, predicament, plight, problem, matter, quandary, fix, pinch, strait, pickle, jam, spot, ordeal, mischief ➡ **hardship, nuisance**
2. *vb* inconvenience, distress, afflict, ail, harry ➡ **bother, disturb, worry**

truce *n* cease-fire, armistice, stand down ➡ **peace**

truth 1. *n* truthfulness, verity, authenticity, veracity, candor, sincerity, openness ➡ **accuracy, honesty, certainty** ⇨ *lie*
2. *n* ➡ **certainty**

try 1. *vb* attempt, strive, struggle, essay, endeavor, venture, undertake, tackle, take on
2. *vb* test, sample, check, taste, experiment
3. *vb* prosecute, sue, indict, adjudicate, impeach, arraign ➡ **blame**
4. *n* attempt, bid, endeavor, go, effort, trial, shot, stab, whirl

tryout *n* audition, trial, reading, screening, hearing

If the word you want is not a main entry above, look below to find it.

trophy ➡ prize

tropic ➡ tropical

troposphere ➡ air

trot ➡ run

troubadour ➡ musician

troublemaker ➡ bully

troublesome ➡ inconvenient

trough ➡ channel

troupe ➡ troop

truancy ➡ absence

truant ➡ runaway

truck ➡ vehicle

trudge ➡ walk

true ➡ correct, faithful, sincere, real, straight

truffle ➡ fungus

truism ➡ cliché

truly ➡ certainly, sincerely

trunk ➡ luggage, chest, body, nose

truss ➡ support

trust ➡ belief, duty, monopoly, inheritance, believe, depend

trust company ➡ bank

trustee ➡ guardian

trusting ➡ naive

trustworthiness ➡ virtue

trustworthy ➡ reliable, sincere, faithful

trusty ➡ faithful

truthfulness ➡ truth

trying ➡ hard

tryst ➡ meeting

tsar ➡ emperor

tsarina ➡ empress

tub ➡ barrel, container

tube ➡ pipe, container

tubing ➡ pipe

tuck ➡ fold

tuft ➡ lock, lump

tug ➡ pull

tuition ➡ education

tumble ➡ fall

tumbler ➡ glass, acrobat

tumbling ➡ gymnastics

tummy ➡ stomach

tumor ➡ growth

tumult ➡ noise, excitement

tumultuous ➡ stormy

tun ➡ barrel

tundra ➡ plain

tune ➡ song

tuneful ➡ musical

tunnel ➡ cave, mine, dig

turbine ➡ engine

turn 1. *vb* spin, revolve, rotate, twirl, swirl, whirl, wheel, swivel, pivot, gyrate, wind, coil, hinge, flip
➡ **bend, swing, swerve**
2. *n* ➡ **curve, corner, round**

tycoon *n* financier, magnate, capitalist, industrialist, entrepreneur, millionaire, businessman, businesswoman, businessperson

type 1. *n* kind, sort, class, nature, manner, style, category, species, variety, race, breed, strain, genre
➡ **make**
2. *n* ➡ **print**
Note that **type**, **kind**, *and* **sort** *are close synonyms and are usually*

interchangeable. **Sort** *is more often used in negative or critical contexts than* **type** *and* **kind**: *"He's just the sort of person who would cheat."*
Class *and* **category** *are more precise in suggesting the nature of the group referred to: "Platypuses are in a* **class** *by themselves;" "These books are divided into two* **categories**—*fiction and nonfiction."*

tyranny *n* oppression, repression, despotism, fascism, totalitarianism, dictatorship, absolutism
➡ **government**

If the word you want is not a main entry above, look below to find it.

turbulence
➡ disturbance

turbulent ➡ stormy, wild

tureen ➡ bowl

turf ➡ dirt

turgid ➡ pompous

turmoil ➡ confusion

turn up ➡ appear

turncoat ➡ rebel

turnout ➡ productivity

turnpike ➡ highway

turquoise ➡ blue

turret ➡ tower

tussle ➡ fight

tutor ➡ teacher, teach

twaddle ➡ nonsense

twang ➡ accent

tweak ➡ squeeze

twiddle ➡ tinker

twig ➡ stick, shoot

twilight ➡ evening

twin ➡ duplicate

twine ➡ string, weave

twinge ➡ pain

twinkle ➡ blink, shine, light[1]

twinkling ➡ moment

twins ➡ pair

twirl ➡ turn, swing, bend, hurt, braid, dance

twisted ➡ bent

twisting ➡ indirect

twitch ➡ fidget, jump

two-by-four ➡ board

two-faced
➡ hypocritical

twosome ➡ pair

typescript ➡ print

typhoon ➡ storm

typical ➡ common, normal, model

typically ➡ regularly

typify ➡ embody

tyrant ➡ dictator, bully

tyrannical
➡ dictatorial

tzar ➡ emperor

tzarina ➡ empress

U

ugly *adj* unsightly, repulsive, hideous, grotesque, loathsome, revolting, repellent, repugnant, horrid, grisly ➡ **plain** ⇨ *pretty*

unanimous *adj* undivided, unified, united, universal, common, undisputed, harmonious, concerted

unaware *adj* ignorant, oblivious, obtuse, unmindful, unconscious, unconcerned, blind, deaf, heedless ➡ **naive**

unbelievable *adj* incredible, unimaginable, implausible, improbable, indescribable, unlikely ➡ **impossible, doubtful**

unbreakable *adj* indestructible, durable, rugged, resistant ➡ **strong, tough** ⇨ *breakable*

uncomfortable *adj* ill at ease, discomfited, cramped, painful, distressful, disagreeable, agonizing ➡ **anxious, nervous** ⇨ *comfortable*

If the word you want is not a main entry above, look below to find it.

ubiquitous ➡ universal

ulcer ➡ sore

ultimate ➡ last, best, top

ultimately ➡ finally

ultimatum ➡ rule, order

ultraviolet ray ➡ X ray

umber ➡ brown

umpire ➡ judge

unable ➡ incompetent

unabridged ➡ complete

unaccompanied ➡ alone

unaccountable ➡ impossible

unaccustomed ➡ strange

unadorned ➡ plain, bald

unanimity ➡ unity

unapparent ➡ inconspicuous

unappreciated ➡ thankless

unappreciative ➡ thoughtless

unarmed ➡ vulnerable

unassuming ➡ humble

unattached ➡ single

unattainable ➡ impossible, inaccessible

unattended ➡ alone

unattractive ➡ plain

unavailable ➡ inaccessible

unavailing ➡ useless

unavoidable ➡ certain

unawareness ➡ ignorance

unbalanced ➡ insane

unbearable ➡ intolerable

unbeatable ➡ invincible

unbecoming ➡ improper

unbefitting ➡ improper

unbeliever ➡ skeptic, atheist

unbend ➡ straighten

unbent ➡ straight

unbiased ➡ fair

unblemished ➡ clean, perfect

unbolt ➡ open

unbounded ➡ infinite

unbroken ➡ complete, continual

uncanny ➡ mysterious

uncaring ➡ apathetic, insensitive

unceasing ➡ continual

uncensored ➡ complete

uncertain ➡ doubtful, variable

uncertainty ➡ doubt, suspense

unchanging ➡ continual

uncivilized ➡ primitive

unclad ➡ naked

unclean ➡ dirty

unclear ➡ obscure, doubtful

unclothe ➡ undress

unclothed ➡ naked

uncommon ➡ rare

unconditional *adj* unrestricted, unqualified, outright, absolute, unequivocal ➡ **complete, certain**

unconscious *adj* insensible, stunned, comatose, out cold, senseless, insensate, inanimate ➡ **asleep, unaware**

under 1. *prep* below, beneath, underneath ⇨ *above*
2. *prep* less than, lower than, inferior to, subject to, subordinate to

underdeveloped *adj* undeveloped, disadvantaged, impoverished, deprived, backward, depressed

underestimate *vb* underrate, undervalue, deprecate, belittle

underground 1. *adj* subterranean, covered, buried, sunken, belowground
2. *adj* ➡ **secret**

undress *vb* disrobe, strip, unclothe, undrape, divest

If the word you want is not a main entry above, look below to find it.

uncomplicated ➡ plain

uncompromising ➡ resolute, strict

unconcern ➡ apathy

unconcerned ➡ apathetic, unaware

unconfined ➡ free

uncongenial ➡ unfriendly

unconquerable ➡ invincible

unconsciously ➡ accidentally

uncooked ➡ natural

uncoordinated ➡ clumsy

uncouth ➡ rude

uncover ➡ discover, reveal

uncovered ➡ open

uncritical ➡ indiscriminate, superficial

unctuous ➡ self-righteous

uncultivated ➡ wild

uncut ➡ complete

undaunted ➡ brave

undecided ➡ unresolved

undeniable ➡ certain, conclusive

undependable ➡ unreliable

underage ➡ young

underbrush ➡ brush

undercover ➡ secret

underfed ➡ hungry

undergo ➡ experience

undergraduate ➡ student

undergrowth ➡ brush

underhanded ➡ sly

underline ➡ emphasize

undermine ➡ weaken

underneath ➡ under

undernourished ➡ hungry

underpinning ➡ basis

underrate ➡ underestimate

underscore ➡ emphasize

undersized ➡ short

understand ➡ know

understandable ➡ articulate

understanding ➡ patient, belief, wisdom, patience, agreement

undertake ➡ try, bear

undertaking ➡ act, work

undervalue ➡ underestimate

underweight ➡ light²

undesirable ➡ bad

undetectable ➡ invisible

undetermined ➡ unresolved

undeveloped ➡ underdeveloped, latent

undeviating ➡ straight

undisciplined ➡ wild

undisputed ➡ unanimous

undisturbed ➡ calm

undivided ➡ unanimous

undo ➡ separate, open

undoubtedly ➡ certainly

undrape ➡ undress

undressed ➡ naked

undulate ➡ swing

undying ➡ eternal

➡ = synonym cross-reference • ⇨ = antonym cross-reference   235

unemployed *adj* jobless, idle, inactive, unoccupied, out-of-work ⇨ **employed**

unfaithful *adj* false, traitorous, treacherous, disloyal, perfidious, false-hearted, fickle ➡ **dishonest** ⇨ **faithful**

unfortunate *adj* unlucky, unhappy, hapless, disastrous, catastrophic, tragic, adverse, hapless, regrettable, lamentable, deplorable ➡ **sad, poor, pitiful**

unfriendly *adj* quarrelsome, antisocial, unsociable, uncongenial, inhospitable, combative, antagonistic ➡ **belligerent, cool** ⇨ **friendly**

unhealthy 1. *adj* unwholesome, harmful, injurious, noxious, unsanitary, toxic, bad ➡ **dangerous** 2. *adj* ➡ **sick**

unify *vb* unite, integrate, merge, fuse, consolidate ➡ **join**

If the word you want is not a main entry above, look below to find it.

unearth ➡ discover, reveal

unearthing ➡ discovery

unearthly ➡ supernatural

uneasy ➡ anxious

uneducated ➡ ignorant

unending ➡ long, eternal

unequal ➡ different

unequivocal ➡ unconditional

unerring ➡ infallible

unessential ➡ unnecessary

unethical ➡ immoral

uneven ➡ rough, variable, different

unexceptional ➡ average

unexciting ➡ trite

unexpected ➡ sudden

unexplainable ➡ impossible

unfailing ➡ faithful

unfair ➡ prejudiced

unfamiliar ➡ strange

unfashionable ➡ unpopular

unfasten ➡ open

unfastened ➡ open

unfavorable ➡ ominous, destructive

unfeasible ➡ impractical

unfeeling ➡ insensitive

unfettered ➡ free

unfinished ➡ partial, unresolved

unfit ➡ weak, incompetent

unflagging ➡ diligent

unfold ➡ spread

unforeseen ➡ sudden

unforgettable ➡ memorable

unforgiveable ➡ inexcusable

unfounded ➡ superstitious

ungainly ➡ clumsy

ungraceful ➡ clumsy

ungracious ➡ rude

ungrateful ➡ thoughtless

unguarded ➡ vulnerable

unhappy ➡ sad, unfortunate

unhearing ➡ deaf

unheeded ➡ unnoticed

unhinged ➡ insane

unification ➡ union

unified ➡ unanimous, inseparable

uniform ➡ same, suit

unimaginable ➡ unbelievable

unimaginative ➡ dull

unimpeachable ➡ reliable

unimportant ➡ trivial

uninhabited ➡ empty, abandoned

unintelligent ➡ stupid

unintelligible ➡ illegible

unintentional ➡ accidental, automatic

unintentionally ➡ accidentally

uninterested ➡ bored

uninteresting ➡ dull, trite

union 1. *n* unification, fusion, amalgamation, coupling, confluence, combination, marriage, merger, consolidation ➡ **link, wedding**
2. *n* association, alliance, federation, league, partnership, guild ➡ **organization**

unique *adj* unprecedented, incomparable, singular, peerless, unparalleled, unrivaled, unsurpassed, matchless, idiosyncratic ➡ **different, special, only**

unity 1. *n* identity, homogeneity, sameness, integrity ➡ **similarity**
2. *n* unison, concord, harmony, unanimity ➡ **agreement**

universal 1. *adj* worldwide, international, global, cosmic
2. *adj* ubiquitous, limitless, catholic ➡ **common, general, unanimous**

unnecessary *adj* needless, unessential, irrelevant, extraneous, superfluous, redundant, optional, gratuitous, pointless, extra, surplus, leftover ➡ **useless, excessive**

unnoticed *adj* unheeded, unobserved, disregarded, unseen, overlooked

unpopular 1. *adj* disliked, despised, unwelcome, friendless
2. *adj* unfashionable, outmoded ➡ **old**

If the word you want is not a main entry above, look below to find it.

uniqueness ➡ novelty

unison ➡ unity

unit ➡ troop, team

unite ➡ join, unify

united ➡ unanimous, inseparable

universe ➡ space

university ➡ college

unjust ➡ prejudiced

unjustifiable ➡ inexcusable

unkempt ➡ messy

unkind ➡ mean

unknown ➡ strange, anonymous

unlawful ➡ illegal

unlearned ➡ ignorant

unlettered ➡ ignorant

unlike ➡ different

unlikely ➡ unbelievable

unlimited ➡ infinite

unlit ➡ dark

unload ➡ empty

unlocked ➡ open

unloose ➡ free

unloosen ➡ free

unlovely ➡ plain

unlucky ➡ unfortunate

unmanageable ➡ clumsy, stubborn, invincible

unmarried ➡ celibate, single

unmindful ➡ unaware

unnamed ➡ anonymous

unnatural ➡ strange

unnerve ➡ disturb, scare, discourage

unnerving ➡ scary

unnoticeable ➡ inconspicuous

unobjectionable ➡ harmless

unobserved ➡ unnoticed

unobstructed ➡ open

unobtainable ➡ inaccessible

unobtrusive ➡ inconspicuous

unoccupied ➡ empty, unemployed

unpack ➡ empty

unpaid ➡ amateur, due

unparalleled ➡ best, unique

unpardonable ➡ inexcusable

unplanned ➡ accidental, spontaneous, arbitrary

unpleasant ➡ bad

unpolished ➡ provincial

unprecedented ➡ unique

unpredictable ➡ arbitrary

unprejudiced ➡ fair

---

unprepared *adj* unready, unsuspecting, inexperienced, napping, unwary

unreliable 1. *adj (used in reference to persons)* untrustworthy, irresponsible, fickle, undependable ➡ **unfaithful, dishonest** ⇨ *reliable*
2. *adj (used in reference to ideas and inanimate objects or things)* deceptive, unsound, misleading, flimsy
➡ **wrong**

unresolved *adj* unsettled, undecided, undetermined, indeterminate, unfinished, pending, incomplete ➡ **doubtful**

unsteady *adj* unstable, wobbly, shaky, insecure, precarious
➡ **variable**

If the word you want is not a main entry above, look below to find it.

unpretentious
➡ **common, humble**

unprincipled
➡ **immoral, dishonest**

unprocessed ➡ **natural**

unprofitable ➡ **useless**

unprotected
➡ **vulnerable**

unqualified
➡ **incompetent, unconditional**

unquestionable
➡ **certain**

unquestionably
➡ **certainly**

unravel ➡ **solve**

unreachable
➡ **inaccessible**

unread ➡ **ignorant**

unreadable ➡ **illegible**

unready ➡ **unprepared**

unreal ➡ **imaginary**

unrealistic
➡ **impractical**

unrealized ➡ **latent**

unreasonable
➡ **illogical**

unrelenting
➡ **stubborn**

unremarkable
➡ **average**

unresponsive
➡ **apathetic**

unrest ➡ **disturbance**

unrestrained ➡ **free**

unrestricted
➡ **unconditional**

unrewarded
➡ **thankless**

unrewarding
➡ **thankless**

unrivaled ➡ **unique**

unruly ➡ **mischievous, stubborn, wild**

unsafe ➡ **dangerous**

unsanitary ➡ **dirty, unhealthy**

unsatisfactory ➡ **poor**

unsavory ➡ **bad**

unschooled
➡ **ignorant**

unscientific
➡ **arbitrary**

unscramble ➡ **solve**

unscrupulous
➡ **dishonest**

unsealed ➡ **open**

unseat ➡ **oust**

unseeing ➡ **blind**

unseemly ➡ **improper**

unseen ➡ **invisible, unnoticed**

unselfish ➡ **generous**

unselfishness
➡ **generosity**

unsentimental
➡ **practical**

unsettle ➡ **disturb**

unsettled
➡ **unresolved, variable**

unshackled ➡ **free**

unshaken ➡ **faithful**

unsharpened ➡ **dull**

unsociable
➡ **unfriendly**

unsightly ➡ **ugly**

unsigned
➡ **anonymous**

unskilled ➡ **amateur**

unsoiled ➡ **clean**

unsolvable
➡ **impossible**

unsophisticated
➡ **naive, primitive, provincial**

unsound ➡ **unreliable, imprudent**

unsparing ➡ **generous**

unspoiled ➡ **new**

unstable ➡ **unsteady**

unsuccessful
➡ **useless**

unsuitable ➡ **improper**

unsure ➡ **doubtful**

unsurpassed ➡ **best, unique**

unsuspecting
➡ **unprepared**

unsympathetic
➡ **insensitive**

until 1. *prep* till, before, up till, up to, to
2. *conj* till

upset 1. *vb* overturn, capsize, topple, upend, invert, tip
2. *vb, n* ➡ **defeat**
3. *vb* ➡ **worry, disturb, anger**
4. *adj* ➡ **angry**
5. *n* ➡ **shock**

upside down *adv* inverted, topsy-turvy, head-over-heels, reversed

urban *adj* city, metropolitan, municipal, civic, cosmopolitan

urchin *n* waif, ragamuffin, brat, imp, gamin ➡ **child**

urge 1. *vb* coax, encourage, goad, prod, spur, egg (on), press, prompt, push, inspire, incite, instigate, provoke ➡ **persuade, suggest**
2. *n* ➡ **desire, beg**

urgent *adj* crucial, pressing, imperative, compelling, desperate, dire, acute ➡ **important**

If the word you want is not a main entry above, look below to find it.

untamed ➡ wild, primitive

untangle ➡ comb

unthinkable ➡ impossible

untidy ➡ messy

untie ➡ open

untimely ➡ early, inconvenient

untouched ➡ new

untrained ➡ amateur

untrodden ➡ impassable

untroubled ➡ calm, carefree

untrue ➡ wrong

untrustworthy ➡ dishonest, unreliable, fickle

untruth ➡ lie

untruthful ➡ dishonest

untwist ➡ straighten

unusable ➡ useless, broken

unused ➡ clean, new

unusual ➡ strange, special, striking

unusually ➡ very

unvarnished ➡ plain

unvarying ➡ continual

unveil ➡ reveal

unwary ➡ unprepared

unwavering ➡ resolute

unwed ➡ single

unwelcome ➡ unpopular

unwell ➡ sick

unwholesome ➡ unhealthy

unwieldy ➡ clumsy

unwilling ➡ reluctant

unwind ➡ rest

unwise ➡ imprudent

unwittingly ➡ accidentally

unwrap ➡ empty

unwritten ➡ spoken

unyielding ➡ resolute, tight, strict

up ➡ above, awake

upbraid ➡ scold

upcoming ➡ future

update ➡ renew

upend ➡ upset

upgrade ➡ promote

upheaval ➡ disturbance

uphill ➡ steep

uphold ➡ support

upkeep ➡ support

upland ➡ plateau

uplift ➡ lift

upon ➡ above

upper ➡ best

upper class ➡ aristocracy

upper hand ➡ advantage

upright ➡ vertical, post

uprising ➡ revolution

uproar ➡ noise, disturbance

uproarious ➡ loud

upscale ➡ expensive

upshot ➡ effect

uptight ➡ nervous

up till ➡ until

up to ➡ until

up-to-date ➡ modern, new

upward, upwards ➡ above

urbane ➡ suave

---

use 1. *vb* employ, utilize, wield, practice, exercise, exert, apply, expend, exploit, refer to, resort to ➡ **operate**
2. *vb* consume, deplete, exhaust, expend ➡ **finish**
3. *n* application, utilization, utility, usefulness, usage, purpose, operation, employment, consumption, expenditure, exercise ➡ **function, worth**

useful *adj* helpful, practical, handy, beneficial, desirable, advantageous, profitable, pragmatic, utilitarian, versatile ➡ **efficient** ⇨ *useless*

useless 1. *adj* futile, vain, fruitless, unavailing, hopeless, desperate, abortive, unsuccessful, ineffectual, unprofitable ➡ **unnecessary** ⇨ *useful*
2. *adj* worthless, unusable, ineffective, counterproductive ➡ **broken**

usual *adj* regular, customary, accustomed, habitual, ordinary, normal, set ➡ **normal**

usually *adv* ordinarily, customarily, regularly, normally, generally ➡ **often, regularly**

utopia *n* paradise, Eden, Shangri-la, Camelot, promised land ➡ **heaven**

If the word you want is not a main entry above, look below to find it.

usable ➡ available	use up ➡ finish	utility ➡ use	utter ➡ pronounce, complete
usage ➡ habit, use, treatment	usher ➡ guide, lead	utilization ➡ use	utterance ➡ remark, speech, word
used ➡ old	usurp ➡ take	utilize ➡ use	
usefulness ➡ use	utensil ➡ tool	utmost ➡ most	utterly ➡ completely
	utilitarian ➡ useful	utopian ➡ idealistic	

V

vacation *n* holiday, recess, leave, furlough, sabbatical, respite, rest, R & R ➡ **break, leisure**

vaccinate *vb* inoculate, immunize

valid 1. *adj* sound, convincing, logical, cogent, telling ➡ **fair**
2. *adj* ➡ **legal, official**

valley *n* vale, glen, dell, dale, hollow, gap, basin, lowland ➡ **canyon** ⇨ *hill, mountain*

valuable *adj* precious, dear, cherished, prized, beloved, inestimable, important, worthwhile, priceless ➡ **expensive, rare**

vandal *n* hooligan, hoodlum, hood, tough, punk, thug, delinquent, savage, barbarian ➡ **criminal, bully, pirate**

variable *adj* changeable, unsettled, mutable, erratic, uncertain, uneven, inconsistent ➡ **arbitrary, fickle, unsteady**

vegetable *n* green, produce ➡ **plant, fruit, herb**

vehicle 1. *n* automobile, car, truck, transportation, transport, wheels (*informal*) ➡ **airplane, boat, taxi**
2. *n* ➡ **tool**

If the word you want is not a main entry above, look below to find it.

vacant ➡ empty, blank

vacate ➡ leave, empty

vaccine ➡ medicine

vacillate ➡ hesitate

vacuous ➡ blank, stupid

vacuum ➡ sweep

vagabond ➡ traveler, homeless

vagrant ➡ homeless, beggar

vague ➡ obscure, doubtful

vain ➡ proud, empty, useless

vainglory ➡ pride

vale ➡ valley

Valhalla ➡ heaven

valiant ➡ brave

validate ➡ approve

validation ➡ justification

valise ➡ luggage

valor ➡ courage

valorous ➡ brave

value ➡ worth, importance, appreciate, respect

valve ➡ faucet

van ➡ front

Vandyke ➡ beard

vanguard ➡ front, patrol

vanish ➡ disappear

vanity ➡ pride

vanquish ➡ defeat

vantage ➡ advantage

vapid ➡ trite

vapor ➡ smoke, cloud

variance ➡ difference

variation ➡ change, difference

varied ➡ different

variegated ➡ speckled

variety ➡ assortment, type

various ➡ many, different

variously ➡ differently

varnish ➡ finish

vary ➡ change, differ

vassalage ➡ slavery

vast ➡ huge

vat ➡ barrel, pot

vault ➡ jump, safe, grave

vaulting ➡ gymnastics

vaunt ➡ boast

veer ➡ bend, swerve

vegetate ➡ rest

vegetation ➡ plant

vehemence ➡ strength

vehement ➡ certain

verify *vb* determine, prove, confirm, ascertain, ensure, assure, show, demonstrate, establish, authenticate, corroborate, substantiate, vindicate, defend ➡ **decide**

vertical *adj* perpendicular, upright, erect, plumb ➡ **steep**

very *adv* extremely, unusually, greatly, absolutely, immensely, terribly, awfully, rather, really, quite, most, too ➡ **much**

vibration *n* quiver, quaver, quake, oscillation, tremor, tremble, shake, shock

victory *n* triumph, conquest, subjugation, mastery, overthrow, ascendancy, win ⇨ **defeat**

view 1. *n* sight, glimpse, scene, scenery, vision, panorama, outlook, spectacle, perspective, prospect, vista ➡ **look**
2. *n* ➡ **belief**
3. *vb* ➡ **look, study**
4. *vb* ➡ **believe**

If the word you want is not a main entry above, look below to find it.

veil ➡ scarf, divider, hide

vein ➡ mood, band, blood vessel

vellum ➡ paper

velocity ➡ speed

velvety ➡ fuzzy

vend ➡ sell

vendor ➡ seller

veneer ➡ coat

venerable ➡ old

venerate ➡ worship

veneration ➡ worship

vengeance ➡ revenge

vengeful ➡ revengeful

venom ➡ poison

venomous ➡ deadly

vent ➡ hole, say

ventilate ➡ fan

ventilation ➡ air

venture ➡ try, bet, adventure, pastime

veracity ➡ truth, honesty

veranda ➡ porch

verbal ➡ spoken

verbalism ➡ word

verbalize ➡ say

verbatim ➡ literal

verbose ➡ talkative

verdant ➡ green

verdict ➡ decision

verge ➡ edge

veridian ➡ green

verification ➡ proof

veritable ➡ real

veritably ➡ really

verity ➡ truth

vermilion ➡ red

vermin ➡ bug

vernacular ➡ dialect

versatile ➡ talented, useful

verse ➡ poem, stanza

versed ➡ expert

version ➡ translation, story

versus ➡ opposite

vessel ➡ boat, bowl

vestibule ➡ hall

vestments ➡ clothes

veteran ➡ soldier

veto ➡ rejection, abolish

vex ➡ bother

vexation ➡ nuisance

viable ➡ alive, possible

viaduct ➡ bridge

vibes ➡ xylophone

vibrant ➡ active

vibraphone ➡ xylophone

vibrate ➡ shake, swing

vicar ➡ priest

vice ➡ fault, dishonesty

vicinity ➡ neighborhood, place

vicious ➡ mean

vicissitude ➡ change

victim ➡ casualty, prey, patient, tool

victimize ➡ abuse

victor ➡ winner

victorious ➡ successful

victuals ➡ food

video ➡ movie

vie ➡ compete

viewer ➡ observer

viewers ➡ audience

viewpoint ➡ perspective

violence *n* brutality, destruction, destructiveness, savagery, aggression ➡ **disturbance, confusion, fight, strength**

violent 1. *adj* savage, fierce, furious, fuming, enraged, berserk ➡ **angry, belligerent, mean, wild, destructive** 2. *adj* ➡ **strong, stormy**

virtual *adj* implied, implicit, practical

virtue 1. *n* integrity, morality, honor, trustworthiness, principle, decency, goodness ➡ **truth, honesty, kindness**

2. *n* innocence, purity, modesty, chastity, virginity
3. *n* ➡ **advantage, worth**

visible *adj* observable, discernible, perceptible, perceivable, visual, optical, graphic, illustrative ➡ **obvious**

visit 1. *vb* call on/upon, stay with, drop by/in, sojourn ➡ **frequent, travel**

2. *n* call, stay, appointment, sojourn, visitation, get-together

visitor *n* guest, caller, company, houseguest, tourist

If the word you want is not a main entry above, look below to find it.

vigil ➡ watch

vigilant ➡ alert

vigor ➡ energy, health

vigorous ➡ lively, strong, healthy

vile ➡ bad

vilify ➡ curse

villa ➡ home

village ➡ town

villain ➡ rascal

villainous ➡ bad

vim ➡ energy

vindicate ➡ revenge, forgive, verify

vindication ➡ revenge, justification

vindictive ➡ revengeful

vine ➡ flower

violate ➡ disobey

violation ➡ crime

violet ➡ purple

VIP ➡ celebrity

viper ➡ snake

virgin ➡ new

virginal ➡ celibate

virginity ➡ virtue

virile ➡ masculine, strong

virtually ➡ practically

virtuoso ➡ expert, genius

virtuous ➡ good

virulent ➡ deadly

virus ➡ disease, poison

visa ➡ ticket

visage ➡ face, appearance

viscid ➡ thick, sticky

viscous ➡ thick, sticky

vision ➡ sight, view, foresight, imagination

visionary ➡ idealistic, idealist

visionless ➡ blind

visitation ➡ visit

visor ➡ bill

vista ➡ view

visual ➡ visible

visualize ➡ imagine

visually impaired ➡ blind

vital ➡ lively, alive

vitality ➡ energy, health, life

vivacious ➡ lively

vivid ➡ bright, explicit

vocable ➡ word

vocabulary ➡ dictionary

vocal ➡ spoken, straightforward

vocalist ➡ singer

vocalize ➡ pronounce, sing

vocation ➡ profession

vociferous ➡ loud

vogue ➡ fashion

voice ➡ speech, choice

voiced ➡ spoken

voiceless ➡ dumb

void ➡ empty, space

➡ = synonym cross-reference • ⇨ = antonym cross-reference

voluntary *adj* intentional, deliberate, willful, willing, freely, spontaneous, optional

vomit *vb* throw up, retch, regurgitate, gag, heave, puke (*informal*), barf (*informal*)

vote 1. *n* ballot, election, referendum, poll, polls, tally
➥ **choice**
2. *vb* ➥ **choose, decide**

vulnerable *adj* defenseless, unarmed, unprotected, unguarded, susceptible, prone, disposed ➥ **weak**

If the word you want is not a main entry above, look below to find it.

volatile
➥ inflammable, temperamental

volition ➥ will

volley ➥ flood

voltage ➥ energy

voluble ➥ talkative

volume ➥ size, book, measure, productivity

voluminous
➥ abundant

volunteer ➥ soldier

vomiting ➥ nausea

voodoo ➥ magic

voracious ➥ predatory, greedy

vouch ➥ testify

voucher ➥ ticket

vouchsafe
➥ condescend

vow ➥ promise

voyage ➥ trip, travel

voyager ➥ traveler

vulgar ➥ common, dirty, sensational

vulgarity ➥ rudeness

vying ➥ competitive

W

wage *n* salary, pay, allowance, fee, tip, compensation, income, earnings, profit, intake, stipend, revenue, return ➡ **pension**

wagon *n* carriage, buggy, cart, coach, stagecoach ➡ **vehicle**

wait *vb* remain, linger, loiter, stay, tarry, await, abide, dally ➡ **delay, hesitate** ⇨ *leave*

wake *vb* wake up, waken, rouse, arouse, awaken

walk 1. *vb* amble, stroll, march, step, hike, stride, trudge, plod, lumber, file, trek, traipse, tramp ➡ **wander, strut, crawl**
2. *n* ➡ **gait**
3. *n* ➡ **path**

wall *n* partition, fence, parapet, stockade, rampart, palisade, barricade ➡ **divider, dam**

wallet *n* billfold, change purse ➡ **bag**

wander 1. *vb* roam, meander, ramble, saunter, rove, range, drift ➡ **walk, travel**
2. *vb* stray, deviate, meander, ramble, digress, diverge

want 1. *vb* wish, desire, crave, yearn, long, pine, hanker, itch ➡ **envy, hope, prefer**
2. *vb* ➡ **need**
3. *n* lack, dearth, paucity, shortage, scarcity, deficiency ➡ **absence, hardship, poverty**

warehouse *n* storehouse, stockroom, depot, depository, granary, grain elevator, silo, armory, arsenal, magazine

---

If the word you want is not a main entry above, look below to find it.

wad ➡ pile	waif ➡ urchin	wallow ➡ fumble	ward ➡ neighborhood
waddle ➡ swing	wail ➡ cry	wan ➡ pale	ward off ➡ repel
wader ➡ bird	wait on ➡ help	wand ➡ stick	wardrobe ➡ clothes, closet
waft ➡ blow²	wakeful ➡ awake	wanderer ➡ traveler	
wag ➡ shake	waken ➡ wake	wane ➡ decrease	wares ➡ product
wager ➡ bet, lottery	walker ➡ pedestrian	wanton ➡ thoughtless, wasteful	warfare ➡ fight
wagering ➡ gambling	walk out ➡ protest		warily ➡ carefully
waggle ➡ shake	walkway ➡ path	war ➡ fight	warlike ➡ military
	wallop ➡ blow¹	warble ➡ sing	warlock ➡ magician

➡ = synonym cross-reference • ⇨ = antonym cross-reference   245

warm 1. *adj* lukewarm, tepid, heated, mild ➡ **hot**
2. *adj* ➡ **friendly**

warn *vb* forewarn, caution, alert, tip off, advise, admonish, exhort, counsel ➡ **scare, tell**

warning *n* alarm, signal, admonition, caution, advice, caveat, premonition, forewarning, omen, threat ➡ **notice, sign**

waste 1. *vb* squander, fritter away, dissipate, misuse, misspend ⇨ *save*
2. *vb* ➡ **decrease**
3. *n* ➡ **trash**
4. *n* ➡ **desert**
5. *adj* ➡ **sterile**

wasteful *adj* extravagant, lavish, profligate, prodigal, reckless, wanton, spendthrift

watch 1. *n* ➡ **clock**
2. *n* ➡ **period**
3. *n* guard, lookout, vigil, surveillance ➡ **attention**
4. *n* ➡ **patrol**
5. *vb* ➡ **look**
6. *vb* ➡ **protect**

wave 1. *n* billow, swell, surge, tidal wave, ripple, breaker, roller, whitecap, comber, surf
2. *vb* motion, gesture, signal, beckon, flag, salute
3. *vb* flutter, flap, ripple, sway ➡ **blow, swing**

weak *adj* frail, feeble, infirm, invalid, helpless, powerless, unfit, impotent, puny, delicate, fragile, flimsy, rickety ➡ **breakable, thin, sick, vulnerable** ⇨ *strong*

If the word you want is not a main entry above, look below to find it.

warmhearted ➡ kind

warmth ➡ hospitality, feeling

warp ➡ bend

warped ➡ bent

warrant ➡ promise, guarantee, deserve

warren ➡ den

warrior ➡ soldier

wary ➡ suspicious, careful

wash ➡ clean, cleaning, laundry

washbasin ➡ sink

washcloth ➡ cloth

washed ➡ clean

washing ➡ cleaning, laundry

washroom ➡ bathroom

washstand ➡ sink

wasted ➡ hungry

wasteland ➡ desert

watchdog ➡ guardian

watchful ➡ alert

watchman ➡ doorman

water ➡ liquid, wet

water down ➡ weaken

waterfowl ➡ bird

waterpipe ➡ pipe

waterspout ➡ gargoyle

watertight ➡ tight

waterway ➡ channel

watery ➡ liquid

waver ➡ hesitate

wax ➡ shine, finish, grow

wax paper ➡ paper

waxy ➡ slippery

way ➡ course, distance, choice, method

wayfarer ➡ traveler

waylay ➡ attack

wayward ➡ mischievous

waywardness ➡ disobedience

---

weaken 1. *vb* flag, wilt, droop, sag, wither ➡ **tire**
2. *vb* cripple, undermine, impair, sabotage, subvert, erode, incapacitate ➡ **destroy**
3. *vb* dilute, thin, water down, adulterate, attenuate ➡ **decrease**

wealth *n* riches, affluence, means, opulence, luxury, prosperity, assets, fortune, treasure, hoard ➡ **money, property, abundance**

weather 1. *n* climate, conditions, clime (*literary*)
Use **weather** *to refer to what is happening in the atmosphere at a particular time or in general:* "I don't like this rainy **weather**." "Is the **weather** being affected by global warming?" Use **climate** *to refer to the average state of the atmosphere in a place or region:* "Florida has a warm **climate**."
2. *vb* age, season, wear, endure ➡ **harden**
3. *vb* expose, overcome ➡ **bear**

weave 1. *vb* braid, knit, interlace, plait, twine, intertwine ➡ **sew**
2. *n* ➡ **cloth**

weight 1. *n* heaviness, heft, mass, substance, pressure, load ➡ **density, measure**
2. *n* ➡ **importance**

welcome 1. *vb* greet, receive, salute, address, herald, hail ➡ **call, entertain, appreciate**
2. *n* greeting, salutation, reception
3. *n* ➡ **hospitality**

welfare 1. *n* well-being, prosperity, good ➡ **health**
2. *n* public assistance ➡ **help**

well 1. *adv* properly, thoroughly, competently, satisfactorily, adequately, excellently, splendidly
2. *adv* favorably, kindly, approvingly, highly
3. *adj* ➡ **healthy**
4. *n* spring, reservoir, cistern ➡ **fountain, source**
5. *n* shaft, bore ➡ **hole**

If the word you want is not a main entry above, look below to find it.

weakness ➡ fault	weary ➡ tired, tire	wedlock ➡ marriage	weir ➡ dam
wealthy ➡ rich	web ➡ net	weed ➡ plant	weird ➡ strange
weapon ➡ gun	webbing ➡ net	weekly ➡ paper	weld ➡ join
weaponry ➡ arms	wed ➡ marry, married	weep ➡ cry	well-behaved ➡ good
weapons ➡ arms	wedded ➡ married	weigh ➡ consider, measure	well-being ➡ welfare
wear ➡ dress, damage, decay, weather	wedding ➡ marriage	weightless ➡ light²	well-informed ➡ educated
weariness ➡ exhaustion	wedge ➡ block, push, embed	weighty ➡ heavy, important	well-known ➡ famous

---

wet 1. *adj* soaked, drenched, saturated, sodden, soggy, dripping ➡ **damp, liquid** ⇨ *dry*
2. *adj* rainy, drizzly, stormy, inclement, misty, showery, snowy, slushy
3. *vb* moisten, soak, dampen, sprinkle, saturate, drench, douse, water, steep, immerse, rinse

wheel 1. *n* tire, roller ➡ **tool**
2. *n* steering wheel, helm, tiller, controls, reins, driver's seat
3. *vb* ➡ **turn**

whip 1. *n* lash, crop, switch, cane, scourge, cat-o'-nine-tails, bullwhip
2. *vb* spank, paddle, lash, thrash, flog ➡ **hit, punish**

3. *vb* ➡ **defeat**
4. *vb* ➡ **mix**

white *adj*, *n* ivory, milky, snowy, silvery, snow-white, frosty, creamy ➡ **fair, pale** ⇨ *black*

wicked *adj* evil, malevolent, diabolical, fiendish, demonic, devilish, heinous ➡ **bad, immoral, mean**

width *n* breadth, girth, wideness, diameter, span ➡ **measure**

wig *n* hairpiece, fall, toupee, periwig (*historical*), rug (*informal*) ➡ **hair**

If the word you want is not a main entry above, look below to find it.

well-mannered ➡ polite, good

well-meaning ➡ kind

wellness ➡ health

well-off ➡ rich

well-read ➡ educated

wellspring ➡ source

well-to-do ➡ rich

well-versed ➡ educated, expert

welt ➡ sore

wetness ➡ humidity

whack ➡ blow[1], knock, hit

wharf ➡ dock

wheatfield ➡ field

wheedle ➡ persuade

wheels ➡ vehicle

wheeze ➡ breathe

whelp ➡ dog

wherefore ➡ therefore

whet ➡ sharpen

whiff ➡ smell

whim ➡ fancy, impulse

whimper ➡ cry

whimsical ➡ funny, arbitrary

whimsicality ➡ humor

whimsy ➡ impulse

whine ➡ complain, cry

whir ➡ hum

whirl ➡ turn, dance, swing, try

whirlwind ➡ wind

whisk ➡ sweep

whiskers ➡ beard

whisper ➡ mumble, rustle

whitecap ➡ wave

whiten ➡ bleach

whittle ➡ carve

whiz ➡ hurry, genius

whole ➡ total, complete, all, healthy

wholehearted ➡ sincere

wholesaler ➡ seller

wholesome ➡ healthy

wholly ➡ completely

whoop ➡ cry

wickedness ➡ immorality

wide ➡ broad

wide-awake ➡ alert

widen ➡ spread

wideness ➡ width

widespread ➡ common, general

wield ➡ swing, use

wife ➡ spouse

wiggle ➡ fidget, crawl

wild 1. *adj* untamed, fierce, ferocious, savage, raging, turbulent, fiery ➡ **violent, mean, rough, stormy**
2. *adj* uncultivated, overgrown, rampant, overrun
3. *adj* disorderly, unruly, obstinate, undisciplined ➡ **stubborn**
4. *n* ➡ **country**

will 1. *n* willpower, determination, resolution, volition, conviction, resolve, willfulness ➡ **ambition**
2. *n* testament, bequest ➡ **inheritance**
3. *vb* ➡ **leave**

win 1. *vb* triumph, prevail, succeed, overcome ➡ **defeat** ⇨ *lose*

2. *vb* score, achieve, earn ➡ **get**
3. *n* ➡ **victory**

wind 1. *n* breeze, gale, tempest, gust, zephyr, draft, blast, whirlwind, blow, puff, breath ➡ **air, storm**
2. *vb* ➡ **bend, turn**

windy *adj* breezy, blustery, airy, drafty, wind-swept ➡ **stormy**

winner *n* champion, victor, hero, medalist, prizewinner, conqueror, champ (*informal*)

wisdom *n* judgment, reason, understanding, appreciation, intelligence, intellect, comprehension, sagacity, perception, discernment, sense, common sense ➡ **knowledge, experience, depth**

If the word you want is not a main entry above, look below to find it.

wilderness ➡ country, desert

wildflower ➡ flower

wildlife preserve ➡ zoo

wile ➡ trick

willful ➡ voluntary, arbitrary

willfully ➡ purposely

willfulness ➡ will

willing ➡ ready, voluntary

willpower ➡ will, discipline

wilt ➡ dry, weaken

wilted ➡ stale

wily ➡ sly

wince ➡ jump

windbreak ➡ hedge

windbreaker ➡ coat

windfall ➡ luck

wind-swept ➡ windy

wind up ➡ finish

wing ➡ limb, branch, fly

wink ➡ blink, moment

winning ➡ attractive

winnings ➡ booty, prize

winnow ➡ sift

wino ➡ drunkard

winsomeness ➡ beauty

wipe ➡ dry, sweep

wire ➡ rope

wiry ➡ thin

wise ➡ smart

wisecrack ➡ joke

wish ➡ want, hope

wistful ➡ thoughtful

wistfulness ➡ desire

wit ➡ humor

witch ➡ magician

witchcraft ➡ magic

with ➡ beside

with child ➡ pregnant

withdraw ➡ leave, retreat, extract

withdrawal ➡ departure, privacy

withdrawn ➡ private

wither ➡ dry, weaken

withhold ➡ subtract, hide, deprive

with-it ➡ fashionable

without ➡ minus

withstand ➡ repel

witness ➡ observer, look

witticism ➡ joke

witty ➡ funny

wizard ➡ genius, magician

wizardry ➡ magic

---

woman n lady, girl, female, gentlewoman, matron, maiden, gal (*informal*), lass ➡ **human being, humanity, adult**

wood n lumber, log, timber, plank, firewood, kindling ➡ **forest**

word 1. n term, expression, locution, utterance, vocable, verbalism, articulation, syllable
2. n ➡ **talk**
3. n ➡ **promise**

work 1. n labor, toil, effort, drudgery, exertion, industry, endeavor, pains, elbow grease (*informal*), travail
2. n ➡ **job, profession**
3. n accomplishment, undertaking, composition, creation, opus ➡ **act, book, picture, poem**
4. vb toil, labor, strive, struggle, slave, strain ➡ **act, do**
5. vb work out ➡ **solve**

worker n laborer, employee, hand, help, colleague, breadwinner, jobholder ➡ **helper, farmer**

worm n earthworm, nightcrawler, angleworm, inchworm ➡ **larva**

worry 1. n concern, care, anxiety, apprehension, burden ➡ **fear**
2. vb upset, concern, trouble, fret, brood, stew ➡ **disturb, bother**

worship 1. vb sanctify, venerate, glorify, exalt, praise, laud, adore, revere, reverence
2. vb ➡ **love**
3. n devotion, prayer, veneration, adulation

worst adj meanest, lowest ➡ **bad, least** ⇨ **best**

If the word you want is not a main entry above, look below to find it.

wobble ➡ shake, swing

wobbly ➡ unsteady

woe ➡ sorrow

woeful ➡ pitiful

wolf ➡ eat

womanhood ➡ maturity

womanly ➡ feminine

women's room ➡ bathroom

wonder ➡ surprise, doubt, miracle, respect

wonderful ➡ great

wont ➡ habit

woo ➡ court

woodcut ➡ print

wooden ➡ prim

woodland ➡ forest

woods ➡ forest

woof ➡ bark

wool ➡ coat

woolly ➡ fuzzy

woozy ➡ dizzy

word-for-word ➡ literal

wordless ➡ dumb

working ➡ employed

work out ➡ exercise

workout ➡ exercise

workplace ➡ office

workshop ➡ factory

world ➡ earth

worldly ➡ cosmopolitan

worldwide ➡ universal

worn ➡ old

worn out ➡ tired

worn-out ➡ old

worried ➡ anxious

worsen ➡ relapse

worth n value, benefit, merit, virtue, estimation ➡ **importance, price, use**

wrap 1. vb gift wrap, cover, bind, envelop, shroud, clothe, swathe, sheathe, swaddle ➡ **bandage**
2. n shawl, muffler, cloak, cape, mantle, stole ➡ **scarf**

wrapper n covering, cover, envelope, jacket, dust jacket, folder ➡ **container**

wrinkle 1. n crease, rumple, crinkle, crimp, crumple, pucker ➡ **fold**
2. vb crease, rumple, crumple, crinkle, crimp ➡ **fold**

write 1. vb inscribe, jot, record, scribble, scrawl, transcribe ➡ **sign**
2. vb compose, draft, indite, pen, author, publish, edit, compile ➡ **print**

writer n author, novelist, poet, playwright, historian, biographer, essayist, humorist, scriptwriter, screenwriter ➡ **reporter, artist**

wrong 1. adj incorrect, false, mistaken, inaccurate, untrue, erroneous, invalid, bad, corrupt, amiss, awry ➡ **improper, illogical, immoral** ⇨ *correct, right*
2. n ➡ **crime**

If the word you want is not a main entry above, look below to find it.

worthless ➡ poor, useless

worthwhile ➡ valuable

worthy ➡ good, noble, praiseworthy

wound ➡ hurt, cut

wraith ➡ ghost

wrangle ➡ argue

wrath ➡ anger

wreak ➡ inflict

wreath ➡ crown

wreck ➡ destroy, collision

wreckage ➡ damage, trash

wrench ➡ pull, hurt

wrest ➡ seize

wrestle ➡ fight

wretch ➡ beggar, rascal

wretched ➡ sorry, poor, awful

wriggle ➡ fidget, crawl

wring ➡ squeeze

wristwatch ➡ clock

writ ➡ order

writhe ➡ fidget

writing ➡ print, handwriting, literature

writing paper ➡ paper

wrongdoer ➡ criminal

wrongdoing ➡ crime

wrongful ➡ illegal

wry ➡ dry

wunderkind ➡ genius

➡ = synonym cross-reference • ⇨ = antonym cross-reference

X·Y·Z

X ray 1. *n* radiation, ultraviolet ray, gamma ray
2. *n* radiograph, encephalogram ➡ **photograph**

xylophone *n* marimba, vibraphone, vibes, glockenspiel

yell *vb, n* call, shout, scream, shriek, screech, bellow, thunder, rant, rave, harangue, boo, hiss, jeer, hoot, squall ➡ **cry**

yellow 1. *adj, n* gold, lemon, sandy, saffron, flaxen, blond, blonde
2. *adj* ➡ **cowardly**

yes *interj* aye, okay, OK, affirmative, amen, yeah (*informal*), yup (*informal*), okey-dokey (*informal*) ➡ **certainly** ⇨ **no**

young *adj* youthful, immature, juvenile, adolescent, boyish, girlish, underage ➡ **childish, new** ⇨ **old**

zero *n* nothing, naught, nought, none, nil, love (*in tennis*), zip (*informal*), zilch (*informal*), goose egg (*informal*), cipher

zigzag *adj* crooked, askew, jagged, oblique, meandering, erratic ⇨ **straight**

zone 1. *n* area, region, district, belt, band, quarter ➡ **place**
2. *vb* ➡ **divide**

zoo *n* menagerie, animal farm, game farm, wildlife preserve, game preserve, aviary, terrarium, aquarium ➡ **park**

If the word you want is not a main entry above, look below to find it.

x ➡ tick
yachting ➡ nautical
yachtsman ➡ sailor
yahoo ➡ boor
yank ➡ pull
yap ➡ bark
yard ➡ property
yardarm ➡ gallows
yardstick ➡ measure
yarn ➡ string, story
yawn ➡ spread
yeah ➡ yes

yearn ➡ want
yearning ➡ desire
yelp ➡ bark
yen ➡ desire
yeoman ➡ farmer
yesterday ➡ past
yesteryear ➡ past
yet ➡ but, more, before
yield ➡ surrender, give, growth
yielding ➡ passive
yip ➡ bark
yo ➡ hello

yoke ➡ team, pair
yonder ➡ far
yore ➡ past
youngster ➡ child
youth ➡ teenager, child, childhood
youthful ➡ young
yowl ➡ cry
yup ➡ yes
zany ➡ funny
zeal ➡ enthusiasm
zealot ➡ extremist

zealous ➡ ambitious, patriotic
zenith ➡ top
zephyr ➡ wind
zest ➡ enthusiasm, spice, excitement
zestful ➡ lively
zesty ➡ spicy
zilch ➡ zero
zip ➡ hurry, energy, zero
zipper ➡ clasp
zippy ➡ lively
zoom ➡ hurry

n = noun • *vb* = verb • *adj* = adjective • *adv* = adverb • *prep* = preposition • *interj* = interjection